WOMEN
AND AMERICAN
FOREIGN POLICY

Volumes Published in the America in the Modern World Series

Lawrence Spinelli, *Dry Diplomacy: The United States, Great Britain, and Prohibition* (1989). ISBN 0-8420-2298-8

Richard V. Salisbury, *Anti-Imperialism and International Competition in Central America, 1920–1929* (1989). ISBN 0-8420-2304-6

Gerald K. Haines, *The Americanization of Brazil: A Study of U.S. Cold War Diplomacy in the Third World, 1945–1954* (1989). ISBN 0-8420-2339-9

Harry Harding and Yuan Ming, eds., *Sino-American Relations, 1945–1955: A Joint Reassessment of a Critical Decade* (1989). ISBN 0-8420-2333-X

Lawrence S. Kaplan, Denise Artaud, and Mark R. Rubin, eds., *Dien Bien Phu and the Crisis of Franco-American Relations, 1954–1955* (1990). ISBN 0-8420-2341-0

Michael L. Krenn, *U.S. Policy toward Economic Nationalism in Latin America, 1917–1929* (1990). ISBN 0-8420-2346-1

Akira Iriye and Warren Cohen, eds., *American, Chinese, and Japanese Perspectives on Wartime Asia, 1931–1949* (1990). ISBN 0-8420-2347-X

Edward M. Bennett, *Franklin D. Roosevelt and the Search for Victory: American-Soviet Relations, 1939–1945* (1990). Cloth ISBN 0-8420-2364-X   Paper ISBN 0-8420-2365-8

James L. Gormly, *From Potsdam to the Cold War: Big Three Diplomacy, 1945–1947* (1990). Cloth ISBN 0-8420-2334-8   Paper ISBN 0-8420-2335-6

Lloyd E. Ambrosius, *Wilsonian Statecraft: Theory and Practice of Liberal Internationalism during World War I* (1991). Cloth ISBN 0-8420-2393-3   Paper ISBN 0-8420-2394-1

Edward P. Crapol, ed., *Women and American Foreign Policy: Lobbyists, Critics, and Insiders* (1992). Second Edition. Cloth ISBN 0-8420-2431-X   Paper ISBN 0-8420-2430-1

WOMEN AND AMERICAN FOREIGN POLICY

LOBBYISTS, CRITICS, AND INSIDERS

EDITED BY

EDWARD P. CRAPOL

SECOND EDITION

A Scholarly Resources Inc. Imprint
Wilmington, Delaware

The paper used in this publication meets the minimum requirements of the American National Standard for permanence of paper for printed library materials, Z39.48, 1984.

Scholarly Resources Inc.
104 Greenhill Avenue
Wilmington, DE 19805-1897

Copyright Acknowledgment

We gratefully acknowledge the Franklin D. Roosevelt Library for its permission to reprint material from the Eleanor Roosevelt Papers. By permission of Franklin D. Roosevelt, Jr.

Library of Congress Cataloging-in-Publication Data

Women and American foreign policy : lobbyists, critics, and insiders /
   edited by Edward P. Crapol. — 2nd ed.
      p. cm. — (America in the modern world)
   Includes bibliographical references (p.   ) and index.
   ISBN 0-8420-2431-X (alk. paper). — ISBN 0-8420-2430-1 (pbk. : alk. paper)
   1. United States—Foreign relations. 2. Women diplomats—United States. 3. Women—United States—Political activity—History. I. Crapol, Edward P. II. Series: America in the modern world (Unnumbered)
E183.7.W85 1992
327.73—dc20   91-46045
                                                CIP

Contents

Contents

Preface to the Second Edition

The republication of this book five years after its original printing is important and timely. It comes at a propitious moment when the historical profession specifically and the scholarly community generally need accessible, reasonably priced works on women and gender to sustain the lurching, halting, but nonetheless ongoing effort to acknowledge the role of gender in society and to redefine the nation's history as a process in which both men and women participated.

The need for a second edition was impressed upon me by several contributors to this collection as well as by my colleagues in diplomatic history and women's studies. Repeatedly they expressed their belief that *Women and American Foreign Policy* has a potential readership much beyond that which has been reached thus far. The fact that the book was originally available only in hardback made it inaccessible to a wider readership and severely restricted its use as a required reading in various courses crossing several disciplines. They continually urged that this study be made available to a broader audience and for general classroom use by undergraduate and graduate students alike. Richard Hopper of Scholarly Resources agreed with these assessments, and I wish to thank him for his support in making a second edition possible.

Finally, it should be noted that all too frequently women's history is dismissed as a peripheral and unimportant diversion that distracts from the true concerns of the diplomatic historian. This collection is the only book available on the role of women in the foreign policy sphere. It is my hope that printing a second edition will overcome the resistance of the historical community, especially within the craft of diplomatic history, to integrating women's history and issues of gender into our study and teaching of American foreign relations.

Williamsburg, Virginia   *EPC*
December 1991

Introduction

This book resulted from my experience in the classroom teaching the history of American foreign policy to undergraduates at the College of William and Mary. In the late 1960s and early 1970s women students in my classes frequently asked to do their research papers on women and women's role in the history of American foreign policy. When I replied that women played no role and had not been a factor in American foreign relations, their reactions ranged from incredulity to barely veiled hostility. My immediate retort was to challenge these women to prove me wrong. Skeptically I suggested: "You go ahead and do your paper on women or an individual woman's influence on foreign policy. See what you can find." Obviously I was passing the buck and invariably after some frustrating hours in the library, my women students would concede that indeed I had been correct: "There is nothing on women and foreign policy." Occasionally a female undergraduate doggedly might try to do something on Abigail Adams, and later in the mid–1970s, one or two grappled with the career and activities of Jane M. Cazneau. Usually their efforts were less than satisfactory to either student or teacher.

Despite my students' discouraging lack of success, I remained intrigued by the problem. Quite by accident I discovered I had been wrong. In doing research for an ongoing project on abolitionists and their impact on foreign policy I encountered Lydia Maria Child. Here, to my surprise, was a female critic who through the power of her ideas and the force of her actions had played some role in American foreign policy. As I read her personal correspondence, novels, antislavery broadsides, and, above all, the brilliant and courageous *An Appeal in Favor of That Class of Americans Called Africans*, I began to understand how she had, within the severe constraints of law, cultural mores and male hostility, attempted to influence the course of American diplomacy. It slowly dawned upon me that Child was not unique, and that her experience in seeking to influence foreign policy probably was paralleled by countless other American women over the last century and a half.

I actively began to locate other diplomatic historians with similar interests and gradually became aware that several were struggling with some of the same problems as they tried to uncover evidence of female participation in the foreign policy decision-making process. A decade ago Joan Hoff-Wilson attempted to document the extent to which women have influenced American diplomacy. She concluded that while United States foreign policy has had "enormous impact on women all over the world, American women have been scarcely involved in its formulation at the top decision-making levels."[1] While it was difficult to dispute Hoff-Wilson's disheartening conclusion, at least in 1977, I remained confident that at a *different* level women played some role and perhaps even had some impact. My continued optimism was fostered in part by Gerda Lerner's insight about nineteenth century women who she maintained were involved in the political struggles of their day, "but the form of their participation and their activities were different from that of men." In her 1976 article "The Majority Finds Its Past" Lerner also observed, accurately I think, that "The involvement of American women in the important events of American history—the political and electoral crises, the wars, expansion, diplomacy—is overshadowed by the fact of the exclusion of women from political power throughout 300 years of the nation's life."[2] Taking a cue as well from the new social history and those social historians who were demonstrating the relevance and importance of non-elites and minorities to the fabric of the national experience, I altered my perspective and tried to extend the boundaries and limits of traditional diplomatic history. Keeping that objective in mind, I plugged along continually inspired by Maria Child's example, confident that while atypical of her gender, she was not alone.

Eventually I came to understand that what was true of women's history in general, was also true of diplomatic history. Women had been ignored or overlooked. In the area of foreign policy the majority still needed to find its past. With that realization, the idea for this collection of essays on women and foreign policy began germinating. The work of other historians, such as Robert E. May's provocative 1979 article on Jane and William Cazneau, sustained my faith in the project.[3] In the fall of 1980 I publicly began presenting my case that women had been historical actors in shaping the nation's foreign policy. At the invitation of my mentor, William Appleman Williams, I delivered a paper at Oregon State University entitled "Women, Slavery, and American Foreign Policy." An early version of the essay on Lydia Maria Child that appears in this collection, my presentation received an encouraging and heartening response. The following year at the annual meeting of the Organization of American Historians in Detroit, I participated in a panel on "Teaching Political and Diplomatic History in an Age of Social History." In my remarks I suggested how one might incorporate the role of women into courses on diplomatic history. On that occasion the small,

all-male audience was openly skeptical and my ideas about women and foreign policy received a chilly reception. I perfectly understood their doubts, having myself originally shared much the same outlook.

By 1983 I had determined that a collection of original essays on the role of individual women in foreign policy was justified and long overdue. The next step was to locate and invite scholars to participate. How to proceed—should I seek well-established scholars to suggest a woman to be included or should I determine the subjects and match them to scholars I had reason to believe would willingly join such a project? As might be expected I followed both procedures. I began on the assumption that my essay on Lydia Maria Child and another on Jane Cazneau would be the opening chapters in the book. Then I decided that several prominent twentieth century women who had been or were actors in the nation's diplomacy, such as Eleanor Roosevelt and Jeane Kirkpatrick, had to be included in such a venture. I first contacted scholars who I knew had been or were engaged in research on prominent American women and invited them to contribute. Simultaneously I coaxed and cajoled a colleague and encouraged one or two graduate students at William and Mary to participate. In a relatively short period of time I lined up an impressive slate of female subjects and corresponding list of contributors for this collection. The present volume is the result of that rather eclectic process.[4]

As editor I did provide each of the contributors with suggestions as to how to proceed and offered several questions for them to consider in preparing their essays. The most important question I posed for each author was central to the purpose of the book: to what extent did the woman influence the foreign policy of the United States? If there was no measurable direct influence, I asked the authors to demonstrate the extent to which their subject's activities, speeches, writings, etc., helped shape the intellectual and political consciousness of other individuals and groups as well as the society at large by defining the issues and developing alternatives. Finally, I asked them to determine whether or not their woman presented or represented a special or different women's perspective. In my estimation, those guidelines have been fairly well met in the essays that follow.

This approach has avoided one of the pitfalls of current scholarship on women identified recently by Hilda Smith. She argues that the concurrent popularity and applicability of women's history and social history have operated to the disadvantage of women because females have been treated as a unit and not as individuals. According to Smith, "When women are lumped together as a unit, while men are studied both as individuals and members of groups, historians and students come to view men as historical actors and women as a group which merely reacts to historical events."[5] The essays in this collection avoid and correct that imbalance by showing that individual women over a long span of the nation's life have been historical actors and have not simply reacted to events.

The opening essay on Child focuses on her intellectual formulation of the slave power thesis as the core of her critique of antebellum diplomacy. Her ideas led countless men and women into the fight against slavery and guided their petition campaigns of the 1830s and 1840s, which in my opinion represents the first truly democratic grass-roots lobbying effort dedicated to restructuring the nation's foreign policy. Child's influence repeatedly was acknowledged by her male and female contemporaries, among them Senators Charles Sumner and Henry Wilson. Admittedly she never directly formulated or executed American diplomacy, but she is a perfect example of a female who shaped and defined the political consciousness of her era by clearly defining foreign policy issues and offering alternative courses of action.

In contrast to Child, Jane Cazneau "stressed the utility of power and force in international relations" and sought to influence foreign policy in distinctly masculine terms. Robert E. May's essay demonstrates the effectiveness of Cazneau's lobbying efforts in behalf of territorial expansion as well as her role in nurturing a transition in the American outlook that emphasized overseas commercial expansion. On foreign policy issues she represented positions that were diametrically opposed to those of her contemporary Maria Child. This was most dramatically illustrated by their differing and opposing viewpoints on Texas and Santo Domingo. What is also apparent is the absence of any gender-related pattern in the foreign policy stances each adopted. Child and Cazneau disagreed on the issues, but their disagreements were mirrored throughout the dominant male population. Cazneau operated as lobbyist and quasi-insider and apparently was more influential in swaying the decisions of policy-makers than was perennial critic Child, or for that matter Anna Ella Carroll, a woman who shared many of Cazneau's views on foreign policy

In her essay on Anna Carroll, Janet Coryell provides another example and mode of female political participation in the man's world that was the mid-nineteenth century. On the surface Carroll's foreign policy outlook, with its emphasis on commercial expansion, appeared quite similar to that of Cazneau, but she was noticeably less consistent as publicist and more mercurial as activist than either of her contemporaries. A woman with a strong sense of duty and passionate devotion to America's mission in the world, Carroll resembled an early version of female jingo dedicated to a chauvinistic spread-eaglism, the American way, and Anglo-Saxon superiority. Despite their different political agendas Carroll and Cazneau clearly adapted to men's rules and norms, and operated as men did in their foreign policy activities. Neither one became a feminist. In post-Civil War years only Maria Child of the three came to see the "woman question" as "decidedly the most important question that has been before the world."[6]

Certainly the "woman question" dominated the career of Lucia Ames Mead, an early twentieth century suffragist and pacifist. As John Craig illustrates, Mead combined an ongoing commitment to women's equality with an activist program of antiimperialism and antimilitarism. Her ambitious pacifism was designed not only to change radically the course of American diplomacy, but to alter completely the accepted pattern of the use of force to settle international disputes.

However, much like Child, who earlier placed abolitionism before women's rights, Mead chose "peace first" over suffragism. She rationalized her position by arguing that women would achieve true equality only through the acceptance of pacifist principles. On that level Child and Mead appear to fulfill what apparently is the most common stereotype about women, which is the belief that American females are predisposed by their socialization to favor peaceful and negotiated settlements to international problems rather than resort to war.

Eleanor Roosevelt initially was attracted to a similar vision of world peace and international harmony, although unlike Mead, she never was a bona fide, full-fledged pacifist. In Blanche Wiesen Cook's essay, Eleanor Roosevelt emerges as a "realistic pacifist" who believed in power, understood power, and sought it throughout her public life. Primarily an insider who also unwaveringly functioned as critic of international injustice and lobbyist for human rights, Roosevelt frequented the corridors of power at both the national and international levels. Eleanor Roosevelt, as Cook shows, was "the First Lady of the World" who "more than any other woman of her era influenced policy from positions of power." In many ways Eleanor Roosevelt's career mirrored the transition that was taking place in women's lives in the twentieth century as her generation saw the victory of woman's suffrage and the dawn of a new era when women would be elected to state legislatures and Congress, serve as members of presidential cabinets, and be appointed ambassadors and ministers of the United States abroad.

As a contemporary of Roosevelt's, Eleanor Lansing Dulles anticipated that her gender would be inconsequential as a barrier to a successful career in the State Department and other government agencies. Certainly as the sister of·two prominent male members of the foreign policy elite she was well-connected and superficially on the threshold of power. But, as Lynne Dunn illustrates, even a female insider with connections who aimed to join the boys' club was denied entrance to the inner sanctum of the foreign policy establishment. Throughout her career Eleanor Dulles remained on the periphery. She was confined to a mid-level status at State and only her presumed importance in the eyes of German leaders allowed her to temporarily finesse the old boy network during her highly successful Berlin assignment. Even then, as Dunn reveals, Eleanor Dulles's male colleagues were using the power of her name to make the Germans believe the United States was greatly concerned about the Berlin issue.

Unlike insider Dulles, who patiently played by men's rules, Jane Fonda boldly and publicly challenged the male establishment to change its policies and withdraw from Vietnam. In her essay Jeanne Zeidler presents Fonda as an example of a contemporary female critic who, outraged by her country's actions in Southeast Asia—just as Child and Mead had been appalled at the moral costs of expansion and imperialism—attempted to parlay her media fame and fortune into political clout and grassroots mobilization for change. While recently a male or two has been able to transfer media power into political power with direct access to decision-making circles, this has yet to be true for a woman. And in

Fonda's case, the fact that she had not duplicated the intellectual efforts of Child and Mead in formulating her opposition to American foreign policy partially explains why her influence on American diplomacy was limited and her activism shortlived.

Among the women discussed in this collection, Jeane Kirkpatrick was the sole female to enter the inner circle of foreign policy decision-makers. As the former United States Ambassador to the United Nations noted shortly after leaving the Reagan administration: "I was the only woman in our history, I think, who ever sat in regularly at top-level foreign policy making meetings." But, as Judith Ewell argues, mere attendance at cabinet or National Security Council meetings assured neither direct influence nor measurable power in the decision-making process. As a general rule the U.N. Ambassadorship, even when occupied by males, has not been a policy-making job. Kirkpatrick's tenure was no exception to this rule as her gender only proved a further limitation on her effectiveness in the male bastions of the foreign policy establishment. It is apparent from Ewell's essay that even with Ambassador Kirkpatrick's pathbreaking elevation to the inner circle, sexist attitudes still restrict women's access to the top levels of decision-making in American diplomacy.

In her concluding essay "Of Mice and Men," Joan Hoff-Wilson provides a historical overview of women in the State Department, some observations about the pattern of the careers of Frances Willis and Jeannette Rankin, and a summary evaluation of the significance of the foreign policy activities of all the women included in this collection. She finds that while in the past decade there has been some improvement in the overall status of women in the State Department, in the Foreign Service women "continued to be markedly underrepresented at the senior levels" and career women have neither filled the major diplomatic posts nor have they headed the various bureaus of the Department. The sketches of Willis and Rankin further verify, as do the other essays in this collection, the absence of any gender-related pattern in the foreign policy positions taken by women throughout the nation's history. In evaluating what the other essays demonstrate about the influence and role of women in foreign policy formulation, Hoff-Wilson is struck by the marginality of women in the decision-making process, obviously attributable to the fact that women traditionally have been excluded from the upper echelon of policy-makers.

Indisputably the formulation and conduct of American diplomacy remains male-dominated and male-oriented. Throughout the nation's existence United States foreign policy has been the domain of white, Anglo-Saxon, Protestant males. The following essays reveal, however, that since the 1830s a number of American women have attempted to shape and influence the nation's foreign policy. They have done so with varying, often limited, degrees of success. But in the process women have expanded their role in the public sphere, helped shape the public's consciousness about the nation's diplomacy, and frequently offered alternative policies that ultimately have infiltrated the inner sanctum of the foreign policy establishment. They have done this as lobbyists who employed intelligence, charm, and tenacity to persuade powerful men to accept their views, as insiders who subtly and effectively influenced the men who were their husbands, bosses, and confidants, and as critics who publicized their ideas and politically mobilized women and men in the pursuit of changing the nature of American foreign policy.

NOTES

1. Joan Hoff-Wilson, "Foreign Policy Trends Since 1920," *SHAFR Newsletter* (September, 1977), 1.

2. Gerda Lerner, *The Majority Finds Its Past: Placing Women in History* (New York, 1979), 165.

3. Robert E. May, "Lobbyists for Commerical Empire: Jane Cazneau, William Cazneau, and U.S. Caribbean Policy, 1846–1878," *Pacific Historical Review* (August, 1979), 383–412.

4. Earlier versions of the essays on Child, Dulles, and Kirkpatrick in this volume were presented at a session entitled "Women in American Foreign Policy" at the annual meeting of the Society for Historians of American Foreign Policy at Stanford University on June 25–28, 1985.

5. Hilda L. Smith, "Women's History and Social History: An Untimely Alliance," *OAH Newsletter* (November, 1984).

6. Lydia Maria Child to Sarah Shaw, September, 1869, in Patricia G. Holland, and Milton Meltzer, *The Collected Correspondence of Lydia Maria Child*, microfiche edition.

1

Lydia Maria Child:
Abolitionist Critic of
American Foreign Policy

Edward P. Crapol

One of the pioneer female critics of American diplomacy was the nineteenth century abolitionist Lydia Maria Child. Born in Medford, Massachusetts, in 1802, she was the youngest of the six children of David Convers Francis, a baker who obtained modest fame and fortune as the producer of the "Medford cracker," and Susannah Rand Francis. Before reaching the age of thirty, Maria Child, as she preferred to be called, had made her mark as an intellectual who was at once a successful novelist, a noted author of "how to" books for women, and the editor of *Juvenile Miscellany*, the first children's magazine to appear in the United States. An advocate of what the English historian J. H. Plumb has labeled the idea of modernity, Mrs. Child viewed slavery as an inhumane, outmoded institution and adhered to the belief that the betterment of humankind, including the elimination of slavery, would be attained through the "acceptance of man's rationality and control over nature."[1] She also operated on the belief that the institution of chattel slavery was acceptable in a society where the status of women and children in the family resembled a form of slavery. As a consequence, Maria Child championed the cause of women's rights on its own merits as well as being a means to undermine black slavery. In *The Mother's Book* (1831) she warned against the overemphasis on romance in young women's lives, urged instead that they cultivate their intellects, abandon their timidity and overcome their dependence on men.[2] Maria Child practiced what she preached. In an extraordinary reversal of roles for nineteenth century America she, admittedly more as a matter of necessity than of choice, financially supported her husband, David Lee Child, for most of their married life.

In the early 1830s at what appeared to be the height of her initial literary fame, Maria Child consciously endangered her public reputation by choosing to become an abolitionist. It was not an easy decision. Her husband made the first move, but she resisted and expressed serious reservations about the antislavery cause. An introduction to William Lloyd Garrison arranged by husband, David, led to her conversion. As she recalled years later, "I little thought then that the whole pattern of my life-web would be changed by that introduction. I was then all absorbed in poetry and painting, soaring aloft on Psyche-wings into ethereal regions of mysticism. He got hold of the strings of my conscience and pulled me into reforms."[3] Once committed to a life of intellectual activism for social reform, Child's critique of the nation's diplomacy flowed naturally from her newly acquired antislavery beliefs. For more than forty years as writer, petitioner, organizer, pamphleteer, and editor she fought slavery, sought racial and sexual equality, and decried "the insane rage for annexation in this country" and the propensity to seize "the territory of our neighbors by fraud or force."[4]

The event that signaled Child's public debut as an abolitionist was the publication in July 1833 of her *An Appeal in Favor of That Class of Americans Called Africans*. Not only was it the first book by an American, either male or female, to call for immediate emancipation, but it also included the first systematic exposition of the slave power thesis to appear in the United States. Pathbreaking as well were Maria Child's unflinching denunciation of white racism in the North and South and her plea for a national policy of racial equality. Not surprisingly the *Appeal*'s harsh attack on slavery, its indictment of white racism, and its demand for racial equality shocked and offended a large number of Mrs. Child's faithful readers. Unquestionably the majority of Americans found her analysis too radical, certainly it was not the sort of thing a respectable American woman should be writing. The *North American Review*, previously among her admirers, regretted that Mrs. Child had diverted her pen from its "legitimate spheres of action."[5] She had anticipated such negative responses to her *Appeal*. In the book's preface Child stated defiantly that "I am fully aware of the unpopularity of the task I have undertaken; but though I *expect* ridicule and censure, it is not my nature to *fear* them."[6] Her prediction was correct. Sales of her books plummeted and the *Juvenile Miscellany* enterprise folded. With the publication of the *Appeal* Child courageously embarked on a lifelong struggle for blacks; but her abolitionism exacted a heavy financial toll as she never fully regained the broad popularity she once enjoyed among the reading public.

Despite its unpopularity with the general public and the political establishment in the United States, the *Appeal* represented a milestone in antislavery annals. It probably converted more women and men to the abolitionist cause than any other publication. Many northern antebellum women acknowledged their intellectual and moral debt to Mrs. Child both publicly and privately. In 1835 antislavery women in Lynn, and Salem, Massachusetts, sent her a gold watch in appreciation of her noble "first appeal in behalf of the American slave."[7] Initially converted or strengthened in their commitment to the antislavery cause after reading the *Appeal* were such prominent and influential male opponents of slavery as William Ellery Channing, Theodore Weld, Wendell Phillips, Charles Sumner, Henry Wilson, Thomas Wentworth Higginson, and John Gorham Palfrey. Two members of this band of Child disciples, Republicans Charles Sumner and Henry Wilson, ultimately wielded considerable political power as senators from Massachusetts, and in Wilson's case as vice president in the second Grant administration. Of all Maria Child's male "pupils," Sumner came closest to being her intellectual protégé and he fondly referred to her as "his teacher."[8]

Child's exposé of the influence of the slave power in her *Appeal* updated the old Federalist argument that stressed the inequity of the three-fifths clause of the Constitution. In her view that clause, which counted a slave as three-fifths of a person in the population tabulation for representation, gave the South twenty undeserved members of the House of Representatives, allowing Southerners to be the "ruling power of this government" as evidenced in their control of the presidency, the vice presidency, the federal judiciary, and the Congress. The detrimental impact on the North as a result of this Southern dominance in the national councils was all too evident, Child alleged, and was reflected most clearly in the South's historical unfriendliness to commerce and that region's opposition to the growth of an American navy. She repeated another standard Federalist charge by claiming that the War of 1812 had been fought for southern, not national, interests. On the question of the tariff, Mrs. Child found the South to be totally inconsistent, first using duties to inhibit commerce and then objecting when the North favored the tariff to protect is nascent industries. Her partisan reading of the history of the United States's fifty year existence led to the conclusion that the South had a stranglehold on the levers of federal power, which guaranteed "the preservation and extension of slave power."[9]

In concluding her analysis of slavery's political influence on the republic, Child decried the slave power's restrictive grip on the nation's diplomacy. Her concerns about foreign policy focused on the issues of Haiti and Texas. More than a quarter of a century after the creation of the western hemisphere's first black republic, the United States still withheld formal diplomatic recognition of Haiti. Child not only argued that official recognition was long overdue, but justified, because Haiti was a political and economic success, "fast increasing its wealth, intelligence and refinement." In her call for recognition she highlighted the commercial benefits that would accrue to the United States from such action. American trade with the black republic, impressive even without the benefit of formal diplomatic ties, would be greatly expanded after recognition and the exchange of representatives. In the early 1820s it was estimated that America's exports to Haiti were as large as its combined exports to Sweden, Russia, Denmark, Prussia and Ireland and more shipping entered American ports from Haiti than any other nation except Great Britain, the British North American colonies, and the island of Cuba. In 1831 total trade with Haiti approached $3,000,000, much of it moving through New England's ports.[10] But, according to Mrs. Child, neither simple human justice nor commercial logic would prompt the Andrew Jackson administration or the Congress to support recognition. The "existence of slavery among us" prevents it, she lamented, and even more distressing, "our Northern representatives have never even made an effort to have her independence acknowledged, because a colored ambassador would be so disagreeable to our prejudices."[11]

Prior to Child's demand for recognition, several politicians had warily and obliquely raised the issue, most notably Caleb Cushing and Henry Clay. In response to these cautious soundings, public opinion remained hostile to the idea, and in that context Child's advocacy of Haitian recognition proved as courageous as it was ingenious. What she did was to employ a foreign policy issue to emphasize the central paradox confronting the citizens of antebellum America. The demand for the recognition of Haiti uncovered the basic contradictions inherent in prevailing American ideology, whereby a republic based on the principle of human liberty, defended and promoted racial inequality and sanctioned chattel slavery for several million human beings. The fact that the Haitian issue forced Americans to accept or reject black equality, and indirectly acknowledge the humanity of American slaves, probably explains why that issue, which appears so innocuous on the surface, became one of the primary objectives of the early abolitionist political program.

Southern designs aimed at acquiring Texas from Mexico emerged as another foreign policy issue that agitated Mrs. Child to action. On this question she was following the lead of the Quaker abolitionist, Benjamin Lundy, and her husband, David Lee Child, both of whom had warned her of this danger earlier. "The purchase or the conquest of Texas is a favorite scheme with Southerners," she said, "because it would occasion such an inexhaustible demand for slaves." At the time of the publication of the *Appeal* in 1833, she was gratified that "the jealousy of the Mexican government places a barrier in that direction."[12] To help ensure that Texas remained Mexican and not new territory for the expansion of slavery, Maria Child during the next several years personally helped gather 45,000 signatures against the annexation of Texas on petitions that were sent to the United States Congress.[13] That prodigious feat was paralleled by her direct influence on the future direction of the antislavery enterprise, for Mrs. Child identified and pinpointed two of the key foreign policy issues—recognition of Haiti and opposition to the annexation of Texas—that became central to the petition campaigns mounted by men and women abolitionists in the 1830s and 1840s.

Despite her unprecedented achievement in so clearly defining the issues and projecting the line of intellectual attack for the antislavery forces, Child's critique of the slave power was not without flaws and partisan exaggeration. Her comments on the War of 1812, the question of Southern opposition to commerce and a navy, and her view of the South's flip-flop on the tariff were often simplistic, inaccurate, and one-sided. And although the three-fifths clause may have allowed the South to elect twenty additional members to the House of Representatives, at no time between the adoption of the Constitution in 1789 and 1833, when her book appeared, did the South as a section have a majority in that body. But her *Appeal* should not be dismissed as a paranoid jeremiad. The basic thrust of her argument was correct. The South did dominate the national government. Northern political support was necessary to maintain that domination, but dominate the South did. Mrs. Child recognized that reality, and while imploring the South to abandon slavery for its and the nation's moral and ideological salvation, concentrated on persuading her northern brethren that it was in their self-interest to work to eliminate slavery and its restraints on the nation's diplomacy.

As a trailblazing critic of foreign policy Mrs. Child consistently throughout her career expressed misgivings about the national mania for territorial expansion. Child was a resolute champion of the underdog, who instinctively sought to protect the reds and the blacks. Future expansion could only come at their expense. It would deprive the Indians of their land and destroy their culture, and it would tighten the bonds of slavery for blacks by opening ever more territory to the "peculiar institution." Child was deeply troubled by what she foresaw as the dire impact of future expansionism. In 1838 she confided to her friend Henrietta Sargent: "What God is preparing for us along the Indian frontier, in Mexico, Cuba, Hayti, I know not; but I think I see 'coming events cast their shadows before.' We certainly have done all we could to secure the deadly hostility of the red man and the black man everywhere." And she added this apocalyptic afterthought: "I think God will overrule *events* to bring about a change, long before the moral sense of this nation demands it as a matter of justice and humanity."[14]

Once she reached the forefront of the antislavery enterprise, Mrs. Child found herself in a whirlwind of activity that ran the political gamut from the tedious chore of circulating petitions to the emotionally and intellectually more satisfying task of dashing off polemical tracts such as *An Anti-Slavery Catechism*. Shortly after the appearance of the *Appeal* she joined the Boston Female Anti-Slavery Society and proceeded to organize, with the help of her close friend Louisa Loring, the first antislavery fair to be held in the country. These bazaars became an annual affair where women contributed needlework, cakes, jellies, preserves, and other goods to be sold to raise money for the cause. The expanding public role played by antislavery women caused some consternation within the movement's ranks as well as among the general public. Mrs. Child assured her sisters that while "some will tell you that *women* have nothing to do with this question . . . where women are brutalized, scourged, and sold, shall we not inquire the reason? My sisters, you have not only the right, but it is your solemn duty."[15] Until her death in 1880 Child would be driven to do something for her oppressed brothers and sisters, be they black, red, white, or yellow.

As a leading antislavery couple the Childs were much in demand during the 1830s heyday of abolitionist activity. In recognition of their commitment they were among the group that hosted the controversial 1835 visit of the British antislavery leader George Thompson. Then in rapid succession the Childs were nominated or volunteered for three overseas ventures ostensibly designed to broadcast the antislavery message, but aimed as well to relieve their increasingly precarious financial straits. A grateful Thompson offered David Child a position in England as an antislavery editor, but before they could sail the entire scheme collapsed for lack of funds. Primarily to overcome the burden of debt, the Childs in early 1836 made plans to join Benjamin Lundy's free labor settlement in Tamaulipas, Mexico. The Texas revolution and the creation of the Lone Star Republic aborted those plans, since the territory Lundy's band was to settle was claimed by Texas. Mrs. Child saw the hand of the slave power at work as she complained that "the troubles in Texas have been got up by bad, ambitious men, stimulated by offers from Southern planters, who want that fine territory for slave markets." Disappointed and depressed at the turn of events, her spirit was "sorely tried concerning Texas" for "if this territory be acquired" by the United States she feared it would "throw back abolition half a century."[16] Still hoping to go abroad, Maria and David volunteered at the 1836 annual meeting to be emissaries for the American Anti-Slavery Society on a fact-finding mission to Haiti and the British West Indies to gather information on the condition of free blacks in those islands. Once again they were thwarted as the Executive Committee of that organization thought the Childs, especially Maria, would be more valuable if they remained at home writing antislavery tracts and articles for the press.

Frustrated in his scheme for a Mexican free labor colony, their friend Benjamin Lundy initially became the major antislavery spokesman against Texas annexation. His two broadsides on the Texas insurrection were standard texts for opponents of further territorial expansion in slavery's behalf, and John Quincy Adams relied on Lundy's expertise and advice while waging the fight against annexation in the House of Representatives. Lundy's analysis of the events and forces that led to the Texas rebellion, while drawn from his own personal experience in that Mexican province, unmistakably was cast in the polemical mold of Mrs. Child's slave power thesis. The Jackson administration's swift recognition of the Texas Republic in March, 1837, in glaring contrast to its established policy of non-recognition of the black republic of Haiti, led Mrs. Child and her compatriots to identify the action as irrefutable evidence of the slave power's dominance in Washington. In the midst of this first Texas crisis the signs of slave power's influence were alarmingly visible. Perhaps most ominous was an action by the House of Representatives in 1836 that directly threatened the constitutional guarantee of the right of petition. The House's so-called gag rule, which automatically tabled all antislavery memorials and petitions, was a rude awakening for many in the antislavery enterprise since it exposed the precarious nature of their own civil liberties.

The Southern-inspired use of the gag in the House, which so blatantly threatened the civil liberties of white male protesters, had the political effect of linking "the claims of emancipation and free discussion." This prompted large numbers of Northerners to flock to the antislavery banner, although Mrs. Child believed many of these new recruits "care little or nothing for the poor slave."[17] And even as it made new converts to the cause, the gag rule did little or nothing to abate the flood of petitions that continued to pour into Congress, which by April 1838 "filled a room 20 x 30 x 14 feet, closely packed to the ceiling." Just over half of those petitions were circulated and signed by women. That year in Northampton, Massachusetts, residents Maria and David Child also were busy at what she considered "that most odious of all tasks, that of getting signatures to Petitions."[18] During the third session of the Twenty-Fifth Congress, December 1838–March, 1839, abolitionist petitions with a total of 500,000 signatures were presented on eight separate topics, including the issues of opposition to the annexation of Texas, and for the first time, the call for the recognition of Haiti.[19] Actually the inauguration of petitions for Haitian recognition was a ploy to evade the gag rule, as abolitionists hoped to force a debate on the diplomatic and commercial merits of the Haitian case and ultimately the evils of slavery, to the floor of Congress. The tactic failed as petitions for Haitian recognition were routinely tabled in the same manner as other antislavery memorials.

Some historians of the pre-Civil War period have argued that the shift in the antislavery outlook from an earlier focus on black equality to one primarily concerned with the political, economic and social rights of northern white men led to the creation of an implicitly racist ideology based on the concept of free men, free soil, and free labor.[20] Although an accurate assessment, what this interpretation ignores is that the gag rule as an overt challenge to white civil rights probably represented an even greater immediate political threat to female than to male abolitionists. Unable to vote or to participate in the various activities associated with the electoral process, antislavery women saw the activity of circulating petitions as the most important form of political action open to them in antebellum America. To thwart that activity would deprive women of even that marginal political voice. The case for petitioning as being crucial to expanding women's public sphere was made repeatedly by abolitionist women and put most clearly by the Third Anti-Slavery Convention of American Women in 1839:

It is our only means of direct political action. It is not ours to fill the offices of government, or to assist in the election of those who shall fill them. We do not enact or enforce the laws of the land. The only direct influence which we can exert upon our Legislatures, is by protests and petitions.[21]

Admittedly women's petition campaigns by and large failed in their objectives of changing domestic and foreign policy. But as historian Nancy Woloch asserted in her recent study of women in American history, antebellum women did succeed "in appropriating and feminizing a portion of the public sphere."[22]

Maria Child reluctantly had attended the first Anti-Slavery Convention of American Women in New York in May 1837. She had come to doubt the wisdom of separate female organizations, believing they reinforced the false notion of the legitimacy of separate spheres for men and women and feeling they were "like half a pair of scissors." After heavy pressure from female friends in the movement, Child went as a delegate from Massachusetts. Honored by being elected one of its six vice presidents of the convention, she actively participated in the proceedings, offering several resolutions on slavery and the right of petition that were adopted by the assembly. Although she did not attend the second women's meeting at Philadelphia the following year, Mrs Child agreed to author the convention's "Address to the Senators and Representatives of the Free States," which was to be distributed to all northern members of Congress. Noting that various Congressional resolutions betrayed a belief in the ephemeral nature of the antislavery feeling, she denied that the abolitionist effort was simply a "fanatical and temporary excitement." She also chastised northern legislators for their passivity in the face of the slave power's encroachments. It was their "timid subserviency" that had allowed for Texan independence to be "so hastily acknowledged" by the American government. But not all Northern members of Congress were spineless, and in her "Address" Mrs. Child singled out Representative William Slade of Vermont and Senator Thomas Morris of Ohio for their political courage.[23]

It was fitting that Mrs. Child should praise the work of Slade and Morris in Congress. Both men were staunch opponents of slavery and the slave power, and probably had been influenced in their antislavery beliefs by the analysis presented in her 1833 *Appeal*. Within months after Child's recognition of their service to the cause, each man would champion issues that she had helped bring to public attention. In December 1838 Representative Slade recommended that a memorial of the citizens of West Randolph, Vermont, be forwarded to the Committee on Foreign Affairs, "with instructions to report bill for recognizing independence of Hayti, and making provision for customary diplomatic relations with said republic."[24] Slade's motion to bring the issue of recognition before the House provided a storm of protest from his Southern colleagues. John Quincy Adams and a few others nonetheless supported Slade's action, but in early 1839 the Foreign Affairs Committee asked to be discharged of further consideration of Haitian recognition, effectively killing the issue in that session. For his part, Senator Morris in February 1839 delivered a famous speech that ostensibly was a defense of the right of petition for abolitionists. In reality the speech proved to be one of the more comprehensive attacks on the slave power, which in its line of argument drew heavily on the intellectual formulation developed by Mrs. Child in her earlier critiques. Widely reprinted, Morris's speech gained a certain notoriety among the faithful and was to become required reading in the growing antislavery library.

After completing the "Address to the Senators and Representatives of the Free States," Mrs. Child temporarily curtailed her public activities primarily because of financial difficulties brought about in good part by her husband's total lack of "business sense." She devoted her energies to aiding her husband in the latest of his unprofitable experiments with sugar beet cultivation, which he hoped would become an alternative to slave-produced cane sugar. In 1841 she emerged from a brief self-imposed exile to accept the position as editor of the *National Anti-Slavery Standard*, a weekly abolitionist newspaper based in New York City. As the first woman to edit a major antislavery publication, Mrs.

Child labored for two years to set a moderate and reasoned tone at the *Standard* in hope of calmly persuading more Americans to the antislavery banner. Initially Mrs. Child's editorials reflected her determination to steer a middle course between the Garrisonians and the Liberty Party men, the two factions that split abolitionist ranks in the early 1840s. In the end she became identified with the Garrison faction, going so far as to endorse his call for disunion in an 1842 editorial. A disunionist stance had been unthinkable to her just nine years earlier when she issued the *Appeal*, but in the interim she had become radicalized by the experience of incessantly confronting the slave power's arrogant and aggressive domination of the existing union. Privately she went even further, confiding to her close friends that violence would be necessary to end slavery and purify the American republic.

The major foreign policy concern of the *Standard* during her tenure as editor was the prevention of the annexation of Texas. The newspaper covered in detail the Congressional debates on the Texas question and kept up the abolitionist drumbeat against taking the Lone Star Republic into the Union. Her husband, David, shared the commitment to antiannexation, writing a major broadside on the issue and traveling to Washington in the fall of 1842 to serve as informal correspondent for both the *Standard* and Garrison's *Liberator*. Mrs. Child also tried to coax non-abolitionist editors to oppose annexation, particularly the transcendentalist Parke Godwin of the *Pathfinder*. She sent Godwin her husband's pamphlet on Texas urging him "to tell the people the truth" because "slavery is making a desperate effort for the extension and permanence of its power on this continent."[25] Although the abolitionists had prevented Texas annexation since the 1836 insurrection against Mexico, Mrs. Child became rather fatalistic about continued antislavery success on the issue. In 1843 just after leaving the *Standard* she confided to fellow abolitionist Ellis Gray Loring that organizations, presumably her newspaper as well, "have about done their work" on Texas, but their effort "will be carried to its full completion by events they can neither foresee nor regulate."[26] And in the hectic period before the Tyler administration's successful annexation of Texas in 1845 by joint resolution of Congress, Maria Child again prophesied that the slave power juggernaut would only be stopped through bloodshed and violence.

Child's prediction of internecine violence was premature. The slave power seemed invulnerable as it rolled on in its territorial quests, and not being satisfied with Texas was now engaged in an unjust war with Mexico for territory stretching as far as the Pacific Ocean. Her pen was once again active in opposition to the Mexican War, but not in any official antislavery capacity. As a result of her exhausting and disillusioning experience as editor of the *Standard*, with the continual strain and tension of factional disputes and feuds, Mrs. Child had privately announced to close friends her retirement from the antislavery cause. Despite this semiformal retirement, Lydia Maria Child never really left the antislavery enterprise either emotionally or intellectually. Thereafter she may have operated independently, free of institutional and organizational constraints, but she was no less instrumental in promoting the cause of the slave, and after the Civil War, the freedman.

As an independent critic perhaps her most effective bit of writing during the Mexican War appeared in one of her "letters from New York," a more or less regular column that ran in the *Boston Courier*. In this particular letter Mrs. Child recounted how a new hotel in the city had attracted her attention because of an unusual sign mounted on its facade. The sign depicted a great bird with outstretched wings and in its beak was a banner with the motto: "The American Eagle allows little birds to sing." This "pompous annunciation of our national condescension and forbearance" caused her to smile, but only halfheartedly since her "perverse thoughts jumped from the eagle to Indian treaties and negro slaves." At that moment she heard martial music from a nearby park where recruits were being assembled for service in the war against Mexico. The tune beckoned "the brave and the free" to do battle for their country "without hinting that their mission would be to extend slavery, and rob a *weaker* nation; because little birds must not be allowed to sing."[27] To Maria Child the American sense of mission to benighted little nations seemed irrepressible, as did the slave power's incessant drive for territory.

After what amounted to very limited participation in the opposition to the Mexican War, Mrs. Child retreated further from the public limelight. For nearly a decade she rarely engaged in the formal organizational activities of the anti-slavery cause. Although she never wavered in her abolitionist convictions, the need to overcome nagging personal financial difficulties and to restore some order to her marriage after years of intermittent separation from her husband demanded most of her time and energy. It was not until the passage of the Kansas-Nebraska Bill in May 1854, with its popular sovereignty provision that nullified the 1820 Missouri Compromise's prohibition on the extension of slavery above the 36° 30′ parallel, that Maria Child once again was stirred to action in defense of the slave. She and her husband entered the fray together—David as lecturer and organizer for the Kansas Aid Society; Maria as author of a serialized tale on "The Kansas Emigrants" published in Horace Greeley's *New York Tribune*, and as fundraiser for the antislavery settlers in Kansas.

Predictably, Mrs. Child held the slave power responsible for passage of the Nebraska Bill, but on this occasion she was as harshly critical of Northern members of Congress for being completely servile to the slave interest. Apparently she was totally ignorant of Illinois Senator Stephen A. Douglas's role, which had little to do with slave power, in formulating the legislation to further his political and financial schemes to guarantee that Chicago would be the northern terminus of the projected transcontinental railroad. Although she distrusted Senator Douglas it was not his shenanigans that most bothered her. What Mrs. Child feared above all was that continued northern servility would allow the nation's diplomacy to be manipulated by the slave power to acquire Cuba and Haiti, either through war, or in the case of Cuba, through the liberal use of bribes among Spanish officials. Her fears were not unfounded. Southerners dreamed of Caribbean empire for slavery's expansion and in recognition of the political appeal of those dreams, the Democrats in their 1856 campaign platform endorsed "American ascendancy in the Gulf of Mexico" as one of their foreign policy objectives.[28]

Now in her mid-fifties at the time the Kansas crisis erupted, Mrs. Child occasionally expressed a sense of despair at the successes of the "ever-encroaching Slave-Power." The emergence of the Republican Party with its modest antislavery stance of free territories and the selection of John C. Fremont to head its 1856 presidential ticket did offer Child renewed hope. It was gratifying for this old foe of slavery to see after almost a quarter century of "labor, discouragement, unpopularity, and persecution" that abolitionist principles at last were beginning "visibly to sway the masses." Mrs. Child's long experience in the cause had converted her to the need for organized political action to assure antislavery victory. In her view Garrisonians and the American Anti-Slavery Society were too narrow and intolerant and had little popular appeal. But in Child's elation over Fremont's nomination, she was not uncritical of the Republican candidate or, for that matter, of all politicians. He had been a filibuster who helped bring on the Mexican War. Despite the fact Fremont may have been deluded "by a blaze of false glory," in her eyes that was little excuse for the unjust aggression against Mexico.[29]

If bleeding Kansas and the presidential contest between Fremont and the victorious James Buchanan rekindled Maria Child's desire to act against the slave power, her response to John Brown's raid at Harper's Ferry in late 1859 evoked national attention that rivaled, and probably surpassed, the public response to the *Appeal* in the 1830s. Upon hearing the news of the attack and Brown's capture, she wrote him offering to come to Virginia to nurse and aid him during his convalescence and trial. Captain Brown graciously declined her offer. In the meantime she had written Governor Henry Wise seeking permission to enter Virginia on her errand of mercy. Wise's reply to her request touched off a correspondence on the moral questions surrounding Brown's raid and the issue of slavery that quickly appeared in the pages of the *New York Tribune*.

The publication of the Child-Wise letters led Margaretta Mason, wife of Virginia Senator James M. Mason, to join the fray. Mrs. Mason accused Maria Child of gross hypocrisy in seeking to aid the "old murderer of Harper's Ferry." In her famous response condemning the evils of slavery Mrs. Child, reacting to Mrs. Mason's discussion of the kindnesses southern ladies heaped on slave women during childbirth, caustically noted that in Massachusetts "the pangs of maternity" met with generous support from neighbors, "and here at the North, after we have helped the mothers, *we do not sell the babies.*"[30] The entire Child-Wise-Mason exchange was printed in 1860 as a pamphlet for circulation by the American Anti-Slavery Society. Over 300,000 copies were distributed throughout the North, with a number of copies reaching southern readers as well. An enormous circulation for that day, the pamphlet made Mrs. Child a national figure in the bitterly enflamed sectional dispute over slavery.

The election of Abraham Lincoln in 1860 guaranteed that the raging sectional conflict that had been fueled by John Brown's Harper's Ferry attack would bring disunion and civil war. For almost two decades Maria Child had forecast the horror of civil strife as the inevitable outcome of the struggle between freedom and slavery. As the nation hung on the brink of war after the secession of the lower South and prior to Lincoln's inauguration, Maria Child confidently wrote fellow abolitionist Lucretia Mott in late February 1861 that "whatever turn affairs may take, the term of slavery is sure to be abridged by the present agitation. The blind fury of the Secessionists have [sic] converted them into the most valuable Anti-Slavery Agents."[31] When war came the bloodshed and loss of life appalled her. But President Lincoln and the Republican-led Congress did proceed to enact many of the long-sought reforms on the abolitionist agenda. In rapid succession during 1862 slavery was abolished in the District of Columbia and the territories of the United States, a preliminary emancipation proclamation was announced by the President, and the Lincoln administration granted diplomatic recognition to Haiti and Liberia. Mrs. Child was "infinitely cheered" by these actions that she "had long given up the expectation of living to see." She applauded Charles Sumner, who was in the forefront of the Senate drive for Haitian recognition, for his long-time devotion and service to the abolitionist cause. The Civil War may have been "an awful thing" but it did represent a "visible step of progress" for Mrs. Child and thousands of her antislavery brethren.[32]

Abolitionist satisfaction at the progress achieved during the war could not conceal the political expediency inherent in not a few of the government's actions. There were several political and commercial reasons for Lincoln's support of Haitian recognition. One that played a key role was his desire to find a location for the colonizaion of freed slaves. The island of Haiti had long been touted as a logical choice for colonization and shortly after the United States extended official recognition a scheme for colonization at Ile-à-Vache, Haiti, was approved by the Lincoln administration. The Haitian colonization effort proved to be a disaster for the several hundred freedmen who staged the resettlement effort. Mrs. Child apparently was unaware of either Lincoln's support for the plan or the human tragedy that resulted during the project's brief existence. Had she and the other abolitionists who originated the 1830s campaign for Haitian recognition been attuned to the racist implications of Lincoln's action, they would have realized that victory was purchased at the expense of one of their most cherished goals—black equality.[33]

Mrs. Child, to her credit, did recognize and decry the widespread disdain for the freedmen's rights that was all too common both during and after the war. Her concern that black equality would be thwarted was apparent from the onset of the conflict. In late 1862 just before the official release of the Emancipation Proclamation, she labeled it merely a "war measure" and lamentably "no recognition of principles of justice or humanity surrounded the public act with a halo of moral glory." Even Union victory was bittersweet, as Mrs. Child seemed haunted by the devastating human cost of the war. In August 1865 she confessed to her old friend Sarah Shaw, a mother who had lost her only son in the war, that had she been told slavery would be abolished in her day, "I should have anticipated such enthusiastic joy as would set me half crazy." But in reality that did not occur, "what with the frightful expenditure of blood" and the emancipation of slaves "being forced upon us by *necessity*." What troubled and angered her as well was "the shameful want of protection to the freedmen since they have been emanicipated." With all that on her mind Mrs. Child admitted "there has been no opportunity for any out-gushing of joy and exultation."[34] But as in the past her unflinching intellectual honesty did not immobilize this intrepid reformer or lead to total despair. Undaunted she went on to become a leading advocate of education for the freedmen as a way to secure their political and social rights.

Just as she realized the immediate legacy of the Civil War would not be one of full political and social equality for the recently emancipated blacks, Maria Child doubted that Union victory and the destruction of the slave power would usher in a new diplomatic era marked by a less aggressive, less expansionist foreign policy. Although Child's antiexpansionist outlook originally evolved from her slave power analysis, defeat of the slavocracy did not lead her to abandon her opposition to territorial expansion, especially if it came through fraud or force and at the expense of a weaker nation. If the Union triumph brought the nation no nearer racial equality, it also only temporarily curbed the lust for territory and the spirit of annexation so central to the nineteenth century American psyche. One recent historian of Civil War diplomacy in fact has argued that the North's victory assured the United States' imperial hegemony in North America and the Western Hemisphere, and enabled it "to continue its headlong rush into superpowerdom."[35] While Maria Child in the post-Civil War period continued to object to morally tainted schemes of territorial expansion, she initially did not place the northern victory in the broad imperial context suggested by some twentieth century historians.

When the United States purchased Alaska from Russia in 1867 the transaction did not arouse any opposition from Mrs. Child. Presumably the Alaska deal was unobjectionable because it came under the category of a mutually arrived at diplomatic agreement for territorial transfer between two nations of roughly equivalent power and strength. Such was not the case when President Ulysses S. Grant's administration sought to annex Santo Domingo. The actions of the United States were those of a bully, as the nation used its superior naval and military power to intimidate a weaker, essentially defenseless, neighbor. Filibusters who were sponsored by northern business and commercial interests were being used to prepare the way for American annexation. It was "a bad business," angrily wrote Mrs. Child in 1871, "a real filibustering project, twin brother to our taking Texas from the poor Mexicans. This Republic will sink rapidly to degeneracy and ruin, if we go on thus seizing the territory of our neighbors by fraud or force."[36] There was another reason for Child's anxiety about affairs in

Santo Domingo and her concern for the future of the American republic. Quite at variance with her genuine and lifelong racial tolerance, she was vehemently anti-Catholic and feared that annexation would bring into the Union a sizable Catholic population that was ignorant of and hostile to republican ideals. Her Yankee, Protestant antipathy for the recent Irish Catholic immigrants that arrived in such large numbers in New England prior to the Civil War apparently extended to Catholic Latins in the Caribbean as well. In the midst of her outcry against Dominican annexation she privately informed Senator Sumner that it would be "exceedingly dangerous to add anything to the weight of Roman Catholic influence" in the United States since "the Roman Catholic Church in its spirit and its form, is utterly antagonistic to republican institutions." Sumner ignored this atypical lapse of tolerance in his aging mentor. But for Mrs. Child anti-Catholicism remained an emotional ingredient in her reaction to Grant's effort at Caribbean expansion.[37]

The pages of the *National Standard*, post-Civil War successor to *The National Anti-Slavery Standard*, served as Child's forum in the campaign against Dominican annexation. In the public debate she downplayed anti-Catholicism, focusing squarely instead on the issue of the injustice of American aggrandizement at the expense of a weaker neighbor. Sumner, engaged in what amounted to a personal crusade in the Senate to thwart Grant's plans, received her continued praise and frequent moral support. She was much relieved when the annexation scheme died, thanks primarily to Sumner's opposition as chairman of the Senate Foreign Relations Committee. The entire Dominican episode, favored as it was by a President she otherwise admired and respected, left the seventy-year-old reformer ever more wary of American leadership's thirst for imperial glory and overseas expansion. Mrs. Child was distressed further upon reading Grant's second inaugural address with its confident prediction that the civilized world was progressing toward republicanism under the aegis of the United States. Writing to Mrs. Shaw in late March 1873, Child confided that she liked the President's remarks on Indians and blacks, "but I am very sorry to see him so infected with the greed for annexation; and I thought it very injudicious to blurt out that prophecy about a Universal Republic."[38]

Later that year when the *Virginius* affair became a *cause célèbre* it appeared Grant might annex Cuba. That island was wracked by a protracted insurrection against Spanish rule. A crisis with the United States erupted when Spanish authorities seized the *Virginius* in the fall of 1873 and summarily executed its predominantly American crew on the charge the ship was carrying arms and supplies to the Cuban revolutionaries. A national furor arose that prompted calls for the American takeover of Cuba. *Harper's Weekly* highlighted its coverage of what it labeled "the butchery in Cuba" with illustrated sketches of crew members and political cartoons urging the Grant administration to take action against the Spanish. One cartoon by Thomas Nast depicted Secretary of State Hamilton Fish boosting Uncle Sam into a bull ring as President Grant handed him a sword with the caption: "THE SPANISH BULL IN CUBA GONE MAD. It must be stopped. If Spain can't do it, WE MUST!"[39] Maria Child was sorely "vexed" at Nast's "mad bull" rendition. In her view the Spanish had not acted as a mad bull; they simply had defended themselves against filibusters and marauders. She also believed "our talk about humanity, and the vindication of our national honor, is all pretense—too flimsy to disguise our eagerness to grab at the possessions of Cuba." In Child's exasperation with American territorial lust she exclaimed "I do believe if we could annex the whole world, we should try to get a quarrel with Saturn, in order to snatch his ring from him."[40] It would appear that within a few short years after the Civil War ended, Mrs. Child had accepted the verdict of later historians that Union victory had set the stage for the creation of an American overseas empire.

In the 1870s Child concluded a lengthy and impressive career as foreign policy critic and champion of the underdog by adopting the cause of the Chinese immigrant. Through the tried-and-true methods of public letter writing and the lobbying of influential male politicans she opposed federal attempts to exclude Chinese from entering the United States. Frequently skeptical of "spread-eagle" nationalism with its inflated sense of mission, Child on this issue revealed her own somewhat romanticized vision of the mission of a republican United States recently cleansed of the taint of slavery. America now had "a glorious mission" to serve as "a High School for all the nations" by accepting, embracing, and assimilating all comers to its shores. In seeking to make the nation a pluralistic model of racial tolerance and political freedom, Mrs. Child denounced what she identified as a cresting wave of native Americanism, apparently unbothered by the inconsistency of opposing further Catholic additions to the population while urging open access for the Chinese.[41] The focus of the anti-Chinese campaign was repeal of the 1868 Burlingame Treaty with China, an agreement that allowed for unrestricted immigration and movement between the two countries. In the end the forces of American nativism triumphed when Congress passed the Chinese Exclusion Act in 1882. Mrs. Child, who died in 1880, did not live to see the defeat of the last of her many foreign policy crusades.

Any assessment of Maria Child's impact on American foreign policy would have to begin with the recognition that she was ever the suspect outsider and unwelcome critic. At no time in her career did she formulate or execute the nation's diplomacy. At no time did she assume the burden of day-to-day decision-making or the challenge of long-range policy formulation. What influence Mrs. Child did have was necessarily indirect and difficult to gauge or measure precisely. As the voice of the oppressed and disfranchised in nineteenth century America she appealed to her contemporaries through the intellectual power and moral force of her ideas. From the public and private testimony of Child's peers it was apparent that the 1833 *Appeal* successfully presented antislavery's initial critique of slave power and its control of American politics and diplomacy. It served as primer for countless men and women who entered the fight against slavery in the 1830s and 1840s. In that sense she did help shape the intellectual, racial, and political consciousness of a generation of the rank and file of the abolitionist enterprise.

Further proof of the intellectual impact of Child's ideas appeared over the next two decades as the core of her pathbreaking synthesis was adopted and expanded upon by abolitionist men and remained the basis of the antislavery argument until the Civil War. One of the first males to expand upon Child's analysis was Judge William Jay, son of founding father John Jay. Judge Jay extensively reiterated Mrs. Child's argument that American diplomacy was "subservient to the interests of the slaveholders."[42] The Child-Jay slave power analysis had further political influence when it became the ideological foundation of the platform of the Liberty Party in the 1840 campaign. James Birney, the party's presidential candidate, and Joshua Leavitt, editor of the party organ the *Emancipator*, were active proponents of Haitian recognition and in the forefront of the struggle against the annexation of Texas. In their speeches and writings Salmon Chase of Ohio and William Goodell of New York carried the argument through the 1850s. Goodell's 1852 book, *Slavery and Anti-Slavery*, represented the polemical epitome of the antebellum slave power conspiracy thesis. In the immediate post-Civil War years Child's acknowledged disciple, Henry Wilson, authored an insider's three volume retrospective on the rise and fall of the slave power.[43] Although the initial formulator of the slave power thesis, Lydia Maria Child has not received the full historical recognition accorded these men primarily because as a woman she was denied equal access to the political arena. She now must be acknowledged as the leader of the cadre of antebellum intellectuals who demanded and secured the demise of slavery and the slave power.

During the Civil War era when Mrs. Child was at the peak of her national prominence she probably had some sway on foreign policy issues with at least two prominent Republicans—Charles Sumner and Henry Wilson. Just how much influence she had in bringing the Lincoln administration to bestow Haitian recognition or in preventing President Grant from annexing Santo Domingo is virtually impossible to determine, much less measure in any quantifiable way. Her voice undoubtedly was heard, if only to reinforce Sumner, Wilson, and others in their previously held abolitionist convictions. Mrs. Child recognized the limitations under which she labored. As she grew older, the frustration of being unable to participate fully and equally in the nation's political affairs led her to become a tough public advocate of female suffrage and women's rights. At the twilight of her forty-year career she complained to Senator Sumner: "I have keenly felt my limitations as a woman, and have submitted to them under perpetual and indignant protest." When appraising her own influence on public affairs within the constraints placed upon her sex, Mrs. Child used the idiom of "the little mouse" ever active behind the scenes, rejoicing "over her work with infinite satisfaction" on the infrequent occasion when one of her crusades met with success. But in what may well be the most revealing testimony to what it was like to be a female challenging America's male-dominated foreign policy in the nineteenth century, Mrs. Child once confessed that "at times, my old heart swells to bursting . . . for it is the heart of a man imprisoned in a woman's destiny."[44]

NOTES

1. J. H. Plumb, "Spreading the News," review of David Brion Davis' *Slavery and Human Progress, New York Review of Books* (January 17, 1985), 31.

2. Lydia Maria Child, *The Mother's Book* (Boston, 1831), 168.

3. Lydia Maria Child to Anne Whitney, June 1879, in John Greenleaf Whittier (ed.), *Letters of Lydia Maria Child* (Boston, 1883), 255.

4. Lydia Maria Child to Charles Sumner, July 4, 1870, in Milton Meltzer and Patricia G. Holland (eds.), *Lydia Maria Child Selected Letters, 1817–1880* (Amherst, 1982), 495; Lydia Maria Child to David Ricketson, February 15, 1871, in Patricia G. Holland and Milton Meltzer, *The Collected Correspondence of Lydia Maria Child*, microfiche edition. Curiously, throughout her long career as social activist and foreign policy critic Maria Child steadfastly refused to lecture publicly. For example, see Lydia Maria Child to William Lloyd Garrison, *The Liberator*, March 6, 1840.

5. *North American Review*, 41 (1835), 193.

6. Lydia Maria Child, *An Appeal in Favor of That Class of Americans Called Africans* (Boston, 1833), Preface.

7. Anna Purinton to Lydia Maria Child, August 8, 1835, *Collected Correspondence*, microfiche edition.

8. Ibid. Charles Sumner to Lydia Maria Child, September 19, 1856; on the influence of the *Appeal*, see also Lydia Maria Child to Lucy and Mary Osgood, May 11, 1856, to Charles Sumner, July 7, 1856, and to Aaron M. Powell, June 6, 1868.

9. Child, *Appeal*, 112.

10. *Niles Register*, XXVII, 31; Timothy Pitkin, *Statistical View of the Commerce of the United States of America* (New Haven, 1835), 219.

11. Child, *Appeal*, 121.

12. Ibid.

13. Patricia G. Holland and Milton Meltzer, eds., *Guide and Index, The Collected Correspondence of Lydia Maria Child 1817–1880* (Millwood, N.Y., 1980), 28–29.

14. Lydia Maria Child to Henrietta Sargent, November 18, 1838, *Collected Correspondence*, microfiche edition.

15. Lydia Maria Child to the Boston Female Anti-Slavery Society [October?—before 19 November 1835], *Selected Letters*, 41.

16. Lydia Maria Child to Lydia Bigelow Child, March 10, 1836; Lydia Maria Child to Louisa G. Loring, May 30, 1836, *Collected Correspondence*, microfiche edition.

17. Ibid., Lydia Maria Child to Henrietta Sargent, November 18, 1838.

18. Ibid.

19. Gilbert H. Barnes, *The Antislavery Impulse 1830–1844* (Gloucester, Mass., 1957), 266.

20. See, for example, Eric Foner, *Free Soil, Free Labor, Free Men: The Ideology of the Republican Party Before the Civil War* (New York, 1970).

21. *Proceedings of the Third Anti-Slavery Convention of American Women, Held in Phildelphia, May 1st, 2d and 3d, 1839* (Philadelphia, 1839), 26.

22. Nancy Woloch, *Women and the American Experience* (New York, 1984), 182.

23. *Address to the Senators and Representatives of the Free States, in the Congress of the United States, by the Antislavery Convention of American Women* (Philadelphia, 1838).

24. *House Journal*, 25th Cong., 3d Sess, 111; 143.

25. Lydia Maria Child to Parke Godwin, May 2, 1843, *Collected Correspondence*, microfiche edition.

26. Ibid., Lydia Maria Child to Ellis Gray Loring, June 26, 1843.

27. *Boston Courier*, October 27, 1846.

28. See: Robert E. May, *The Southern Dream of a Caribbean Empire, 1854–1861* (Baton Rouge, 1973).

29. Lydia Maria Child to Sarah Shaw, November 9, 1856, *Collected Correspondence*, microfiche edition.

30. *Correspondence Between Lydia Maria Child and Gov. Wise and Mrs. Mason, of Virginia* (Boston, 1860), 26.

31. Lydia Maria Child to Lucretia Mott, February 26, 1861, *Selected Letters*, 377.

32. Ibid., Lydia Maria Child to Charles Sumner, June 22, 1862, 412.

33. Ludwell L. Montague, *Haiti and the United States, 1714–1938* (Durham, 1940), 76.

34. Lydia Maria Child to Sarah Shaw, August 11, 1865, *Selected Letters*, 457–58.

35. David P. Crook, *Diplomacy During the American Civil War* (New York, 1975), 9.

36. Lydia Maria Child to Daniel Ricketson, February 15, 1871, *Collected Correspondence*, microfiche edition.

37. Lydia Maria Child to Charles Sumner, July 4, 1870, *Selected Letters*, 495; for her anti-Irish sentiments, see Lydia Maria Child to Maria Chapman, April 26, 1842, 169.

38. Ibid., Lydia Maria Child to Sarah Shaw, March 24, 1873, 513.

39. *Harper's Weekly*, November 29, 1873, 1068.

40. Lydia Maria Child to Sarah Shaw [1873, after March 24?], *Collected Correspondence*, microfiche edition.

41. Lydia Maria Child to John Greenleaf Whitter, July 31, 1870, *Selected Letters*, 497.

42. William Jay, *A View of the Action of the Federal Government in Behalf of Slavery* (New York, 1839), 47.

43. Henry Wilson, *The Rise and Fall of the Slave Power in America*, 3 vols. (Boston, 1872).

44. Lydia Maria Child to Charles Sumner, Wayland, 1870, in Whittier, *Letters*, 208; Lydia Maria Child to Charles Sumner, July 7, 1856, *Selected Letters*, 283.

2

"Plenipotentiary in Petticoats": Jane M. Cazneau and American Foreign Policy in the Mid-Nineteenth Century

Robert E. May

For American women in the mid-nineteenth century, governmental service was supposed to be forbidden fruit. Deprived of the suffrage, women were subject to advice that their sex be content with its lot and beware the pitfalls awaiting "female politicians." Since they supposedly lacked both the time and "strength of mind" essential to "form decisions on public matters," women were assured of happiness if they found their challenges in the "needle, the broom, the mustard-cup," and other domestic chores. They could make *their* contribution to the national well-being by inculcating republican values at home. Female historical personages who had crossed the sexual boundary line into politics, women such as Empress Catherine II of Russia and Queen Marie Antoinette of France, had suffered guilty consciences and passed "conspicuously unhappy" lives.[1]

Given such mores, it is not surprising that women rarely appear in accounts of nineteenth century American foreign relations. Foreign affairs, a sphere of government often associated with guile and manipulation, was an inapprorpiate realm for a sex who was assigned custodianship of religious and moral virtue. Most women who turn up on the pages of our nineteenth century diplomatic historiography, like the "Gardiner and Tyler ladies" who "cajoled, wheedled, flirted, danced . . . and buttonholed every walking vote [on the Texas annexation congressional resolution of 1845] that came within polka distance," gained entree as flirts. Substantive matters were reserved for men.[2]

One striking exception was Jane M. Cazneau, a New York native of strong ideological convictions, who devoted a great share of her life to influencing the *direction* of American foreign relations. She may well have been attractive. Louisville editor Henry Watterson described her as "still comely at fifty" and surmised that she "must have been a beauty in her youth."[3] However, evidence is compelling that she confronted male politicians and diplomats on their own terms. Her many letters to policy-makers are businesslike in content; address ("Dear Sir," "My Dear Sir," "Mr. President," etc.) and closing ("Very Respectfully," "Truly and respectfully yours," etc.) are usually formal; and there was nothing peculiarly "feminine" about her way of dealing with men who resisted her solicitations—her correspondence is peppered with threats of individual ruin and political party oblivion. Perhaps more significantly, she stressed the utility of power and force in international relations. Certainly male policy-makers—given the sexual stereotypes of the day—characterized her in distinctly masculine terms. To Aaron Burr, who may have had an affair with her at one time, she nonetheless was a "woman of business" with a rare amount of "courage Stability and perseverance" for one of her sex. Thomas Hart Benton remembered her "masculine stomach for war and politics." The New Orleans *Delta* emphasized that she spoke her own mind. A hostile journal satirized that she had become the "better man" of her marriage and bore her husband's name rather than yoke![4]

Unfortunately, surviving documents provide few clues about those circumstances, if any, in Jane Cazneau's childhood and youth that would later cause her to deviate so sharply from gender norms. We know that she was born Jane McManus in 1807, in a Scotch-Irish Troy, New York, household; that her father William, an attorney, had considerable prominence in local public affairs and later served a term in Congress; that she had three brothers; that she was baptized a Lutheran and converted to Catholicism sometime prior to November 1832; and that though her mother lived until Jane was in her thirties, an aunt in Brookfield, Connecticut, had a lot to do with her upbringing. Relationships with siblings and parents, and significant events, remain obscure.[5]

The record is even more muddled regarding Jane Cazneau's young adulthood. She apparently married a William F. Storms in 1825, bore him a son (William Mount), and was divorced in 1831. But there has been some confusion about her husband's name and the dates of marriage and divorce, and she contributed to the confusion by using her maiden surname in the years immediately following the divorce before reverting to Storms in the years prior to her second marriage (to William L. Cazneau) in 1849.[6] Little has surfaced about the first marriage and her doings during those years.

When Jane Cazneau finally emerges on the historical record with some clarity in 1832, she is already prepared to confront challenge and take risks in a man's world. In that year, troubled by declining family fortunes, her father sent her to see Aaron Burr, an old family friend, about the family's resettling in "some new Country." Burr recommended the Austin colony in Mexican Texas, and soon she, her brother Robert (a surveyor), and her father were engaged in a settlement scheme involving a group of German immigrants. Although the plan went amiss when the settlers insisted on stopping at Matagorda on Texas' eastern coast instead of proceeding to the more westerly lands that had been designated for their colonization, her brother and she acquired a variety of landholdings in

Texas, and Robert made Galveston his permanent residence. Jane spent a considerable amount of time in the 1830s either in Texas or managing her Texas properties from the States by mail.[7]

Jane Cazneau felt her way into diplomacy through the back door of journalism, and she came carrying her Texas credentials. Living in New York City in the mid–1840s at the time of the national debate over whether or not Texas should be annexed to the United States, she began feeding pro-annexation pieces, under a pseudonym, to Moses Yale Beach's New York *Sun*, a popular penny newspaper. Beach ran the pieces, and after annexation was consummated, welcomed contributions from her on other foreign policy issues such as the Oregon and Texas/Mexico boundary questions.[8]

Diplomacy fascinated Jane Cazneau and she was receptive when a chance for more direct participation in foreign affairs came her way. On November 21, 1846, about a half year after the commencement of the Mexican War, Moses Yale Beach received an appointment from President James K. Polk—communicated by Secretary of State James Buchanan—as "confidential [that is, secret] agent to the Republic of Mexico." Under innocuous instructions (Beach was to hide his identity, keep in mind the president's desire for peace on "just and honorable terms," make contact with "some high officer" of the Mexican government who might be similarly inclined to peace, and report back to the State Department), Beach left within days. Posing as an Englishman, he traveled to Havana, Cuba, and, procuring a British passport, made his way on an English packet to Mexico. He reached the capital of Mexico City in January 1847. Accompanying the *Sun* proprietor were his daughter Drusilla, and, as an American consul in Cuba observed, one "Mrs. Storms."[9]

Buchanan's bland directive for this mission made no mention of Jane Storms. The secretary's words imply that the president chose Beach simply because of random information that the journalist was intending a trip to Mexico on "private business." However, according to a later explanation by Beach's son, Moses Sperry, what really prompted the president, whose desire for territorial expansion had so much to do with the coming of the war, was news that certain political and clerical elements in Mexico City now favored a negotiated settlement with the United States, which would have included Mexico's cession of all California above the 26th parallel latitude.[10] This information had been leaked to Mirabeau Buonaparte Lamar, former president of the Republic of Texas, and William Leslie Cazneau, a prominent Texas entrepreneur/politician, and eventually, was conveyed to the administration through Beach and Catholic Bishop John Hughes of New York City.[11]

However Jane Storms may have been responsible for the appointment. Not only did she know Beach and Bishop Hughes, but she also had ties to the two Texans who were serving as go-betweens. She had met Cazneau, then a storekeeper, in Matagorda in 1832. Whether or not Cazneau fell in love with her at that time, as a Matagorda inhabitant later reminisced, their relations were cordial enough for another mutual acquaintance in 1844 to refer to Cazneau as one of her particular "friends." Lamar's relationship with Jane Storms is both more obscure and in some ways more intriguing: he later dedicated a collection of his poetry to her.[12] When the time came for Cazneau and Lamar to reach the administration, they likely worked through Jane Storms. Certainly she had contact with the administration that year. She wrote letters to and visited with Secretary of the Navy George Bancroft. Anna Kasten Nelson, moreover, has uncovered ties between Jane and Nicholas Trist, chief clerk of the State Department, and discovered that Jane Storms appeared at a White House reception prior to the appointment. There is every reason to suspect her involvement. Even Moses Sperry Beach—who was anxious to inflate his own father's importance—acknowledged that Jane Storms was expected to be a helpful accomplice on the mission. After all, she not only was a Catholic, but she spoke Spanish and was thoroughly familiar with Latin culture by virtue of her Texas residence.[13]

In his official report following the mission, Beach made only indirect reference to Jane Storms. Rather, Beach emphasized his own activities at the enemy capital, asserting that he had been close to a breakthrough in talks with the clergy and Mexican politicians before the whole scheme collapsed. According to Beach's account, he had indeed been able to open peace discussions centering on the 26th parallel with members of the Mexican Congress. And he claimed being instrumental in civil disturbances at Mexico City and other municipalities that disrupted the enemy war effort. Then Mexican leader General Antonio López de Santa Anna had arrived at Mexico City and suppressed the resistance, causing Beach, fearing for his life, to flee to the sanctuary of American military forces at Tampico on the coast.[14] But scattered evidence suggests an active role for Jane Storms also. For one thing, a Baltimore *Sun* reporter in Washington, D.C., at the time of her return, noted that she had mentioned her *own* conversations with the Bishop of Puebla; according to her account, she had extracted a promise that the Mexican clergy would submit to American authority once guarantees were extended to church property and the practice of the Catholic faith. For another, in March 1847, prior to his own flight from Mexico City, Beach did entrust Jane Storms with the important mission of reporting on his situation to the American military command then involved in the siege of Veracruz on the coast. Traveling alone down Mexico's dangerous National Highway, she not only reached American lines and made her report to General Winfield Scott, but was even presumptuous enough to make suggestions about the route Scott should take in his forthcoming campaign to conquer Mexico City. Finally, she had an hour's audience about the mission with President Polk, following her return to Washington, an unlikely circumstance had she merely been Beach's translator.[15]

At the least, the mission whetted Jane Storms' appetite for diplomacy, and led her to believe that she now had a special understanding of Mexico. Perhaps in reaction to the precipitate collapse of Beach's negotiations and certainly in response to the anarchy she had witnessed, she returned convinced that the absorption of Mexico into the United States offered the only permanent solution to the Mexican problem. In a letter posted to the *Sun* from Veracruz on April

16, she opined that Mexico was too disunited to survive the war intact, and that Americans faced the choice of either encouraging separatism by effecting treaties with individual Mexican states anxious to sever relations with their central government, or annexing the entire country to forestall its conquest by "some European prince." Gradually she concluded that total annexation would be best, and she became one of the nation's opinion makers in what became known as the "All Mexico" movement. To Buchanan, in letters that July and August, she warned that the war would decide the 1848 presidential race and that the administration would forfeit its standing with the public should it conclude "too liberal" a treaty with Mexico: war proponents would never be sated with limited acquisitions, while war dissenters could only be appeased when convinced that the war brought "commensurate acquisition" to compensate for its cost. Later that year, she offered the State Department some fresh suggestions as to how the U.S. might enlist the Mexican clergy in arranging enemy submission, and when news of the Trist Treaty, which arranged extensive—but still partial— acquistions arrived in the States, she jumped on Buchanan again with her All Mexico convictions. "New York City and the West," she admonished, wanted "a *very large slice*" of enemy domain, and would "count the country defrauded by such a mockery as this treaty." Letters to Bancroft and President Polk followed a similar line (the American people would never "disgrace their Saxon lineage by letting territory escape their grasp"), and when Polk accepted Trist's work, Jane lamented that he had sacrificed his political influence.[16]

Even before the Trist Treaty was ratified, Jane Storms was involved in another facet of U.S. foreign relations—American diplomacy vis-à-vis the Spanish-ruled sugar island of Cuba. Over the course of almost ten years, through both print efforts and lobbying in Washington, she tried to influence the direction of American policy. Had there been no stopover in Havana during the Beach mission, she probably would have promoted the annexation of Cuba anyway. An ideological imperialist at this point in her life, she was convinced that even British Canada belonged within the American "area of freedom." But the Havana visit did little to enamor her with Spanish authority in the island. She could not help but notice agencies of authoritarian control: "You can go no where, in Cuba, without meeting soldiers. At church, at the theatre, at the mad house, at market, every where soldiers are on duty." Petty trade, press, and travel restrictions, moreover, stifled the freedom of movement, commerce, and expression essential to enlightened society.[17]

Beach, however, took a hand in Jane Storms' growing absorption with Cuba. On his way back to the States from the war, he had returned to Havana, where he fell in with John L. O'Sullivan, another expansionist New York journalist. O'Sullivan, whose sister had married a wealthy Cuban, had developed contacts with what was known as the Havana Club—a group consisting primarily of planters favoring American purchase of Cuba from Spain. Beach was brought into this circle, and convinced to lend the *Sun*'s weight to a propaganda campaign for annexation.[18]

Then, too, residence in New York City may have conditioned Jane Storms to an awareness of Cuban affairs. The metropolis was pulsating with Cuban exiles anxious to liberate their homeland from the Spanish yoke. Some hoped to create an independent republic; others anticipated Cuba's eventual annexation to the United States; many became involved in planning for what evolved into the López "filibusters"—military expeditions to Cuba commanded by exile Narciso López, intended to spark an uprising against Spain. When one of several landings, in 1851, resulted in the deaths of López and hundreds of followers (many of them Americans), the exiles in New York and other urban centers in the East and South turned to John A. Quitman, a Mexican War hero and former Mississippi governor, as their "Chief." From 1853 to April 1855, Quitman was immersed in conspiratorial planning for a new expedition; but he never quite put it all together.[19]

Jane Storms/Cazneau lobbied for Cuba with all three presidential administrations between her return from Mexico and the collapse of Quitman's scheme. She always presented herself as a political independent, so the sequence of Democratic-Whig-Democratic triumphs in the presidential elections of 1844, 1848, and 1852 posed no particular difficulties for her. In the case of Polk, she exerted considerable effort to commit administration officials to an annexation policy. To Buchanan, she wrote that a "Cuba fever" was erupting, and hinted that Buchanan could make himself the next president by arranging an agreement with Spain (presumably purchase) that would tie a "knot" between the United States and Cuba. To Bancroft, now U.S. minister to Great Britain, she suggested that the United States cut a deal with England, which had been hostile to American acquisition of the island, by giving the British a free hand in Puerto Rico and the Philippines—other possessions of the Spanish crown—in return for the British acceding to American annexation of Cuba. She also facilitated contact between exile leaders and Polk administration officials as well as Democrats in Congress. Thus she alerted Buchanan to a "gentleman from Cuba" with whom she wanted the secretary to meet, who could "prove of inestimable use to this country and Cuba, if his services and information are properly understood." She apparently believed her associate could help work out a purchase treaty with Spain, because she wanted Buchanan to provide him a courier's passport so that he might help both his "native island" and "future country."[20]

When Zachary Taylor succeeded Polk in 1849, Jane prepared to renew her efforts. Taylor, as a general in Mexico, had gained fame conquering Spanish-speaking peoples, and she looked upon him as a *"representative of progress and acquisition."* But Taylor proved a disappointment. In August 1849, the president issued a proclamation warning Americans against participation in the López movement. Whig officials also used military personnel and legal procedures to interfere with filibuster preparations. Further, Taylor, unlike Polk, who at least tried to purchase Cuba, took no diplomatic initiatives regarding annexation. Perturbed, she wrote Senator William Seward of New York, who was known to have considerable influence with the president, that the decision to "throw away Cuba" would destroy the Whigs at the polls. She was relieved when the 1852 election returned the Democrats to power, and tried to influence policy even prior to the new administration's taking office. In January 1853, she asked Buchanan to arrange a private interview between her and President-elect Franklin Pierce. Denouncing the "mischievous inter-regnum" of the past four years, she alerted Buchanan that insurrection would "blaze forth" in Cuba as soon as the New York exile leadership gave the word, but that England might intercede. She needed to brief Pierce, and learn what action he might take if the British interfered, so that she could advise the exiles whether they should go ahead with invasion preparations. When Pierce, in mid-administration, followed Taylor's precedent and adopted antifilibustering policies, Jane worked to preserve room for Pierce to change his mind if he so desired, in the hope that the president remained sympathetic to the Cuba annexation cause. Upset at an attack on Pierce in the expansionist *New York Herald*, she wrote to Moses Sperry Beach, who had become *Sun* proprietor in 1852, pleading that *his* journal not point fingers. Arguing that Pierce might simply have succumbed to misinformed advice from a hostile cabinet member or two, she predicted that he might reconstitute the cabinet and that it would be impolitic to alienate him without proof of his genuine hostility.[21]

Simultaneous with these lobbying efforts, Jane Storms/Cazneau mounted a print onslaught designed to arouse a popular passion for Cuba, which might compel officials in Washington to act. Probably no journalist in the country at the time surpassed her in faith that public opinion could sway decision-making; she expressed this confidence in letter after letter. Certainly she tried to demonstrate the point regarding Cuba. First, her Mexican War letters from Havana appeared in the *Sun*, letters that noted Cuban progress in industrialization (thus contravening the impressions of some Americans that Cubans were stupid and unfit for American institutions), and argued that only American control could provide Cuban planters with the kind of security they required against slave revolts. Later she became editor of a Cuban exile Spanish-and-English-language newspaper called *La Verdad*, which commenced running off the *Sun* press in January 1848. For some time, the paper carried a column headed "THE TRUTH, BY CORA MONTGOMERY." Under this heading, Jane discussed such matters as Cuba's economic and strategic/geographical importance to the United States as "warden of the Mexican Gulf" and defined the 1852 presidential election as a mandate for Cuban annexation. She also devoted much of a book, one of several that she produced as "Cora Montgomery" during her lifetime, to Cuba. *The Queen of Islands and the King of Rivers* portrayed Cuba as a paradise "[b]orne by foreign soldiers," extorted by taxes, deprived of elementary freedoms, and peopled by inhabitants ready for republicanism, and explained how the incorporation of Cuba would bring economic benefits to the United States. And Jane Cazneau founded her own magazine, obviously intended, in part, as a mouthpiece for her views about Cuba. The October 1852 issue of *Our Times* carried three distinct articles that were Cuba-related.[22]

Meanwhile, in the fall of 1849, Jane Storms had married William Cazneau. No documents have survived about what prompted the union, but it is obvious from a public letter she wrote soon afterward that Jane anticipated no retreat to the "mustard-cup." A January 8, 1850, two-page draft of a "Montgomery" piece denouncing Henry Clay for failing to support a Senate resolution calling for a break in U.S. relations with Austria over Austria's repression (with Russian aid) of the Kossuth revolution in Hungary in the previous August, exhibits not only her sympathy with the "Young America" movement of that time, but more importantly that she did not even take a temporary respite from public issues after matrimony. There is no reason to suspect that William, whatever his romantic inclinations may have been, ever desired Jane's withdrawal from national affairs. An entrepreneur with ambitious plans, who had known his prospective spouse and observed her activities for almost two decades, he most likely saw her as an accomplice in his speculations.[23]

Initially, the main effect of marriage upon Jane Cazneau was to bring her back to the southwestern frontier. William Cazneau sensed opportunity in the vast territory of New Mexico, acquired in the cession ending the Mexican War. Americans populating New Mexico and western Texas would require supplies, and commerce beckoned with north Mexican states where independence movements erupted regularly and where inhabitants willfully evaded trade restrictions imposed by the far-off government in Mexico City. Then, too, prospects of applying Anglo methods and entrepreneurship to undeveloped gold and silver lodes intrigued William Cazneau. Any landholdings he might acquire on the frontier, moreover, would skyrocket in value with the construction of a Pacific railroad and the annexation of northern Mexico—developments that his wife and he expected within years and occasionally tried to hurry along. In the summer of 1849, backed by some New Orleans investors, William Cazneau led an eighty-vehicle wagon train stacked with goods from Corpus Christi to El Paso, and on into the New Mexico territory.[24] Convinced of the region's potential, he decided to establish a trade depot on the Texas frontier at Eagle Pass, a site on the Rio Grande just below the U.S. army post of Fort Duncan. There, to a "neat cottage," which he had constructed for his spouse, William Cazneau either summoned or brought her in early 1850. Ultimately the Cazneaus would claim title to some 1000 acres at Eagle Pass.[25]

Though Eagle Pass was very remote from the corridors of power in Washington, and though Jane Cazneau complained that being 150 miles from a mail route made her feel "excommunicated," she nonetheless discovered new diplomatic causes to agitate before she returned to New York City in 1852. When she got settled, she discovered that raiders from both New Mexico and Mexico had been in the custom of crossing the Rio Grande into Texas, apprehending Mexican laborers—even some who had become U.S. citizens—and kidnaping them into debt peonage. Her moral outrage merged with fears for her own servants to provoke her to send a series of letters to Senator Seward complaining of the practice. She not only implored Seward to take up the issue in the Senate and with Secretary of State Daniel Webster, but also sent evidence regarding an abducted Eagle Pass resident direct to Webster. She taunted Seward by declaring that if Webster dragged his heels, she would provide enough case history material to her "democratic friends" for the Democrats to make political capital. Webster would then "face the music—unless the press dies." She urged that Webster negotiate an extradition treaty with Mexico and that the administration police against peonage in its own New Mexico territory. As usual, she also relied on print methods to arouse the public, writing to Horace Greeley of the *New York Tribune* and indicting peonage in page after page of a book called *Eagle Pass; or Life on the Border*—an account of her experiences, which she published in New York in 1852 and which *did* lambast Daniel Webster for suppressing the issue.[26]

In late 1853, for the second time in her life, Jane Cazneau traveled to a foreign land as the accomplice of a secret agent of the United States government. On November 2, the State Department commissioned William Cazneau "special agent" to the Dominican Republic, a Caribbean country that took up the eastern two thirds of an island—Hispaniola or "St. Domingo"—that it shared with the black republic of Haiti. By December 9, Jane Cazneau had located in Santo Domingo City, and she was joined several weeks thereafter by her husband.[27]

Surely whatever the circumstances may have been regarding the Beach escapade, this second secret agent mission must have been Jane Cazneau's doing. She had been harping on conditions in Hispaniola in print and political correspondence for the last two years. Marriage to a Texan had made her into something of a Southerner,[28] and she identified with southern antipathy to Haiti and fears that the kind of violent race revolt that had once wracked Haiti and destroyed its planter class might be exported to other Caribbean areas and even the southern United States. In *Our Times* she had warned that Haitian Emperor Faustin Élie Soulouque intended to "devour" the Dominicans, and she endorsed a planned American filibustering invasion (she called it "armed colonization") of Hispaniola known as the "Dominican Encampment of the Brotherhood of the Union." In her January letter to James Buchanan, she had urged the State Department to tie up "in brown wrappers the colored magistrates of Hayti." In addition, she had longstanding ties to New Yorker William L. Marcy, Pierce's Secretary of State; Marcy had referred to her as an "old friend" many years earlier. Given these circumstances, as well as the timing of Jane Cazneau's arrival in the Dominican Republic before her husband, there is no reason to quarrel with a report in the *New York Evening Post*, a journal hostile to the mission, that William Cazneau had been in Texas when the appointment was originally procured, and that the State Department had mailed the commission direct to Jane Cazneau in New York. The *Post* believed Jane Cazneau the "real" commissioner.[29]

Though Marcy's mission instructions discussed Dominican relations with Haiti as an important matter for William Cazneau to investigate, there was more to the assignment. The United States had never recognized and established official relations with the Dominican Republic, primarily because Dominican rulers, though generally lighter skinned than Haitian authorities, nonetheless were looked upon as Negro by American officials. Southerners, in particular, had no desire to see their national leaders treat black diplomats as equals. This failure to recognize the Dominican Republic, in turn, had damaged U.S.-Dominican trade. Marcy, noting that Hispaniola was the only major island in the West Indies that was not a dependency of a European nation, wanted Cazneau to investigate the possibility of trading recognition of the Dominican Republic for commercial concessions.[30]

Despite a decade-long career as rabid territorial imperialist, Jane Cazneau embraced Marcy's stricture that "commercial intercourse" be William's principal objective. A fervent unionist, Jane had been obliged for years to reconcile her love of country with the intersectional hatred generated by territorial gains such as Texas, New Mexico, and California, a rather hopeless ideological endeavor as would be confirmed eventually by the American Civil War. The Dominican mission suggested alternative ways of conceptualizing American expansion, ways that appealed not only to Jane Cazneau but also to her husband and his entrepreneur mentality. As the Dominican mission progressed, Jane Cazneau emerged as a promoter of what recent historians have identified as "commercial expansion" or "informal empire." That is, she came to believe that American economic penetration of foreign lands through trade and investment opportunities would prove as beneficial as imperialism, yet avoid all the military complications and sectional friction intrinsic to territorial expansion. There was nothing absolute about the break in Jane's thinking. She had understood the concept of commercial expansion for a long time: in an 1850 article in *Hunt's Merchants' Magazine*, for instance, she had dwelled upon the need to build a railroad or canal across Mexico's Isthmus of Tehuantepec so that Mississippi Valley merchants could undersell Europeans in Asian markets; she had also affirmed that trade and fast communication were methods to hold the Union together. She did not entirely forswear territorial acquisitions after the Dominican assignment, but even began pushing the purchase of Cuba anew when James Buchanan became president in 1857. Nevertheless, the Dominican mission marked an important transition in Jane's outlook.[31]

She all but announced the change with "Cora Montgomery's" next contribution to the public weal, a letter designed to stimulate popular enthusiasm for her husband's mission, which she got off to the *New York Tribune* soon after her arrival in Santo Domingo City. In it, she dwelled on how the "enterprise of the North" should learn the way "money is to be made in St. Domingo." She reported that Frenchmen and other foreigners had been reaping vast profits from cutting Dominican mahogany, and also how European merchants and industrialists had been monopolizing Dominican foreign trade:

The best results of these [mahogany] cuttings find the way to Europe chiefly through the free port of St. Thomas, and the productions of European industry come back in return, and supersede American fabrics in the markets of St. Domingo. Our cheap, strong and well-adapted cotton goods ought to clothe all the working population of the island. It is but 1,400 miles from the best ports of the manufacturing States of the Union, where everything wanted in the Antilles—flour, fish, furniture, machinery and farming implements—can be made and exported to the very best advantage.

She attributed American laggardness to the "glaring impolicy" of non-recognition. There was nothing in the piece about annexation.[32]

Jane Cazneau's main contribution to William's mission came in a letter that she despatched to Secretary Marcy the following February. Having found that Dominican authorities would not conclude a treaty with an agent lacking official credentials, she entreated Marcy to give William Cazneau the authority he needed ("I was astonished to find there was no credential whatever to the Dominicans in my husband's instructions") so that he could proceed with the negotiations that, she felt, would both gain the United States favored status in a Dominican port and open the country to American immigrants and investors. She had particular hopes that her husband would gain mining concessions. If the United States would agree to an arbitration treaty, she was confident that Dominican ruler General Pedro Santana would in return concede to American citizens and their descendants "the *fullest rights of nationality* to hold lands and mines, without losing their [American] nationality." Marcy responded by promoting William Cazneau to full Commissioner giving him the authority to trade recognition for the lease of a coaling station, and this did facilitate the talks; the following October, he concluded a treaty of amity and commerce. However, pressure from the British and French consuls led the Dominicans, subsequently, to add some amendments that were unacceptable in Washington, and Marcy, that December, recalled his commissioner.[33]

With the collapse of the Dominican mission, Jane and William Cazneau plunged into a veritable maze of speculations. Some of the projects, such as a scheme to establish a line of first class steamers between Europe and the Chesapeake, bore little immediate relationship to diplomacy.[34] But most of the ventures did have a link to foreign relations. During the Buchanan administration, for instance, Jane Cazneau pushed for informal empire in Mexico. She urged him, as soon as the Pennsylvanian took office, to try to negotiate free American transit rights across Mexico's Isthmus of Tehuantepec, which, in an age when there was no transcontinental railroad, promised lucrative profits in trade and passenger travel between America's coasts. The next year, when two Mexican factions—the Liberals and Conservatives—were fighting for control of Mexico, Jane drew on her influence in the press and with Buchanan in an effort to get U.S. recognition of the Liberals in return, apparently, for the Liberals granting her husband concessions in Mexico. She assured the president that for $2,000,000 the United States could acquire both transit and settlement rights in Tehuantepec, and transit privileges in northern Mexico. Since Benito Juárez, the Liberal leader, was willing to make northern Mexico to the 28th parallel neutral territory, the United States would have virtual control without a formal transfer.[35]

If Jane and William Cazneau respected boundaries betweeen private gain and public policy, they certainly hid their tracks. The Cazneaus conceptualized the benefits of commercial expansion in terms of opportunities for investors, and they demonstrated this connection very openly regarding Nicaragua, their consuming passion between 1856 and 1858.

Ever vigilant for new opportunities south of the border, they could not help but take notice of William Walker, an American filibuster who, with a small group of fellow adventurers—contracted as mercenaries (land was to be the reward) in a Nicaraguan civil war—incredibly, in 1856, managed to get control of the entire country. The Cazneaus, from the start, saw the "gray-eyed man of destiny" as a potential agent of informal empire. Turning down an invitation to a pro-Walker rally in May because of "severe indisposition in my family" (presumably Jane was ill; they had no children), William attacked British support for Costa Rica, whose forces, as part of a general campaign to expel Walker from Central America, had taken San Juan del Sur, the Pacific outlet of Nicaragua's Isthmian transit route—a route involving road, river, and lake transportation that had been operated for years by an American firm called the Accessory Transit Company. To William Cazneau, reports of British firearms shipments to Costa Rica confirmed an English plot to control American seas and "hold a rod over our inter-coast commerce." His response was that the United States government should relax enforcement of the neutrality law, so that Americans could aid "the lion of Spanish American regeneration."[36]

Once the Cazneaus learned that Walker had made himself president, they threw caution to the wind. That summer they traveled to Nicaragua. They may have been present for Walker's staged inauguration on July 12, for Jane Cazneau posted a letter just three days later from Granada (where the ceremony took place) that everything seemed to be progressing well and that she believed Walker's government stable. Perhaps there was wishful thinking in her hopeful appraisal. A newspaper clipping in the scrapbook of John P. Heiss, Walker's appointee as special commissioner to the United States and Great Britian, alludes to William and Jane Cazneau purchasing "a great track of of land" while there, and William, the next year, made reference to his financial interest in "valuable" Nicaraguan mines. When the Cazneaus departed for New York City in late August, moreover, they not only carried with them some of Walker's official diplomatic despatches, but also a formal contract, dated August 15, in which William agreed to recruit 1000 male "colonists" (i.e., soldier reinforcements) for Walker.[37]

That fall, from rooms at the St. Nicholas Hotel, the Cazneaus drummed up support for Walker in New York. Jane worked the press. William solicited recruits and helped plan a major Walker rally. When the time came on December 24 for the steamship *Tennessee* to take away the several hundred (*not*, it should be noted, 1000) recruits whom William Cazneau had managed to enlist, and

William learned that U.S. District Attorney John McKeon was on the verge of interfering with the departure, he intruded into McKeon's office and handed the official his contract from Walker, insisting that these were bona fide emigrants anxious to get eighty-acre homesteads that Walker had stipulated in the contract. Later that day, McKeon let the vessel sail, but his posting deputies on shore and a revenue cutter near Staten Island apparently inhibited a substantial number of filibusters from embarking.[38]

Remaining in New York after the *Tennessee*'s departure, the Cazneaus continued striving for Walker, even as his tenure in Nicaragua became precarious. In December, Costa Rican forces had seized the San Juan River steamers of the Accessory Transit Company, vessels on which Walker depended for supplies and reinforcements from the Caribbean coast. Early in 1857, Central American allied forces defeated Walker's men in several pitched battles, and, in March, succeeded in putting the filibuster under siege in the town of Rivas. In April and into the first days of May, Jane and William swamped U.S. Attorney General Jeremiah Black with pleas that the new Buchanan administration embrace Walker's cause, and sometime that spring Jane traveled to Washington and spoke personally with Black. Jane and William demanded several policy changes. First, they insisted that Walker, despite his reverses, remain *de facto president* of Nicaragua and that he merited official recognition (diplomatic relations had been severed by Pierce after Walker's initiation as president); Fermin Ferrer, Walker's minister-designate, was staying with them at the St. Nicholas and was ready to be received. Second, citing the 1850 Clayton-Bulwer Treaty with England, which guaranteed the neutrality of Isthmian transit, they urged that the U.S. pressure Costa Rica either to return the river steamers or pay compensation. When Jane heard a rumor that the administration had sent the warship *Saratoga* to Nicaraguan waters to force restitution, she exulted that it would strike "a braver and more effectual blow for American interests than has ever before been made in that quarter." Third, they called for implementation of the Wheeler treaty with Nicaragua, negotiated by U.S. Minister John Wheeler prior to the break in relations, which offered Americans the right to hold lands and work mines in Nicaragua without forfeiting their American citizenship.

Behind these specific requests lay the vision of commercial empire. Jane Cazneau claimed that after the Wheeler treaty was activated, its effect, in combination with various colonization land grants that Walker had extended to attract immigrants, would "call into existence a permanent array of prosperous American settlements along the entire line of Transit." Once this occurred, the United States would have virtual control over one of the most important commercial highways of the world, without any of the "cares and entanglements" attached to actual sovereignty. And behind the commercial empire lay, of course, the Cazneaus' own speculations. Their land and mining claims would be worthless should the filibuster regime collapse.[39]

Even had Buchanan been willing to reverse U.S. policy, the Cazneau letter barrage came too late. Rather than suffer starvation or annihilation, William

Walker, in early May, surrendered to U.S. naval captain Charles Henry Davis, on an understanding that Davis had worked out with Costa Rican forces, which guaranteed the safe evacuation of Walker and his men from the country.

Yet Walker's capitulation by no means terminated the Cazneaus' involvement in Nicaraguan affairs. The previous August, Congress had passed legislation permitting U.S. citizens discovering guano deposits on any "island, rock, or key not within the lawful jurisdiction of any other government," to take possession of such places, collect the guano, and sell it to U.S. citizens at up to eight dollars per ton. Guano, or sea bird dung, could be found on various Pacific and Caribbean islands, and had become very important in U.S. farm fertilizing over the past few years. The legislation seemed to promise great profits to enterpreneurs who located unclaimed guano islands, and one such group of speculators organized a firm called the Atlantic and Pacific Guano Company to develop some claims at Swan Island, located in the Caribbean about 100 miles off the Central American coast. When Walker returned to the United States and began organizing an expedition to reconquer Nicaragua, these entrepreneurs struck a deal with him by which he would support their claims and they would back his bid to return to power in Nicaragua, an arrangement that became increasingly important to them since the State Department rejected their Swan Islands claims.[40]

William and Jane Cazneau were active in the Company-Walker machinations, though it is unclear whether they actually held Company stock. Their interest may have derived primarily from their prior land and mining investments in Nicaragua, as is indicated by the following excerpt of correspondence between two Company officials:

I write now to advise you not to write to General Walker till we know what his plan of operations is to be. Ferrer remains at St. Nicholas with Cazneau. His [Cazneau's] mines & property offer a good basis for an operation. But nothing can be done until Walker has moved.

Jane Cazneau, that fall, wrote letters on Nicaragua to Black and Buchanan. To Black, she urged rescue of the Wheeler agreement from its "unexplored recess of the State Depart.," and the permanent deployment of an American man-of-war off Central America so that the "anarchies" governing the area would respect American trade and citizens. To Buchanan, she suggested that the administration force the new Nicaraguan provisional government of Tomás Martínez into guaranteeing American rights on the Nicaraguan transit by threatening to unleash William Walker. She wanted the United States to hold off recognizing Martínez, send a commission to Nicaragua with its demands, and then convert Walker's imminent departure into leverage for Nicaragua's concurrence. The letter was a marvelous example of Jane Cazneau's inclination to realpolitik, as was a remarkable epistle she wrote about Nicaragua the following spring. By then Walker's expedition had been frustrated by U.S. naval interference, and her old Texas

associate, Mirabeau Buonaparte Lamar, had become U.S. minister to the Martínez government. She asked Lamar to arrange for her a colonization grant with
Nicaraguan authorities, which would allow her to bring American families to
settle on the island of Ometepe in Lake Nicaragua. Amazingly, for a woman
who had worked on behalf of filibusters for ten years, she boasted that Americans
were really "anti-filibuster" and suggested that Lamar press the scheme with
the logic that the colonists would become peaceful cultivators of coffee groves
and help defend Nicaragua from future American freebooting schemes![41]

From 1859 until the ends of their lives, Jane and William Cazneau settled on
Hispaniola for their informal empire. Prior to leaving the Dominican Republic
in 1855, they had purchased an estate called the Esmeralda just outside the walls
of Santo Domingo City. The estate gave them a vested interest in the country,
and the collapse of the 1854 mission still rankled. When a change of Dominican
administrations in January 1859 brought Pedro Santana, whom they belived pro-
U.S., back to the presidency after his being out of power for some time, the
Cazneaus determined that the propitious moment had come for a renewal of
negotiations along the lines of the 1854 agreement. According to Jane's later
account, William won the concurrence of "many leading Dominicans" to a plan
by which Samaná Bay—on the Republic's northeastern coast—would be opened
to American commerce as a neutral port, and then he and Jane took their scheme
directly to Buchanan, meeting twice with him at the White House library. Buchanan, in turn, involved Secretary of State Lewis Cass in the discussions and
Cass, that April, appointed William Cazneau to a new stint as U.S. special agent
to the Dominican Republic.[42]

In many ways, the Cazneaus' 1859 mission demonstrated that history can
approximate, if not repeat, itself. Once again, Jane and William Cazneau found
themselves trying to market their recognition policy with cautious Washington
officials. William Cazneau reported how "heavy discrimination in favor of those
nations who have treaties with the Dominican government" had chased American
ship companies out of the passenger business to the country, and that he had
been obliged to take passage on a British vessel. Timber resources and silver
and copper mines still awaited American "science, capital, and enterprise";
"European bottoms" were carrying off to European ports all the tobacco produced in the Republic's north—tobacco that held its own against the best Cuban.
Jane Cazneau, similarly, pressed commercial empire on the president, stressing
that "access" to Dominican mines would immediately follow recognition. She
praised her husband for disabusing inhabitants of the notion that the United States
sought annexation, calling such apprehensions the "black phantom" of the
Republic's "colored races." A "free commercial entrepot at the gates of the
Gulf of Mexico and Caribbean Sea" remained the Cazneaus' objective, and they
wondered how their government could pass up such opportunities.[43]

Unfortunately the similarities transcended the Cazneaus' boosterism. As in
1854, William believed himself on the verge of a diplomatic breakthrough. On
July 2, he wrote Cass that he had been passed information that Samaná Bay

would soon be opened to foreign merchant vessels, and announced that he would try to get American ships put on a most favored nation basis when that event occurred. Later letters expressed hopes that the Dominicans would negotiate making Samaná Bay an American coal depot and announce export duty exemptions for minerals extracted from Dominican soil. However, the Cazneaus also discovered that as in 1854, the Republic was plagued by a pervasive fear of a Haitian takeover. This time they encountered a lot of sentiment for allowing Spain, which had once ruled the country, to assume a protectorate as a strategy for averting Haitian control.

The Cazneaus hoped that recognition and demonstrations of American concern and power might yet keep Santana out of Spain's grasp. In November 1860, during the waning months of the Buchanan administration, Jane turned alarmist in a last-ditch attempt to redirect American policy. Informing Attorney General Black that rule by weak Spain was only intended as a transition to dominion by powerful Napoleon III of France, she also contended that "Africanization" by Haiti remained an alternative possibility. If the latter occurred, the contagion of black rule could be expected to spread to Cuba and Puerto Rico, where coolie labor would supplant slavery. Surely, she argued, the administration, particularly Southern cabinet members, would be unable to justify acquiescence in such a "sacrifice." Southerners linked to such a development would lose credibility in their home states and witness the destruction of their own political futures.[44]

But Buchanan, like Pierce, refused to give Jane and William Cazneau the one diplomatic tool they most coveted. They watched helplessly as President Santana, in March 1861, proclaimed the Dominican Republic reannexed to Spain. That same month, William Cazneau's commission as secret agent was canceled by William Seward, Secretary of State in Abraham Lincoln's administration, which had just assumed office; he sadly predicted that Spanish suppression of free speech and press, and other restrictions, would soon provoke massive Dominican uprisings, and that the ultimate result might well be a "merciless war of races." American citizens who had invested in Dominican businesses, under such circumstanes, could not "hope to escape their share of suffering."[45]

Despite their prophecies of Spanish rule being a calamity, Jane and William Cazneau stayed on at their Esmeralda estate rather than return to civil conflict in the United States. In time, concluding that seeming political stability, rising land values, and new opportunities for investment offset authoritarian excesses, they even became champions of the new order. Jane, in late 1862, described Spain as being on its "best behavior" in the Protectorate. Both Cazneaus that year became active in schemes to colonize the country with Americans. Jane penned a new book, to be released in serial form in the *Sun*, about what it was like to pass a year in "St. Domingo," informing Moses Sperry Beach that her positive depiction was intended to prod American poor whites and blacks into emigrating there. William, meanwhile, in cooperation with Joseph W. Fabens (a New York merchant originally from Salem, Massachusetts, who had served William Walker as a colonization agent), managed to get land concessions from

Spanish authorities, and played a role in the workings of a New York based colonization corporation, the American West Indies Company, which was organized in October 1862. The company did arrange the emigration of small groups of Americans, though their settlement proved a fiasco. The Cazneaus' accommodation to the protectorate ended only when Spanish officials in Santo Domingo, plagued by a growing insurgency throughout the country, which they mistakenly attributed to American subversion, destroyed Esmeralda in October 1863 on the rationale that it lay within a military zone. Leaving behind a claim of $10,000 against Spanish authorities, the Cazneaus fled to Keith Hall, a country house in Jamaica.[46]

The Cazneaus had fewer than two years to wait before renewing their Dominican connections. Even before they evacuated their pillaged estate, an insurgent Dominican government had been announced. In 1864, the rebels gained the upper hand, and by July of the next year, Spanish troops had left the country. That September, Jane Cazneau's restless pen was at work again, summoning yet another American administration to take up the unfinished work of commercial empire in Hispaniola. This time, bending the ear of Andrew Johnson's Secretary of the Interior James Harlan, Jane claimed that the newest men who controlled "the action of the Dominican Republic" were ready to accede to terms giving the United States a naval station and opening a belt of territory seven to nine miles wide for American colonization. She urged Harland to look over her husband's despatches from 1859–60 about what might be accomplished, and to lay her suggestions before the president.[47]

Returning to the Dominican Republic, William Cazneau, presumably with his wife's concurrence, gambled on some new investments—speculations that dwarfed in scale his earlier financial endeavors in foreign countries. Dominican governments following the overthrow of the Spanish Protectorate were desperate for funds, and anxious to encourage American investment and trade in their country. This was particularly true of Buenaventura Baez, who took over the presidency in December 1865, was ousted the following May, and then returned to authority in March 1868 for a six-year stint. But it also held for José Maria Cabral, who held power for part of 1865 and then again after Baez gave up the presidency in May 1866. William Cazneau and his associate Joseph Fabens were among the main beneficiaries of the Dominican largesse. Their most impressive coup came in a contact with Baez of July 1868, in which Cazneau and Fabens formed the San Domingo Survey and Mining Company. The contract stipulated that in return for making a geological and mineralogical survey of the public lands of the Dominican Republic, the Company would be granted title to one fifth of the lands that it examined, an incredible bonanza considering that three fifths of the entire country consisted of public land, and that the actual choice of land was reserved to the Company. But this was only one of several ventures. After Spofford, Tileston & Co., a New York merchant house, gained a concession for a steamship line between New York and Dominican ports, Cazneau and Fabens went in with the Company in obtaining title to a thirty-acre tract fronting

Samaná Bay. Then, too, Cazneau invested in copper mines, was involved in a chartered National Bank of Santo Domingo, took on some new colonization ventures (involving land grants for settlements on the frontier with Haiti), and organized a camel transportation scheme. Jane Cazneau's will also alludes to the fact that the Cazneaus owned a square of land within Santo Domingo City.[48]

These transactions framed the backdrop for the Cazneaus' last fling in American diplomacy. For one thing, both Baez and Cabral found in William Cazneau an agency to convey to Washington their message that the Dominican Republic was receptive to American influence and would grant concessions to revitalize American-Dominican trade and to encourage Americans to invest in Dominican development; for another, the Cazneaus were sensitive that their speculations would remain precarious unless American involvement helped stabilize Dominican government.[49]

Whether or not William and Jane Cazneau engineered a December 12, 1865, petition from New York City merchants to the Department of State that William be made commissioner to the Dominican Republic for the purpose of negotiating a treaty "for the protection of American interests," the Cazneaus were already in the thick of U.S.-Dominican affairs. In January, Secretary of State William Seward, accompanied by his son, Assistant Secretary of State Frederick Seward, put in at Santo Domingo City during a Caribbean cruise. He may have included the stop in his itinerary because of Jane Cazneau's letter in September to Interior Secretary Harlan, and while on the island he conferred with both William Cazneau and President Baez about America's non-recognition policy. The visit, and talk about possible Dominican concessions, contributed to President Johnson's recommending formal recognition in a January 30, 1866, message to Congress, and the president's nominating William Cazneau as American Commissioner and Consul-General. Despite William's subsequent rejection by the Senate, which was based, in part, on reports that he had been a Confederate sympathizer, the Cazneaus kept up the pressure. On April 9, Jane wrote Frederick Seward a letter signed, "Your Very Sincere Friend," warning that Haiti was stirring up new rebellion in the country and reiterating Baez's openness to American influence. "Every vessel," she enthused, "brings in parties from the United States in quest of mines & c. President Baez receives them cordially and whom brings a fair show of responsibility is sure of getting the right to do some." In September, the United States finally recognized the Dominican Republic, and the next winter Frederick Seward returned to Santo Domingo City, under instructions from his father, to try to arrange a treaty giving the United States a lease or grant of Samaná Bay for a naval and coaling station in return for either cash or surplus Civil War arms. After Seward's Samaná project fell through, William Cazneau became involved in the efforts of the Grant administration to annex the Dominican Republic—a scheme that failed in no small part because reports linked the proposal to the Cazneau speculations.[50]

Jane Cazneau's direct involvement in American diplomacy seems to have ceased with the exit of William Seward from the State Department in 1869.

Despite her husband's notoriety in President Grant's Dominican scheme, Jane Cazneau's name rarely surfaced in the public record, an exception being an allusion in a Senate committee investigation report to a brief visit paid on her by Grant's private secretary, Orville E. Babcock, during one of Babcock's visits to Santo Domingo City. It is hard to believe, however, that she stayed aloof from the annexation project. Certainly she retained her interest in U.S. foreign affairs, and particularly the role of Americans in the Dominican Republic, to the end of her life. She contributed letters to the *New York Herald* on Dominican affairs, and in 1878, two years after her husband's death and just prior to her own, came out with one last volume of travel information and diplomatic advice. *Our Winter Eden: Pen Pictures of the Tropics* lauded the resources of Samaná Bay, insisted that biracial colonization of the tropics would work, and renewed her husband's call for an American naval depot at a Samaná Bay cove, which would evolve into "the guardian sentinel of great American trade centre."[51] On December 12, 1878, Jane Cazneau died en route from New York to the Dominican Republic in the sinking of the steamer *Emily B. Souder*.

Since the United States had no female ministers, ambassadors, or foreign service officers until the twentieth century, it is likely that Jane Cazneau came as close to a formal role in American diplomacy as any woman in the nineteenth century. She may, in fact, at times have either fantasized herself an actual U.S. diplomat or contemplated soliciting a formal assignment. "By the way," she announced to Buchanan during the heady days for U.S. expansionists prior to Franklin Pierce's inauguration, "I mean to be an office-seeker myself if there is any stir in Mexico or Central America and I see positively a way to be of use there." The next year, in her letter to William Marcy about the Dominican mission, she alluded to what steps she might take to block American interests were *she* the French consul. Certainly diplomats from other nations were forced to grapple with Jane Cazneau as an untitled U.S. diplomat. Thus John F.T.C. Crampton, British minister to the United States, conveyed to his home government in 1854 his concern that William Cazneau sought a naval base in the Dominican Republic in order to service a U.S. invasion of Cuba, and grounded his apprehensions on anticipated machinations by William's "Lady," who went along on the mission and was "notoriously in favor of the annexation by any means of Cuba to the United States."[52]

Yet, it would be wrong to define Jane Cazneau as a pathbreaker for her sex. Her participation in American political and diplomatic life may have inspired some other women to achieve new things, but the best evidence of this is only an 1844 letter from a *male* acquaintance who exulted that her columns in the press on Texas were winning influence for herself "and the ladies." Jane Cazneau was less than enthusiastic about those of her gender who became active in the women's suffrage movement, and her obituary was close to the mark in saying that she had not been "a 'woman's rights woman' in any sense." She demonstrated that a determined woman did not have to adhere to male prescriptions for feminine behavior, but she brought little in the way of a feminine perspective to diplomacy and apparently did nothing to open up diplomatic opportunities for her oppressed sisters. In many ways she was sui generis, and any final assessment needs to measure her actual impact upon American diplomacy rather than her example as sexual pioneer—a difficult task since hardly any of her incoming correspondence has survived.[53]

Some rather grandiose claims have been made for Jane Storms/Cazneau. Henry Watterson stated that she actually wrote the Trist Treaty, while Thomas Hart Benton asserted in his reminiscences that she was solely responsible for generating the All Mexico movement. The historian Edward S. Wallace recorded that General Scott determined his route of campaign to Mexico City on the basis of her advice. Jane herself, on more than one occasion, suggested that she had started the Texas annexation movement through her columns in the *New York Sun*. Watterson's assertion, however, is absurd, and the other claims cannot be substantiated. Jane Cazneau may have been a "pioneer in the cause of 'manifest destiny,' " as the *Herald* put it, but she was one of many.[54]

What can easily be demonstrated is that Jane Cazneau's views over a period of approximately twenty years were intermittently before U.S. policy-makers, and that American leaders felt compelled to confront her opinions. Thus Secretary of the Navy Gideon Welles in December 1865 noted in his diary how Jane's name cropped up at a cabinet meeting. "Seward," he recorded, "had a long story about Mrs. Cazneau and St. Domingo. I judge from his own statement or manner of stating, and from his omission to read Mrs. C's communication, that he has committed some mistakes which he does not wish to become public." Sometimes Jane Cazneau's specific requests won quick endorsement, such as when Secretary of State Marcy promoted her husband from agent to full commissioner. Often she was simply listened to with politeness. President Polk reflected following her May 1847 exposition on Mexican matters at the White House, "She is an intelligent woman, but I confess when she retired I did not feel that I was enlightened by any information which she had given me." Some policy-makers, bothered by her daring to act in a field monopolized by men, undoubtedly found her irritating. Winfield Scott supposedly criticized Moses Y. Beach for allowing a "plenipotentiary in petticoats" to convey his diplomatic messages, and Jane seems to have been sensitive to her own abrasiveness. She confessed an awareness that "one of my sex" was not supposed to "deal" in politics in one letter, and alluded to her "seeming officiousness" when she made a consulship request of Seward.[55]

Regarding broad policy objectives, Jane Cazneau rarely got her way. If she met success in her Texas advocacy, she also encountered disappointment in her crusades for All Mexico, early recognition of the Dominican Republic, the annexation of Cuba, U.S. support for William Walker, and activation of the Wheeler treaty. Yet she did influence U.S. policy, and it would be a mistake to dismiss her as ineffective. She affected such decisions as President Polk's attempt to purchase Cuba, President Buchanan's recognition of the Liberals in Mexico, and Secretary of State Seward's attempt to acquire Samaná Bay. State Department documents, moreover, reveal that Daniel Webster (as well as William Marcy) did eventually take action with Mexican authorities upon her complaints regarding peonage in Texas.[56]

Certainly enough evidence survived about Jane Cazneau's mysterious career to justify a conclusion that she played as important a role—and in many cases a more prominent role—in American foreign policy than many male diplomats of her time. Her unrelenting endorsement of commercial expansion at a time when manifest destiny had stalled helped push her nation in a new direction. It would be a disservice to her career and women's history if we stressed the symbolic aspects of Jane Cazneau's participation in foreign affairs. That one woman refused to cater to sexual norms is in itself of limited consequence. That she actually affected the substance of American diplomacy says a great deal.

NOTES

1. (Natchez) *Mississippi Free Trader*, March 1, 1838; [Anon.], "Female Politicians," *Democratic Review*, XXX (April 1852), 355–59.

2. Paul A. Varg, *United States Foreign Relations, 1820–1860* (East Lansing: Michigan State University Press, 1979), 139, quoting a passage in Robert Seager, *And Tyler too: A Biography of John and Julia Gardiner Tyler* (1963).

3. Henry Watterson, *"Marse Henry": An Autobiography* (2 vols.; New York: George H. Doran, 1919), II, 57. Little is known about Jane Cazneau's physical features, though she apparently was dark-complexioned. *Ibid.*; *New York Sun*, January 11, 1879.

4. Aaron Burr to James Workman, November 16, 1832, Moses Austin Bryan Papers, Barker Texas History Center Archives, University of Texas [the Barker Texas History Center Archives are cited hereafter as BC]; Thomas Hart Benton, *Thirty Years View; or, A History of the Working of the American Government* . . . (2 vols.; New York: D. Appleton and Company, 1897), II, 704; New Orleans *Delta* quoted in (Natchez) *Mississippi Free Trader*, January 12, 1853; *New York Evening Post*, May 24, 1854; *New York Tribune*, December 31, 1878. For the possible affair with Burr, see Milton Lomask, *Aaron Burr: The Conspiracy and Years of Exile, 1805–1836* (New York: Farrar, Straus, Giroux, 1982), 395–403.

5. Merton L. Dillon, "Jane Maria Eliza McManus Storms," in Edward T. James, ed., *Notable American Women 1607–1950: A Biographical Dictionary* (3 vols.; Cambridge: Harvard University Press, 1971), I, 315; Arthur James Weise, *Troy's One Hundred Years, 1789–1889* (Troy: William H. Young, 1891), 244, 338; Aaron Burr to James Workman, November 16, 1832, Moses Austin Bryan Papers, BC.

6. Dillon, "Storms," 315; Watterson, *"Marse Henry,"* II, 56; *Baltimore Sun*, June 7, 1847; *New York Tribune*, December 31, 1878.

7. Aaron Burr to James Workman, November 16, 1832, Aaron Burr to Jane [McManus], [no date], Moses Austin Bryan Papers, BC; Jane M. McManus to Samuel Williams, July 29, 1834, June 19, 1835, Jane M. Cazneau Papers, BC; Jane McManus to [?], Ethel Mary Franklin, ed., "Memoirs of Mrs. Annie P. Harris," *Southwestern Historical Quarterly*, XL (January 1937), 239; William Solyman Coons, comp., *Koon and Coons Families of Eastern New York* . . . (Rutland, Vt.: Tuttle Publishing Company, 1937), 200. In 1849, Jane claimed to have already made nine trips "to & from & through

Texas." Jane M. Storms to Moses S. Beach, February 25, 1849, Jane M. Cazneau Papers, New-York Historical Society [all references to manuscripts in this collection are to copies of originals owned by Brewster Y. Beach, of New York City; the New-York Historical Society will be cited hereafter as NYHS].

8. Tom Reilly, ''Jane McManus Storms: Letters from the Mexican War, 1846–1848,'' *Southwestern Historical Quarterly*, LXXXV (July 1981), 24, 25–26, 25n; Walter Prescott Webb, *The Handbook of Texas* (2 vols.; Austin: Texas State Historical Society, 1952), II, 122.

9. James Buchanan to Moses Y. Beach, November 21, 1846, John Bassett Moore, comp. and ed., *The Works of James Buchanan* (12 vols; Philadelphia: J.B. Lippincott Company, 1908–11), VII, 119–20; John Parrott to James Buchanan, February 8, 1847, Despatches from U.S. Consuls in Mazatlan, John Black to James Buchanan, January 28, 1847, Despatches from U.S. Consuls in Mexico City, Record Group [Record Group in cited hereafter as RG] 59, Records of the Department of State, National Archives [cited hereafter as NA], Microcopy [cited hereafter as M] 159, Roll 1, M 296, Roll 5.

10. Moses Sperry Beach, ''Origin of the Treaty of Guadalupe Hidalgo,'' *Scribner's Monthly*, XVII (December 1879), 299–300; Beach, ''A Secret Mission to Mexico,'' *Scribner's Monthly*, XVIII (May 1880), 136–40.

11. Beach, ''Secret Mission,'' 137.

12. Franklin, ed., ''Memoirs,'' 239; James Morgan to Mrs. [Jane M.] Storms, January 26, 1844 [typewritten copy], James Morgan Papers, Rosenberg Library, Galveston, Texas; Mirabeau Buonaparte Lamar, *Verse Memorials* (New York: W. P. Fetridge & Co., 1857).

13. Jane M. Storms to George Bancroft, July 23, September [no exact date], George Bancroft Papers, Massachusetts Historical Society; Anna Kasten Nelson, ''Mission to Mexico—Moses Y. Beach, Secret Agent,'' *New-York Historical Society Quarterly*, LIX (July 1975), 232–33; Beach, ''Secret Mission,'' 137.

14. Moses Y. Beach to James Buchanan, June 4, 1847, RG 59, Despatches from Special Agents of the State Department, NA, M 37; Beach, ''Secret Mission,'' 139–40.

15. *Baltimore Sun*, June 7, 1847; Edward S. Wallace, *Destiny and Glory* (New York: Coward-McCann, 1957), 245–48; James M. Polk Diary, May 13, 1847, Milo M. Quaife, ed., *The Diary of James K. Polk, 1845–1849* (4 vols.; Chicago: A. C. McClurg & Co., 1910), III, 25. More is known about Jane's continuing role as newspaper contributor during the war. The *only* American correspondent to report from behind Mexican lines, she not only despatched thirty-one letters to the *New York Sun* during her mission, but even managed to get off several pieces to the *New York Tribune* and the *Philadelphia Public Ledger*. Reilly, ''Storms,'' 30–34, 30n, 36–38.

16. *New York Sun*, May 13, 1847; Jane M. Storms to James Buchanan, July 8, August 24, November [no exact date], December 12, 1847, 1848 [no exact date], [microfilm copies], James Buchanan Papers, Historical Society of Pennsylvania; Jane M. Storms to George Bancroft, February [no exact date], June 20, 1848, Bancroft Papers; Jane M. Storms to James K. Polk, February 8, 1848, James K. Polk Papers, Presidential Papers, Library of Congress [the Library of Congress is cited hereafter as LC]. Prior to the Beach mission, Jane had advocated that American troops create an independent republic in northern Mexico, which would be annexed to the United States at a later date. Jane M. Storms to George Bancroft, July 23, and September [no exact date] 1846, Bancroft Papers.

17. Jane M. Storms to George Bancroft, June 20, 1848, Bancroft Papers; *New York Sun*, April 8, 1847; Reilly, ''Storms,'' 30.

18. Basil Rauch, *American Interest in Cuba, 1848–1855* (New York: Columbia University Press, 1948), 48–58.

19. Rauch, *American Interest, passim*; Charles H. Brown, *Agents of Manifest Destiny: The Lives and Times of the Filibusters* (Chapel Hill: University of North Carolina Press, 1980), 21–144; Robert E. May, *John A. Quitman: Old South Crusader* (Baton Rouge: Louisiana State University Press, 1985), 270–95.

20. Jane M. Storms to James Buchanan, August 24, 1847, Buchanan Papers; Jane M. Storms to George Bancroft, February [no exact date], 1848, Bancroft Papers; Jane M. Storms to James K. Polk, August 26, 1847, Jane M. Storms to Daniel S. Dickinson, January 4, 1849, both in James K. Polk Papers, Presidential Papers, LC.

21. Jane M. Storms to George Bancroft, June 20, 1848, Bancroft Papers; Jane M. Storms to [William H.] Seward, September 27, 1849, William H. Seward Papers, University of Rochester Library; Jane M. Cazneau to James Buchanan, January 18, 1853, Buchanan Papers; Jane M. Cazneau to Moses S. Beach, June 25, 1855, Jane M. Cazneau Papers, NYHS.

22. *La Verdad*, File, February 1853–April 1854, Cadwalader Papers, Historical Society of Pennsylvania; Cora Montgomery, *The Queen of Islands and the King of Rivers* (New York: C. Wood, 1850), 3–27; *Our Times*, I (October 1852), 115–18, 187–88; Rauch, *American Interest*, 58, 60. I have been unable to determine the exact chronology of Jane Cazneau's tenure with *La Verdad*. Her column, for instance, appeared from February 10–April 20, 1853, but then disappeared. Her exact connection with *La Verdad* prior to 1853 has not been delineated.

23. January 8, 1850, letter draft, unaddressed, in Jane M. Cazneau Papers, NYHS; Donald S. Spencer, *Louis Kossuth and Young America: A Study of Sectionalism and Foreign Policy, 1848–1852* (Columbia: University of Missouri Press, 1977), 27, 31–34. The marriage occurred sometime between September 27 and December 10. Jane M. Storms to William H. Seward, September 27, December 10, 1849, Seward Papers.

24. James Reed to Thomas Reed, July 15, 1849, Thomas Reed Papers, Louisiana State University Library; Montgomery, *Queen of Islands*, 15; Cora Montgomery, *Eagle Press; or Life on the Border* (New York: Putnam, 1852), 179–81; Jane M. Cazneau to [Moses S. Beach], September 30, 1850, Jane M. Cazneau Papers, NYHS.

25. Montgomery, *Eagle Pass*, 48–50; Jane M. Cazneau Will, January 27, 1877 [typewritten copy]; Jane M. Cazneau Papers, BC. On other occasions, Jane Cazneau described her Eagle Pass Home as a tent. See, for instance, *New York Tribune*, July 15, 1850.

26. Jane M. Cazneau to William H. Seward, January 16, June 3, December 30, 1851; Population Schedules of the Seventh Census of the United States, 1850, Roll 908, Texas, Bexar County; Montgomery, *Eagle Pass*, 10, 34–39, 59, 80, 86–90, 95, 113–18; *New York Tribune*, July 15, October 17, December 11, 13, 1850, February 1, March 6, 8, August 2, 1851. Jane Cazneau apparently returned east, in part, for the purpose of lobbying the federal government to provide border settlers more military protection against Indian attacks. Jane M. Cazneau to Thomas J. Rusk, July 7, 1852, Thomas J. Rusk Papers, BC.

27. William L. Marcy to William L. Cazneau, November 2, 1853 [copy], RG 59, Diplomatic Instructions, Special Missions, NA; *New York Tribune*, January 6, 1854; *Vicksburg Weekly Whig*, March 15, 1854.

28. See particularly Montgomery, *Eagle Pass*, 20; Jane Cazneau letter, February 27, 1853, in *La Verdad*, February 28, 1853.

29. *Our Times* I (October 1852), 115; Jane M. Cazneau to James Buchanan, January

18, 1853, Buchanan Papers; William L. Marcy to Jane M. Storms, June 11, 1847 (accession #7543), New York State Library, Albany; *New York Evening Post*, May 24, 1854. Presumably the *Our Times* piece that mentioned the Haiti filibuster referred to the abortive plot discussed in Spencer, *Louis Kossuth*, 166–67. She also interjected Dominican commentary into her *La Verdad* columns. *La Verdad*, March 20, 30, 1853.

30. William L. Marcy to William L. Cazneau, November 2, 1853 [copy], RG 59, Diplomatic Instructions, Special Missions, NA.

31. *Ibid.*; *Our Times*, I (October 1852), 154; Jane M. Storms to Daniel S. Dickinson, January 4, 1849, in Polk Papers; Montgomery, *Queen of Islands*, 26; Jane M. Cazneau to James Buchanan, November 14, 1857, Buchanan Papers; Cora Montgomery, "The Union of the Seas," *Hunt's Merchants' Magazine and Commercial Review*, XXII (February 1850), 146, 154.

32. Jane M. Cazneau letter, December 9, 1853, in *New York Tribune*, January 6, 1854.

33. Jane M. Cazneau to William L. Marcy, February 7, 1854, Miscellaneous Letters, William L. Marcy to William L. Cazneau, June 17, 1854, Diplomatic Instructions, Special Missions, William L. Cazneau to William L. Marcy, October 9, December 6, 1854, William Cazneau to Jonathan Elliott, November 23, 1854, Jonathan Elliott to William Cazneau, November 16, 1854, Special Agents, all in RG 59, NA. Jane Cazneau also lobbied for the mission with New York Senator Hamilton Fish, a member of the Senate Foreign Relations Committee, and made some inquiries about establishing a pro-American press in Santo Domingo City. Allan Nevins, *Hamilton Fish: The Inner History of the Grant Administration* (New York, 1937), 252; Jane M. Cazneau to Moses S. Beach, December 28, 1854, Jane M. Cazneau Papers, NYHS.

34. William L. Cazneau to T. J. Green, July 24, 1857; William L. Cazneau to Ambrose Dudley Mann, August 3, 1857, William L. Cazneau Miscellaneous Manuscripts, NYHS.

35. Jane M. Cazneau to James Buchanan, March 20, 1857, June 5, 1858, Buchanan Papers; Donathon C. Oliff, *Reforma Mexico and the United States: A Search for Alternatives to Annexation, 1854–1861* (University: University of Alabama Press, 1981), 98–101. On April 1, 1859, the Mexican Liberals granted William Cazneau land and right-of-way concessions for a wagon road connecting the Gulf of California with the Sonora-American frontier. Five days later, the United States granted formal recognition to the Liberals. Oliff, *Reforma Mexico*, 124–25.

36. *Cincinnati Daily Enquirer*, June 3, 1856; Brown, *Agents*, 340. Jane Cazneau, meanwhile, supported a series of lectures in New York City, which were intended to drum up American emigrants for Nicaragua. Jane M. Cazneau to Moses S. Beach, May 31, 1856, Jane M. Cazneau Papers, NYHS.

37. Jane M. Cazneau to John P. Heiss, July 16, [?], 1856, paraphrased in John P. Heiss to Stephen A. Douglas, Stephen A. Douglas Papers, University of Chicago Library; Undated clippings in John P. Heiss Scrapbook, Tennessee State Library and Archives; *Daily Vicksburg Whig*, December 5, 1856; *Baltimore Sun* September 2, 1856; *New York Times*, December 5, 1856.

38. William L. Cazneau to Appleton Oaksmith, September 13, 1856, Appleton Oaksmith Papers, William R. Perkins Library, Duke University; T. N. Carr to William L. Marcy, December 16, 1856, William L. Marcy Papers, LC; Jane M. Cazneau to Moses S. Beach, October 6, 1856, Jane M. Cazneau Papers, NYHS; *New York Times* December 25, 1856. The *Tennessee* encountered difficutlies at sea and never made it to Nicaragua.

39. William L. Cazneau to Jeremiah S. Black, March 18, April 3, 1857, Jane M.

Cazneau to Jeremiah S. Black, April 8, May 4, and undated, Jeremiah S. Black Papers, LC.

40. U.S. Statutes at Large, vol. XI, 35 Cong., 1 Sess., 119–20. The doings of the Atlantic and Pacific Guano Company can be followed in a large number of letters between April and July of 1857 in the Duff Green Papers, Southern Historical Collection, University of North Carolina.

41. Joseph W. Fabens to Duff Green, April 29, July 16, 1857, Green Papers; Jane M. Cazneau to Jeremiah S. Black, September 10, 1857, Black Papers; Jane M. Cazneau to James Buchanan, November 14, 1857, Buchanan Papers; William L. Cazneau to Mirabeau Buonaparte Lamar, January 3, 1858, Jane M. Cazneau to Mirabeau Buonaparte Lamar, April 2, 1858, Mirabeau Buonaparte Lamar Papers, Texas State Archives and Library.

42. William G. W. Jaeger to William H. Seward, December 27, 1863, RG 59, Despatches from United States Consuls in Santo Domingo, NA, T 56, Roll 4; Edmund Ruffin Diary, April 20, 1858, LC; Mrs. William Leslie Cazneau, *Our Winter Eden: Pen Pictures of the Tropics* (New York: Authors' Publishing Co., 1878), 117–19.

43. William L. Cazneau to Lewis Cass, June 19, July 30, 1859, Jane M. Cazneau to James Buchanan, October 17, 1859, RG 59, Special Agents, NA.

44. William L. Cazneau to Lewis Cass, July 2, 1859, February 22, May 12, July 31, October 13, November 17, 1860, RG 59, Special Agents, NA; Jane M. Cazneau to Jeremiah S. Black, November 6, 1850, Black Papers.

45. William H. Seward to William L. Cazneau, March 11, 1861, Diplomatic Instructions, Special Missions, William L. Cazneau to Lewis Cass, January 11, 1861, William L. Cazneau to William H. Seward, May 13, June 28, 1861, Special Agents, RG 59, NA; James W. Cortada, *Spain and the American Civil War: Relations at Mid-Century, 1855–1868* (Philadelphia: American Philosophical Society, 1980), 37–38.

46. Jane M. Cazneau to Moses S. Beach, April 24, June 7, July 6, September 24, October 7, 1862, Jane M. Cazneau to Mrs. Beach, December 1, 1865, Jane M. Cazneau Papers, NYHS; Charles Callan Tansill, *The United States and Santo Domingo, 1798–1873* (Baltimore: Johns Hopkins Press, 1938), 216–20; protest of William Cazneau, October 15, 1863 [copy], enclosed with William G. W. Jaeger to William H. Seward, December 27, 1863, RG 59, Despatches from United States Consuls in Santo Domingo, NA, T 56, Roll 4.

47. John Edwin Fagg, *Cuba, Haiti, & the Dominican Republic* (Englewood Cliffs, New Jersey: Prentice-Hall, 1965), 149–150; Jane M. Cazneau to James Harlan, September 6, 1865, in Seward Papers.

48. Barry Ross Rigby, "American Expansion in the Pacific and Caribbean Islands, 1865–1877" (Ph.D. dissertation, Duke University, 1978), 59–63, 67b, 69, 72; Tansill, *United States and Santo Domingo*, 345–46; Nevins, *Fish*, 245–56; Jane M. Cazneau Will [typewritten copy], Jane M. Cazneau Papers, BC.

49. According to one contemporary source, William Cazneau even felt it necessary that Americans come and work his Dominican mines, and by January 1866 he had imported American laborers. He claimed that idle Dominicans, needing few clothes in their tropical environment and being able to find fruit at will, would not accept the two-to-four-dollar daily wage he was offering. Frederick W. Seward Journal, January 14, 1866, in Frederick W. Seward, *Reminiscences of a War-Time Statesman and Diplomat, 1830–1915* (New York: G. P. Putnam's Sons, 1916), 313–14.

50. Petition and George W. McLean to Henry Raymond, December 12, 1865, enclosed

44 Robert E. May

with Richard B. Kimball to Frederick W. Seward, December 18, 1865, RG 59, Letters of Application and Recommendation for Appointment to Federal Office, NA; Tansill, *United States and Santo Domingo*, 227–28, 232–45; Jane M. Cazneau to [Frederick W. Seward], April 9, 1866, Seward Papers; Seward, *Reminiscences*, 346–55. William Cazneau was also involved in an effort late in the Johnson administration to annex the Dominican Republic. See Tansill, *United States and Santo Domingo*, 249–50.

51. "Report of the Select Committee to Investigate the Memorial of Davis Hatch," Senate Report No. 234, 41 Cong., 2 Sess., p. 50; Nevins, *Fish*, 260; Cazneau, *Our Winter Eden*, *passim*.

52. Lois Decker O'Neill, *The Women's Book of World Records and Achievements* (Garden City, New York: Anchor Press/Doubleday, 1979), 90, 91; Jane M. Cazneau to James Buchanan, January 18, 1853, Buchanan Papers; Jane M. Cazneau to William L. Marcy, February 7, 1854, RG 59, Miscellaneous Letters, NA; John F.T.C. Crampton to Lord Clarendon, October 9, 1854, quoted in Tansill, *United States and Santo Domingo*, 192–93.

53. James Morgan to Jane M. Storms, January 26, 1844, Morgan Papers; Montgomery, *Eagle Pass*, 59; *New York Tribune*, December 31, 1878. There *are* indications that Jane Cazneau's letters to policy-makers were often answered. See for instance Jane M. Storms to James Buchanan, July 24, 1848, Buchanan Papers, which was endorsed "answered."

54. Watterson, *"Marse Henry,"* 56; Benton, *Thirty Years View*, 704; Wallace, *Destiny and Glory*, 248; Jane M. Cazneau to Moses S. Beach, August 25, 1865, Jane M. Cazneau Papers, NYHS; Thomas W. Streeter, ed., *Bibliography of Texas, 1795–1845* (3 vols.; Cambridge: Harvard University Press, 1960), II, 527; *New York Herald*, May 26, 1854.

55. Gideon Welles, *Diary of Gideon Welles*, December 26, 1865 (3 vols.; Boston: Houghton Mifflin Company, 1911), II, 404; James K. Polk Diary, May 13, 1847, Quaife, ed., *Diary of James K. Polk*, 25; Beach, "Secret Mission," 140; Jane M. Storms to Thurlow Weed, March 23, 1841, Jane M. Storms to William H. Seward, December 10, 1849, Seward Papers. By Jane's own admission, William Seward was initially indifferent to her Samaná ideas. Cazneau, *Our Winter Eden*, 124.

56. William L. Marcy to Alfred Conkling, May 5, 1853, William R. Manning, ed., *Diplomatic Correspondence of the United States: Inter-American Affairs, 1831–1860* (12 vols.; Washington: Carnegie Endowment for International Peace, 1932–39), IX, 130–31.

3

Duty with Delicacy: Anna Ella Carroll of Maryland

Janet L. Coryell

"The sight of your 'atrociously scrawling' handwriting was very cheering to our hearts," wrote J. S. Serrill to his friend Anna Ella Carroll in 1869, "But I quarrel with it from one end of your letter to the other—you ought to give us three sheets instead of one. Your galloping letters cheat us out of half that you might say," he scolded. "Write *small* & lines *close together* & don't take a whole *line* to write three words."[1]

Serrill's advice went unheeded—Carroll had been writing for too many years and had too much to say to waste time improving her penmanship. Through books, pamphlets, articles and editorials, Carroll promoted her political policies in a valiant attempt to sway leaders and influence decisions. At times a paid writer, at times a concerned citizen, Carroll worked as both critic and lobbyist. She never quite made it into the inner circles of power, and by many measures, she was a failure. But although she did not achieve her goals, her involvement in nineteenth century political life provides historians with a case study of how the unfranchised could work within a system without a ballot.

Carroll was born in Maryland, daughter of future governor Thomas King Carroll and Julianna Stevenson of Baltimore. She came from good stock: Thomas Carroll's grandfather had been kin to Charles Carroll, a signer of the Declaration of Independence, and to the Most Reverend John Carroll, first Roman Catholic archbishop in the United States. Thomas Carroll had briefly practiced law in Baltimore with Robert Goodloe Harper, the son-in-law of Charles Carroll of Carrollton, and about 1814, he met and married Julianna Stevenson of that city. Her father, Dr. Henry Stevenson, was a prominent physician and leading advocate of smallpox innoculation.[2]

Thomas King Carroll was a Southerner, a Whig, and a plantation owner. His father died shortly after his marriage, so Carroll moved from Baltimore to his inheritance, the family estate of Kingston Hall, Somerset County. There on August 29, 1815, Anna Ella Carroll was born. The eldest of nine children, and her father's favorite, Carroll received a substantial education that included Blackstone and Coke on law, Kantian philosophy, and Shakespearean drama. Thomas Carroll had entered the Maryland legislature about the time of Anna's birth, a move that ensured a continual exposure to politics for his precocious daughter. By 1829, when the legislator became a one-term governor, Carroll's political education was such that letters to her "wisest and dearest of fathers" were sprinkled with political comments amongst the news of home: "It is my principle, as well as that of Lycurgus," she wrote at age fourteen, "to avoid 'mediums'— that is to say, people who are not decidedly one thing or the other. In politics they are the inveterate enemies of the State."[3] Such antipathy toward moderation would characterize Carroll's political views throughout her life.

Nine children, a sickly wife and fifty slaves on a southern plantation could mean financial problems to anyone, and Thomas Carroll was a poor manager who compounded his problems by refusing to sell unneeded slaves farther South. This humanitarian gesture, however, did not prevent him from using those same slaves as collateral for mortgages required to pay off loans he had co-signed for improvident friends.[4] By the mid–1830s, "Miss Anne" took the first step of what would be a lifelong job of trying to help her family stay afloat financially as she opened a boarding school on the plantation. Her attempts postponed the inevitable by only a few years. In 1837, Thomas Carroll was forced to sell Kingston Hall and move to a smaller house at Church Creek, Dorchester County, Maryland, where he would live till his death in 1873, and where his daughter would retreat whenever her political fortunes temporarily declined.[5]

Little is known about Anna Carroll in the decade from 1840 to 1850. She lived in Baltimore and Washington during that period, apparently working as a writer and lobbyist for railroad interests. In 1848, after arranging for a mortgage on some Maryland real estate, she left Washington to care for her ailing mother, who died soon afterward. Carroll's departure from Washington was only temporary, and by April of 1849, she had returned to the city. Her petition to the new Whig Secretary of State John M. Clayton resulted in a job for her father as Naval Officer of Baltimore. With her father's immediate financial future more stable, Carroll began to involve herself and her pen more deeply in national politics.[6]

Politics had fascinated Carroll since childhood and by 1850, at the age of thirty-five, unencumbered by husband and child, she took full advantage of her intelligence and education to participate in the political life of the nation's capitol. Carroll never married—a surprising fact for an attractive and vivacious woman of a distinguished family—and her letters to politicians and family alike lack any sense of the domesticity that was the usual lot and focus of most women in the mid-nineteenth century. Instead, her letters are full of political news and gossip, of reports and opinions, of articles and editorials she had penned under a pseudonym or anonymously. She never hesitated to introduce herself to political leaders. Millard Fillmore in April of 1852 and William Henry Seward in September of the same year both received effusive letters in which Carroll "could not refrain" from addressing them, sure their "noble" characters would overlook her presumption. The letters were characteristic of Carroll's first literary contact with the leading politicians that made up much of her correspondence. Her stated goal was admiration of their intelligence and political acumen; her eventual hope was another patronage position for her family or friends.[7] Other political contacts she no doubt made through her family name and her father's reputation. By 1852, Carroll's correspondents included not only Fillmore and Seward, but Thomas Corwin and Elisha Whittlesey of Ohio and Kenneth Rayner of North Carolina. To this group she would later add John Minor Botts of Virginia, Attorney General Edward Bates, Jefferson Davis, Abraham Lincoln, Edward Everett, Salmon P. Chase, and others.

The overriding characteristic of Carroll's work—correspondence, political comments, criticism, and lobbying efforts—was her belief in the superiority of the American way of life. For Carroll, the way of life was white, Anglo-Saxon, and Protestant, in spite of her familial linkage with the very Catholic line of Carrolls. While she honored "that paternal ancestry," she feared the influence of foreign Catholics on the government. As a bulwark against their "Jesuitical" influence she pleaded for the preservation of what she called "the Protestant Institutions" of Constitution and civil government that would foster the end and goal of America's existence: to establish "the only true principles of liberty the world has ever known." That mission, in Carroll's eyes, was from God, who "had raised this Independent Nation upon which to foster his own glorious Truth. . . ."[8] By "spreading their Protestant Bible and their American Constitution on the wings of the American eagle," Americans could throw their weight "in behalf of equality and justice, over the countries of the world. . . ."[9] Not incidentally those actions would also mean that "our own strength shall increase, our own resources expand, and an additional impetus be given our moral, commercial, and political greatness."[10]

Spread-eaglism in Carroll's views on international affairs was paralleled by her domestic policy. She took political positions that represented national, not sectional, interests. As did many Marylanders in the 1850s, Carroll turned for political succor from the growing sectionalism and dying force of the southern Whigs and from the threatening influx of immigrants to the pro-Union nativism of the American, or Know-Nothing, Party.

Carroll embraced the American Party for a number of different reasons. Her father was a Whig supporter, as was she, and both had been disheartened when Henry Clay lost the 1844 presidential race to James K. Polk. Many Maryland political leaders blamed the foreign Democratic vote in Baltimore for helping to give the victory to Polk, even though Maryland had gone Whig as a state and Baltimore had given Polk a plurality of only 473 votes, or .02 percent of the popular total.[11] Although Thomas Carroll had benefited from a Whig patronage position in 1849, by 1853 the Whigs were out of office and he was out of a job.

The Whigs' continued decline by the mid–1850s made the Know-Nothings an attractive, non-Democratic alternative. An additional influence on Anna Carroll was Robert Breckinridge, an ardent anti-Catholic, and Carroll's Presbyterian minister during her days in Baltimore. His powerful tirades against foreigners and Catholics made a deep and long-lasting impression.[12] The pro-Union stance of the American Party was also important to Carroll, who feared occasional secessionist talk in the Capitol.

By 1855, Carroll was active in the American cause, lobbying party leaders for Millard Fillmore's nomination to the presidency, and then applying her literary talents to churning out at least seven different books and pamphlets in support of the American Party and the ticket of Fillmore and Donelson, all published in 1856. It was a prodigious amount of work: the first production of that year, *The Great American Battle*, was 365 pages long; the last, *The Star of the West*, was over 500. In between came shorter works, all designed to criticize the Democrats and promote the Know-Nothings.[13] Carroll considered the Republicans as too sectional to attract many voters, and therefore only a minor threat.

Carroll's works, like most political tracts of the time, were less than literary masterpieces. She showed a tendency for overly dramatic prose, hyperbole, italics, and exclamation points. Combined with essays in her papers, however, her published works give a sense of who she was and what she believed in. She was an ardent, sometimes fanatical, Unionist, a partisan zealot, and a firm believer in the traditions of manifest destiny and Anglo-Saxon superiority. Yet she was also a Southerner who worked to protect the interests of her section against attacks from northern abolitionists and southern disunionists. She was quite capable of arguing both sides of a question if it suited her purpose. A consummate political animal, she was dedicated to achieving and maintaining whatever hold she could on political power. She loved politics; she loved being on the fringes of, or as she usually perceived herself, in the midst of, political decisions. While aware of the restrictions placed upon her by her sex, she worked around them by declaring herself above them. "I am a *lady*," she wrote to William Henry Seward in 1852, "but by *blood & name* and *spirit identified* with those who contributed greatly to establish and perpetuate our free institutions— . . . . By education & association my interest is more than that of ladies ordinarily. I *read, think & write.* . . ."[14]

And so she did. Two of Carroll's 1856 works give the most coherent and comprehensive view of her criticisms of United States foreign policy in the 1850s: *Review of Pierce's Administration* and *The Star of the West*. Her opinions were characteristic of the antebellum expansionists such as Matthew Fontaine Maury, Asa Whitney, and William Henry Seward. Not limited to the continentalism of Manifest Destiny, not interested in the Young Americans' call for intervention in Europe, Carroll was primarily a commercial expansionist. She argued strongly for a foreign and domestic policy that would benefit trade, a consular and diplomatic service that would promote the expansion of American markets, a strong navy to protect Americans abroad, reciprocity treaties with South America, and peace with Europe to avoid the disruptions of trade any war would bring.[15] These were all points upon which she attacked the Pierce administration in her *Review*.

Her biggest target was Louisiana Senator Pierre H. Soulé, minister to Spain for the first half of the Pierce administration. Easily Pierce's most disastrous appointment, Soulé had been exiled from France as a radical republican, and was seen by the London *Times* as "a declared enemy" of Spain "in the guise of a foreign envoy." Carroll saw him as trouble. Not only was Soulé a "French Jacobin," but worse, a "disunionist," and worst of all, a *"fillibustero* sent with the desired aim of war with Spain over Cuba."[16] Spain's first measure of Soulé's less-than-diplomatic behavior came as Soulé dueled with the French ambassador over comments about Mrs. Soulé's immodest appearance (although Carroll, the essence of tact and propriety, claimed it was fought over a coat). Soulé then compounded Spanish dismay as he manifested his desire to acquire Cuba during the *Black Warrior* affair. In February of 1854, the merchant ship *Black Warrior* was detained in Havana harbor for an incomplete manifest until a $6000 fine was paid. Soulé meant to escalate what was a minor incident into a war by an uncompromising attitude and a forty-eight-hour ultimatum for reparations. Though war was averted, Soulé's desire for the island exacerbated the Cuban crisis of 1854 that eventually resulted in the unauthorized issuance of the Ostend Manifesto, which called for the United States to "wrest" the island from Spain.[17]

In keeping with Carroll's general ideas regarding foreign policy, her criticism of Soulé's actions regarding the *Black Warrior* reflected her concept of the proper role of an American minister. As the country's representative, Soulé's task was to promote American interests, particularly trade, keep the peace with Europe, and maintain the honor of Americans abroad. Carroll argued that Soulé had gone to Spain with designs on Cuba as his primary interest, instead of designs to promote American trade. Soulé's threats and schemes during the *Black Warrior* affair made those designs evident. But Carroll also had to answer those who said that the seizure of the *Black Warrior* was an infringement on the rights of Americans abroad, the protection of whom was part and parcel of Pierce's foreign policy—and supposedly hers as well.[18] Something had to be done to avenge American honor, and for Know-Nothing Carroll, that something had to show up the Democrats' ineptitude.

What to do was the problem. A demand for reparation for the losses incurred by the *Black Warrior* to the Spanish crown was the obvious choice of both Carroll and the government. But Soulé's demands for reparation were ignored by the Spanish government, Carroll said, because Spanish Secretary of State Calderon de la Barca knew Pierce and his cabinet could not and would not back up Soulé's claims, and thus "had divested Spain from all fear or terror in the delay." Why did Spain not quake at the thought of American displeasure? Because the administration had failed in another inaugural promise to rebuild the navy to protect its far-flung interests and citizens. Without a proper navy, the United States could not hope to enforce its demand for reparation.[19] What was needed, according to Carroll, was prompt action, presumably in the form of a U.S. warship in Havana harbor to impress Spain with the seriousness of the American demands.

By using this particular line of logic, Carroll was able to score political points in an election-year pamphlet and still appear consistent in her foreign policy. However partisan her interpretations, Carroll tended to maintain her private world view in her public writings. One way she achieved this was by isolating the event and ignoring the long-range effect, a literary trait no doubt valuable to the American Party. For instance, Carroll could admit the danger that Soulé was a filibuster with ignoble and greedy designs on Cuba, and then ignore the probable effects of Soulé's imperious demands on the Spanish government. She could ignore the wisdom of Pierce's choice of peace over war, and concentrate on the isolated failure to keep an inaugural promise. She could ignore the interconnections of the Cuban issue with the slavery question and the territorial question. She could ignore as well the desire for peace with the world that Pierce had expressed in his inaugural address, by turning the focus of her criticism on his failure to fulfill other inaugural promises.

In this manner, Carroll, who supported building a Pacific railroad, could excoriate Pierce for the Gadsden Purchase. Instead of providing land for the railroad, it was a "humbug" that "served no better purpose than to set up Santa Anna in Mexican style."[20] The Gadsden Treaty conveyed an overly expensive, "worthless strip of land, and the privilege of fighting the Apaches Indians [sic] on our own soil!" when the money should have been used "to fit out a suitable navy. . . ."[21] Once again, she ignored what was part of her own policy aim, the Pacific railroad, which would lead "to political and commercial greatness,"[22] as it completed the link between the United States and the China market. Yet she still maintained her own views by choosing another aspect of her ideas on foreign policy—a strong navy—as a support for her criticism. As a political writer, Carroll was not so interested in logical consistency as in producing a polemic against the Democrats. Yet she never entirely divorced her own world view from her criticisms.

Upon occasion, that world view became paramount even within her political polemic. This was true in Carroll's interpretation of the Ostend Manifesto. This curious document was issued in October of 1854 by Soulé, James Buchanan, the American minister to England, and John Mason, the American minister to France. A statement of intent to purchase Cuba or, barring Spanish compliance, to "detach" it from Spain, the Manifesto provided plenty of ammunition for Carroll. She clearly saw its ramifications, and used the incident to form her harshest criticism of Pierce's term.

On this issue, Carroll showed a clear, intelligent, and fairly non-partisan grasp of the possible repercussions of the Ostend Manifesto. Supposedly, it was designed to meet a threat to American security from Cuba. That threat was the "Africanization" of Cuba, a term that referred to Cuban Captain-General Marques Juan de la Pezuela's plan to emancipate all blacks brought to the island since 1835, and to train and arm free black men for the militia. Such a move would heighten southern fears of an armed rebellion led by foreign freed blacks. But Pezuela's plan was imaginary, said Carroll, and the imaginary plan was supported by an imaginary conspiracy of the French and English. To meet that conspiracy by relieving Spain of its ownership of the island by whatever means necessary was the supposed object of the Manifesto.[23]

But since neither threat nor conspiracy existed, what was left was a "refractory" Minister Soulé who had neglected his duties and had to be disciplined by the other two signing diplomats, Buchanan and Mason. All three then conspired to "adjust" any differences with Spain. That adjustment, in accordance with "*DIVINE LAW*," meant the United States would grab Cuba by purchase or force and provide the slave states with expansion territory.[24]

It was madness, argued Carroll, to pursue such a course as suggested by the Manifesto. In the first place, the *raison d'être*—the supposed conspiratorial French and English support for Spanish "Africanization"—did not exist. Second, the Manifesto would mean "war, immediately, with England, France, and Spain." That war would mean a cessation of commerce between Europe and the United States, precipitating economic anarchy and political revolution among the European nations, and destroying America's "best customers abroad." Third, the United States already possessed an area of territory only one-sixth less than the area of the fifty-nine states of Europe. It needed no more territory. Carroll believed it made far more sense to make treaties and send missionaries, "to enlighten . . . benighted papists . . . than to bring a population of ignorant paupers and criminals, who could never appreciate our Anglo-American liberty, under the aegis of American laws."[25]

Carroll's brand of American expansion was rife with references to America's mission and the superiority of the American way of life. The principles that had guided America thus far must not be limited to Americans only, she wrote. "Our examples, our ideas, our discoveries, our inventions, our habits of life, our social, political and religious institutions must ultimately extend our form of government."[26] But the missionary work could not be done in a haphazard or sectional fashion. The Ostend Manifesto was too sectional a method to extend "Americanism." Here, as with her earlier criticism, Carroll did not override all of her foreign policy. Although taking Cuba provided for the expansion of American markets by controlling Gulf trade, as well as a chance to "save" Cuba by converting its population to Protestantism and the American way, Carroll was more concerned about the sectional antagonisms raised by the proposal. The Manifesto threatened to split the country over slavery expansion, and Unionist Carroll could never support such a move.[27]

Carroll's analysis of the dangers inherent in the issuance of the Manifesto was largely correct. The Ostend Manifesto was a threat, pure and simple. The desire to annex territories such as Cuba was not an aberration in American foreign policy—after all, Texas and California had been "detached" from Mexico by aggressive support from the United States. But the Manifesto was an aberration in language. Supporting a revolution from the outside by filibusters and funds or by nonenforcement of neutrality laws was one thing; threatening a forceful takeover of the property of a sovereign nation was another. Had not Secretary of State William Marcy repudiated the Manifesto in no uncertain terms and Soulé subsequently resigned, war with Spain would have been a distinct possibility. And Spain, according to Carroll, would have been justified in the eyes of the international community.[28]

What Carroll wanted was an opportunity to export American ideals without the territorial expansion of slavery, such as had been sought in Cuba by southern radicals like Soulé. America's mission was to spread its ideals and, in consequence, to make itself "formidable" to Europe. Fear of European interference in American affairs had led the country "to the *westward*" from the first, Carroll wrote. As early as 1787 it was clear to American forefathers (she cited Patrick Henry) that the Atlantic seaboard could never be adequately fortified.[29] Westward lay the course of an empire conquered by rail; that done, as she believed it would soon be, the course would move southward to the Caribbean and South America. A policy emphasizing trade would lead to reciprocity treaties, trade agreements, and eventually a form of economic annexation by which one could "*American-ize*" a "race of savage idolators" so that they could both enjoy the benefits of liberty that the American mission spread, and become good trading partners as well.[30]

An opportunity for that variety of expansion presented itself upon the occasion of William Walker's invasion of Nicaragua, an event Carroll reviewed in glowing terms in her last major work of 1856, *The Star of the West*. Subtitled "National Men and National Measures," it was a collection that illustrated Carroll's fascination with the idea of American mission. There were long essays on the navy, exploring expeditions, the Pacific railroad, various anti-Catholic and anti-European warnings and diatribes, and on William Walker's filibustering adventures in Nicaragua. There is no evidence to explain why Carroll chose this particular episode to write about, but Walker's actions would certainly appeal to her sense of mission and duty that were so much a part of her expansionist outlook.

Carroll compared Walker's work with what "Lafayette, de Kalb, Pulaski, Kosciusko had done for American liberty. . . . Who, then, can repress patriotic emotion, or deep sympathy for his triumph?" America was right to "extend the protection" of its laws and systems of government to a people who had supposedly "invited" the United States "to take up their cause."[31] The triumph of self-government in the American tradition for such a people tied in well not only in spiritual terms with American interest in liberty and justice, but in economic terms as well. To Carroll, Walker in Nicaragua meant that "our stars and stripes will yet float over the Pacific gate of the Nicaraguan transit" on the road to the China market, and thus the key to the Gulf of Mexico would "never fall into the hands of savages." The Central American states, so "essential to the commerce of the United States" must never be "owned" by the "enemies" of those

United States.[32] Walker's activities provided Carroll with the perfect example of the nobility of the American mission in action in Central America, restoring order and peace through American systems of government, and at the same time ensuring the preservation and promotion of United States trade.[33]

Walker's own account of his invasion of Nicaragua, not published until 1860, took the same general tone as Carroll's earlier defense. His motives, he declared, even in his earlier attempts to set up republics in Lower California and Sonora were "not to destroy but to reorganize society." He saw his landing at Realejo in northern Nicaragua as opening a "new epoch" of constitutional, peaceful government. The only reason he had declared the Rivas government of Nicaragua dissolved in June of 1856 was because it was discriminating against the "people" and therefore "no longer worthy of existence." His own provisional government would last only until Nicaragua could "exercise its natural rights of electing its own rulers."[34]

Carroll must have been greatly pleased to receive Walker's note thanking her for the copy of *The Star of the West* that she had sent him. It was "a source of consolation as well as of encouragement . . . to receive such assurances as you manifest in the cause of Nicaraguan regeneration." He promised her he would try to see her when and if he revisted New York City, where Carroll was working. There is no indication that the two ever met. Her description of his public speaking presence, however ("an expression of meekness, accompanied by a nasal tone and sluggish utterance, which would arrest attention in any assembly"), is peculiar enough to suggest she might have returned to Washington in time to meet with him before his last invasion of Nicaragua and subsequent execution by a Honduran firing squad in 1860.[35]

But if she did meet with him or hear him speak, she would have had considerable difficulty with the second half of his defense of his actions in Nicaragua: his attempt to make Nicaragua a field for slavery expansion. Walker's decree of September 22, 1856, had repealed the abolition of slavery and repaved the way for its reestablishment; desperately seeking recognition for his government to stave off defeat at the hands of a union of the Central American states and Cornelius Vanderbilt, whose transit company's lucrative concession in Nicaragua was threatened by Walker, he intended the decree to appeal to southern pro-expansion sentiment.[36]

The profundity of Walker's desire to restore slavery to Nicaragua would not have been apparent to Carroll in the summer of 1856 as she wrote *The Star of the West*. But by fall, she no doubt knew about the September decree. As was true in her other political writings, though, she chose to deemphasize the contradiction between the American ideals and sense of mission she had found in Walker's exploits and his work to extend slavery. Instead, she focused on the enemy: the ready and familiar scapegoat of Pierre Soulé. Soulé had come to Nicaragua in August of 1856, ostensibly to facilitate the sale of public lands in Nicaragua. But Carroll saw a sinister conspiracy: Soulé had been sent by James Buchanan and the Democratic Party to reintroduce slavery into Nicaragua.[37] By

taking this approach, Carroll was once again able to score political points against
the Democrats, while still maintaining the overall validity of her own opinion
of Walker.

Whether Buchanan and the Democrats had anything to do with Soulé's trip
is doubtful. But the combined factors of Walker's need for recognition of his
government, Soulé's desire to secure slavery in the South through expansion
farther south, and the short time between Soulé's visit and the issuance of the
September decree that opened the door for slavery's reestablishment in Nicaragua
suggest a legitimate connection between the aims of Walker and Soulé. By re-
establishing slavery, Walker would put pressure on the United States to recognize
his government as a response to the southern lobby. He could also thus provide
himself with an adequate labor force, which would help to ensure the profitability
of American investments in Nicaragua, and, in the event the Union was dissolved,
he would have the basis for a powerful alliance with a confederacy of the southern
states.[38]

Carroll could blame the Democratic corruption of Walker for his disunionist
sentiment and pro-slavery expansionism. But Walker's conversion to the Catholic
faith in 1859 no doubt put an end to Carroll's support entirely. Walker's earlier
presidency had used Catholic rites during his inauguration, but actual conversion
would have been too much for anti-Catholic Carroll to tolerate.[39]

By 1859, moreover, Carroll was becoming concerned with the growing sectionalism in the United States. In 1860, to her dismay, Abraham Lincoln was
nominated as the Republican presidential candidate—far too sectional a candidate, Carroll felt, to please any part of the country. She thought him an abolitionist, and not to be trusted; still he was the duly elected candidate and the
Union was what was important. After the returns were in, she wrote to her good
friend Governor Thomas Hicks of Maryland, and urged him to stand faithful to
the Union—on him and Maryland depended the successful inauguration of Abraham Lincoln.[40]

Lincoln's first few months in office did nothing to assuage Carroll's fears.
His failure to convince any southern Unionist to come into his Cabinet on his
terms, Carroll regarded as an "irreparable blunder." In constructing his Cabinet
on "partisan grounds," she wrote, Lincoln had made a "fatal error," resulting
in the increase of the power of the Confederate rebellion a "hundred fold!" He
had driven "from the support of the government all the able men of the South,"
by his sectional policies. The South would never be restored to the fold of the
Union without southern Unionist "allies on the soil" of the South, Carroll argued,
and that would never be achieved so long as Lincoln acted "exclusively on his
anti-slavery prejudices."[41]

Like many border-state slaveowners, Carroll hated the institution of slavery,
but saw no feasible way to rid the South of it. She well knew the economic
consequences of keeping slaves. In an 1854 letter to Gerrit Smith, a philanthropist
and advocate of compensated emancipation, Carroll had asked for his aid in
raising money to continue buying her father's mortgaged slaves to prevent their

sale South. At the end of her "mental elasticity," she wrote, "I regard all my own misfortune—or that, in which I am involved, on acct. of my family, to that inheritance of slavery, to which for so many generations my family have been subjected."[42] Economics aside, there were emotional considerations as well. Her memories of the days when the slave traders came to buy those whom the plantation would no longer support made her in later years

shudder . . . at the sight of such horrors as came before my own eyes—a daughter, clinging to her parents . . . with screams that were frantic, the whole white family of females, in tears, yet powerless to interpose . . . the most tender and devoted of mothers too far bereft by the sale of her first born boy to shed a tear. . . . Scenes like this no years have ever effaced—no time can ever make me forget—. . . .[43]

Carroll's antipathy toward the horrors of slavery led her to search constantly for a way out. She succeeded in raising funds to buy about twenty of her father's slaves, and she liberated her own slaves at the outbreak of the Civil War. But Lincoln's leanings toward abolition, which she viewed as part and parcel of his political policy, were too much of an attack on the South. The southern economy and its society would be destroyed. For Carroll, compensated emancipation with colonization was the answer. Though apparently not a member of the American Colonization Society, Carroll had friends who were. Like them, she believed that once colonized and protected from exploitation, freed blacks "would be able to develop all the elements of their nature, believing as I do that they are capable of attaining a high degree of civilization; much higher than they ever can attain, in competition with the white race."[44]

Unlike her work on behalf of the American Party, for which there is no indication she was ever paid, Carroll's work for colonization would be paid labor even while it combined a personal interest with her professional career.[45] By April of 1861, Anna Carroll had established a working relationship with Aaron Columbus Burr, a leading New York merchant. Burr, in March of that year, had become the agent for James Grant of Belize, British Honduras, to sell Grant's 150 square miles of land in "Stand" [Stann] Creek, to found a colony for free blacks. Aside from what he viewed as the humanitarian motive of colonization, Grant was asking $65,000 for the land, which included considerable stands of mahogany, rubber trees, "cocoa nut trees" and a brickworks.[46]

Burr had originally made a land-lease agreement with Grant for a mahogany-cutting company formed in 1860. The political unrest in the area scared off investors, but Grant had received several offers for the land itself, which Burr privately valued at $100,000. In the spring of 1861, Burr proposed to Carroll, "known as a practical advocate of colonization," that a company be formed "for the purchase of this land for the benefit of the free persons of color in the United States." Also to benefit Burr's pocket—he offered the land at what he called a "reduced price" of $75,000, but since he had never actually purchased the land from Grant, he stood to make $10,000 on the sale of the land to the government, some of which undoubtedly would go to Carroll.[47]

Burr apparently hired Carroll to help him present his case to the government. Throughout the spring and summer of 1862, she wrote to President Lincoln, voluminous letters of ten to fifteen pages of her widely spaced scrawl. But she wrote with little apparent effect. Her first step to push for colonization by the federal government was to lobby against the Washington, D.C., emancipation bill of April 16, 1862. She argued that it too closely followed John C. Calhoun's series of feared abolitionist measures (first the District, then the territories, then federal property, then internal slave trade, finally Abolition entire) that Calhoun had warned the South to watch out for. Signing the bill, warned Carroll, would prove to the country that, in spite of his public declarations supporting colonization, Lincoln was really a northern abolitionist. The bill would free only 1500 slaves, yet would reinforce the South with 50,000 fighting men from the Border States who could not swallow any form of abolition, or anything that would look like the beginning of an abolition process, no matter how great their love for the Union. Colonization would have to follow emancipation to be an acceptable policy for the Border States.[48]

The D.C. Bill passed, but Carroll gave up neither hope nor the lobbying activities Burr employed her to pursue. She wrote to the president proposing the colonization of British Honduras. Carroll presented the colony as attractively as possible: close to the United States, direct trading track, easy access, friendly government, tropical climate, and fertile soil. There was an added, and perhaps overstated, attraction: "the desire of the government" of British Honduras "to develop its vast resources of wealth, by receiving upon a social and political equality, the very class of persons which it is the interest of this country to furnish." It was also a way for the United States "to remove the colored race and make them useful to themselves and retain them as friends" of the whites.[49]

The formal proposal was finally made by Burr himself on May 6 to the Department of the Interior, which was in charge of all colonization projects. For $75,000 Burr would transfer title, found a settlement colony named the "Lincoln Colony," and "if the government desire my services" he would "receive these freedmen as they are transported, and superintend their location upon the land, upon whatever principle may be determined by the government." On May 13, Carroll wrote to Secretary of the Interior Caleb Smith with a full accounting of the improvements on the land and included a map of Scotland Town, the main settlement. The matter was laid before Lincoln by the 19th.[50]

At this point, there may have been a meeting between Carroll and Lincoln regarding the colonization project. Reminiscing late in life, Carroll recalled a touching scene in which Lincoln asked her what he should do about the matter of colonization.

I was perfectly charmed with his cordial and simple remarks, free from every semblance of ambition. He, in the most exalted office upon earth, deferring as humbly to another, as if he had no power or aim! He was patient and gentle as a woman could be, nothing brusque about him. He got up and took a large map which he hung in the room and sat down on a small low stool by the fire place, spread the map on his knees, and asked me to point out the place I recommended for the colonization of the freedmen. I pointed to British Honduras, in Central America, and gave all the reasons for this as the then proper locality. . . . [51]

Such a domestic scene may have been fact, or fancy created by the passage of time and presidential martyrdom. At any rate, she did continue to contact Lincoln through letters, writing to him on the 19th of May. In that long missive, she argued against Liberia as disadvantageous: transportation costs to the colony were too great, and the opposition of freed blacks to leave the United States for Africa was too strong. Haiti, another suggested site, was just as objectionable. The island was too small for the "American element" (who were presumably used to the vastness of the North American continent, and who were now four million in number). No doubt a "few, shrewd" colonists would succeed, but only "by sinking their Americanism and becoming thoroughly European in their caste . . . the majority . . . would be held only as laborers and producers. . . ." In addition, the "arbitrary" government of the island would give colonists "no more chance for elevating their social and political positions" than in the United States. British Honduras was the answer. Large enough "to found an empire for many millions," it was the only country in Central America that would not require civil and military support and protection from the United States for its colonists. Life, liberty, and property were secure in British Honduras and its government would "interpose no barrier" to colonization. [52]

It is difficult to tell exactly when Lincoln rejected the choice of British Honduras as a possible colonization site, if he did indeed consider it seriously. Carroll had just sent him a box of "Central American goods" to convince him of the plenty that awaited colonists, and she thought it was still alive as a choice on August 30. She wrote to Burr telling him she was sure the Chiriqui colonization project, another Central American site that Lincoln had proposed to a delegation of free blacks on the 14th, was dead. [53] This was in spite of Lincoln signing the Confiscation Bill of July 17, which Carroll had viewed as another step that seemed to indicate Lincoln's preference for outright abolition instead of colonization. Such a bill, she vainly protested, would serve only to alienate southern Unionists and would change the whole meaning of the war. "It will no longer be regarded, as a war for the maintainance [sic] of the American Constitution, but as one, for the subjugation of the Southern States, and the destruction of their social system. And the judgment of the civilized world will then decide, that the South is in a just struggle for Constitutional Liberty, against an arbitrary and revengeful government." Jefferson Davis and the Confederates would, as a result, "be regarded, like Washington and his copatriots, as founders of a new empire," while the president and his cabinet would become the new George III and Lord North. Furthermore, Europe would never intervene on the side of the Union, if that was what the president was hoping to accomplish with the Confiscation Bill, and any suggestion that it would, would soon "prove a *deception, and a snare.*"[54]

She was right, of course: Lincoln's emancipation policies did change the nature of the war. At the same time that Carroll was pushing for British Honduras colonization as a way to keep the purpose of the war limited so southern Unionists would not be alienated, Lincoln was using the country's growing awareness of the military importance of slavery to the Confederacy, and the value of armed freed blacks to the Union cause as a way to push toward emancipation. Lincoln's "paramount object in this struggle," he wrote to Horace Greeley on August 22, was "to save the Union." While he knew his official duty had to override personal feelings and any full-scale emancipation measure had to come "as a practical War measure," his personal wish was that all men be free.[55] Lincoln could see a way to accomplish that with his approach that entailed emancipation with or without colonization. Carroll could not wield such a double-edged sword. In her opinion, emancipation without colonization would mean the loss of the Border States and, in the end, the death of the Union itself.

After a September 13 meeting with Senator Samuel C. Pomeroy, head of the still-lively Chiriqui project, Carroll wrote Burr that the British Honduras colonization proposal was dead. Instead, the "Chiriqui property will be bought & fortunes made for the *white* speculators through the poor Africans who will hew the wood & draw the water." The Chiriqui site was not the final choice, but the administration's two-pronged attack on slavery continued with the issuance of the Preliminary Emancipation Proclamation on September 22. This setback to Carroll's plans kept her subdued for a month, but on October 21, she made a last-ditch effort as she asked for a meeting with Lincoln as "a sincere friend of the colored" to argue once more for the British Honduras site. If she did meet with him, her arguments failed to sway him, for the announced site was the Haitian island of Ile-à-Vache.[56]

That October 1862 meeting appears to have been the last between Lincoln and Carroll. Earlier, she had tried to take advantage of his knowledge of her writing abilities by offering in August to go to Europe and write on behalf of the Union cause. Lincoln had thought her proposition for $50,000 for her work as a propagandist the "most outrageous one ever made" and Carroll had replied stiffly that "the difference between us, was in our views, upon the value of intellectual labor in the administration of government."[57] No doubt some of the president's outrage was occasioned by the high price of Carroll's work. But Lincoln's rebuff did not appear to have been forgiven lightly by a woman whose sense of self came from her intellectual and literary labors. Carroll, after her contact with him in October over the colonization issue, turned her efforts and interests toward military affairs and collecting payment from the government for literary services rendered the War Department. She apparently did not correspond with Lincoln again.[58]

In interpreting Carroll's activities as a critic and lobbyist, determining the extent to which Carroll had access to Lincoln and the degree of attention he paid her ideas are difficult to ascertain. On the surface, it appears as though she only rarely reached him; when she did make contact, she failed to sway him. Yet Carroll did articulate soundly the concerns of the Border States regarding emancipation and colonization, and Lincoln did recognize and speak to those concerns, if not in direct reply to her. In September, 1862, for example, he pointed out his fear to a visiting interdenominational delegation of Christians from Chicago that "fifty thousand bayonets" from the Border States might be turned against the Union in consequence of a proposed emancipation proclamation. This was an argument and a figure that Carroll had used in her letters to Lincoln the preceding April and July.

The rest of the war years for Carroll were focused on the domestic rather than foreign policy, as she turned to state politics and family problems. After the war, Carroll's literary output declined considerably. She was in her fifties, suffered from bouts of ill health and was growing deaf. Still she felt up to a trip West with her constant companion, former representative from Texas Lemuel D. Evans, in the winter of 1868–69, where she reported on the Texas Reconstruction Convention to President-elect Ulysses Grant. And she continued to pen anonymous articles on nepotism, corruption, and reconstruction politics. Her rabid anti-Catholicism and nativism mellowed but slightly over time. As late as 1880, she wrote Republican presidential candidate James Garfield, warning him of an alliance between the Catholic church and the Democratic party to destroy civil and religious liberty in America.[59] She also kept up her correspondence with congressmen throughout the 1880s, and her interest in national politics never waned.

Educated as a man would be, trained in law and constitutional theory, and possessed of enough self-confidence and energy to push her way into the political world she loved, Anna Carroll was a fascinating example of the degree of political participation a nineteenth-century woman could achieve without the franchise. Her greatest strength as a critic of American foreign policy was that she perceived and articulated well the ideas of large political groups such as the American Party and the Border States. When not overburdened by partisanship, her arguments for their positions were logical, sound, and coherently expressed. Her writings represent ideas held by a substantial minority in the United States. The American Party, for example, pulled in 21.53 percent of the popular vote in 1856, a third-party record not even approached until it was surpassed by the 27.93 percent of the Progressive Party in 1912.[60]

Another important facet of Carroll's life was that she developed a compromise method of working within the political system that did not threaten her own sense of femininity, or the male-dominant power structure. She was very aware that she was a female operating within a male sphere. She either used or ignored this fact, as it suited her purpose. At first, she used it: she apologized for her intrusion into the masculine world of politics. She was not a feminist when it came to the franchise, for instance; rather, she argued that "the interests and destiny of mothers and daughters are common with those of their fathers and brothers." Duty was her motivation, she reassured her readers, perhaps because she knew that claiming a right to participate fully in politics would raise a backlash that could shut her out completely.[61]

She recognized the limits of "feminine delicacy," yet the "unwillingness to recognize by formal act the indebtedness of the Government to a woman" for her work during the Civil War finally led her to ask for help from the feminists. "Truth is what concerns mankind," she wrote, and even when truth was from a woman's pen, all should welcome it, "especially when its aim is for the welfare and highest good of individuals, of society, and of the nation."[62]

A particularly feminine political method, the imagery of the "republican mother," was present in Carroll's writings as well. It was "mothers who make the men in a nation," and her approach when analyzing William Walker's life was a good example of this imagery. She gave credit for Walker's favorable behavior in Central America to the fact that he had "a *good* mother." Walker, in fact, "by the amiability of his disposition, and the sweetness of his temper, supplied the place of a daughter" to his widowed mother.[63]

Carroll's communication through print, rather than confrontation, was typical of what historian Linda Kerber refers to as "prepolitical" behavior. With no franchise to serve for political expression, Carroll used books, pamphlets and letters—all of which were forms of petitioning, an archaic and honored form of political method employed by women and men through the ages. Her style was similar to the parameters set by Kerber: the acknowledgement of inferiority or subordinate status, the "rhetoric of humility," and the individual nature of the act of petitioning.[64] With this style of presentation, Carroll could share her ideas without threatening those in power.

Through apology, duty, imagery, and petition, Carroll presented her case to those in office. She was unsuccessful in achieving her political goals: her ideas were not popular enough, her information was limited, her presentation was often paranoid.[65] Yet she kept on, despite the disappointments of the Know-Nothings' demise, of Walker's corruption of American principles by his slavery expansionism, of colonization's failure. She remained active and interested in politics for over forty years. Far from being discouraged by her exclusion from a part of the political system, she found a way to live her life the way she wanted, doing what she wanted. While the end results may not have been all she desired, she presented a useful methodology for any who cared to follow.

NOTES

1. J. S. Serrill to Anna Ella Carroll, 12, July 1869; 21 September, 1869, Anna Ella Carroll Papers, Maryland Historical Society, Baltimore, Maryland.

2. Elias Jones, *Revised History of Dorchester County, Maryland* (Baltimore: Read-Taylor Press, 1925), pp. 296–301.

3. Anna Ella Carroll to Thomas King Carroll, 17 February, 1830, cited in Sarah

Ellen Blackwell, *Life of a Military Genius: Anna Ella Carroll of Maryland* (Washington, D.C.: Judd & Detweiler, 1891), p. 18.

4. Anna Ella Carroll to Gerrit Smith, 26 June, 1854, Gerrit Smith Collection, The George Arents Research Library, Syracuse University, Syracuse, New York.

5. Jones, *Revised History*, p. 298; Blackwell, *Life*, pp. 19–27; Charles McCool Snyder, "Anna Ella Carroll, Political Strategist and Gadfly to President Fillmore," *Maryland Historical Magazine* 68 (Spring 1973): 37.

6. Anna Ella Carroll to John Young Mason, 6 November, 1848, Mason Family Papers, Virginia Historical Society, Richmond, Virginia; Snyder, "Anna Ella Carroll," p. 38; Anna Ella Carroll to John M. Clayton, 13 April, 1849, John M. Clayton Papers, Library of Congress, Washington, D.C.

7. Anna Ella Carroll to Millard Fillmore, 27 April, 1852, Millard Fillmore Papers, Buffalo & Erie County Historical Society and State University College at Oswego, Oswego, New York; Anna Ella Carroll to William Henry Seward, 15 September, 1852. William Henry Seward Papers, Rus Rhees Library, University of Rochester, Rochester, New York. (Seward Papers reprinted by permission.).

8. Anna Ella Carroll, *The Great American Battle; or the Contest Between Christianity & Political Romanism* (New York: Miller, Orton & Mulligan, 1856), pp. iii-vi.

9. Ibid., p. 28; Anna Ella Carroll, *The Star of the West; or, National Men and National Measures*, 3d edition (Boston: James French & Co., 1857), p. 346.

10. Carroll, *Star*, pp. 346–47.

11. W. Darrell Overdyke, *The Know-Nothing Party in the South* (Baton Rouge, Louisiana: Louisiana State University Press, 1950), p. 12; Harry J. Carman and Richard H. Luthin, "Some Aspects of the Know-Nothing Movement Reconsidered," *South Atlantic Quarterly* 39(1940): 216–17; Michael Holt, "The Antimasonic and Know Nothing Parties," in *History of U.S. Political Parties*, ed. Arthur M. Schlesinger, Jr., 4 vols. (New York: Chelsea House Publishers in association with R. R. Bowker Co., 1973), 1:596–97; W. Dean Burnham, *Presidential Ballots 1836–1892* (Baltimore: Johns Hopkins Press, 1955), p. 504; Anna Ella Carroll, *Which? Fillmore or Buchanan!* (Boston: James French & Co., 1856), p. 24.

12. Robert J. Breckinridge, "To the Citizens of Baltimore!" n.d., Breckinridge Family Papers, Library of Congress, Washington, D.C.

13. In addition to these two massive tomes, Carroll wrote *American Nominations Fillmore and Donelson* (New York: Orton & Mulligan, 1856), an extract of *The Great American Battle*; *Review of Pierce's Administration; Showing Its Only Popular Measures to Have Originated with the Executive of Millard Fillmore* (Boston: James French & Co., 1856); *The Union of the States* (Boston: James French & Co., 1856); *Which? Fillmore or Buchanan!*, and *Who Shall Be President? An Appeal to the People* (Boston: James French & Co., 1856).

14. Anna Ella Carroll to William Henry Seward, 15 September, 1852, Seward Papers.

15. Charles Vevier, "American Continentalism: An Idea of Expansion, 1845–1910," *American Historical Review*, 65 (January 1960): 323–35; Carroll, *The Star of the West*, pp. 162–86; Carroll, *Which? Fillmore or Buchanan!* pp. 13–16, 34–35.

16. London *Times*, 26 August, 1853, cited in Allen Nevins, *Ordeal of the Union: A House Dividing* (New York: Charles Scribner's Sons, 1947), pp. 67–68, n.78; Carroll, *Review*, p. 25. Pierce needed to appoint a Southerner to a major diplomatic post to continue his sectional balancing act. Louisiana Representative John Slidell was offered a Latin American post, which he rejected as a form of exile; in relief, Pierce met his

obligation with the more personable Soulé, Slidell's rival in Louisiana politics. See Nichols, *Franklin Pierce: Young Hickory of the Granite Hills* (Philadelphia: University of Pennsylvania Press, 1969), pp. 256, 276–77; David Potter, *The Impending Crisis*, edited by Don E. Fehrenbacher (New York: Harper & Row, 1976), p. 14.

17. Carroll, *Review*, pp. 43–44, 73–91; Henry L. Janes, "The Black Warrior Affair," *American Historical Review* 12 (1907):280–98, Nevins, *A House Dividing*, p. 68; Potter, *Impending Crisis*, pp. 184–87.

18. Janes, "The Black Warrior Affair," p. 290; Potter, *Impending Crisis*, p. 184, Franklin Pierce, "Inaugural Address and Message to Congress," 15 March, 1854, in James D. Richardson, ed., *A Compilation of the Messages and Papers of the Presidents, 1789–1902*, 10 vols. (Washington, D.C.; Bureau of National Literature and Art, 1905), 5:199, 234–35.

19. Carroll, *Review*, pp. 51–52, 54; Nevins, *A House Dividing*, pp. 350–51.

20. Carroll, *Review*, pp. 37, 56.

21. Ibid., pp. 56, 52.

22. Carroll, *Star*, p. 186.

23. Carroll, *Review*, pp. 74–75. This curious attempt to take over Cuba is interpreted as a drive for slavery expansion by southern radicals in Robert May, *The Southern Dream of a Caribbean Empire, 1854–1861* (Baton Rouge, Louisiana: Louisiana State University Press, 1973); for "Africanization" see pp. 35–36, 176. See also Potter, *Impending Crisis*, pp. 184–193, as he holds the Ostend Manifesto responsible for putting the nails in the coffin of Manifest Destiny as a viable movement because of its link with blatant aggression.

24. Carroll, *Review*, pp. 74–78, 85; Potter, *Impending Crisis*, p. 191, n.30. The rumors of the French and English conspiracies are discussed and dismissed also in Amos A. Ettinger, *The Mission to Spain of Pierre Soulé 1853–1855* (New Haven, Connecticut: Yale University Press, 1932).

25. Carroll, *Review*, pp. 134–36.

26. Carroll, *Star*, pp. 346–47.

27. Carroll, *Which? Fillmore or Buchanan!*, pp. 16–17, 22; *Review*, pp. 72–78, 92–93; *Who Shall Be President?*, pp. 4–5. Potter, *Impending Crisis*, pp. 196–97, blames the rapid decline of expansionism in the 1850s with its link to sectional interests.

28. Carroll, *Which? Fillmore or Buchanan!*, p. 23. See also Nichols, *Franklin Pierce*, pp. 340–42; Nevins, *A House Dividing*, pp. 368–79.

29. Anna Ella Carroll, Historical notes [MDHS:3654–622], n.d., Carroll Papers.

30. Carroll, *Star*, p. 390.

31. Ibid., pp. 379, 384.

32. Ibid., p. 385.

33. Ibid., pp. 378, 386.

34. William Walker, *The War in Nicaragua* (Mobile, Alabama: S. H. Goetzel & Co., 1860; reprint ed. Detroit: Blaine Ethridge-Books, 1971), pp. 23, 34, 228.

35. William Walker to A. E. Carroll, n.d., Anna Ella Carroll Papers; Carroll, *Star*, p. 349.

36. Walker, *War*, pp. 255–56. For the precarious nature of Walker's hold on power, see Thomas L. Karnes, *The Failure of Union: Central America, 1824–1975* (Tempe, Arizona: Arizona State University Press, 1976), p. 140; Potter, *Impending Crisis*, p. 194; May, *Southern Dream*, pp. 77–99; Walker, *War*, pp. 255–56, 266, 279–80.

37. Ibid., pp. 238–39; Carroll, *Who Shall Be President?*, pp. 10–11. See also William

O. Scroggs, *Filibusters and Financiers: The Story of William Walker and His Associates* (NY: Macmillan Co., 1916), p. 211.

38. Scroggs, *Filibusters & Financiers*, pp. 209–13; Potter, *Impending Crisis*, pp. 193–95; May, *Southern Dream*, pp. 106–08, 112–13.

39. Carroll, *Star*, p. 390; May, *Southern Dream*, p. 130.

40. Anna Ella Carroll to Thurlow Weed, 11 December, 1856, Thurlow Weed Papers, Rus Rhees Library, University of Rochester, Rochester, New York (Weed Papers reprinted by permission); John Minor Botts to Anna Ella Carroll, 9 October, 1859, Carroll Papers; J[osiah] F. Polk to Anna Ella Carroll, 11 October, 1859, Carroll Papers; Anna Ella Carroll to Thomas H. Hicks, November 1860, Carroll Papers.

41. Anna Ella Carroll, incomplete manuscript essay [MDHS:3650–178], circa August 1861, Carroll Papers.

42. Anna Ella Carroll to Gerrit Smith, 26 June, 1854, Smith Collection.

43. Anna Ella Carroll, Manuscript on slavery, post–1864, Carroll Papers.

44. Blackwell, *Life*, p. 27; Anna Ella Carroll, Loose papers [MDHS:3622–103, p. 13], circa 1865, Carroll, Craddock, Jensen Collection, Maryland Historical Society, Baltimore, Maryland.

45. The lack of payment apparently rankled; in a letter to Thurlow Weed regarding the 1860 campaign, for example, Carroll sent him a bill for her work: "I should be glad to know if I can be well & handsomely paid for my service. . . . My ability as a writer is conceded here by men of all parties & I don't mean ever to throw my time & talent away for any cause again." Anna Ella Carroll to Thurlow Weed, 20 April, 1860, Weed Papers.

46. John B. Fry to Anna Ella Carroll, 5 April, 1861, Carroll Papers; James Grant to A. C. Burr, 31 August, 1860, Aaron Columbus Burr Papers, Yale University, New Haven, Connecticut (Burr Papers reprinted by permission); James Grant to A. C. Burr, 13 September, 1861, "General Records of the Department of the Interior," U.S. Department of the Interior, Record Group 48, National Archives, Washington, D.C.; Anna Ella Carroll to Abraham Lincoln, 23 April, 1862, Dept. of Interior, Record Group 48.

47. A. C. Burr to Interior Secretary Smith, 6 May, 1862, Dept. of Interior, Record Group 48.

48. Anna Ella Carroll to Abraham Lincoln, 15 April, 1862, Carroll Papers.

49. Anna Ella Carroll to Abraham Lincoln, 23 April, 1862, Anna Ella Carroll to Secretary Caleb Smith, 27 April, 1862, Dept. of Interior, Record Group 48. One group eager to accept blacks for labor in British Honduras was a colony of pro-Southern expatriates. See Wayne M. Clegern, *British Honduras: Colonial Dead End, 1859–1900* (Baton Rouge, Louisiana: Louisiana State University Press, 1967), pp. 30, 38.

50. A. C. Burr to Secretary Smith, 6 May, 1862; Anna Ella Carroll to Secretary Smith, 13 May, 1862, Dept. of Interior, Record Group 48.

51. Anna Ella Carroll, unpublished manuscript on Lincoln [MDHS:3655–722, pp. 105–20], n.d., Carroll Papers.

52. Anna Ella Carroll to Abraham Lincoln, 19 May, 1862, Robert Todd Lincoln Papers, Library of Congress, Washington, D.C.

53. William Mitchell to A. E. Carroll 13 May, 1862, Carroll Papers. Mitchell's letter, which describes the President's delighted reaction to the box sent and praises Carroll's abilities as a writer, is a copy in Carroll's hand, and may have been used at a later date in her claim against the government for monies owed. It is one of three copies, none of which are exactly alike, and therefore must be viewed cautiously. Anna Ella Carroll to

A. C. Burr, 30 August, 1862, Burr Papers; Roy P. Basler, ed., *The Collected Works of Abraham Lincoln*, 9 vols. (New Brunswick, New Jersey: Rutgers University Press, 1953–59) 5:370–75.

54. Anna Ella Carroll to Abraham Lincoln, 14 July, 1862, Carroll Papers.

55. Abraham Lincoln to Horace Greeley, 22 August, 1862, in Basler, *Works*, 5: 388–89; Benjamin Quarles, *Lincoln and the Negro* (New York: Oxford University Press, 1962), p. 155; Stephen W. Sears, *Landscape Turned Red: The Battle of Antietam* (New Haven, Connecticut: Ticknor & Fields, 1983), pp. 42–43.

56. Anna Ella Carroll to A. C. Burr, 13 September, 1862, Burr Papers. Burr protested the decision to both Pomeroy and Lincoln and warned of dire consequences if colonization proceeded elsewhere, but to no avail. See A. C. Burr to Senator Pomeroy, 20 September, 1862, 5 October, 1862, and A. C. Burr to Abraham Lincoln, 6 October, 1862, Burr Papers; Basler, *Works*, 5:433–36; Anna Ella Carroll to Abraham Lincoln, 21 October, 1862, Lincoln Papers. A substantial work on the Ile-à-Vache colony is by Jayme Ruth Spencer, "Abraham Lincoln and Negro Colonization: the Ile-à-Vache, Hayti Experience, 1862–1864" (unpublished master's thesis, College of William and Mary in Virginia, Williamsburg, Virginia, 1971).

57. Anna Ella Carroll to Abraham Lincoln, 14 August, 1862, Lincoln Papers. Carroll claimed to have done considerable work contracted by the War Department for which she remained unpaid; she discussed this in the 14 August, 1862 letter to Lincoln, Lincoln Papers. See also Basler, *Works*, 5:381–82.

58. Basler, *Works*, 5:423; Anna Ella Carroll to Abraham Lincoln, 15 April, 1862 and 14 July, 1862, Carroll Papers.

59. Anna Ella Carroll to General Grant, 26 December, 1868, Carroll Papers; Anna Ella Carroll to James A. Garfield, 21 August, and 11 September, 1880, James A. Garfield Papers, Library of Congress, Washington, D.C. There is no good biography of Carroll. Snyder's excellent article on her relationship to Fillmore is the first balanced work on Carroll. Most of the biographies done have concentrated on her claim that she developed the invasion strategy used in the Civil War's Tennessee Campaign during the winter and spring of 1862. Highly romanticized and popularized, Carroll's claim has managed to obscure the rest of her career, just as it became her obsession, eventually to the exclusion of almost everything else, to prove herself as author of the invasion plan and worthy of national recognition of such. See Hon. John D. White, Speech in House of Representatives, 7 February, 1884 (Washington, D.C.: n.p., 1884); Alice Stone Blackwell to Kitty Barry, 23 August, 1885, Carroll File, National American Woman Suffrage Association Papers, Library of Congress, Washington, D.C.; Kenneth P. Williams, "The Tennessee River Campaign and Anna Ella Carroll," *Indiana Magazine of History* 46 (September 195):221–48; Sydney Greenbie and Marjorie Barstow Greenbie, *Anna Ella Carroll and Abraham Lincoln* (Manchester, Maine: University of Tampa Press in cooperation with Falmouth Publishing House Inc., 1952).

60. Carroll's book, *The Great American Battle*, had sold 10,000 copies by May of 1856. Anna Ella Carroll to Thomas King Carroll, 23 May, 1856, Carroll Papers. Congressional Quarterly, *Guide to U.S. Elections* (Washington, D.C.: Congressional Quarterly, Inc., 1975), pp. 231, 306, 411.

61. Carroll, *Review*, pp. iii–iv.

62. Carroll, *Review*, p. iv; Anna Ella Carroll, Memo [MDHS:3650–178, p. 7], n.d., Carroll Papers.

63. Carroll, *Review*, p. iv. For an examination of women's political methodology prior

to enfranchisement, see Mary Beth Norton, *Liberty's Daughters: The Revolutionary Experience of American Women 1750–1800* (Boston: Little, Brown & Co., 1980), Chapter 6; Linda K. Kerber, *Women of the Republic: Intellect and Ideology in Revolutionary America* (Chapel Hill, North Carolina: The Institute for Early American History and Culture by the University of North Carolina Press, 1980), Chapter 9; Carroll, *Star*, pp. 349–350.

64. Kerber, *Women of the Republic*, pp. 85–98.

65. For characteristics of paranoid political style, see Richard Hofstadter, *The Paranoid Style in American Politics and Other Essays* (New York: Alfred A. Knopf, 1966), pp. 29–40; David Brion Davis, *The Fear of Conspiracy: Images of Un-American Subversion from the Revolution to the Present* (Ithaca, New York: Cornell University Press, 1971), particularly pp. xviii-xxiii.

4

Lucia True Ames Mead: American Publicist for Peace and Internationalism

John M. Craig

In 1926, Dr. Aletta Jacobs asked her colleagues in the Women's International League for Peace and Freedom, "Is it not time to appoint someone to write a history of the part played by women in war . . . and in international relations?" Otherwise, the Dutch feminist and internationalist warned, "the only records will be histories written by men of what the men did." Needless to say, the fears of Holland's first female physician proved well-founded. Even studies of the American peace movement, where women have played a significant role since the nineteenth century, usually suffer from myopia based on gender. During the early years of the twentieth century, men actually found themselves in the minority. Though most women failed to serve in visible public capacities, some acted as lobbyists, publicists, and officers of various peace societies. Among these leading female activists, few contributed more talent and energy to the cause than Lucia Ames Mead, who helped found the American branch of the organization that Jacobs addressed in 1926.[1]

Between 1897 and World War I, Lucia Mead earned a place "in the front rank among women peace advocates." For the Boston reformer and intellectual, peace activism became a vocation. Her considerable efforts on the lecture platform and as a writer won her recognition as one of the movement's most effective publicists and prompted one famous women's activist, Carrie Chapman Catt, to label Mead "the best informed woman in the United States on the subjects of war and peace."[2] Yet in spite of her deserved reputation, peace activism had not represented a life-long pursuit for the reformer from New England, for she paid scant attention to the cause until she had passed her fortieth birthday. The daughter of a yeoman farmer, Lucia True Ames was born in New Hampshire in 1856. Though her family was of modest means—she once noted that her father raised four children "on $300 a year"—Lucia Ames received a sound education at public schools and through private instruction in Chicago and Boston. After spending ten years in Illinois, she moved back East in 1870 to live with older brother Charles, a recent graduate of Amherst College, who worked for a publishing house.[3]

Charles Ames' interest in philosophy, literature, and similar scholarly pursuits encouraged his sister's passionate intellectual curiosity. He introduced the young student to idealist philosopher and noted educator William Torrey Harris, who later became Secretary of Education. She began a course of study under Harris's tutelage, which awakened her to sophisticated theological, metaphysical, legal, political, and social thought. Ames also attended the Concord Summer School of Philosophy, which Harris directed after 1880. Here, she heard first hand the teachings of Ralph Waldo Emerson and other intellectual giants of the period. Ames later organized a "Saturday Club"; they met regularly to hear Harris discuss a variety of topics. As an outgrowth of these sessions, she began offering her own classes on "Nineteenth Century Thought" to women in Boston in 1886. Within six years, she instructed "eleven classes of mature women, mothers and teachers, numbering in all about two hundred and twenty-five to whom [she lectured] for an hour and a quarter weekly."[4]

Even before meeting Harris in 1878, Ames had devoted all her spare hours studying history, literature, theology, and other topics. Ames also studied music under the private instruction of noted teacher Benjamin Lang, whose "class of private pupils upon the pianoforte belong[ed] to the very elite of Boston."[5] Between 1875, the year of her nineteenth birthday, and 1886, she earned a living as a piano teacher herself. As she suggested in one of her earliest articles, for Lucy Stone's *Woman's Journal*, "If a woman who is strong and capable feels herself to be dependent in pecuniary matters she is sure not to be independent in her thought. She will be lacking the self-poise and self-confidence, I might almost say the self-respect, necessary to independent, impartial judgement."[6] Not surprisingly, Ames possessed the very qualities that she believed reliance on males undermined. Stubbornly independent and self-assured, her outspoken, assertive posture often shocked new male acquaintances. While on her first visit to London in 1884, for example, a young man expressed disbelief "about how extremely independent about receiving attention or assistance" the Bostonian seemed to be.[7]

In the best New England tradition, Lucia Ames merged her literary and scholarly interests with social activism. Both sides of her family contained abolitionists and women's suffrage advocates, including her famous uncle, Charles Carleton Coffin. Like Uncle Charles, Lucia Ames worked as "an earnest, outspoken advocate of woman suffrage" as a member of the Massachusetts Woman Suffrage Association (MWSA). In the early 1880s, as one of the society's rank and file, she presented petitions to her state representative and contributed occasional pieces to the *Woman's Journal*, the leading periodical devoted to women's rights during the period. Ames became an early convert to the point of view identified by historian Aileen Kraditor as the suffrCalifist "argument from expediency."

Claiming that women already won the "argument from justice," Ames urged women to demonstrate how they would use the ballot. This could be accomplished by supporting other reforms. In 1886, she advised other suffragists to become "the first and foremost leaders" in raising the age of consent for young girls from ten years old to a more suitable age. "Nothing would unite all women more completely," she argued, and "it would do more directly for suffrage than conventions, or addresses, or petitions."[8]

When Lucia Ames published her third book in 1898, she enjoyed a local reputation as "an earnest, enthusiastic, progressive" writer, lecturer, and activist. Her first book, written in 1888 and designed for children, presented current liberal thought on a variety of religious and scientific issues. Reviewers found her second long work, the novel *Memoirs of a Millionaire*, "cleverly written," "suggestive," and "imaginative," but pointed out some organizational problems and flawed literary technique. Ames modeled the protagonist of *Memoirs* after her perception of her own personality. This character, Mildred Brewster, was an unmarried, bookish, outspoken teacher from Boston who inherited a fortune and then used her millions to further a number of reforms. Through the medium of fiction, Ames advocated housing reform for the urban poor. Influenced by John Ruskin, and later, Jacob Riis, she urged the construction of model tenements that would include resident agents, day-care services for young children, kindergartens, communal parlors, laundry facilities, and even central cooking. A number of Ames' articles echoed these ideas, while she also called for a proper education system to meet the needs of all Americans, increased economic opportunity for blacks and recent immigrants, and municipal reform efforts.[9]

Lucia Ames's next book, *To Whom Much Is Given*, expanded upon two favorite lecture themes, "extravagant self-indulgence" on the part of the wealthy and the reluctance of privileged women to commit their time to social justice causes. In addition to her classes devoted to great literature, Ames often spoke to female and mixed audiences. She delivered addresses under the auspices of the Twentieth Century Club of Boston, a unique discussion group devoted to social and political reform. Founded in 1893 by Edwin Doak Mead, whom Ames married in 1898, the TCC contained notable writers, artists, and other intellectuals who worked actively for change. That Ames was accepted into such a club, which included Unitarian minister and author Edward Everett Hale, the president of the Associated Charities of Boston and the Boston Children's Aid Society, Robert Treat Paine, and leading public school administrator Samuel Train Dutton, is testimony to her stature as a reform-minded intellectual in Boston.[10]

In 1897, Lucia Ames received an invitation to Albert K. Smiley's third annual Lake Mohonk Conference on International Arbitration. The teacher and social activist could hardly have anticipated that her acceptance of this invitation would transform her life dramatically. Edwin Mead no doubt secured the invitation for her to the highly select affair, which also included other Twentieth Century Club members. Mead, as secretary of the conference, and other organizers prevailed upon the Boston intellectual to deliver an address during a session devoted to

"The Education and Influencing of Public Opinion." The only woman so honored, Ames responded with an informed and, at times, humorous speech.

Lucia Ames struck a responsive chord among her audience when she began by noting how some failings of the American education system produced the difficulties faced by the arbitrationists. Too few Americans received an adequate introduction to history, civics, ethics, and great literature, she observed, thus they could not make informed choices on important matters. Worse yet, this condition reinforced the "natural bigotry" in children, which only a knowledgeable teacher could eradicate. Ames recalled her own feelings as a narrow-minded child of eight who "marvelled that the Almighty did not annihilate all Roman Catholics, Jews, Unitarians, and all other obnoxious and dangerous persons who did not hold my father's creed [Congregationalism]." Her reference sparked a burst of laughter when she turned to her current minister, Unitarian E. E. Hale, and warned, "I would have had no mercy on you, Dr. Hale. I wouldn't have let you cumber the ground."

Ames also touched on some "remedies for ignorance," particularly those that women, as teachers and mothers, could effect. Teachers should, she urged, instruct their students about the economic aspects of war. Even in peacetime, she noted, European powers spent nine hundred million dollars annually to support their armies and navies. In the event of a major war, not only would this sum increase, but the indirect losses due to war would be staggering. Ames also suggested that teachers deal with the subject of patriotism "in a new way," not simply as "pride in our country or of boasting about our country, but . . . service for our country." Calling upon the philosophy of Emerson, whom she admired greatly, Ames urged all women to "teach faith and hope" and to recognize that all people enjoyed the same rights and privileges under God.

During her first address at Mohonk, Lucia Ames foreshadowed an obsession that would later command a great deal of her attention—the need for a campaign of public education on behalf of the peace and arbitration movement. The economic disasters that a major war would unleash could be illustrated, she advised, "in some graphic form where people could read and consider them," such as in the street cars "between advertisements of 'Columbia Bicyles' and 'Ayers Sarsaparilla.' " This approach would have a greater impact, she predicted, then issuing fifty thousand copies of the proceedings of the conference.[11]

In subsequent years, Ames always dated her involvement in the peace movement to this single trip to Albert Smiley's scenic Catskill Mountain resort. Though initially peace advocacy represented just one more concern to add to a large list of reform interests, a series of events between 1897 and 1901 galvanized her commitment to a movement that embraced Ames as a leader with remarkable alacrity. How she achieved a prominent position so easily is a complex question, but the work of historian David S. Patterson sheds some light on the issue. As his study of the peace movement's leadership shows, the social origins of its movers and shakers were virtually identical. They were, almost to the man or woman, Anglo-Saxon, Protestant, Eastern-urban professionals who entertained a firm faith in progress, placed exalted value on a thorough education, and believed in moral absolutes. Nearly all could be labeled "cosmopolitans," to borrow a term employed by Samuel P. Hays and other scholars, whose social vision transcended local community concerns and the narrow goals of interest-group politics. Besides the Twentieth Century Club members, other Mohonk participants included prominent Protestant ministers such as Hale, Congregationalist Frederick Lynch, and Unitarian Jenkin Lloyd Jones; economist John Bates Clark; and most national officers of the American Peace Society. Within a half dozen years of Ames's first visit, the Mohonk Conference could also boast the participation of a Supreme Court Justice, a former Secretary of State, members of the Hague Court, and various other architects of American foreign policy.[12]

Lucia Ames readily fit into this group. As one who embraced many of the tenets of Fabian Socialism, she proved far less conservative on social issues than many other Mohonk participants. But for the most part, her ideas, values, and background mirrored others in attendance at the conference. Some fellow Bostonians, as members of the Twentieth Century Club, were also personal friends. Moreover, her gender provided less of a barrier in achieving a leadership position compared with most other reform movements. Contemporary thinking counted peace activism among a number of special "women's causes," like work in settlement houses, temperance societies, and purity leagues. In the wake of the positive reception afforded Ames's address at Mohonk, she undoubtedly recognized the opportunity to follow on the footsteps of Julia Ward Howe, Hannah Bailey, and Belva Lockwood.[13]

One other crucial factor that helps explain Ames's conversion to peace advocacy also deserves note. Her burgeoning interest in the movement cannot be understood without recognizing the importance of her relationship to Edwin Doak Mead. Twenty-five years before her first trip to Mohonk, Charles Ames had introduced his sister to "Ned" Mead, a friend from the publishing trade. From that point onward, Mead became her close adviser and friend. Like his future wife, Mead was a deeply religious and introspective individual who lived for the world of ideas and to reform the world's evils. By the 1890s, he enjoyed a much deserved reputation as a skilled orator, author, and reformer. He not only helped found the Twentieth Century Club, but also the Massachusetts Society for Promoting Good Government and Boston Municipal League. As editor of the *New England Magazine* after 1890, a prestigious journal devoted to the area's "life, thought, and history," Mead contributed a monthly column on current issues, literature, history, and other topics. He seldom mentioned the peace movement or critizied aspects of American foreign policy before 1897, though he had attended a few arbitration conferences before that date. His desire to see better Anglo-American relations had sparked his interest in the cause, but domestic reform remained Mead's primary concern.[14]

On September 29, 1898, Edwin Mead and Lucia Ames exchanged marriage vows in West Newton, Massachusetts. This event inaugurated a long, equal

partnership of progressive activism. Within three years, the couple chose to
devote all their collective energies to the peace movement. The fin de siècle
burst of militarism and imperialism on the part of the United States focused their
attention on international issues and each believed they had much to offer the
crusade to end war. During the months between the couple's visit to Mohonk
and their marriage, the United States had crushed the weak Spanish empire in
battle, and the "Great Debate" over what to do with the spoils of war erupted.
Lucia Mead dismissed the contest with Spain as "the product of a jingo press"
who misrepresented the "*Maine*" catastrophe to inflame misguided nationalist
passions. Edwin Mead adopted an overt antiwar stance in the "Editor's Table"
of the *New England Magazine*, but a trip to Europe by Ames in the summer of
1898 precluded any direct antiwar activism on her part. She returned in time to
participate in the debate over the Philippines, however. She spoke at rallies
sponsored by the Anti-Imperialist League and contributed articles on the subject
to various journals; one of these written for the *Outlook*, published in 1900,
attacked the McKinley administration's Philippine policy in no uncertain terms
and called upon participants on both sides of the "imperialism" debate to begin
defining their terms.

As one historian has aptly observed, "In some respects the great debate over
imperialism sounded like *Alice in Wonderland*. Both sides used the same words,
but the words seemed to mean different things."[15] Oddly, few involved in the
war of words tried to clarify the semantic muddle, but Lucia Mead suggested
that the time had come by 1900 for "the advocates and opponents of the Administration's policy [to] understand once and for all what they are talking about."
Defenders of McKinley's position clouded the issue, she insisted, by claiming
that an American presence in the archipelago served the interests of the native
peoples, thus American behavior was not "imperialistic." Yet Mead argued that
the establishment of a few schools or extension of some limited self-government
had little to do with the question of imperialism, which "is not [one] of beneficent
administration or assimilation . . . [or] granting civil rights, but solely a question
of political rights. "The anti-imperialist holds," she claimed, "that any nation,
whether it be monarchy or republic, which buys or takes by conquest another
people, and dominates them without promise of granting them independence or
. . . explicitly guaranteeing future Statehood, has adopted an imperialist
policy."[16]

When the Anti-Imperialist League finally named three women to its executive
board in 1904, Lucia Mead joined Jane Addams and Josephine Shaw Lowell as
its first female vice presidents. She also continued to criticize America's colonial
policy in the Philippines. Among a small number of true dissidents who articulated fundamental critiques of expansionism, Mead believed that imperial policies abroad would ultimately proscribe domestic reforms. Most Progressive
reformers, as William Leuchtenberg has shown, saw little inconsistency between
the United States flexing its muscles as an imperial power and efforts to achieve
social justice. But as an uncompromising adherent to "free trade" economic

theories, Mead deplored the exploitation of foreign peoples by American companies (such as tobacco and sugar interests in the Philippines), opposed the rapid growth of the United States Navy, and advocated scrapping the Monroe Doctrine. She objected not only to colonialism, but to other practices that modern historians have included under the rubric of "market expansionism."[17]

If Mead's distaste for her nation's behavior in the Philippines stirred powerful negative emotions, another event provided some cause for optimism. On the morning of August 29, 1898, while in England, Mead opened her London *Times* only to read one article "with a thrill never to be forgotten." The Russian tsar had issued an Imperial Rescript calling for a disarmament conference for all nations with ministers at the Romanov Court. Like most peace advocates and arbitrationists, she hailed the resulting Hague Peace Conference as the first step toward permanent world peace. She wrote articles publicizing the event, upon returning to the United States. In one, she called upon a rich philanthropist to offer prizes of fifty thousand dollars each to the individual in every major nation to be represented at the Hague Conference who submitted "the best plan for gradual disarmament and for a method of settling present and future international difficulties without war." She believed this scheme would inspire widespread public interest in the conference.[18]

Lucia and Edwin Mead's final decision to limit their other efforts on behalf of domestic reforms and devote their lives instead to the peace movement came as the result of a visit to Europe in 1901. America's war with Spain and brutal suppression of the Philippine insurrection left Mrs. Mead "with a sad heart to be an American," and she departed the United States "craving for something deeper in our life [*sic*]." Six months later, the couple returned from abroad "with a cheerful, hopeful outlook," certain they had "spent the summer in the wisest way that would ensure permanent rest." What had transformed their attitudes so dramatically? Part of the answer lies in the reception afforded the Meads by leading European pacifists. Private meetings with flamboyant "Pro-Boer" editor William T. Stead, noted Russian internationalists Jacques Novicow and Jean de Bloch, and British economist John A. Hobson provided Lucia Mead with what she called, rather obliquely, an "intellectual Thanksgiving." The wealth of ideas emanating from these great thinkers gave her cause for hope. She visited Hobson, for instance, while he worked on his forthcoming *Imperialism* (1902), and found "the quality and quantity of [the British economist's] work remarkable." Hobson claimed that the Boer War and other British imperial policies had checked social and political reform in England, a trend Mead saw appearing in the United States. In her view, which bears little consistency with commonly accepted notions about the "Progressive Era" in America, the nineteenth century had witnessed great advances in furthering "the rights of women, children, and all within our midst who need protection." After the mid-1890s, however, the nation "departed from this tendency" because its surge of militarism, nationalism, and imperialism slowed the quest for social justice.[19]

A major reason behind the Meads' lengthy sojourn abroad in 1901 was to participate in their first Universal Peace Congress, scheduled for September in Glasgow. Here they enjoyed a warm reception from other delegates. Mrs. Mead played a "significant" role as an American representative, as the *Woman's Journal* reported back home in the United States. She displayed a thorough grasp of international affairs and an ability as a public speaker. On two occasions, Congress leaders prevailed upon the Boston activist to speak on behalf of all the women in attendance at nightly banquets, where she toasted the men and made some brief comments on the international peace movement and the problems faced by American reformers. In addition, she helped work out a compromise over the language to be employed in condemning British actions in southern Africa. During the morning session of September 12, W. T. Stead offered a bitter and potentially divisive resolution "damning" England for brutalizing the Boers. When the Congress adjourned for lunch, Edwin Mead composed a more discreet resolution, which his wife offered in his absence at the outset of the afternoon session. In a short talk, she told the assemblage that as an American disturbed deeply by her own nation's suppression of the Filipinos, she sympathized with Stead's "earnest repudiation of his country's wrong." Mead proposed a "more gentle condemnation" nonetheless, Stead acquiesced, and the amended version passed unanimously.[20]

When the Meads arrived back in Boston in November of 1901, Edwin Mead resigned as editor of the *New England Magazine* and from that point onward, the couple concentrated on writing and speaking for the peace movement, and working within the established and newly formed peace organizations in the United States. Lucia Mead's pattern of activism changed little between this point and the outbreak of World War I. Though she spoke to a wide variety of groups over the years, she often singled out women as the focus of her attention. Traditional assumptions about "women's proper place" allowed her few choices, of course, and she often found it easier to have her writings published in women's journals and to secure speaking engagements in front of female audiences. But regardless of the sexist barriers she encountered, which she seldom complained about, fertile ground existed for peace activism among women's organizations. Even many years later, she continued to express a preference for speaking to "mothers and teachers" because those groups "may largely shape the ideals of future generations."[21]

No major American women's organization had ever formulated and acted upon a peace agenda, but Lucia Mead converted many individuals to the cause. Fanny Fern Andrews, the guiding force behind the American School Peace League, represented the most famous of Mead's converts. On Christmas Eve, 1907, Mead visited Andrews's house to talk to the recent college graduate about the peace movement. After an hour and a half "session," she left a pile of literature, and promised to return in a few days. When Mead came back, the younger woman was already "hooked." She went on to play a leading role in the movement for many years. None of Mead's other converts enjoyed the prominence of Fanny Fern Andrews. But any peace-minded woman able to devote a few spare hours to studying the subject could contribute useful service to the cause. Female schoolteachers could teach "history and patriotism, literature and geography . . . in the spirit of the new internationalism which the times demand," Mead also urged, "lest race prejudice and national conceit and arrogance lead us into great international blunders."[22]

A long-time suffragist, Lucia Mead believed a logical connection existed between that crusade and peace reform. She predicted that women would achieve true equality only in a world that did not settle its disputes on the battlefield. Therefore, she argued that pacifism should take precedence over suffragism. Most women's rights activists of the era disagreed, but Mead's "peace first" posture failed to injure her reputation within suffrage circles. The Boston Equal Suffrage Association for Good Government, organized in 1901 by Pauline Agassiz Shaw and Maud Wood Park, appointed her chairperson of its peace and arbitration committee. Mead also would hold similar positions in the National Council of Women (NCW) and National American Woman Suffrage Association (NAWSA), and in 1903 she became the head of the Massachusetts Woman's Suffrage Association "with the full understanding that she would not be a 'working president' owing to the demands of the [American] Peace Society upon her time." From Mead's perspective, the MWSA post provided a chance to discuss the peace movement's goals in the company of the most influential women's rights activists of the day. Consequently, her term as president, from 1903 to 1909, proved mutually beneficial to the Massachusetts Woman's Suffrage Association and Mead.[23]

In 1902 Lucia Mead returned to Mohonk again to address the convention. Her address in 1902 bore little resemblance to the optimistic, somewhat facetious tone of her maiden speech. She condemned the rising tide of militarism in the United States, as evidenced by increased naval and armament expenditures. Mead noted "not merely an increase in militarism" but a decrease "of the democratic spirit, an apathetic attitude toward injustice, and a callousness toward cruelty" in both England and America. She also accused the popular press of pandering to the "business interests of this country," and ridiculed parasitic women of leisure for wasting their lives on the golf course and at the whist table.[24]

During the opening years of the century, Lucia Mead also emerged as an active, outspoken member of the American Peace Society's (APS) Board of Directors. At the organization's annual banquet in 1903, Mead developed some of the issues she raised at Mohonk the previous summer. She warned her colleagues of the mounting "big navy" craze, "spreading like a prairie fire over dry grass." Proponents of naval expansion pointed to America's newly won position in the Pacific to justify increased spending. According to Mead, this trend simply invited conflict. In the Western Hemisphere, she urged replacing the "dangerous" and "outworn" Monroe Doctrine with a defensive alliance of American nations. She called upon the friends of peace to pressure trade unions, churches, bar associations, and political representatives to resist the trend toward military "preparedness." In addition, Mead proposed the founding of a "School of Diplomacy" in Washington, D.C., to train diplomats and consuls, and the creation of a "peace budget." If the peace and arbitration movement had the cost of one large battleship at its disposal, seven million dollars, Mead predicted it could fund an effective public campaign to stem the tide of militarism.[25]

The last point represented an issue of great import in the mind of Lucia Mead. At the APS banquet, she stressed the need for "a campaign of education, [which] every great cause requires." Mead admonished her fellow peace workers for failing to make a genuine effort to enlist new members and spread the gospel of peace among the general population. Like its guiding force, the scholarly and dignified Benjamin Trueblood, the APS nonetheless maintained a highly respectable, elitist posture. This lack of interest in generating mass support caused Lucia Mead to reemphasize her thoughts on mass publicity at conference after conference for the next decade. On the eve of World War I, she still found it necessary to exhort her colleagues to supplement "our present dignified organs of international law and of the peace societies, read by few [with] a popular illustrated journal with colored cover to be sold upon all news stands. We need to follow the example of almost every other reform movement but our own and learn how to advertise our doctrines [and] tell our story graphically."[26]

With little support from other peace advocates, Mead created several exhibits for mass viewing that attempted to portray the choice of "law or war" in a striking manner. She prepared an exhibit for the American Peace Society's display at the 1904 St. Louis Exposition. On a series of twenty-five cards, with "distinct headings and illustrated by many striking pictures" of the Hague Court, evils of war, and famous pacifists, among other scenes, Mead presented a "most telling arraignment of the war system and the history of the peace and arbitration movement." The APS subsequently turned the text of the exhibit into a lengthy pamphlet, A Primer of the Peace Movement, which sold ten thousand copies in three months and went through many editions in a number of languages. The Primer received high praise at the next meeting of the Universal Peace Congress in Boston, and some peace advocates sent copies to leading American citizens, including Robert Erskine Ely, who gave a copy to Woodrow Wilson in 1907.[27]

Mead's booklet for peace workers, designed for newcomers to the cause or to convert people to the movement, presented "ammunition" for use against opponents of the peace reform. In the opening section, Mead outlined the six requisite steps to precede permanent world peace. The first two, she suggested, had already seen fulfillment, representative government in most Western nations and the birth of a World Court. These must be followed by general arbitration treaties between all major countries, the creation of a "Stated World Congress," gradual proportionate disarmament, and the establishment of a small international police force. Few other peace advocates favored the latter but most others agreed with the need for the other parts of her "practical program." The Primer included historical information on the peace movement, antiwar quotations from leading statesmen and military men, and a list of the causes of war. According to Mead, a large military class "ambitious for activity and promotion," racism, false

Biblical interpretations, and the sensational press helped bring about wars. Quoting J. A. Hobson, she also attacked certain business interests, such as munitions makers, who benefited from wars, and those who desired the high interest-yielding investment opportunities that war loans provided. Mead noted some dangers of market expansionism, as well. "Foreign investments are enormously increasing in weak and poorly governed nations," she observed. This financial involvement, just as with direct colonialism, often led to native resistance, which in turn caused armed conflicts.[28]

Though American peace advocates might praise Lucia Mead's *Primer* or pay lip service to the need to generate public support, most "deliberately discouraged participation by the lower classes . . . or gave little emphasis" to non-elites, as David S. Patterson has suggested.[29] Discouraged but undaunted by their overly respectable posture, Mead took her case directly to the people, through her writings for popular journals and daily newspapers and exhaustive efforts on the lecture platform. Mrs. Mead had developed her skill as a public speaker over the course of many years. Not only had she lectured to adult women on a regular basis in her own courses, but her long involvement with the Massachusetts Woman Suffrage Association, Twentieth Century Club, and similar organizations had allowed her countless chances to speak in front of diverse audiences. Often her talks drew members of both sexes, and when she addressed mixed groups her ability usually surprised the men in attendance. During a lecture tour in 1907, she noted in her diary with satisfaction that "a professor of elocution complimented me highly on my use of voice" and at the University of Rochester a sociology teacher labeled her speech "a statesman's address." In the same year, the head of the American delegation to the First Hague Peace Conference, Andrew Dickson White, introduced Mead to a group in Ithaca, New York, expecting "just a little womanly talk on peace." At the close, he admitted his mistake to the audience and claimed "it was the best presentation he had ever heard on the subject" of international cooperation.[30]

Probably the most useful description of Lucia Mead's talent as a speaker came from Jane Addams, who first met the Boston reformer in the 1890s. Many years after Mrs. Mead first began lecturing on peace, Addams observed that "No one in the United States has done more through that most valuable method of instruction, direct speech, to educate the public in the history of the peace movement, nor has any one been more successful in securing new adherents to the unremitting efforts of substituting law for war than has Lucia Ames Mead." Addams explained Mead's success as the result of a thorough grasp of the issues and "historical perspective" derived from studying the great metaphysicians and political thinkers of all ages. Because of this background, her lectures were "always characterized by a tone of 'Let us reason together' with an appeal to the logic of the situation."[31]

During the decade before World War I, Mead traveled the country spreading the gospel of peace. She spoke to at least 200 audiences every year on subjects such as "The End of International Dueling," "The New Internationalism,"

"National Dangers and National Defense," Imperialism, Social Darwinism, the economic disaster that a major war would initiate. In her appearances throughout the nation Mead also might discuss some current crisis in Latin America, the need either to support a particular arbitration treaty pending in Congress or to resist some present aspect of American foreign policy.

In one "typical" season, in 1909 and 1910, Lucia Mead traveled throughout Massachusetts, Connecticut, New York, Vermont, New Hampshire, Ohio, Illinois, Pennsylvania, and elsewhere. Between February and the middle of May, 1909, she addressed 75 audiences including over 25,000 people; late that fall, she embarked on another tour, where she delivered 65 speeches at schools, colleges, churches, private homes, and in front of a variety of groups. Mead kept a careful record of each address, estimating the number present and the audience's response, which she usually found favorable. On occasion, she would feel that a group might have little to offer the peace movement, because they lacked time, money, and influence, as was the case with a visit to the Bay Ridge Unitarian Church in Brooklyn on February 21. But most often, she distributed leaflets, encouraged people to join the American Peace Society or local peace organization, and generally sparked some interest.[32]

During what she called a "fruitful season" in 1909 and 1910, Mrs. Mead delivered about half of her addresses to school groups, including colleges. While speaking to younger students, she tried to interject some humor into the talk and encouraged active participation, such as her success in having her listeners "shout with me 3 times 'Organize the world' " at Lafayette High School in Buffalo, New York, in the fall of 1908. Mead seldom lectured under the auspices of any peace organization, preferring to maintain a degree of independence by making all her own arrangements. She asked for rail fare from the groups that sponsored her talks, but would accept any other contribution toward her "salary." This remained quite small throughout her life, though the Meads had other sources of money from savings, Mr. Mead's (much larger) salary drawn from a number of peace groups, and royalties from published material.[33]

Lucia Mead supplemented her efforts on the lecture platform with an endless stream of published works. She turned out scores of short articles and letters to editors each year. Employing a highly systematic procedure, Mead became the "most successful newspaper letter writer in the United States," at least according to noted pacifist Frederick J. Libby. The Boston author maintained a list of potential sources for publication among dailies, weeklies, and monthlies. Writing a minimum of two pieces per week, she sent each to a half dozen appropriate places in widely separated areas. She enclosed a postcard with each, requesting publication information. Upon learning that a particular letter or article appeared, she could acquire a copy through the clipping services to which she belonged.[34]

Lucia Mead also published two books on peace and international cooperation before World War I. The first appeared in 1906, *Patriotism and the New Internationalism*. She designed this work for teachers to encourage the inclusion of material about the peace movement and internationalism in classroom instruction.[35] Her second book, *Swords and Ploughshares*, nicely summed up her thinking on peace-related issues. In the book, written for a popular readership, she lashed out at militarism, imperialism, blind nationalism and attacked the trend toward mounting military expenditures. She conceded that all nations must be prepared to defend themselves, but called upon national leaders in the United States to get ready for real threats, not "hypothetical, theoretical dangers." The United States, she pointed out, was the safest country on earth, protected by two oceans. She therefore accused national leaders of "putting the greatest defence where it is least needed and our least defence where it is most needed." The true enemies of America were, she noted, not Japan or Germany, but "ignorance, recklessness, waste, preventable disease, and crime." She further blamed armament makers, the press, and the military establishment for consciously promoting militarism. "As regularly as the month for naval appropriations arrives," she noted caustically, "we are infected with Japanophobia and columns about . . . 'our absolute unpreparedness.' "

Mead singled out the arguments of Admiral Alfred Thayer Mahan for special attention in *Swords and Ploughshares*. Among the most influential expansionists of the period, and a vocal critic of arbitration schemes and the peace movement, Mahan provided much of the intellectual rationale for the dramatic growth of the United States Navy after 1889. In the era of the First World War, the nation's navy ranked third or fourth in the world. Yet Lucia Mead pointed out a number of, in her view, "misconceptions and errors" in Mahan's thinking. She accused the naval expert of intentionally blurring his definitions of war and violence to support his case against arbitration schemes. Mahan claimed that "all organized force is by degree war" and insisted that no form of violence, including war, could end until all violence ended. Mead countered by demonstrating the difference between "thrashing a schoolyard bully" and organized mass killing, which was not a difference in degree but in kind. Moreover, she predicted, only a small fraction of the world's population, "the leaders of thought," could bring about international cooperation without waiting for human nature to achieve perfection.

According to Mead, Mahan's belief that armies and navies were national police represented his most dangerous fallacy. Genuine police undertook protective work or "getting with the minimum of force a criminal before a court law." They did not assume the role of judge, jury, and executioner. On the other hand, she suggested, "a navy is a tool of government which is created for the settlement of difficulties through the maximum of force . . . irrespective of justice." A body composed of international judges sitting on an arbitration tribunal would be far more likely to render a fair verdict.

Mead also attacked American imperialism and, not surprisingly, Admiral Mahan proved a useful target of her barbs, particularly his statement that a "moral elevation comes to every citizen in the membership of a great empire." Mrs. Mead ridiculed Mahan's assertion and pointed out it was "no mere coincidence that race hatred and civic corruption have had such a recrudescence among us since we became imperialistic in our foreign policy.'' As elsewhere, she advocated discarding the Monroe Doctrine and called for Philippine independence. Then the United States could ''build one less battleship and put its cost onto our first real gift for the Filipinos,'' that for public education.

''False patriots'' usually represented a favorite target of Lucia Mead's displeasure, and they failed to escape her acrimony in *Swords and Ploughshares*. Herself the descendant of Revolutionary ancestors, she nonetheless deplored the boom in ''Patriotic'' societies that began in the 1890s. Instead of spending their time cultivating antiquarianism, undertaking genealogical projects, and exhibiting artifacts, she urged patriots to show ''far more willingness to serve their country.'' Mead suggested that the women might find better ways of proving their patriotism, such as providing meaningful assistance to the foreign-born poor. ''Is it not,'' she asked ''personal friendliness which can alone bridge the chasm which yawns between culture and ignorance, between privilege and privation? Is it not that spirit of democracy which goes an arrow's flight above noblesse oblige and welcomes'' new citizens to America?[36]

G. P. Putnam's published *Swords and Ploughshares* in 1912, at a time when American peace advocates expressed universal optimism about the possibilities of achieving permanent world peace. The movement lacked widespread public support, in spite of the efforts of a few publicists like Lucia Mead and the birth of two major, richly endowed, peace foundations. In 1910, wealthy textbook publisher Edwin Ginn contributed fifty thousand dollars a year to found the International School of Peace. He named his close friend Edwin Mead its principal director and under a new name, the World Peace Foundation (WPF), undertook some programs that the Meads had both long advocated. The WPF circulated books and pamphlets in large quantities to young people, sponsored lectures and conferences, and worked closely with other organizations. Not to be outdone by a mere millionaire, Andrew Carnegie then pledged ten million dollars in U.S. Steel bonds to create the Carnegie Endowment for International Peace. Carried away by the optimism of the times, the Carnegie Endowment funded ''scientific'' studies by academicians into the causes and possible cures of war. Little did they know that they would soon find an opportunity to study a major war first hand.

From the point of view of preventing a major war, the international peace movement failed in the era preceding the First World War. But the events of the summer of 1914 were beyond their control and do not represent a measure of the movement's vitality or wisdom. If it failed, it was in its inability, as Michael Lutzker argues, to confront ''the central dilemma of any peacetime movement opposed to war . . . to resist nationalism in its various benevolent guises. This implies a willingness to mobilize public sentiment critical of one's government policies when necessary.'' As respectable luminaries of the religious, educational, legal, business, and political communities, the movement's leaders refused to adopt a stance in opposition to the national government in power. Rather, as cosmopolitans who had a hand in forging national policies or who at least enjoyed the confidence of government insiders, they "looked to government, worked through government, and advanced the policies of government as their mode of working for peace." Consequently, while pressure groups such as organized labor, agricultural organizations, woman suffragists, conservationists, and other contemporary reform movements sought new, experimental methods of political action, the peace advocates clung tenaciously to traditional ideas.[37]

As far back as her first visit to Lake Mohonk, Lucia Mead had urged the peace movement to shed its elitist image. Other voices echoed her sentiments and within this minority of peace advocates a number of women stand out prominently. In a study of the peace movement during the period before World War I, David S. Patterson selected six women as recognized leaders. All six, including Mead, Hannah Bailey, Belva Lockwood, Jane Addams, May Wright Sewall, and Fanny Fern Andrews, favored a search for widespread public support. Obviously, the primary reason for this tendency is gender-related. Mead, like the other women, lacked access to the official channels of policy making. Since maleness represented, for the most part, a prerequisite for "insider" status within government circles, women naturally gravitated toward an area where they could exert influence. The irony of this should not be lost on the modern observer. A movement that was led primarily by "practical" men of power and wealth failed in part because it clung stubbornly to a respectable, establishment status. Had it paid greater attention to the warnings of Lucia Mead, who lacked this "advantage," they might have enjoyed some success in mobilizing public sentiment against war between 1914 and 1917.[38]

As the chairperson of the peace and arbitration committees of both major women's organizations in the country, Lucia Mead seemed the logical choice to lead a women's movement against war, but she was traveling in Europe when the fighting began. While in London, the Hungarian suffragist and pacifist Rosika Schwimmer came to see the Boston reformer. The international press secretary of the International Woman Suffrage Alliance informed Mead of her intention of visiting the United States to urge neutral mediation of the conflict. Part of her mission would include stirring women to action, and Mead provided her with the letters of introduction to various people. During her subsequent visit to the United States, Schwimmer failed to interest Woodrow Wilson in her mediation scheme, but succeeded dramatically in sparking interest among American women. Another prominent suffragist Emmeline Pethick-Lawrence of England also helped inspire women to action. Schwimmer and Pethick-Lawrence, during whirlwind tours of America, met with prominent suffragists and pacifists, lectured on the relationship of suffrage and peace, and urged the formation of "a real organization for women pacifists."[39]

Yet when Lucia Mead returned from London in November, no such organization existed. Soon afterward, however, Jane Addams issued a call for a mass women's demonstration against war, and an organizing convention to consider forming a women's peace party. The origins of this invitation are exceedingly complex, as accounts by many historians testify. Alice Paul's Congressional Union, the National American Woman Suffrage Association's militant rival, had already planned a small peace conference, so Addams's call simply expanded the numbers of prominent women who participated. Notable confusion existed regarding the planned convention, which may have been avoided had Lucia Mead been in the United States, but thanks to the efforts of Addams, Fanny Villard, Carrie Chapman Catt, Anna Garlin Spencer, Crystal Eastman, and Mead, among many others, the organizing convention of the Woman's Peace Party (WPP) finally met in Washington, D.C.

Blame for the long delay, until January 10, 1915, probably belongs on the shoulders of the leading suffragists in NAWSA. Carrie Catt, president of the International Woman Suffrage Alliance and guiding force of the NAWSA, believed that any close association between the suffrage movement and antiwar agitation might delay the final enfranchisement of American women. Though Schwimmer and Pethick-Lawrence argued the opposite point of view, that suffragists could increase their prestige by linking themselves to a call for peace, Catt insisted that "suffragists should not be the prime movers" in antiwar agitation by women. Lucia Mead had long favored the view of Schwimmer and Pethick-Lawrence on this issue, and Catt took steps to prevent the peace leader from assuming control of any movement designed to oppose the war in Europe. Catt saw Mead as "without question exceedingly well informed upon the peace question and a woman of very rare ability." But she also found Mead's forceful manner in dictating to suffragists what they *must* do for the peace cause a tactic that upset many suffragists, rendering Mead an "unpopular woman" among some. Besides, Catt wished to see "The First Lady of the Land," to use Ida Tarbell's label, lead a women's peace party because no one would add greater legitimacy to the undertaking than Jane Addams, and therefore protect the image of the suffragists.[40]

When Addams did preside over the organizational conference of the Woman's Peace Party, she looked out at a legion of talented American women from suffragist, domestic reform, and peace groups. Lucia Mead served on the platform committee with Catt, Addams, pacifist minister Anna Garlin Spencer, pacifist and antiimperialist Alice Thatcher Post, feminist author Charlotte Perkins Gilman, and Fanny Fern Andrews. The resulting organization that emerged that January proved to be the most active antiwar society in the nation over the next three years, and its successes and failures have received adequate attention elsewhere. As president, Addams appointed Mead its national secretary, a position she held until after the war. The experienced peace advocate and recognized expert on international affairs proved the obvious selection for this post. Mead had never proposed the idea of a separate women's peace party before 1914, but welcomed the addition of thousands of new supporters for the cause. As she told her skeptical associates in the American Peace Society, the new group would "add the zest and enthusiasm for a large number of new recruits." If properly financed, she believed the WPP would popularize the crusade to end international war as never before.[41]

Lucia Mead saw in the Woman's Peace Party a chance to fulfill her dream of mounting a major campaign of education; as national secretary, she helped develop policies, wrote many of its public statements, and lectured under its auspices. She also continued to write extensively, often under male pseudonyms to protect the image of the WPP. However, Mrs. Mead was unable to devote the same amount of energy to her work for the WPP, compared with her untiring prewar efforts on behalf of peace. After months of strenuous activity to get the World Peace Foundation to adopt a conspicuous antiwar posture, Edwin Mead suffered a severe nervous breakdown in early 1915. The peace movement lost one of its leading lights while his wife tried to cope with his "strange double personality." He sometimes enjoyed a few hours a day when "he read and talk[ed] in a normal fashion," but most of his time was spent screaming and moaning "in a state of tumultuous excitement and distress which [was] heart rendering to witness." Though restricted to a sanitarium, Edwin Mead's illness limited his wife's freedom for the next seven years, until his full recovery in 1922.[42]

Before the United States entered the war, the Woman's Peace Party fought against rising national expenditures for military "preparedness," the growth of hysterical chauvinism in America, and Uncle Sam's imperialist ventures in the Orient and in Latin America. The WPP called upon the United States to lead the way toward permanent world peace, while advocating a just peace treaty with no annexations or indemnities, a postwar league of nations, and a massive rehabilitation program to relieve the suffering of war victims. Much of the WPP's program represented positions that Mead had long advocated, particularly its campaign against preparedness. As Congress appropriated vast sums to upgrade the country's navy, Mead called upon national leaders to rely on "statesmanship" instead of the "battleship." She pointed out that a victorious Germany, though "pictured in the lurid columns of the jingo press as able to reduce us to humiliation if we do not vote away $500,000,000 of the people's taxes in war preparations," could hardly invade the United States by shipping its army 3,000 miles across the Atlantic.[43]

When the United States declared war in April of 1917, the Woman's Peace Party faced the dilemma all peace organizations confront when their nation chooses a belligerent course. The WPP had called for a referendum on the declaration of war and then opposed conscription. But in the wake of defeat on both issues, the WWP avoided further obvious antigovernment positions. Only a few members, clustered in New York, believed the WPP should adopt a stance in direct opposition to American participation in the war. Even Crystal Eastman, the recognized leader of the "radical" New York branch, believed "common sense as well as loyalty and the habit of obedience to law counseled this course."[44] Fearful of being labeled disloyal, some members chose to resign, particularly women more concerned with suffragism or specific social reforms. Lucia Mead nonetheless believed that the organization "was never more needed." She urged that the party "ought not to depart from our special educational and congressional work."[45]

With the exodus of some of the Woman's Peace Party's more conservative members, the balance of power within the group shifted somewhat in 1917. Dissatisfied with the WPP's continued passive, non-confrontational approach, members of the New York branch desired overt antiwar tactics, such as Eastman, the architect of New York's first workmen's compensation law; trade union organizer Elizabeth Glendower Evans; and a host of militant feminists including Fola LaFollette, Freda Kirchwey, and Margaret Lane. They ridiculed Mead's notion that the WPP should display public "patriotism" to ensure continued credibility in a nation at war, along with the behavior of the moderate Massachusetts branch in general. As antagonism mounted between moderates and radicals in late 1917, Massachusetts leaders including president Rose Dabney Forbes promised to quit if Eastman won election to the WPP national board, or if the moderates lost their majority at the upcoming annual meeting. Though some historians have treated Lucia Mead as a mouthpiece for her friends in Massachusetts, she actually hoped to steer a middle course between the two extremes of membership. Noting that "personally I should not object to Miss Eastman on our board," she nonetheless warned of the imminent withdrawal of the "most influential members who sustain" the Massachusetts branch should Eastman win the election.[46]

The Massachusetts conservatives kept Eastman off the national board, though fortunately for the Woman's Peace Party she continued to add her exceptional talents to the group. Remarkably, this divisiveness failed to destroy the WPP, which reorganized as the American branch of the Women's International League for Peace and Freedom (WILPF) afterward. Mead remained WILPF's national secretary and traveled to the International Congress of Women held in Zurich in May of 1919. Here, each major delegation named a "committee of five" to help organize the conference. Mead joined Addams, Post, Emily Greene Balch, and Florence Kelley on the American organizing committee. As chairperson of the conference's committee on politics, Mead found herself in the minority on a major issue. She condemned the Versailles Treaty as "imperialistic and full of weaknesses," yet accepted the proposed League of Nations Covenant "as it is as the less of two evils." Though some American delegates like Addams, Post, and Balch leaned toward this view, the majority of women on the committee, led by Florence Kelley and Emmeline Pethick-Lawrence, refused to endorse any part of the treaty. The committee finally adopted a compromise statement that withheld full endorsement of the League and criticized the treaty. Mead also served on the committee on education, where she formulated a resolution urging the League to establish a Commission on Education, and again with some difficulty, saw it passed.[47]

Over the next two years, Lucia Mead continued to press for American entrance into the League of Nations. In October of 1920, as she prepared to vote in a national election for the first time, she accompanied a number of famous pro-League Independent Republicans on a nineteen-day rail trip across the United States. Professor Irving Fisher of Yale organized the project, which included participation by former Republican Congressman Herbert Parsons, Secretary of War Newton Baker (the only Democrat), James G. Blaine's daughter-in-law Anita McCormick Blaine, seven other men, and four other women. Fisher asked Mead to come along because of her expressed desire to vote for Democrat James M. Cox, and because she supported Senate ratification of American entrance in the League. As a political "independent," her presence on the "League of Nations Special" seemed appropriate to Fisher, and during the tour she spoke to 89 audiences, totaling 65,000 people.[48]

During the last fifteen years of her life, Mead remained a prolific writer and active lecturer. Peace advocacy continued to be her vocation, and long after her seventieth birthday she traveled extensively throughout the United States each year, while letters to the editors signed "Lucia Ames Mead" seemed to appear everywhere. However, her advancing age, her husband's chronic poor physical health, and a relentless stream of personal attacks emanating from conservative forces reduced Mead's influence within the new peace organizations that emerged in the 1920s. Ironically, these agencies, such as the Women's International League for Peace and Freedom, National Council for the Prevention of War, National Conference on the Cause and Cure of War, and War Resisters League adopted the very tactics long advocated by the aging Boston reformer. They rejected the approach of the "respectable" peace organizations of the pre-World War I era, placed minimal importance on lobbying efforts among top level policy-makers, and instead sought to create widespread public sentiment opposed to war.

To say that Mead's influence declined within the new peace movement does not imply that the reformer whose ideas foreshadowed the new approaches faded into insignificance. When the Women's International League for Peace and Freedom and a host of other women's peace organizations urged Warren Harding to appoint a woman to the upcoming Washington Naval Conference in 1921, Carrie Chapman Catt called upon the president to name Lucia Mead to that post. Though Harding declined to include any women on the negotiating team, the incident indicates the lofty position as an expert on international affairs Mrs. Mead enjoyed in the minds of her activist colleagues. From a "spiritual founder" of the "new" peace organizations of the 1920s, as leading pacifist Fredrick J. Libby labeled her, Mead's written and spoken message (she rarely missed a major peace conference) commanded the respect of her younger associates. Mrs. Mead herself saw her role, after 1920, as primarily "to fertilize the [younger] workers for peace" with her ideas, both substantive and tactical. Her generation had missed a great opportunity to "organize the world," but undaunted, she "strain[ed] every nerve to help arouse our young people . . . to [their] duty."[49]

If the new generation of peace activists looked to Lucia Mead for guidance, her adversaries conversely saw the longtime pacifist as a voice to be silenced. In 1926, the Secretary of the Industrial Defense Association ranked her behind Roger Baldwin and Jane Addams as the third "most dangerous" American. Few blacklists designed to identify subversives failed to include the name of Lucia Mead. Chauvinistic organizations, denouncing the peace advocate as a "dangerous red" or "German agent," prevented and disrupted her talks and even the Boston public schools, where she had lectured for years, banned classroom appearances by Mrs. Mead. She hoped to counter the "wicked, reckless talk" with court cases, to "hail a lie and stand the racket" it would cause, but friends counseled a less combative course in the repressive climate of the twenties. Actually, the Daughters of the American Revolution and the American Legion could only prevent a few addresses, and Mead continued amazingly active as a speaker and writer until late October of 1936, when she suffered a critical fall on a subway platform. She died a few days later, on November 1.[50]

Death spared Mead the trauma of witnessing a second world war. Once again, the American peace movement, despite dramatic changes in its tactics, failed to steer the nation away from belligerency. The Peace reform's ultimate failure to mobilize a large segment of the population against the war, however, does not give historians license to dismiss the movement as simply an impotent force in American society. Rather, the very fact that the movement has enjoyed a prominent "outsider" status makes it worthy of study. As Charles DeBenedetti argued in his recent survey of the peace reform, modern peace advocates have "accept[ed] their distance from the country's dominant power values and realities ... [and] resolved to serve as the most vocal critics of power as traditionally pursued and applied." As unashamed critics who oppose vigorously many government policies, they must be content to "guide forward a subculture of dissent that survives in the certainty that there are working alternatives to the dominant modern power drive toward national self-aggrandizement."[51] Lucia Mead represents one of the few American peace advocates who bridged the gap between the old peace movement of the era before World War I, which prided itself on its "insider" status and avoided direct criticism of government policies in most cases, and the "modern" peace movement described by DeBenedetti that emerged from the rubble of World War I. If Mead failed to reject totally the notion that peace groups could affect national policy by supporting "sympathetic" government insiders, she nonetheless believed this effort would not succeed unless supplemented by a campaign of public propaganda. If specific government policies deserved blunt criticism, she concluded, then so be it.

Lucia Ames Mead enjoyed a notable career as a peace activist and critic of American foreign policy, though, for the most part, historians have thus far ignored her life. Around the turn of the century, she rose quickly to become a prominent officer of the American Peace Society, a leading participant at international and national peace conferences, and the most successful promoter of the peace movement among the principal suffragist and feminist organizations in the United States. She accomplished all this in spite of encountering the barriers faced by every female activist of her period who sought equal status in reform organizations dominated by men. Mead's remarkable life deserves attention because, like too many other publicly active women who overcame formidable sexist barriers, she nonetheless "disappeared" from history. Yet the author and lecturer not only achieved an extraordinary position as a reformer in a man's world, her gender actually helped move her to embrace an alternative perspective on what tactics the male-dominated peace movement should have employed. Thus the ideas and activism of Lucia Mead add further evidence in support of Gerda Lerner's trenchant observation that "Men and women, even when active in the same social movements, worked in different ways and defined issues differently."[52]

NOTES

1. Jacobs quoted in Jo Ann Robinson, "Introduction to Women, War, and Resistance to War: A Transnational Perspective," *Peace and Change* 4 (Fall, 1977), 1. Benjamin Trueblood, Secretary of the American Peace Society, observed in 1910 that "For the last three or four decades women have been, in this country, quite as numerous as men in the peace organizations, and at the present time probably outnumber them." See *Women in the Peace Movement* (pamphlet) Boston, American Peace Society, 1910, n.p.

2. Julius Moritzen, *The Peace Movement in America* (New York, 1912), 309; Catt quoted in *Lucia Ames Mead: Memorial Meeting of the Twentieth Century Club* (Boston, 1937), 32.

3. General information regarding Lucia Ames's background may be gleaned from Frances E. Willard and Mary Livermore, eds., *A Woman of the Century: Leading American Women* (Buffalo, 1893), 23–24; *Principal Women of America*, 2 vols. (London, 1936), II:339; Charles Carleton Coffin, *The History of Boscawen and Webster* (Concord, New Hampshire, 1878), 467, 493; and *Memorial Meeting*, *passim*. The best brief sketch is Warren F. Kuehl, "Lucia True Ames Mead," in *Notable American Women*, 4 vols., edited by Edward T. Jones, et al. (Cambridge, Massachusetts, 1971), II:521–22. Statement on father's income from Lucia True Ames to Wiliam T. Harris, 19 June 1894, William T. Harris Papers, Houghton Library, Harvard University.

4. Lucia True Ames to William T. Harris, 25 November 1892, Harris Papers.

5. William S. B. Mathews, *A Hundred Years of Music in America* (New York, 1889), 429.

6. Lucia True Ames, "No Occupation I Suppose?" *Woman's Journal* 15 (December 20, 1884), 407.

7. Diary of Lucia True Ames, August 2, 1884, Edwin D. and Lucia Ames Mead Papers, Box 7, Swarthmore College Peace Collection.

8. Lucia True Ames, "The Duty of Woman Suffragists," *Woman's Journal* 16 (April 3, 1886), 108. The campaign urged by Ames did succeed in raising the age of consent from ten to sixteen in 1893. For information on Charles Carleton Coffin, see William Elliot Griffis, *Charles Carleton Coffin: a Biography* (Boston, 1898).

9. Lucia True Ames, *Memoirs of a Millionaire* (Boston, 1889). See also "The Home in the Tenement House," *New England Magazine*, n.s., 7 (January, 1893), 394–99; "City Homes for the Poor," *Lend a Hand: a Record of Progress* 12 (March 1894), 163–70. For reviews of *Memoirs* see "Problems of Charity," *New York Times*, 1 December

1889, 19; "Literary Notices," *Woman's Journal* 20 (October 22, 1889), 339; "More Fiction," *The Nation* 50 (February 20, 1890), 159–60.

10. Lucia T. Ames, *To Whom Much Is Given* (Boston, 1898). Information on the Twentieth Century Club can be found in Arthur Mann, *Yankee Reformers in the Gilded Age: Social Reform in Boston, 1880–1900* (New York, 1954), 172.

11. *Report of the Third Annual Meeting of the Lake Mohonk Conference on International Arbitration* (Lake Mohonk, New York, 1897), 95–99.

12. David Sands Patterson, "An Interpretation of the American Peace Movement," in Charles Chatfield, ed. *Peace Movements in America* (New York, 1973), 20–38; Samuel P. Hays, "Political Parties and the Community-Society Continuum," in William Nesbet Chambers and Walter Dean Burnham, eds, *The American Party Systems* (New York, 1967), 152–81; Lloyd Gardner, Walter LaFeber, and Thomas McCormick, *Creation of the American Empire*, 2 vols, 2nd ed. (Chicago, 1976), 193. For the importance of Lake Mohonk, see C. Roland Marchand, *The American Peace Movement and Social Reform, 1898–1918* (Princeton, New Jersey, 1972), 18–21.

13. The noted reformer Howe served on the Board of Directors of the American Peace Society and authored a famous tract on the potential role women could play in ending war, "An Appeal To Womanhood Throughout the World" (1870). Lockwood was the most effective publicist and lobbyist in the Universal Peace Union, America's second most influential peace organizatin in the pre-World War I era, and founded the National Arbitration Association at Washington. Bailey, a Quaker pacifist, served as superintendent of the Woman's Christian Temperance Union's peace and arbitration department and edited two monthly periodicals on peace.

14. Brief accounts of Edwin Mead's life may be found in Mann, *Yankee Reformers*, 159–63 and his article on Mead in Robert L. Schuyler, ed., *Dictionary of American Biography* (1958), 22, Supplement Two, 442–43; Edwin M. Bacon, ed., *Men of Progress* (Boston, 1896), 899–90. See also Mead's "Boston Memories of Fifty Years," in Elisabeth M. Herlihy, ed., *Fifty Years of Boston: A Memorial Volume* (Boston, 1932).

15. Robert E. Osgood, *Ideals and Self-Interest in America's Foreign Relations* (Chicago, 1953), 54.

16. Lucia Ames Mead, "What Is Imperialism?" *Outlook* 66 (October 6 1900), 375.

17. William E. Leuchtenberg, "Progressivism and Imperialism: The Progressive Movement and American Foreign Policy, 1898–1916," *Mississippi Valley Historical Review*, 39 (December, 1952), 483–504. For a discussion of American expansion during the period, see Walter LaFeber, *The New Empire* (Ithaca, New York, 1963), 407–17.

18. Lucia Ames Mead, "How to Cooperate with the Czar," *Woman's Journal* 29 (December 3, 1898), 386.

19. Diary of Lucia Ames Mead, June–November 1901, Box 7, Mead Papers, Lucia Ames Mead, *Patriotism and the New Internationalism* (Boston, 1906), 41.

20. Diary of Lucia Ames Mead, September 12, 14, 1901, Box 7, Mead Papers; "International Peace Congress," *Woman's Journal* 32 (October 19, 1901), 332–33.

21. Lucia Ames Mead to Gladys K. Gould, May 13, 1922, Box 54, National Council for the Prevention of War Papers, SCPC.

22. *Memorial Meeting*, 22–23; Lucia Ames Mead, "In Behalf of Peace," *Woman's Journal* 38 (January 12, 1907), 8.

23. "State Correspondence: Massachusetts," *Woman's Journal* 40 (October 30, 1909), 175.

24. *Mohonk Conference, 1902*, 61–63.

25. Lucia Ames Mead, "What Are We To Do?" *Advocate of Peace* 65 (August 1903), 142–43.

26. Ibid., 143; *Book of the Fourth American Peace Congress* (St. Louis, 1913), 373–79.

27. "A Primer of Peace," *Lend a Hand: A Record of Progress* 22 (December, 1904), 15; Lucia Ames Mead, *A Primer of the Peace Movement* (Boston, 1904); Robert Erskine Ely to Woodrow Wilson, March 25, 1907 in Arthur Link, et al., ed., *The Papers of Woodrow Wilson*, 37 vols. (Princeton, New Jersey, 1974), XVII:93.

28. Mead, *Primer*, n.p.

29. Patterson, "An Interpretation of the American Peace Movement," 27.

30. Diary of Lucia Ames Mead, September 1907, Box 7, Mead Papers.

31. Jane Addams, Review of *Law or War* in *The World Tomorrow* 12 (April 29, 1929), 183.

32. Copy of Announcement, "Lecturer on International Peace," for the Fall of 1913, in Massachusetts Peace Society Papers, Box 8, SCPC. See also Mead's diaries for 1905 and 1906, for example, Box 7, Mead Papers.

33. Diary of Lucia Ames Mead for 1908 to 1910, Box 7, Mead Papers.

34. Libby quoted in *Memorial Meeting*, 26; May Bell Harper, *Breaking into Print for the Sake of Peace* (pamphlet), National Woman's Christian Temperance Union's Publishing House [1937?].

35. Mead wrote one other book before World War I, *Milton's England* (Boston, 1902), designed as a handbook accenting history and culture for American tourists visiting London.

36. Lucia Ames Mead, *Swords and Ploughshares or The Supplanting of the System of War by the System of Law* (New York, 1912), chapters II, IV, V, VI, VIII, X, and XII.

37. Michael A. Lutzker, "The Pacifist as Militarist: a Critique of the American Peace Movement, 1898–1914," *Societas* 5 (Spring, 1975), 103; Lutzker, "The Practical Peace Advocates: An Interpretation of the American Peace Movement, 1898–1917" (Ph.D. Dissertation, Rutgers University, 1969), x-xii, 348.

38. Patterson, "An Interpretation of the American Peace Movement," 34n. In *Newer Ideals of Peace*, Jane Addams found "the hope for the prevention of war in the peaceful instincts of working men and women," says Allen Davis in *American Heroine: The Life and Legend of Jane Addams* (New York, 1973), 146. May Wright Sewall, the long-time president of the National Council of Women, strove for many years to interest women in the cause. See her *Women, World War, and Permanent Peace* (San Francisco, 1915).

39. Lucia Ames Mead, "Thinking Women and the World Crisis," *Femina* 3 (November, 1916), 393; Diary of Lucia Mead, August 17, 1914, Box 7, Mead Papers. A good account of Schwimmer and Pethick-Lawrence's efforts in America is contained in Barbara J. Steinson, *American Women's Activism in World War I* (New York, 1982), 16–23.

40. Carrie Chapman Catt to Jane Addams, 14 December 1914, Container 4, Catt Papers, Manuscript Division, Library of Congress. See also Catt to Addams, 4 January 1915 and 12 November 1915, Container 4, Catt Papers. The standard work on the WPP is Marie Louise Degen, *The History of the Woman's Peace Party* (Baltimore, 1939). Marchand's study, *The American Peace Movement and Social Reform*, deals with the WPP in Chapter 6, "The Maternal Instinct." Marchand overemphasizes the role of Catt, however. The most recent study of the WPP is Steinson's *American Women's Activism*

in World War I. Steinson provides a good account of WPP activities, but inaccurately finds Mead's efforts to keep the organization together motivated by "vindictive nationalism."

41. Lucia Ames Mead, "The Women's Peace Party," *Advocate of Peace* 77 (February 1915), 35–36.

42. Descriptions of Edwin Mead's illness may be found in Lucia Ames Mead to Mrs. Benjamin Trueblood, 2 August 1915, Box 6, American Peace Society Collected Papers, SCPC; Lucia Ames Mead to Charles Levermore, 28 August 1918, New York Peace Society Records, SCPC; Lucia Ames Mead to Jane Addams, 13 August 1919, DG 1, Box 8, Jane Addams Papers, SCPC; Lucia Ames Mead to Henry Longfellow Dana, 29 August, 1918, Box 1, Dana Papers, SCPC.

43. Lucia Ames Mead, "The Immediate Duty of American Patriots," in Mead, ed., *The Overthrow of the War System* (Boston, 1915), 50. See also "Statesmanship or Battleship?" *Survey* 36 (July 8, 1916), 387–88; "America's Danger and Opportunity," *Survey* 35 (October 23, 1915), 90–92.

44. Crystal Eastman, "Two Communications," *Advocate of Peace* 80 (March 1918), 84.

45. "Extracts of Letter of Mrs. Mead [to WPP State Chairmen]," April 6, 1917, Box 13, Mead Papers; Lucia Ames Mead, "Women's Work for Internationalism; the Women's Peace Party," clipping, 1917, Box 14, Mead Papers.

46. Lucia Ames Mead to Jane Addams, 5 November 1917, Box 1, Women's Peace Party Collected Records, SCPC. See also Mead to Addams, 13 November 1917; Mead to Alice Thatcher Post, 17 November 1917, Box 1, WPP Records.

47. Lucia Ames Mead to Jane Addams, 13 August 1919, DG1, Box 8, Addams Papers; Lucia Ames Mead to Charles Levermore, 9 June 1918, NYPS Papers. See also diary of Lucia Mead, April–May 1919, and Lucia Ames Mead to State Chairmen of the WPP, 9 June 1919, Box 10, Mead Papers.

48. Diary of Lucia Ames Mead, October 18–November 7, 1920, Box 8, Mead Papers.

49. "Proposes Mrs. Mead for Big Conference," Boston *Herald*, August 20, 1921, 3; Libby quoted in *Memorial Meeting*, 25; Lucia Ames Mead to Frederick J. Libby, 24 May 1924, National Council for the Prevention of War Records, Box 54, SCPC; Lucia Ames Mead to Elizabeth Glendower Evans, 23 August 1935, Elizabeth G. Evans Collection, The Arthur and Elizabeth Schlesinger Library on the History of Women in America, Radcliffe College. In 1922, some American newspapers and journals compiled lists of the "most respected" women in America and Carrie Chapman Catt topped most lists; see "The Twelve Greatest Women in America," *Literary Digest* 74 (July 8, 1922), 36–45.

50. E. Tallmadge Root to Lucia Ames Mead, 22 September 1926, Box 6, Mead Papers. For Mrs. Mead's response to the actions of superpatriotic societies, see Lucia Ames Mead to Frederick J. Libby, 4 February and 15 April 1924; Mead to Gladys K. Gould-MacKenzie, 27 November 1926, 26 November 1927, and 28 February, Box 54, National Council for the Preservation of War Records. Accounts of attempts to silence Mead can be found in D. Witherspoon Dodge, "Mrs. Mead in Atlanta," *The Congregationalist* (December 30 1926), 793; "They Think Mrs. Mead 'Red'; Cancel Speaking Engagement," *The Christian Register* (December 16, 1926), 1144.

51. Charles DeBenedetti, *The Peace Reform in American History* (Bloomington, Indiana, 1980), 198–200.

52. Gerda Lerner, "The Necessity of History and the Professional Historian," *Journal of American History* 67 (June 1982), 13.

5

Eleanor Roosevelt and Human Rights: The Battle for Peace and Planetary Decency

Blanche Wiesen Cook

Eleanor Roosevelt worked to influence the course of U.S. foreign policy through-out her adult life. For over forty years she promoted her unique vision of decency in world affairs from a variety of public positions—as lobbyist, critic, and insider. She did not become the "First Lady of the World" as a result of her role as the most public, active, and popular first wife of the U.S. Rather, her diplomatic interests and skills and her involvement in U.S. foreign policy developed slowly, and systematically. From 1923 until her death on 7 November, 1962, ER was a key, if often unrecognized, figure in activist international circles.

Passionately committed to peace, ER was not an absolute pacifist. She called herself a "realistic" pacifist and meant by that support for both military pre-paredness and conscription. "In a world that is arming all around us, it is necessary to keep a certain parity," she wrote in 1938. Also, she understood that peace was not merely the absence of war. True peace would continue to be a chimera so long as entire nations and subject peoples within many nations were denied access to economic security: food, clothing, education, work, comfort.

Above all, Eleanor Roosevelt believed in power. She understood power, sought power, and more than any other woman of her era influenced policy from positions of power. She was a practical idealist who understood the complexities of colonial privilege and revolution; the vagaries of competition and compromise. She was an internationalist whose values were profoundly American. She was committed to the precepts of America as codified in the Declaration of Inde-pendence and the United States Bill of Rights. She believed in liberty, democracy, and freedom. But she also believed that no individual, community, or nation could be truly free so long as others were fettered.

With courage and determination ER personally carried her commitment for

human rights into tiny villages and hamlets as well as into the citadels of government authority. She touched the imagination of people everywhere because
she included in her vision people of all economic and social classes. Her capacity
to touch people with the magentism of her profound sincerity was rooted in her
capacity to care, to see, to understand. Her genuine concern "for everyday
people" eventually embraced all the people of the world. It was that gift, that
ability to know and to care, that caused so many to believe, with her, that there
was hope for a more decent future. There was nothing radical really about her
views, or her efforts. But it is amazing how radical simple decency seems in a
period of mean-spirited militarism.

Eleanor Roosevelt's profound commitment to human life, to its value and
variety, was forged out of her understanding of the wants and needs of her own
frequently neglected and discounted childhood. Her vision was strengthened
throughout her life by a rare understanding of alliances and community. ER
understood that politics was not an isolated individualistic adventure. Intimate
friendships and working partnerships formed the essence of her own strength
and were the core of her power.

Throughout her public career, ER had the support of and worked with like-
minded women and men who also operated from positions of privilege, influence,
and power. On issues relating to international peace and civil rights, where her
stands were often far bolder than her husband's, she had from the beginning the
support of a group of political women who were her lifelong friends, and whom
she creditied with "the intensive education of Eleanor Roosevelt."

Esther Everett Lape, a crusader for national health care and a leader in the
fight for American participation in the World Court, and attorney Elizabeth Read
introduced ER to the women's movement for international peace and to such
peace and feminist activists as Agnes Brown Leach, Carrie Chapman Catt, and
Jane Addams.

After World War I, ER became identified with the activist peace movement
that Jane Addams guided until her death in 1935. But during World War I
Eleanor Roosevelt was associated with the interventionist, pro-Allied sentiment
spearheaded by her uncle Theodore Roosevelt and her husband Franklin Delano
Roosevelt—who then led the preparedness movement in Woodrow Wilson's
cabinet. As undersecretary of the navy, FDR bitterly opposed such Wilsonian
pacifists as Secretary of State William Jennings Bryan and his own boss, Josephus
Daniels—who before 1917 equated navalism with imperialism. FDR followed
the teachings of his hero Alfred Thayer Mahan, who popularized the notion that
seapower was the key to world power. FDR was contemptuous of his neutralist
colleagues, and hoped Bryan and Daniels would resign.

Eleanor Roosevelt was not so scornful, and acknowledged that she admired
their principled courage in the face of the well-financed preparedness movement.
But she had nothing to do with such organizations as the American Union Against
Militarism or the Woman's Peace Party, organized by Jane Addams, Lillian
Wald, Crystal Eastman and others, so many of whom later became ER's allies.

Rather, ER spent the war years in full uniform, administering a Red Cross canteen and knitting brigade. She helped found the Navy Relief Society. She lectured and raised money, and was considered "the dynamo" behind the canteen service that greeted as many as ten troop trains a day at Washington's Union Station. Her experiences during World War I changed many of her attitudes toward people, politics, and her own mode of life. She wrote her mother-in-law, Sara Delano Roosevelt, that the war awakened "people to a sense of responsibility and obligation."

In January 1919, ER accompanied FDR on a post-war tour of Europe. She visited hospitals and battlefields, and bore witness to a Europe vastly changed from the time of her pastoral London school days at Allenswood—when the world seemed a simpler, and far more settled place. Great cathedrals had been bombed. Entire towns had been virtually destroyed. The devastation was unbearable. And "every other woman wears a crepe veil to her knees." It was a haunting, unforgettable experience. ER returned home committed to the League of Nations, and eager to work for a more tolerable world. Her first major public effort on behalf of peace involved an intense and unusual effort to promote U.S. adherence to and participation in the World Court.

In 1923 Esther Lape invited ER to help administer Edward Bok's American Peace Award, a vigorously publicized contest for "a practicable plan to achieve and preserve the peace of the world." Bok, the former publisher and editor of *Ladies' Home Journal*, offered a prize of fifty thousand dollars to the best plan, to be followed by a second fifty thousand dollars if the U.S. Senate accepted it. A vast fortune in 1923, the prize was headline news throughout the U.S. It was featured in news columns, editorials, comic strips, and cartoons. Will Rogers and Mutt and Jeff each ran a syndicated series on the award, which became a household issue across the country.

The goal was to encourage a plan that would "provide a practicable means whereby the U.S. can take its place and do its share toward preserving world peace, while not making compulsory the participation of the U.S. in European wars if any such are, in the future, found unpreventable."

Edward Bok's contest raised provocative and critical questions:

"Is there a part America must play in the prevention of future wars?"

"Do the kaleidoscopic changes now taking place with startling rapidity in Europe affect our life here?"

"Can we have a fundamentally changing Europe without a changing America? . . . "

Bipartisan and high-powered, the policy committee set up to administer the peace prize concluded that the "ultimate fate of America is related to the fate of the rest of the world," and they sought "an acceptable WAY by which America's voice can be made to count among the nations for the peace of the world and for the present and future welfare of the United States."[1]

The contest captured the imagination of the American public, created a stir in academic circles, and was taken seriously among leading American interna-

tionalists, especially businessmen who hoped for an expanding economic future
free of both war and the current hysteria that rejected all "foreign entanglements"
including foreign trade. President Calvin Coolidge, who was Bok's personal
friend, wrote: "Edward, don't let them laugh at it."[2]

Esther Lape, Narcissa Vanderlip—an activist philanthropist widely identified
with the League of Women Voters—and Eleanor Roosevelt were the core of the
organizing and policy committee. Several statesmen and international lawyers
served as consultants and jury, including: Secretary of State and former Secretary
of War Elihu Root, Judge Learned Hand, Henry Stimson (subsequently Hoover's
Secretary of State and FDR's Secretary of War), and Roscoe Pound, dean of
the Harvard Law School.

A great optimistic mood regarding the possibility of outlawing war and achieving peace through rational discourse prevailed during the 1920s. Thousands of
plans were submitted from noted legal scholars, businessmen, former and current
public officials, and university presidents. Harvard's President Eliot, for example, saw the path to world peace through increased "family discipline."

Of the 22,165 plans submitted, the committee chose a very simple plan by
Charles E. Levermore, which recommended immediate adherence to the Permanent Court of International Justice, and cooperation with (although not membership in) the League of Nations. The winning plan stimulated a major effort
by Bok, Lape, and ER to promote U.S. membership in the World Court that
lasted for years. Although Bok was initially dismayed by what he considered
the unimaginative modesty of the plan, Lape and ER agreed with Elihu Root
that in matters of "international cooperation, we move forward only slowly."

In 1925 Bok organized the American Foundation to begin a campaign to
educate the American public on issues relating to international peace and the
need for U.S. participation in the World Court. Esther Lape was appointed
member-in-charge, and Eleanor Roosevelt participated in most of its activities.
The American Foundation was to be guided by the conviction that "it is possible
to educate the public"; and that "lasting education is to be achieved by fact and
not by propaganda."

But the reaction to Bok's contest and the Foundation's activities was outrage
on the part of Senate isolationists, who called for an investigation into the un-
American and potentially treasonous nature of the award. Condemned as propaganda, it was alleged to encourage foreign entanglements and communistic
internationalism. All involved with its promotion were suspected of Red tinge.

A Senate committee investigating "propaganda and the use of money in
promoting public questions" was empowered to investigate "whether American
citizens working with foreign Governments are promoting movements to control
or affect the foreign policy of the U.S." The Bok award was criticized as a plot
by unscrupulous women influenced by foreign radicals and their bipartisan hench-
men (Root and Stimson were Republican) to ensnare the U.S. into membership
in that clearly un-American organization the League of Nations. Vapors of the
Red Scare were mixed with traditional misogyny as the *New York Herald* head-

lined: "The great Bok peace prize was managed by two matrons of social distinction [ER and Narcissa Vanderlip] and a highly educated and most efficient young unmarried woman." Lape was in fact older than ER. But unmarried women were generally perceived to be young—or at least younger than matrons of distinction.[3]

While the Senate investigation simply expired, ER continued to work for the League, and for U.S. entrance into the world Court. In 1925, the House voted for U.S. participation, and ER called for a women's crusade to achieve Senate approval. Although she recognized that entrance into the World Court was only a first and rather tiny step on the long road toward international peace, she said wherever she spoke: But remember, "all big changes in human history have been arrived at slowly and through many compromises."

Thoroughout the 1920s, ER divided her political time between movements for international peace and work for the New York State Democratic party. She believed that women were better organized, more efficient, and more systematically political than men. She disparaged "the masculine idea that politics was a passing interest in women," and noted that among women's greatest contributions was their opposition to traditional, dull, formal, ritualistic behavior, and their greater reliance on "spontaneous action" to meet the pressing needs of contemporary politics.[4]

In October 1927 ER hosted a meeting of 400 women at Hyde Park to launch a woman's peace movement and support the Kellogg-Briand Treaty to outlaw war. Carrie Chapman Catt, the keynote speaker, called for a crusade against war as mighty as the antislave crusade, as mighty as the suffrage crusade. "Only by finding a way to arbitrate international disputes can we end this awful menace to civilization, the disgrace to this century, called war."

For the next ten years ER was to be one of the most prominent antiwar women in the U.S., associated with both Jane Addams's Women's International League for Peace and Freedom, and Carrie Chapman Catt's National Conference on the Cause and Cure for War.

Throughout the 1920s ER edited the *Women's Democratic News*, a monthly magazine sent to Democratic Party activists and subscribers. In July 1926 she wrote an editorial calling for bold, spontaneous, anonymous demonstrations for peace by American women: "Have you noticed that in England there have been lately big pilgrimages of women for peace converging on London?" ER was impressed that they seemed unorganized, and no individual women or groups took credit for their creation. "Of course, English women and European women generally feel more deeply than we do the horrors of war. They have lost their husbands and sons in great number." But, she asked: "Cannot we women here even interest ourselves enough to study the possible ways open to us in the world today of eliminating the causes of war and then get behind all the movements furthering these ends with some demonstrations of our own?"

In the early months of 1927, ER's editorials focused on Central America— Nicaragua in particular. In January she wrote: "Our Foreign Policy—What is it?'' Since "we do not wish to be entangled in European difficulties, our government's only concern is to collect what money is due us and constructive effort to build up good feeling is too much trouble since we have an ocean to protect us." But, she pointed out, "on this side of the Atlantic we do nothing constructive to build up good feeling either, and we drift into a very difficult situation."

ER deplored especially the United States reaction to Mexico's decision to nationalize its oil properties: a notice was sent that "our Marines are being issued tropical kits." She asked: "Can it be that we 'the big brother of all nations on this side of the Atlantic' are playing the part of the bully? That is not a part usually admired by our people." Then she turned to Nicaragua: "With the Mexican question is tied up the Nicaraguan question. Just what we are doing there it is hard indeed to understand from the conflicting reports . . . and no matter what happens in both Mexico and Nicaragua we have not shown our Central and South American neighbors a very reassuring picture of a disinterested and magnanimous neighbor. . . . ''

In March ER featured a front page article, "Banks and Bayonets in Nicaragua," with the banner headline: "Do We Deserve the Hatred of the World?"

Subsequently, her attitude toward Central America seems in retrospect vague, and she had no qualms as First Lady about entertaining Nicaragua's dictator Somoza or accepting a medal from him. But she was clear in her opposition to imperialism and her support for the policy of non-intervention. Whenever she spoke as the decade of the 1920s marched with militarist bombast into the turbulence of the 1930s, she spoke at least in part about world peace. Long before the war clouds gathered her message was succinct: "the time to prepare for world peace is during the time of peace and not during the time of war."[5]

There was nothing simple about ER's views on international relations during the 1930s. Moreover, she was most constrained and her influence as First Lady was most limited regarding international issues. Her response to letter after letter appealing to her for help or advice regarding a particular diplomatic matter, or desperate situation as Nazi atrocities began to mount was that international questions were not her area. She would then send the letter to the appropriate State Department official, but generally with little expectation that anything would come of her effort.

Still, she participated in another round of public lobbying and private persuasion on behalf of the World Court between 1934 and 1935. But isolationist sentiment remained strong and a vicious opposition campaign led by the "radio priest" Father Charles E. Coughlin and the Hearst papers overpowered significant congressional support. ER wrote Esther Lape on 12 April, 1934, that Roosevelt's administration was persuaded that the "World Court shall not come up until after the next election as they feel that it would just give Mr Hearst another thing to pin his attack on. So I am afraid there is not much chance."

Despite her husband's passivity during this last-ditch struggle for U.S. adherence to the World Court, ER broadcast a major fifteen-minute talk over NBC to bolster public support:

If you want to see the influence of your country on the side of peace, I beg of you to let your representatives in Congress know at once. It will not make peace certain. It is only one step. But I believe it is the desire of our nation to see virtue done at home and abroad. I make a special appeal to the women of my generation who desire to take any action they can to safeguard the people.

When the votes were tallied, the loss in pro-Court circles was a bipartisan disappointment. On 29 January, 1935, 43 Democrats and 9 Republicans voted for the Court; while 20 Democrats and 14 Republicans, 1 Progressive, and 1 Farmer-Labor voted in opposition. ER did not blame FDR's inaction—although many of her friends, including Esther Lape, were critical. ER wrote to one woman who protested: "I doubt if any public word by the President would have helped matters much. He sent for every Democratic and Independent Senator and talked to him personally, besides sending his message. I am afraid that the pressure must come from the people themselves, and until it does, we will never become a member of the World Court."[6]

When ER addressed Carrie Chapman Catt's National Conference on the Cause and Cure of War in 1934, she asked, "How can we live through the things that we have lived through and complacently go on allowing the same causes over and over again to put us through these same horrible experiences? . . . Anyone who thinks, must think of the next war as they would of suicide."

While in some circles ER was considered the "Number One Pacifist" who equated war with suicide, increasingly, she began to call for unity against fascist atrocities in Spain and Germany. Although she opposed war, she believed that specific international measures such as an economic boycott against the fascists were in order, as was a campaign to enlighten Americans to the dangers of isolationism. Still, she spoke ardently for peace. She hosted a reception at the White House to celebrate the twentieth anniversary of the Women's International League for Peace and Freedom, only weeks before Jane Addams's death in May 1935. On 9 October, 1935, ER chaired a radio broadcast, "Women Want Peace," sponsored by the National Council for the Prevention of War. Her name was associated with the American Friends Service Committee, the Fellowship of Reconciliation, and the War Resisters' League. As late as 1937, she told her radio audience that only women could adequately lead a peace crusade. When enough women organized to work for peace, wars would end, because "a woman's will is the strongest thing in the world."

Eleanor agreed with Senator Gerald P. Nye's 1934–36 committee investigating the Munitions Industry, which found the association between industry and the military treacherous. According to the Nye Committee, World War I mobilization involved "shameless profiteering" and forged "an unhealthy alliance" between business and military interests. ER believed that profiteering promoted war, and argued that the munitions industry should either be nationalized or government-regulated and controlled.

But opposed as she was to war, ER was also opposed to isolation, unpre-

paredness and fascism. Moreover, she was not neutral: Spain was "fighting on
the frontier of democracy." In a "My Day" column she wrote: "I believe in
democracy and the right of a people to choose their own government without
having it imposed upon them by Hitler and Mussolini." She defended the Abraham Lincoln Brigades and all who opposed Franco as fighters for democracy
against fascism. Franco, she told Catholic critics of her views, bombed churches.
Franco controlled the air force, not the American volunteers who sought to
defend democratic Loyalist Spain against Hitler and Mussolini.

In 1938 she wrote a "little book on peace," *This Troubled World*. The book
was dedicated to Carrie Chapman Catt, "who has led so many of us in the
struggle for peace," and introduced several of the themes that remained constant
as ER's vivid presence in global politics unfolded:

"The newspapers these days are becoming more and more painful. I was reading my
morning papers on the train not so long ago, and looked up with a feeling of desperation.
Up and down the car people were reading, yet no one seemed excited. To me the whole
situation seems intolerable. . . .

"We can establish no real trust between nations until we acknowledge the power of
love above all the other powers. . . .

"You laugh, it seems fantastic, but this subject [love] will, I am sure, have to be
discussed throughout the world for many years before it becomes an accepted rule. We
will have to want peace, want it enough to pay for it, pay for it in our own behavior and
in material ways. We will have to want it enough ot overcome our lethargy and go out
and find all those in other countries who want it as much as we do."

But by 1939 ER was persuaded that the U.S. would have to fight. She believed
fascism threatened the future of civilization. To begin with, she wrote, we will
"have to fight with our minds, for this is as much a war for the control of ideas
as for control of material resources."

On 6 September, 1939, ER wrote to her Allenswood schoolmate, Carola von
Schaeffer-Bernstein, who had become a Nazi sympathizer while remaining a
devout Christian. It was a combination of loyalties that dismayed and puzzled
ER: "You who believe in God must find it very difficult to follow a man who
apparently thinks he is as great as any god." ER had listened to Hitler's Reichstag
speech and, she wrote, she knew "enough German" to discern that Hitler "never
mentioned that there was a God whom we are supposed to have." While she
still hoped that the U.S. would "not have to go to war," she concluded: "no
country can exist free and unoppressed while a man like Hitler remains in
power."

One is amazed in this letter to read that the woman who stood above all others
in her generous support for Jews during and after the Holocaust shared, even
until September 1939, the prevailing anti-Semitism that so thoroughly dominated
international and domestic politics. Although she wrote Carola von Schaeffer-
Bernstein that Americans were unable "to understand how people of spirit can
be terrified by one man and his storm troops to the point of countenancing the

kind of horrors which seem to have come on in Germany, not only where the Jews are concerned,'' among Catholics and liberal German Protestants, she wrote: ''I realize quite well that there may be a need for curtailing the ascendancy of the Jewish people, but it seems to me it might have been done in a more humane way by a ruler who had intelligence and decency.''

Eleanor's vision was not fully transformed until after the U.S. entered the war. Even before she recognized the details of the Holocaust, however, her inability to achieve any significant change in U.S. legislation on behalf of Jewish refugees made her aware of the bitter struggle for human dignity that lay ahead.

With several close friends, including Judge Justine Wise Polier, New Deal strategist Ben Cohen, and Clarence Pickett of the American Friends Service Committee, she campaigned for a Jewish Children's Refugee bill introduced by Senator Robert Wagner and Congresswoman Edith Nourse Rogers. The Wagner-Rogers bill would have permitted 20,000 German children, most of whom would have been adopted by Quaker families that had already guaranteed them homes, to enter the U.S. The bill was withdrawn in 1939, during a vicious anti-Semitic crusade by ''restrictionists'' who were sufficiently powerful to persuade FDR that it were better that he said nothing to promote the bill. Such silence was not limited to the president.

Anti-Semitism was so pervasive, many American Jews were afraid that the situation would only be exacerbated by public protest. This astonished ER, who told Judge Polier: ''You know when I ask for help for the sharecroppers, the miners' children, the first people to come forward are the Jews. Now when they need help why do they hesitate . . . '' ''Because,'' Justine Wise Polier responded, ''of the cruelty of the Christian world.'' There was no particular place to turn for help. Outraged and distressed, ER made many private efforts to help indi-vidual Jews reach safety, but she was powerless to modify the Allied acquiescence to the Nazis' ''final solution.'' Not until she toured refugee camps near Frankfurt in 1946 did she fully appreciate the enormity of the human suffering and depravity World War II engendered.[7]

After World War II, Eleanor Roosevelt dedicated the rest of her life to the United Nations and to the struggle for worldwide recognition of the principles of human rights. She believed that the UN would be the best means by which to achieve abiding peace for this fragile and endangered planet, upon which we all do happen to live together. ER had no difficulties imagining a global community that would have at its core what all decent communities of neighbors share: respect for diversity and differences, and an understanding of the need for cooperative support. She believed that the ideal of a global community would be enhanced by a doctrine of intent. Like the U.S. Declaration of Independence, and the Magna Carta, such a doctrine would establish the purpose and intentions of the new world body.

More than any other single person ER is responsible for the Universal Declaration of Human Rights agreed to by the UN General Assembly on 10 December, 1948. Consisting of a preamble and thirty articles, the Declaration was to serve "as a common standard of achievement for all peoples and all nations," a yardstick by which to measure decency and human dignity. Since 1948 it continues to be the most significant, the most far-reaching of all UN declarations on behalf of fundamental freedoms and economic and social rights:

—All human beings are born free and equal in dignity and rights . . .

—Everyone is entitled to all the rights and freedoms set forth . . . , without distinction of any kind, such as race, colour, sex, language, religion, political or other opinion, national or social origin, property, birth or other status . . .

—No one shall be held in slavery or servitude . . .

—No one shall be subjected to torture or to cruel, inhuman or degrading treatment or punishment . . .

—All are equal before the law . . .

—No one shall be subjected to arbitrary arrest, detention or exile . . .

—No one shall be subjected to arbitrary interference with privacy, family, home or correspondence, nor to attacks upon honour and reputation . . .

—Everyone has the right to freedom of movement and residence within the borders of each State . . .

—Everyone has the right to leave any country, and to return . . .

For twenty-two articles the Declaration detailed political and civil rights: free assembly, opinion, expression; "the right to seek, receive and impart information and ideas through any media and regardless of frontiers." The right to religion, and to change religion. The right to marriage, and divorce, and the right to be secure and protected within the family unit.

—"The will of the people shall be the basis of the authority of the government," involving free and secret ballots based on equal and universal suffrage.

Articles 23 to 30 detailed the economic and social rights and obligations of the human community to ensure the free and full development of personality

—Everyone has the right to work, to free choice of employment, . . . and to protection against unemployment

—Everyone, without any discrimination has the right to equal pay for equal work . . .

—Everyone has the right to form and to join trade unions

—Everyone has the right to rest and leisure, including periodic holidays with pay

—Everyone has the right to a standard of living adequate for health and well-being including food, clothing, housing, medical care and necessary social services, and the right to security in the event of unemployment, sickness, disability, widowhood, old age . . .

—Motherhood and childhood are entitled to special care and assistance. All children, whether born in or out of wedlock, shall enjoy the same social protection.

—Everyone has the right to education. Education shall be free, at least in the elementary and fundamental stages . . . and higher education shall be equally accessible to all on the basis of merit. . . .

Eleanor believed that the kind of New Deal agencies created within the U.S. to limit and prevent so many of the personal tragedies engendered by the Great Depression might be applied to the needs of the entire post-war world.

To ensure human rights, political and civil rights, economic and social rights, the UN created or strengthened various agencies, and Eleanor championed during her lifetime the work of each one, especially: the United Nations Educational, Scientific and Cultural Organization (UNESCO), the World Health Organization (WHO), the Food and Agriculture Organization (FAO), and the International Labor Organization (ILO).

Shortly after FDR's death on 12 April, 1945, Eleanor dismissed a young woman journalist eager for an interview with the words: "The story is over." But the fact is that Mrs. Roosevelt's public life hardly missed a beat, and in some aspects the story had just begun. Thoroughout the spring of 1945, she wrote daily columns and long letters to President Truman regarding the post-war future and detailed her understanding of what would be needed to achieve peace. Eleanor was disturbed in May 1945 by the signs of emerging bitterness between the wartime allies.

On 10 May, Truman wrote her an eight-page letter:

I noticed in your good column today you expressed some surprise at the Russian attitude on the close of the European War. . . . I think I should explain the situation to you. On Wed April 25th our Minister to Sweden sent a message to me saying that Himmler wanted to surrender to Gen Eisenhower all their troops facing the Western Front and that the Germans would continue to fight the Russians. Before our State Department could get the message deciphered the Prime Minister called me from London and read the message to me. . . . The matter was discussed with our Staff and the offer was very promptly refused. The Russians were notified of our joint action. . . . Negotiations went on for two more days—me, always insisting on complete unconditional surrender on all fronts. The German idea, of course was to split the three great powers and perhaps make things easier for themselves. We were nearly at an agreement and the famous Connolly statement came out and completely upset the applecart. Himmler was displaced by Admiral Doenitz and a new start was made. Germans delayed and delayed, trying all the time to quit only on the Western Front. They finally offered Norway, Denmark, Holland and the French Ports they still held but wanted to keep resisting the Russians. Our Commanding General finally told them that he would turn loose all we had and drive them into the Russians. They finally signed at Rheims the terms of unconditional surrender effective at 12:01 midnight of 8 May.

In the meantime Churchill, Stalin and I had agreed on a simultaneous release at 9 AM Washington time, 3 PM London and 4 PM Moscow time. Then the Associated Press broke faith with Gen Eisenhower. The Germans kept fighting the Russians and Stalin informed me that he had grave doubts of the Germans carrying out the terms. There was fighting on the Eastern front right up to the last hour. In the meantime Churchill was trying to force me to break faith with the Russians and release on the 7th, noon Washington time, 6 PM London, 7 PM Moscow . . .

When Truman released as originally agreed

fighting was still in progress against the Russians. The Germans were finally informed that if they didn't cease firing as agreed they would not be treated as fighting men but as traitors and would be hanged as caught. They then ceased firing and Stalin made his announcement on the 9th.

He had sent me a message stating the situation at 1 AM 8 May and asking for postponement until 9 May. I did not get the message until 10 AM 8 May, too late of course to do anything.

I have been trying very carefully to keep all my engagements with the Russians because they are touchy and suspicious of us. The difficulties with Churchill are very nearly as exasperating as they are with the Russians. But patience I think must be our watch word if we are to have World Peace. To have it we must have the whole-hearted support of Russia, Great Britain and the United States . . .

Eleanor agreed and replied to Truman's letter with her hope that the spirit of FDR's commitment to the Grand Alliance might prevail:

"Your experience with Mr Churchill is not at all surprising. He is suspicious of the Russians and they know it. If you will remember, he said some pretty rough things about them years ago and they do not forget." (According to Winston Churchill's cousin Clare Sheridan, he so despised the Bolsheviks that, by 1923, he was talked of as the likely leader of a fascist party in England. During the 1920s, Churchill considered fascism the shadow of Bolshevism, and said he would rather be ruled by fascist violence than Bolshevik violence.)

"Of course," ER continued, "we will have to be patient, and any lasting peace will have to have the Three Great Powers behind it." She suggested that Truman "get on a personal basis" with Churchill: "If you talk to him about books and let him quote to you from his marvelous memory everything on earth from Barbara Fritchie to the Nonsense Rhymes and Greek tragedy, you will find him easier to deal with on political subjects. He is a gentleman to whom the personal element means a great deal." She also had practical advice on how Truman might approach the Russians. It was an area in which she considered Churchill unimaginative. He did

not have the same kind of sense of humor that the Russians have. In some ways the Russians are more like us. They enjoy a practical joke, rough-housing and play and they will joke about things which Mr Churchill thinks are sacred. He takes them dead seriously and argues about them when what he ought to do is to laugh. That was where Franklin usually won out because if you know where to laugh and when to look upon things as too absurd to take seriously, the other person is ashamed to carry through even if he was serious about it.

You are quite right in believing that the Russians will watch with great care to see how we keep our commitments . . .

Eleanor never lost her capacity to deal with Russians personally, although she became increasingly dismayed by many of their policies. Their opposition to the fundamental political rights she held sacred, such as the freedom to emigrate and to dissent, was especially abhorrent. But she considered such issues part of a long-range battle to be fought collectively, at the United Nations, and mediated by world public opinion as well as changing needs and abilities. They were the critical issues of a peaceable future. They required debate, vision, economic aid, and widespread public activity on all levels. Distrust, hate, mean-spirited propaganda would render that long-range effort impossible, and could lead to war. ER was above all concerned about the pressures on Truman to disavow the alliance, and to abandon the real efforts required if a peaceful future was to be achieved.

She wrote Truman:

A rumor has reached me that that message from Mr Stalin to you was really reached in plenty of time to have changed the hour but it was held back from you. Those little things were done to my husband now and then. I tell you of this rumor simply because while you may have known about it and decided that it was wise just not to receive it in time, you told me in your letter that you did not receive it and I have known of things which just did not reach my husband in time. That is one of the things which your Military and Naval aides ought to watch very carefully.[8]

ER had replied to Truman's long letter that she "was very much touched" that he had taken "the trouble to write" in longhand, and suggested in the future that he have his letters typed "because I feel guilty to take any of your time." But Truman continued to write in longhand, and to request her advice. ER remained for Truman the First Lady, and he carefully considered her words. On 1 September, 1945, he wrote: "I have just returned to the White House study. . . . The first thing I always do is . . . read the editorial page and your column. Today you've really 'hit the jack pot'—if I may say that to the First Lady. I am asking one of my good Senatorial friends to put it in the Congressional Record . . . for the sake of history."

On 20 November, 1945, she wrote a long letter of opinion to Truman on a variety of troubling issues: she was convinced "that we have an obligation first of all, to solve our own problems at home," since all of our own failures would impact on the rest of the world. America's post-war leadership position was not to be wasted or abused. She hoped that all post-war planning would be fair to labor and business interests alike; and would take into account the U.S.' growing responsibilities in the world. She wanted her trusted friend Bernard Baruch, for example, to be involved in the "survey of our resources"—upon which we were expected to "base not only our national economy, but what we lend other nations." We know today that what was to become the Paley Report, "Resources for Freedom" (June 1952), correctly gave ER cause for anxiety. ("The US must reject self-sufficiency . . . and instead adopt the policy of the lowest priced acquisition of materials wherever secure supplies may be found.")[9]

The issues were complex, and in 1945 ER wanted people she trusted to be involved in the investigation and analyses. Also, she did not approve of Truman's lending policies:

It seems to me that we should lend other nations equally. If we lend only to Great Britain, we enter into an economic alliance against other nations, and our hope for the future lies in joint cooperation. . . .

I am very much distressed that Great Britain has made us take a share in another investigation of the few Jews remaining in Europe. If they are not to be allowed to enter Palestine, then certainly they could have been apportioned among the different United Nations and we would not have to continue to have on our consciences, the death of at least fifty of these poor creatures daily.

The question between Palestine and the Arabs, of course, has always been complicated by the oil deposits, and I suppose it always will. . . .

Great Britain is always anxious to have some one pull her chestnuts out of the fire, and though I am very fond of the British individually and like a great many of them, I object very much to being used by them. . . .

Lastly, I am deeply troubled about China. Unless we can stop the civil war there by moral pressure and not by the use of military force, and insist that Generalissimo Chiang give wider representation to all Chinese groups . . . I am very much afraid that continued war there may lead us to general war again.

Being a strong nation and having the greatest physical, mental and spiritual strength today, gives us a tremendous responsibility. We can not use our strength to coerce, but if we are big enough, I think we can lead.

That would require, she concluded, "great vision and understanding," and "first and foremost . . . the setting of our own house in order."

After Truman appointed ER to the first meeting of the General Assembly of the United Nations in London in December 1945, she addressed every major issue that remains before us today: the violence of apartheid in South Africa; the economic needs and complexities of a post-colonial world; full employment; food for peace; economic security; disarmament; the quality of life in a peaceable world. She wrote at length, she spoke with vigor, and she introduced specific programs and procedures for real change. Her ideas were bold and her vision was clear. She was forthright and unafraid. Although she too became embroiled in the Cold War tides that swamped U.S. politics, she clung to the outer shores of liberal decency, and remained open to new information, new ideas that might change her mind—enlarge her position.

Before leaving for London, ER requested suggestions from her friends and allies, from organizations she had depended upon for information and advice for decades. Carrie Chapman Catt wrote that as far as she was concerned the women wanted peace:

War must be abolished. During the last two thousand years nearly every war has developed new and more destructive weapons than have existed before. . . . It has destroyed more property, devastated more territory, set adrift a larger army of orphans and misplaced persons. It has wrecked more of the institutions designed to aid human progress, such as churches, libraries, universities, museums, and each war has cost more than its predecessor. The cost of the war just closed, for the first time, will be counted in trillions.

Since wars have thus increased their wickedness and destruction, it is clear that the first and greatest problem for consideration at any international conference is the determination to abolish war. . . . No nation which calls itself civilized should consider the question of the abolishing of war debatable. War is not civilized, nor can any nation hereafter be considered civilized if it intentionally contributes to the continuation of war . . . [10]

Vera Whitehouse, chair of the Women's Action Committee for Victory and Lasting Peace, an umbrella organization in which ER had been active and which involved many of her closest friends, was more specific: ER should work to create UNESCO, the incorporation of newly acquired strategic bases into the UN's trusteeship system, effective machinery for the development of international trade, control of atomic energy by the UNO, and acceptance by the U.S. of compulsory jurisdiction of the International Court of Justice.

Walter White and W.E.B. Dubois sent ER a specific list of "desires of American Negroes" in "response to your request":

1. The placing of all colonies mandated after WWI under UNO trusteeship and the development of immediate means of preparing these colonies for self-government and independence.

2. A world-wide and sincere campaign to abolish the entire colonial system as one of the chief causes of war, poverty and disease.

3. A world campaign of education for the uneducated colonial and other peoples.

4. A world campaign to utilize all the resources of science, government and philanthropy to abolish poverty for all people in our time.

5. Denial to the Union of South Africa to annex former German Southwest Africa because the South African treatment of native peoples is undemocratic and uncivilized.

6. The restoration of Eritrea and Somaliland to Ethiopia and the withdrawal of British troops.

7. Freedom and independence for Indonesia, India, Burma, IndoChina and Siam.

8. Democracy for China.

9. Withdrawal of recognition of Franco's Spain.

Esther Lape, director of the American Foundation that coordinated Edward Bok's American Peace Prize in 1923, and ER's first feminist friend and political adviser sent ER a list of very practical concerns:

1. In the League of Nations, the really important questions, the economic questions, were never really faced or discussed in the Assembly or the Council. They were shunted off to "Committees," from which they never came into active and general debate or into any arena in which DECISIONS are made. The League is a very good

example of the old army game of reserving controversial subjects for "study" by appropriate committees. As you know the sessions of the Assembly were completely dead. . . .

The important thing about the UNO will be WHO MAKES THE AGENDA. . . . An international debating society is SOME good; but not much. It won't avert wars.

2. Many of the questions upon which international agreements and treaties are most needed are questions that will require antecedent legislations by the individual nations. How for instance could the USA be a party to an international covenant on citizenship until we had decided whether we are going to continue to exclude Chinese and Japanese? How could we be a party to international agreements regarding refugees so long as we keep our immigration quota system . . . which is really an incorporation of racial discrimination. How could we be a party to international agreements designed to make the raw materials of the earth more equitably available (and this is one of the promises of the Atlantic Charter) unless we are prepared to transfer to an international economic and scientific and allocating body the resources we now hold under strong national possessive control.

On the other hand, Lape concluded, national legislation would be forthcoming if and when international agreements required them, especially concerning "raw materials, trade routes and policies, citizenship, immigration (which can no longer be a purely national question)." Moreover, the economic issues were the key, she wrote. It is not so much "what authority is to handle the atomic bomb" as

how do we handle the economic questions that produce the wars of which the atomic bomb is a final form. It is still the CAUSES of wars that are our major problem, not the ways of fighting. . . . We all know well that the causes of wars are oil, farm products, over-population, the need of Hinterlands, the need of a "place in the sun," etc.

Above all the UNO must address itself to the causes—not in the course of generations, but NOW.

All the old guff will be brought forward to make the approach indirect rather than direct—all the old saws about . . . surveying the problems, about committees for study. . . . Our politicians—and they are dominant in the UNO—know very well that, for instance, an international proposal to allocate raw materials by scientific determination and international agreement to abide by it is a much bigger and a much tougher question than the atomic bomb. So the atomic bomb will certainly be dragged out in front of the other tougher problem.

But the delegates could prevent this. They should make the agenda. . . . I hope all of your magnificent courage will be expended in this direction. Even with the rest of the set up (Connally, etc. and Byrnes) you might prevail. . . . [11]

World leadership meant a great deal to ER. She had a powerful sense of mission and responsibility. As she regarded war-torn Europe, the combined legacies of depression and holocaust, she believed in some variation on the theme of an American Century. But is was not Henry Luce's century—for business expansion and America first. It was a democratic future that recognized the global connectedness of the world's people and the world's resources. She wanted the U.S. to take the lead in a great campaign for planetary decency and peace, and to enable through progressive and supportive economic conditions the United Nations, with all its diversity and despite all the difficulties, to negotiate fairly the direction and priorities of a united world future.

President Truman's decision to appoint ER to the United States delegation to the UN gave her an opportunity to fight for her vision of the future from an official position of leadership for over six years. She considered her appointment to the UN a great victory for women, and a great opportunity. She took every conflict and every decision seriously. She lobbied and cajoled; she compromised and fought. She was an earnest diplomat who frequently succeeded. When she lost, she returned fighting. Convinced that pessimism was politically incorrect, she never gave up.

ER lent considerable dash to the United States's bipartisan and rather ordinary first UN team. Former Secretary of State Edward Stettinius was designated principal representative to the UNO Security Council. Senator Tom Connally (D-Texas), chair of the Foreign Relations Committee, Senator Arthur Vandenberg (R-Michigan), and Secretary of State James Byrnes were joined by five alternates: John Foster Dulles (an international lawyer, who had been at Versailles with Wilson, and served as an adviser to the drafting conference for the UN Charter at San Francisco in April 1945); Representative Sol Bloom (D-NY), chair of the House Foreign Affairs Committee; Rep Charles Eaton (R-NJ); former Postmaster General Frank Walker; former Senator John Townsend, chair of the Republican Senatorial Campaign Committee.[12]

Unused to having a woman participate in a decision-making capacity on important international issues, ER's colleagues treated her with a crude kind of misogyny. She was regarded as an interloper. But she was insistent, and she would not be ignored. The world's press was more interested in her views than in any of her colleagues'. Day after day, in paper after paper her words were sought, and quoted. And then there was the fact of her own daily column, her own radio programs, and all the hours, on a regular basis, she gave to other people's radio programs, as well as the Voice of America. She was a political pro. She understood the game, the political game as well as the game of nations, and she played with rare energy and concerted vigor.

The old boy's ploy of listening politely to the lone woman in the room, and then moving on—never addressing her words, however apt or significant, would not work. ER repeated her words, patiently, frequently, until they were acknowledged. Undoubtedly it drove Dulles wild. Even in the official publication of State Department papers, FOREIGN RELATIONS OF THE US, when references to ER are made, a tone of lofty condescension creeps into the otherwise colorless reports of committee meetings. Her voice is reported to have been shrill; she was strident; or school-marmish.

Eleanor was not, however, overly impressed with her colleagues. They were self-involved, legalistic, and wordy beyond belief. They strutted and preened

and were frequently careless about the sensibilities of other countries. She was
frankly surprised at how undiplomatic some of the diplomats could be. Moreover,
they seemed to her without serious convictions and in many ways thoughtless:
"I like the Vandenbergs more than I do the Connallys but I don't like any of
them much." She was somewhat appalled at Senator Connally's initial response
to England during the drive up to London: He "kept repeating: 'Where is all
this destruction I've heard so much about, things look all right to me.' I started
to point out bombed spots but soon found he just wasn't interested."

ER at first found Vandenberg "difficult." He made no effort to achieve any
coordinated position, and she objected to his having private press conferences.
Even when she agreed with some of his views, she found his behavior "pretty
shoddy." Subsequently, she noted: "Vandenberg's position is funny and I am
interested in the way all the legislators react. I think not having strong convictions
they doubt their ability to defend a position which they may take so they can
not decide on any position and go on arguing the pros and cons endlessly."[13]

ER was pleased that Trygve Lie was elected Secretary General of the Security
Council. He was a compromise candidate, that the U.S. and the USSR could
agree upon. "The papers should not be pessimistic," she wrote her friends and
family, "progress is being made here. Vandenburg and Dulles are largely responsible for pessimism, I think. These representatives of ours don't build friendship for us. They have no confidence so they are rude and arrogant and create
suspicion. Honesty with friendliness [is needed] but they haven't the technique.
Jimmy Byrnes' overcordiality isn't right either. Why can't we be natural and
feel right inside and just let it come out?"

Altogether, ER watched the U.S. delegation "with great concern." Secretary
of State Byrnes "seems to me to be afraid to decide on what he thinks is right
and stand on it. I am going to try to tell him tactfully that everyone has to get
the things they need from us and that is our ace in the hole. We could lead but
we don't." We "conciliate and trail either Britain or Russia and at times I am
sure a feeling that we had convictions and would fight for them would be
reassuring to them. Secretary Byrnes is afraid of his own delegation. He has
held very few meetings and now we begin to need them and yet we have to ask
to see him in separate groups. It isn't that he is leaving me out, for the others
complain to me."[14]

ER considered Sol Bloom an asset, and he gave an important speech to the
UN Relief and Rehabilitation Administration: "Everyone agreed with Sol Bloom
and patted him on the back and he was as pleased as a little boy and [sailed for
home] feeling a hero. I think he felt kindly toward me though he hated not being
a full delegate. He is able but so many foibles! All these important men have
them, however. I'm so glad I never FEEL important, it does complicate life!"[15]

ER was more impressed with the State Department staff and ancillary U.S.
personnel—Alger Hiss, Dr. Ralph Bunche, Adlai Stevenson, Ben Cohen, and
Durward Sandifer. She understood that they had influence and a sense of re-

sponsibility, and tended to talk with them at length: "I said many things which I hope go back to the Secretary and the President."

ER was not at all "convinced that Great Britain and ourselves must line up to keep the Russians in hand. I think we must be fair and stand for what we believe is right and let them, either or both, side with us. We have had that leadership and we must recapture it."[16]

ER took her work seriously, and worked a long and exhausting day. On 31 January she wrote: "Yesterday was the usual pattern. 9:30 delegates meeting; at office, 10:30 committee meeting. Ate and dictated column, saw a doctor on national health organization, went to BBC and did two recordings, 1 for Infantile [Paralysis] and one for American Broadcasting program. Had tea for a Swedish woman and a Jewish refugee; went to Port of London Authority tea and Turkish Embassy. Frieda Miller dined with me and I had all the women delegates here in my room." Occasionally when morning meetings were canceled, she enjoyed an extra hour to read or write her column in the quiet of her room: "No delegates meeting" early this morning "because the boys couldn't agree" last night, "thank goodness!"[17]

ER considered the London meetings a remarkable learning experience. "It is a liberal education in background and personalities." Above all, she learned how differences in background and experience affect perception: "Since the Civil War we have no political or religious refugees fleeing our country and we forget to take it into account. No European or South American forgets it for a minute." Noting Russia's recent history of revolution and counterrevolution, and the Allied intervention of Russia in the 1920s, ER wrote that it seemed that only "years of stability" allowed "you to look beyond your own situation and consider that there are human rights that operate for those who think in a way that you think wrong!" But ER was also aware of the United States's failures concerning human rights. In December she had sent Truman information regarding the dreadful camp conditions among the Japanese-Americans on the west coast. Truman forwarded her letter to the attorney general for action, and wrote: "This disgraceful conduct almost makes you believe that a lot of our Americans have a streak of Nazi in them."[18]

At the UN ER was reminded that she had always enjoyed a good fight, and that she was good at it. "We defeated the Russians on the three points we disagreed on, they were all fundamental." She was brief and "clear in my opposition. Wise Mr Sandifer of the State Department seemed pleased but whispered, 'The Russians won't like that.' "[19]

ER's early victories against the Russians concerned the status of refugees about whom she cared deeply. She had been assigned to Committee Three, the social, humanitarian and cultural committee. It was in the beginning perceived as the domestic sphere of the UN, an appropriate place for a woman, and not especially important.

ER's colleagues were appointed to oversee the tougher, the "stickiest" tasks:

John Foster Dulles sat on the trusteeship committee, which negotiated the future of League-mandated territories, and such controversial new trust territories as the U.S.-claimed Pacific areas like the Caroline and Marshall islands, which were taken over as military bases. Particularly explosive issues such as South Africa's refusal even to provide information regarding conditions in its "non-self-governing" territories were to remain bitterly divisive issues, about which Dulles seemed unconcerned. During briefing sessions when all the representatives reported on their committees, ER frequently protested Dulles's calm. ER "was not very optimistic" about South Africa. In Committee 3, the Union of South Africa "made it very clear that it believed a government had the right to discriminate in any way against any part of its population." But still she "wondered why we should stand against something that will improve the colonies," whether South African or British. Indeed, she noted, there were dreadful conditions in "places where the UK had been for a hundred years" and she "couldn't help wondering what the UK had been doing there for a hundred years. She did not see anything improper, looking at it as a man in the street." But Dulles explained all the U.S. could do was to look at it from a legal point of view, and "there was only one word for the Assembly to use, the word 'recommend.' " Although ER's moral outrage frequently got nowhere in meetings of the U.S. delegation, she never failed to take her perceptions to the public.[20]

Vandenberg was appointed to the administrative and budgetary committee; Connally was named to the political and security committee, which would be involved with such political issues as the status of the Levant, and Soviet claims in Turkey, as well as such security issues as the control of atomic energy; Bloom was appointed to the economic and financial committee; and Walker to the legal committee.[21]

But ER's committee quickly became one of the most controversial and significant. It was concerned with all issues relating to human rights, fundamental freedoms, social progress and world development. It was also the committee that witnessed the first substantial confrontation between the contradictory visions of the U.S. and the USSR, especially relating to refugees. Her chief opponent on the issue was the formidable Andrei Vishinsky, Stalin's chief prosecutor in the Moscow purge trials. The Russians accused Western propagandists of fermenting fear and hatred in the DP camps, by discouraging Central European refugees from returning to their homelands. The Russians claimed that those who refused to return were quislings, traitors or fascists.

ER was outraged at the accusation, denied that these were unsubstantial propaganda issues, and called for the universal recognition of the rights of political asylum and freedom of movement. Although she was victorious, and the General Assembly voted for the right of refugees to choose their destination, her moral outrage and political rectitude was somewhat wilted by the fact that no western country—including Canada or the U.S., for example, welcomed the refugees, and Britain prohibited additional Jews from going to Palestine. The fight at the UN continued for years, while the refugees languished in camps.

ER's firm and extemporaneous capacity to debate and best the Soviets impressed even her Republican colleagues. Dulles told her frankly that he had been appalled by her appointment, and wanted now to acknowledge that her "work had been fine." ER noted in her diary: "So—against odds, the women move forward, but I'm rather old to be carrying on this fight!"

She left London optimistic about the future of the UN. The greatest accomplishment of its first session, she wrote, was "that at the end we still are a group of 51 nations working together." Unlike the League of Nations, the U.S. was in the UN, and from the beginning Republicans and Democrats actively participated. Over the years ER fought virulent U.S. opposition to the UN. In June 1947 she criticized "the unfortunate and irresponsible pessimism" of those who compared the UN to the old League and harmed the cause of international cooperation. She called for an active peace movement energized by "the enthusiasm and optimism of young people to build the UN into a truly great organization."[22]

ER had great faith in the importance of personal diplomacy. Face-to-face contacts mattered:

At the Assembly sessions, our delegation is seated next to the Russians. On the first day I was delighted to find that next to me was V. V. Kuznetsov, president of the All-Union Council of Trade unions of the USSR. He greeted me in a most friendly fashion, and I remembered that he had come to my apartment in NY one afternoon to interpret for a group of Russian women who were part of a workers' delegation sent over from Russia to visit some of our factories. It's funny how a little opportunity like this of seeing someone in your own home, even for a little while, makes you feel much more friendly.

And despite her debates with Vishinsky they remained on entirely cordial terms. ER had also met Ambassador Andrei Gromyko in Washington. Now, during these meetings she "had the pleasure of sitting next to him at lunch. All these little contacts do develop better understanding," she concluded.[23]

But ER realized that it was in the institutional processes that the future peace would be secured. And ER was particularly gratified that fifteen "well distributed" judges were elected to the International Court of Justice, representing the U.S., the UK, Russia, France, China, Belgium, Norway, Yugoslavia, Poland, Egypt, Canada, Mexico, Chile, and El Salvador. ER, who had worked so hard to secure U.S. adherence to the World Court, was particularly pleased with the willingness of these nations in 1945 to deal seriously with the hardest political questions: Russia's interest in Iran, and Britain's military presence in Greece, for example. If that spirit of cooperation could be maintained, ER concluded, the UN would become "a real instrument for peace."

She was also pleased that the UNO decided to place the permanent headquarters in the U.S. There had been some discussion of choosing Hyde Park as the site of the UN, which ER favored but the Republicans rejected. Whatever the site, she was delighted that the U.S. was selected: "Since European nations are more international-minded, they are not apt to forget that peace requires as much attention as war. But the US, because of its early isolation, has lived in what many might call a fools' paradise.'' ER believed that the American public would be more responsive to the UN if it were in the U.S., and that would ''insure, as nothing else would, the active, whole-hearted support of our people for this effort, which is the last and best hope for our civilization.''

After the completion of the first session of the UNO, ER toured the devastated continent. She wrote in *My Day* that she dreaded the journey knowing that the tragic sights of the holocaust would ''fill our souls . . . But sorrow which leads to constructive work and a determination to keep from repeating our mistakes is good for us. It should strengthen us for the battle that must come in these next few years—the battle for peace. And we must pray for victory no less sincerely than we did in time of war.''

In Germany, ER visited two camps for displaced persons. At Zellsheim, a camp for Jewish DPs, she answered their greetings ''from an aching heart'' and wondered: ''When will our consciences grow so tender that we will act prevent human misery rather than avenge it?'' She talked with a man who told her that his entire family had been ''made into soap''; and she met a young boy of ten who looked six, who ''had wandered into camp one day with his brother, so he was the head of his family'' and ''the camp singer.''

He sang for me—a song of his people—a song of freedom. Your heart cried out that there was no freedom—and where was hope, without which human beings cannot live?

There is a feeling of desperation and sorrow in this camp which seems beyond expression. An old woman knelt on the ground grasping my knees. I lifted her up, but could not speak. What could one say in the end of a life which had brought her such complete despair?

From Zellsheim ER went to Wiesbaden and visited a camp of Poles and Balts. ''These are refugees who, because of political differences with their present governments cannot see their way to return to their own countries, and yet they fought against the Nazis, and many of them spent long years in concentration or forced labor camps.'' The political complexities of these political refugees as well as the Jewish refugees would haunt the early years of the UN. Few countries would accept them, and Russia insisted they be returned to their countries of origin. For years the debate went on as the refugees continued to weaken and die or subsisted in the most vile and wretched camp conditions. ER asked in 1946: What is the ''ultimate answer?'' The UNO created a commission within the Economic and Social Council to study the problem, and she predicted it ''will tear at their hearts.'' She approved of the study, and had recommended all due speed. But it was a dreary and protracted process, complicated by disagreements over Palestine, political distrust, and pervasive bigotry.

On her return to Frankfurt ER met with German journalists who asked her if she thought ''the whole German nation was responsible.'' ''I answered what to me seems obvious. All the people of Germany have to accept responsibility for having tolerated a leadership which first brought such misery to groups of people within their own nation, and later created world chaos.''[24]

As chair of the Human Rights Commission from 1946 to 1952, ER was to be continually involved with the needs and the future of refugees, with a global society that created displaced persons through cruel neglect and a persistent refusal to deal honorably or humanely with its own citizens, whether dissenters or religious and racial minorities. But her efforts on behalf of the Declaration of Human Rights laid the unfinished ethical agenda of our time before the world.

The Declaration was a compromise. Every word was an agony of disagreement. In the end it represented the world's best hope. At first ER was instructed to limit the principles to civil and political rights. This she refused to do. And the woman who always advised her friends: if you have to compromise—compromise up, succeeded in persuading her delegation, as well as Truman and Secretary of State Marshall, of the importance of including the Soviet-originated demands for economic and social rights. ER understood the need for an all-embracing document: ''You can't talk civil rights to people who are hungry.'' Moreover, the New Deal had promised freedom from want as well as freeedom from fear. ER believed in the connectedness of the economic and civil, political and social, aspects of human rights.

After endless meetings, each one of them arduous and full of rancor, frequently lasting twelve to sixteen hours a day, Committee 3 presented the Universal Declaration of Human Rights to the General Assembly meeting in Paris in September 1948. Then the Soviets insisted it be taken up again page by page, article by article, ''exactly as though it was all an entirely new idea and nobody had ever looked at it before.''

Finally, after eighty-five meetings at 3 AM on 10 December, the UN General Assembly approved the Declaration. The vote was 48 in favor, 2 absent, 8 abstentions—Russia and its allies, Saudi Arabia, and South Africa. ER was pleased that the Soviets did not vote against it, a testimony in fact to her remarkable personal diplomacy. The Assembly gave her an unprecedented standing ovation. And from that day to this the Declaration stands as a beacon—to stir our imaginations, and prod us on. ER considered it a ''first step,'' and she went to work to negotiate two enabling convenants.[25]

But in 1952 Eisenhower accepted her resignation with cold alacrity and Dulles ended the United States's leadership role in the effort to achieve human rights. The fact is that Dulles never supported Human Rights except as a propaganda ploy. So long as the Soviets opposed Human Rights it served U.S. interests to support the concept. But he never wanted anything binding, and any hint of legal obligation sent him into a frenzy of moral confusion. In September 1948 Dulles wanted to be assured that the Delcaration entailed no ''new obligations, other than those already in the [UN] Charter.'' Persuaded there were none, according to the legal experts of both the State Department and the attorney general's office, Dulles still protested the language. He read from the document: " 'Everyone has the right of access to public employment,' " and then protested that he "had to sign a declaration that he was not a Communist at the time of his appointment to the Delegation." He hoped these words did not mean the U.S. had now to hire communists. Again he was assured that it meant nothing, beyond a declaration of princple, much as the U.S. Declaration of Independence was a declaration of principle.[26]

Just as slavery mocked the U.S. Declaration of Independence, so did U.S. racism and the coils of the Cold War mock the Declaration of Human Rights. Throughout the 1950s Eisenhower's "Southern strategy" prevented any serious advance in the field of human rights. In April 1953 Dulles told the Senate that the State Department no longer cared to ratify the civil and political covenant, or the economic and social covenant. The Department was disinterested in the genocide convention and intended to take no part in the effort to secure a UN treaty on the rights of women. Sandifer told ER that the United States' human rights position at the UN was now limited to: "reports and studies on the status of such human rights issues as slavery; and the creation of an advisory service which would fund seminars and fellowships on human rights." ER replied: "You will excuse me if I thing these [efforts] are really comic."

After ER's official tour of duty at the UN ended, she walked across First Avenue and offered her time and energy to the American Association of the United Nations. From 1953 to 1962 she traveled around this country and around the world with her message of peace and human rights. She went door to door, town by town insisting that the fight for a global standard of human rights, the intrusion of morality and decency into the international arena, was in full swing. ER understood that it would take as much energy and vision, as much money and dedication to win a war for human rights as it took to win any other war. She said so repeatedly. She wrote column after column detailing the needs. In 1958, she wrote:

Where, after all, do universal human rights begin? In small places, close to home— so close and so small that they cannot be seen on any maps of the world. Yet they ARE the world of the individual persons; the neighborhood . . . ; the school or college . . . ; the factory, farm or office . . . Such are the places where every man, woman and child seeks equal justice, equal opportunity, equal diginity without discrimination. Unless these rights have meaning there, they have little meaning anywhere. Without concerned citizen action to uphold them close to home, we shall look in vain for progress in the larger world.

ER's crusade for a future defined by the Declaration of Human Rights was complicated by a lack of support from the U.S. government and by her ever-growing distrust of the Soviet Union. But these conflicting tensions were regulated by a still more overriding concern, the urgent need for arms control and disarmament.

The day the atomic bomb was dropped, she said in October 1945, "we came into a new world—a world in which we had to learn to live in friendship with our neighbors of every race and creed and color, or face the fact that we might be wiped off the face of the earth.'' The escalating Cold War did not alter this nuclear imperative: "Either we do have friendly relations, or we do away with civilization.'' ER was adamant: "We must wake up to the fact that what we really want to do, we can do.''

Errors were made by all sides. She was robustly and routinely critical of them all. She opposed the Truman Doctrine, unilateral intervention, the substitution of military aid for economic aid, and the United States's growing militarism and neocolonialism. She was concerned about food, population, and resources. She predicted that the U.S. would continue to lose influence to the Soviet Union unless it ended racial injustice, changed its food and scarcity policies, and converted to the kind of food-first policy we now associate with Frances Moore Lappe and Joseph Collins' Global Food Institute, and the North-South discussions on resources.

ER believed that the U.S. had to reexamine the repair of its own house. In 1950 she wrote that "our great struggle today is to prove to the world that democracy has more to offer than communism.'' But it cannot do that with bigotry, segregation, unemployment. The U.S. could not have it both ways: world leadership and domestic sloth; the verbiage of liberty without the contents of human contentment. She challenged public opinion to organize, to show what it could do: "We have to develop a courage and a staunchness that perhaps we have never had.'' Civil rights was no longer a "domestic question. . . . It is perhaps the question which may decide whether democracy or communism wins out in the world.'' And there were other factors, imperative economic factors: "We cannot be complacent about unemployment . . . , about injustices.'' And we have to be able to talk with each other and disagree, and learn and contemplate new ideas.[27]

ER opposed the arms race and she oposed the diplomatic losses to commumism each time the U.S. supported an unpopular dictator in the name of anticommunism. Competition between the U.S. and the USSR was, she pointed out, increasingly economic and political. She called for arms control, economic cooperation, world order. In the wake of the failed invasion of Cuba at the Bay of Pigs, she wrote of the popular support for Fidel Castro's government and insisted that Americans must understand the need to end economic exploitation. She opposed the growing U.S. reliance on covert CIA activities and warned against unilateral involvement in Vietnam, urging again that all such conflicts be referred to the United Nations.

On 5 November, 1961, she endorsed the American Friends Service Committee's delcaration of conscience opposing "the present drift toward war.'' In a column "Turn Toward Peace,'' ER affirmed her conviction that "freedom and democracy could not survive nuclear war'' and called for a popular movement that would lead to disarmament. Without explanation, in this same column, she dismissed as "meaningless and ineffective" the idea to organize a "Women's strike for peace."

Human rights was defeated for almost two decades by the contradictory tides of global schism that divided the world between "east" and "west" and within the U.S. condemned all efforts on behalf of international peace and human rights, especially economic and social rights, as suspicious if not overtly communistic. It is important to recall that ER seemed to the right wing of the 1950s a very wild woman. She was a feminist and a unionist, and she promoted civil rights. To the extent that she was a Cold Warrior, she was a moderate anti-McCarthy Cold Warrior. But during the 1950s that was not enough. McCarthyite attacks on New Dealers and Truman's Fair Dealers, on "phoney egg-sucking liberals, Commicrats and Queers" were frequently aimed directly at Eleanor. Even President Eisenhower, who privately opposed McCarthy, publicly mocked ER and noted in 1954 that opposition to the UN's Human Rights agreement was an effort "to save the US from Eleanor Roosevelt."

But the post-war world, as it began to unravel from its colonial grip, had another agenda and at the UN, among the many new nations, the idea of human rights would with each passing year gain in spirit and support. Long before most of America's leadership appreciated the changing needs of this planet, ER did. During the last weeks of her life, in September 1962, she wrote a column that remains today the primary challenge of our time:

It has always seemed to me that we never present our case to the smaller nations in either a persuasive or interesting way. I think most people will acknowledge . . . that we have given far more military aid to these nations than economic aid. It is not very pleasant to palm off this military equipment on people who really are not looking for it. The fiction is that they are being given military aid so that they will be better able to cope with any Communist attack. But all the nations where we do this know quite well that it is pure fiction and nothing else. Practically none of them could withstand a really determined Soviet attack.

In view of this, why don't we offer them something they really want? For one thing, most of them would like food. Many of them, as they watch the development of the bigger nations, want to establish the beginnings of industry. But they know that wider training of their people is essential . . . and hence a primary need is aid to their education system. . . . [28]

Until her death on 7 November, 1962, ER was committed to a liberal vision, and to hope. In *Tomorrow Is Now*, her last book, published posthumously in 1963, she looked to the future with positive optimism. "I am not afraid of 1984." With "proper education . . . a strong sense of responsibility for our own actions, with a clear awareness that our future is linked with the welfare of the world as a whole, we may justly anticipate that the life of the next generation will be richer, more peaceful, more rewarding than any we have ever known." But for the future, she concluded, the U.S. needed to resurrect with conviction and daring the good American word LIBERAL, "which derives from the word FREE . . . We must cherish and honor the word FREE or it will cease to apply to us."

Eleanor Roosevelt's international journey reflects the full range of the complex tides of the twentieth century. Committed to improving the quality of life, she made the noblest values seem globally achievable. She believed particularly in the power of ideas to transform society. In *Tomorrow Is Now*, she wrote that social change required that ideas be faced with imagination, integrity, and courage. That was how she lived her life and pursued the complexities of the most controversial issues of state, none of which have become any less controversial. Ultimately, she embodied her own creed: "The influence you exert is through your own life, and what you've become yourself."

NOTES

To reassess Eleanor Roosevelt's commitment to the UN and to human rights is first of all to reclaim her contribution. It is distressing how rarely in the diplomatic histories, the textbooks and analyses of U.S. foreign relations she is credited. It is even more distressing that in the UN's most recent overview, *The United Nations and Human Rights* (1984, UN #E.84.I.6), ER's name simply does not appear. The men are credited. They are named and their work emphasized. But while ER's work might be detailed, her name has been erased.

1. All correspondence and information concerning the Bok Peace Prize is in the Esther Lape Papers, Franklin D. Roosevelt Library (FDRL). See also Esther Lape's collection of the twenty most interesting entries, *Ways to Peace* (Scribner's, 1924); and The *New York Times*, 21, 22, 24, 25 January, 1924.

2. Ibid.

3. Ibid.

4. The *New York Times*, 25 January, 1927.

5. Ibid., 15 October, 1927; 8 December 1927; 2 November, 1929.

6. ER's NBC radio address, 27 January, 1935; her defense of FDR's inactivity, ER to Mrs. Kendall Emerson, 12 February, 1935; see especially Gilbert N. Kahn, "Presidential Passivity on a Nonsalient Issue: President Franklin D. Roosevelt and the 1935 World Court Fight," *Diplomatic History* (Spring 1984), pp. 137 ff. See also Joseph P. Lash, *Eleanor and Franklin*, chapter 46.

7. Judge Justine Wise Polier, Interview, Eleanor Roosevelt Oral History Project, FDRL. All ER correspondence, Eleanor Roosevelt Papers, FDRL.

8. Eleanor Roosevelt to Harry S. Truman correspondence, May 1945, Eleanor Roosevelt Papers, Box 4560.

9. For a discussion of the Paley Report and its impact on U.S. foreign economic policy, see B. W. Cook, *The Declassified Eisenhower* (Penguin, 1984).

10. Catt to Eleanor Roosevelt, 28 December, 1945, Eleanor Roosevelt Papers, Box 4561.

11. Lape to Eleanor Roosevelt, n.d., December 1945, Eleanor Roosevelt Papers, Box 4562.

12. The *New York Times*, 20 December, 1945.

13. Eleanor Roosevelt's London Diary, 2, 6, 7, 27 January, 1946.

14. Ibid., 16 January.

15. Ibid., 2 February.

16. Ibid., 27, 29, January.

17. Ibid., 6 February.

18. Harry S. Truman to Eleanor Roosevelt, 21 December, 1945, Eleanor Roosevelt Papers, Box 4560.

19. Eleanor Roosevelt, London Diary, 6, 8 February.

20. *Foreign Relations of the United States*, I, 1947, pp. 304 ff; I, 1948, pp. 278–79.

21. The *New York Times*, 8 January, 1946.

22. Ibid., 18 June, 1947.

23. Eleanor Roosevelt, *My Day*, 11, 13 February, 1946.

24. *My Day*, 16 February, 1946; ER's statement on refugees, Committee 3, 28 January, 1946.

25. See Joseph P. Lash, *Eleanor: The Years Alone* (W. W. Norton, 1972), Chapter 3.

26. FRUS, 1948, pp. 290 f.

27. Eleanor Roosevelt, *Congressional Record*, 19 April, 1950, A2802.

28. *My Day*, 14 September, 1962.

6

Joining the Boys' Club: The Diplomatic Career of Eleanor Lansing Dulles

Lynne K. Dunn

Eleanor's talents...include constructive and very concrete qualities. Among all the bureaucratic paper-shufflers I have worked with, she is among the very few who are represented now, even after she has left her post, by buildings that are there because she was there. She fought for these. The Berlin Hospital is there because somebody put it there. It is a lot of concrete and represents a lot of energy and she has this quality. The Conference Center in Berlin, the Free University set-up, student housing, these may have nothing much to do with policy, the glamour term of history, but they are far from insignificant.[1]

—Elwood Williams
Foreign Service Officer

Eleanor Lansing Dulles would not disagree with this assessment, advanced by a former colleague. She is among the first to admit that her mid-level position in the State Department was removed from policy-making: she never achieved the recognition or influence of her older brothers John Foster and Allen. At the apogee of her career she was responsible for the economic revival of one city. Using the power and influence that stemmed from family connections, her own talents, energies and tactics developed during years of bureaucratic service, Eleanor Dulles worked to transform Berlin. Yet her contribution and involvement in United States post-war foreign policy go beyond concrete structures. As a woman, and as a member of a powerful family, Eleanor held positions in both the Truman and Eisenhower administrations that, although lacking rank, made her an active participant in the exercise of American foreign policy.

In the post-war era, as American involvement in European affairs increased dramatically, two programs were of integral importance: the Marshall Plan for European Recovery and the economic revitalization and integration of the Federal Republic of Germany into the western alliance system. As Financial Attaché to the United States Occupation Forces for Austria 1945–1948, and officer in charge of the Berlin "desk" 1952–1959, Eleanor Dulles was involved in both these programs. Because the State Department remained a male preserve her rank remained mid-level. However, as Williams points out, her contribution was far from insignificant.

Born June 1, 1895, to Allen Macy Dulles, a Presbyterian minister, and Edith Foster Dulles, Eleanor, like her siblings John Foster, Margaret, Allen, and Nataline, had horizons extending beyond her father's Watertown, New York, parish. Her maternal grandparents, particularly her grandfather, John Watson Foster, were instrumental in introducing the Dulles children to events and people beyond the confines of upstate New York. Foster, described by his granddaughter as "the dominant personality in our family circle," served as United States Minister to Mexico, Russia, and Spain, Counselor to the State Department, member of the Imperial Chinese delegation to the Hague Peace Conference of 1907, and Secretary of State. Following his retirement from the State Department, he continued to be influential through his connections to Wall Street.[2]

The world Foster opened to the Dulles children was of considerable scope. One of Eleanor's earliest recollections of her grandparents is of being with them in Washington when a telegram arrived announcing the death of Queen Victoria. Eleanor also vividly recalls their drawing room, full of articles from China, Japan, and India, including a magnificent polar bear rug. She recalls that she would go and "sit on this bear, lean up against its belligerent head, and tell myself stories about the wonderful things in this room."[3]

Each summer Grandmother and Grandfather Foster vacationed at Henderson Harbor on Lake Ontario and were joined there by their daughters Edith (and the Dulles children) and Eleanor (Mrs. Robert Lansing). Visitors were frequent: William Howard Taft, John W. Davies, Andrew Carnegie, and Bernard Baruch all came to enjoy the fishing. Biographers stress the impact this had on the ambitions and outlook of John Foster and Allen Dulles, since Grandfather Foster included his grandsons in the outings. Eleanor was never so closely inluded, yet power and prestige clearly impressed her.[4]

Away from Henderson, in Watertown and later in Auburn, where her father taught at the Auburn Theological Seminary, Eleanor recalls a "life that was typical of the professional people of the time." She professes uncertainty about her family's social status, stating that she "never heard the term middle class" until she went to college.[5]

Certainly in economic terms the family was middle class. Allen Dulles earned $3500 in 1905–06, but the financial strains of supporting five children forced him to supplement his income by preaching at the Auburn Second Presbyterian Church. Despite Dulles's financial realities, his position as a theologian and academic provided social status, intellectual stimulation and advantages commonly associated with the American elite. And always in the background was John Watson Foster, whose gifts allowed for better education and trips to Europe, and whose connections provided contact with influential people.

These influences, far more than religious training, shaped Eleanor. As a child, she attended all her father's church services, had regular assignments of Biblical passages to memorize and recite, and she was taught Presbyterian doctrine. Certainly, as a minister's daughter, religion was important to her. Yet transcending the literal message was a code of morality, a sense of cultural obligation, and ambitions that extended beyond traditionally narrow female confines.

Throughout her life, Eleanor felt herself part of an elite, with the ability and responsibility to lead and influence. Her professional life spans the years 1921–78, and is marked by energy, pride, and ambition. Driven by a desire for recognition and acheivement, she, like many women of her generation, embarked on a career believing that the barriers to feminine success were gone. She first sought entry into the world of business after earning a Master's degree in industrial management from Bryn Mawr, only to find that "brute strength in the mills and male dominance in the office were to rule. . . . The world of industry was not mine to conquer."[6]

Eleanor subsequently returned to academe, first as a graduate student at Harvard-Radcliffe, where she earned a Ph.D. in economics in 1926, and then as a professor. She taught at Simmons College, Bryn Mawr, and The Wharton School of Finance until 1936, when she joined the federal bureaucracy.

Initially Dulles worked as an economist for the Social Security Board. She remained with that agency until 1942, when she transferred to the Board of Economic Warfare. Within the year she received another assignment; now she was with the Division of Postwar Planning within the State Department. Eleanor remained with Postwar Planning until mid–1944 when she was appointed to the International Secretariate for the Bretton Woods Conference.

In the spring of 1945, Eleanor was granted a new position. On V-E Day 1945, she stood in Hyde Park and listened to Winston Churchill address the crowd. The war in Europe was over and reconstruction could begin.

Eleanor Dulles had personal reason, beyond the general relief and joy felt at the ending of World War II, to view the future with optimism and satisfaction. She had arrived in Europe to assume responsibilities as Financial Attaché to the United States Occupation Forces for Austria. Having worked on the Bretton Woods Agreements, she felt that the International Monetary Fund and the International Bank for Reconstruction outlined there would prevent the crippling economic difficulties experienced after World War I. She was confident that continued Allied cooperation and the new United Nations Organization would create a workable and lasting peace. And, as a member of the occupation bureaucracy, she would have a chance to participate and influence decisions in a meaningful way.

Eleanor received her orders to join General Mark Clark's headquarters, "Austria Forward," at the end of May 1945. She traveled to Caserta, only to find that headquarters had advanced to Livorno, Italy. Once there, she was granted the military rank of lieutenant colonel, and began her responsibilities amidst disarray. She notes that "only our chief, Erhardt [John G. Erhardt, Political Adviser to the American Occupation Forces], had the appurtenances of a bona fide government man—the In and Out baskets and a real desk." The rest of the staff spent their days at the office—an old tobacco factory—studying German, reading occupation directives and generally putting in time while they awaited permission to enter Austria.[7]

It would be several months before that permission was granted. Although the Allies had determined, in the Moscow Declaration of November 1943, that Austria would be treated as a liberated, rather than a defeated belligerent nation, relatively few decisions had been reached about the logistics of occupation.[8] During July and August 1945, as decisions regarding zonal and sector boundaries, trade in food and fuel, and administrative details were finalized at higher levels, "Austria Forward" moved slowly across Europe—from Livorno to Florence, Verona and Salzburg before entering Vienna.

During this interim, Eleanor frequently wrote to her older sister, Margaret, expressing her dual frustration. The first involved the pervasive sense she noted among the staff that they were "feeling their way," facing the "strain of a constant feeling of destruction." Her letters raised the specter of a devastating winter to come in Europe. She wrote:

Everyone is pessimistic about the food and coal situation. It is probable that most of the industries will have to close down for some time for lack of fuel. If industries are at a low ebb, then there will be less food, less clothes, fewer houses and there are not enough even for summertime.

If I could see some materials, food or coal coming in from the outside, I would feel better about our ability to carry on military government. It is a hard job at best. In finance I think we are pretty well prepared, but there have been questions of jurisdiction which have slowed us up.

In other fields it is perhaps more difficult, anyway our progress does not seem too good.[9]

Eleanor felt strongly that, from a policy standpoint, continued delay in reaching Vienna was detrimental. She was aware that the movement of headquarters had a "considerable amount of political meaning," but lamented that "none but the top few knew exactly what was going on."[10]

Eleanor's second source of frustration stemmed from relations with her male colleagues. Despite her military rank she soon found that she was afforded the same treatment granted the secretaries with whom she shared billets. In late June, John Erhardt gave her permission to join the advance staff in the villa outside Salzburg, where they were housed. However, within the week James Denby, Erhardt's deputy, informed her that "this is a boys' club." Subsequently she was packed off to the Hotel Pitter in the city with the secretaries. Annoyed but undeterred, Eleanor began the search for economic data necessary to determine the economic needs of Austria.

At this juncture, Dulles's concern centered on the complexities and difficulties inherent in the establishment of occupation bureaucracy. She resented her exclusion from "the boys' club," and quickly developed means to circumvent the restraints on her effectiveness. When she finally reached Vienna she installed herself in a large home, where she frequently entertained small groups of public officials, students and women; their conversations gave her a strong sense of the perilous economic and political questions facing Austria. She candidly admits that this type of entertaining made working with European officials easier than working with her American colleagues. She discovered in Vienna, and later in Berlin, that if she acted and entertained as if she had rank, Europeans responded. Thus she found a way to outmaneuver the boys' club and established her own influence within the bureaucracy.

Another source of concern was the seeming lack of progress in Allied negotiations. Dulles recognized the necessity of concluding political agreements, yet she chafed at the slowness of the process. During the late summer and autumn she was optimistic about the continuation of cooperation. Her judgment that continued delay in reaching Vienna was detrimental stemmed from concern about the dire shortages facing Austria if trade was not resumed immediately. Her letters noted the strongly anti-Soviet sentiment of Austrians, a view she did not share. Eleanor attributed this attitude to the excessive brutality of Soviet troops during liberation. Certainly she did not condone the looting, rape, and plunder committed by Russian troops. But she viewed these actions within the context of temporary vengeance (thirty-five of Hitler's divisions that fought on the Eastern Front were formed in Austria and were commanded by Austrian officers) rather than as an indication of Soviet aggressive intent.[11]

Eleanor's subsequent analysis identifies four fundamental errors in judgment that determined policy and outlook during the 1944–45 period. First and foremost, political and military decisions were based on the belief that "the greatest threat to future world peace would be the German people." This led directly to the second error: western leaders were "naive and unmindful" about the "geographic position and political opportunity" granted the Soveit Union in eastern Europe. "It was not recognized by the Western experts in 1945, that the USSR drive to protect the gains of the Soviet revolution and the fear of contamination from freedom would lead to the building of an almost impenetrable barrier between the world of the Communist East and the capitalist freedom beyond."

The third and fourth errors in judgment involved the belief that peace treaties would be concluded rapidly, as soon as conditions stabilized, and that the United Nations Organization "would develop rapidly and exert an effective authority to maintain peace and assure the rights of men, in Germany as well as elsewhere."[12]

Certainly the views she expressed during the period July–November 1945 reflect these conceptions. She was not initially anti-Soviet. She felt that through

Allied cooperation, in the Allied Control Commission for Austria and at higher levels, the Austrian economy would be stabilized, a representative government established, a peace treaty concluded, and Austria restored to normal relations within a reconstructed Europe.

Eleanor believed that it was the Austrian elections of November 1945 that changed the entire context of Allied cooperation and determined the course of Soviet conduct thereafter. Soviet reaction to the election results both changed her attitude toward the Russians and led her to assert that the Cold War began in Austria in 1946.

During the first days of liberation, Soviet leaders had established an Austrian Provisional government, headed by the Socialist Karl Renner. Although the unilateral nature of the Soviet action made British and American leaders hesitant, they extended recognition to the Renner government in October. General elections for a permanent government were scheduled for November.

When the elections took place, the results reflected the strength of the conservative People's Party. That party received 49.8 percent of the vote, the Socialist Party 44.6 percent, and the Communist Party 5.4 percent. On November 28, Karl Renner officially dissolved the Provisional government. Leopold Figl, leader of the People's Party, was named chancellor; Dr. Adolf Schaerf, Socialist Party, was selected vice chancellor. The cabinet, announced in early December, consisted of seven ministers and the chancellor from the People's Party, five ministers and the vice chancellor representing the Socialists, one communist minister of power and electrification, and two non-party ministers.[13]

In Dulles's subsequent appraisal of European events, these election results assume critical importance. She contends that Soviet leaders seriously miscalculated the strength of the communist party in Austria. Citing the statement of the Soviet political adviser that the party would receive 20 percent of the vote, as representative, she concludes that the Soviets were vastly overconfident. They seriously underestimated "the permanent impression . . . of brutality . . . and the independence of spirit of the Austrians." Ultimately, "this failure, in a country with a strong tradition of Socialist support, guaranteed that Moscow would never again permit free elections in any area of occupation, particularly in Germany."[14]

General Mark Clark, United States allied commander for Austria, concurs with this evaluation. In his autobiography, *Calculated Risk*, he asserts that the Soviets changed tactics after the elections, and that there was a "steady deterioration" in cooperation after November. He notes that "Russians who had shown themselves friendly toward Americans seemed to disappear from Vienna, presumably transferred back to the Soviet Union. Those who replaced them were stiff and formal in their contacts with Westerners and resisted all efforts to establish anything other than an official relationship."[15]

Eleanor, too, was quick to note this change. She wrote to Margaret, "the Russians not only won't talk policy, they won't even talk art, music, science, or anything interesting or important. I consider the inability to talk, and for the most part mix socially, as the most serious threat to the future—there is so little chance of compromise on the one hand or understanding on the other.''[16]

Clearly, talking and socializing with other policy-makers was an integral part of Dulles's style. She viewed it not only as the tactic by which she circumvented the boys' club, but also as an essential element of the diplomatic process. She began concentrating all her attention on Austrian officials, entertaining extensively at her own expense.

John Erhardt was aware of these activities and, early in 1946, he challenged her. He recounted rumors that she had met with the Austrian minister of commerce, officials of the National Bank, and the minister of reconstruction. She confirmed this, and he ended the conversation with a stern "Well, don't make any mistakes."

Eleanor did not. After an evening with government and financial leaders, she wrote a report regarding Soviet pressure on public officials and the deprivations of the Austrian economy in the eastern zone. Using materials available to the Austrians, she compiled a report that won her a commendation, recognition that strengthened her position within the bureaucracy and forestalled further criticism by Erhardt.[17]

Following the establishment of the Figl government, Eleanor's responsiblities focused on the negotiation of trade and currency reform. Skillfully maneuvering inside and outside official channels, she oversaw the transfer of vitally needed coal and foodstuffs between Austria and Germany, and was closely involved in the bargaining over currency reform.

The difficult negotiations over the recall of German *reichmarks* and the institution of occupation and national currency in Austria presaged a similar currency reform crisis in occupied Germany that resulted in the Berlin Blockade of 1948. Although the Austrian reform was accomplished without crisis, Dulles's suspicions were confirmed by the events in Vienna. By mid–1946, she was conviced that the Soviet Union was bent on an expansionist and obstructionist policy aimed at the domination of eastern Europe.

Eleanor Dulles was certainly not alone in these perceptions. Indeed with this analysis she joined the emerging consensus within the State Department. Fearing that continued European economic dislocation would inevitably lead to communist regimes, either internally or externally imposed, George Marshall unveiled a proposal for massive U.S. economic assistance in June 1947. The Soviet Union made it equally clear that they viewed the plan as a denigration of sovereignty and that their eastern European allies would not participate.

Austrian leaders found themselves in a quandary. While not dominated by the Soviet Union, Austria remained vulnerable to pressure. Negotiations over reparations, German-owned asets in Austria, and Austrian access to coveted eastern markets were proceeding. If Austria joined the Marshall Plan, bargaining would be more difficult. On the other hand, Austria was in desperate need of continued economic aid. The special credits received under the United Nations Relief and

Rehabilitation Administration (UNRRA) would expire in July. An emergency program of $85 million from the United States and $13 million in credit from the Export-Import Bank merely maintained existence: Austria needed vast resources to reconstruct a healthy, functioning economy.

In no other instance was Eleanor's ability to work with Austrian politicians more opportune. She considers this her greatest accomplishment in Vienna. By using her influence effectively she helped convince the Austrians to oppose Soviet pressure and rely on the West. On April 3, 1948, the Figl government signed a bilateral Austro-American agreement entitling it to Marshall Plan funds. During the first year of assistance Austria received $217 million in Unconditional Aid and $66,600,000 in Drawing Rights.[18]

By its very nature influence in these matters is difficult to document. Although no record of her many conversations exists it is beyond question that Dulles's voice was heard. Despite a mid-level position in the huge complex of occupation government she often drank brandy in her study with Austrian Chancellor Leopold Figl, Vice-Chancellor Adolf Schaerf, Foreign Minister Karl Gruber, Minister of Reconstruction Peter Krauland, future Chancellor Julius Raab, and Oscar Pollack, editor of the influential newspaper *Arbeiter Zeitung*. While visiting Vienna, Walter Lippmann met with Eleanor prior to meeting with other American and Austrian officials. John Foster Dulles, when attending the Moscow meeting of the Council of Foreign Ministers in March 1947, met with his sister to discuss German and Austrian affairs. Certainly Eleanor's connections to higher American policy-making circles were closer than her rank would indicate and the implications of those connections were not lost on Austrian politicians.[19]

Feeling that her job in Europe was complete, Dulles chose to return to Washington, where she was detailed to the Central European Division of the State Department. She notes that ''the months after my return in November of 1948 were to be the worst in my professional experience. They were even more frustrating than my last months at the Social Security Board. There my problems had centered on policy and personality. Now they were . . . rooted in sex discrimination.''[20]

Eleanor had experienced sexual discrimination before and recognized it for what it was. She had, however, one advantage that always helped her overcome the obstacle of her sex: she was a Dulles. But in late 1948, the Dulles political fortunes were at their lowest ebb. The bipartisan spirit, scrupulously maintained during the first Truman administration, was virtually destroyed by the election campaign. Foster had been courted as the future secretary of state for Thomas Dewey, and Allen's record with the OSS during the war gave him hopes of controlling an expanded U.S. intelligence agency. These hopes were dashed by the Republican defeat. Both brothers returned to private law practice in New York.

Eleanor could not dissociate herself from her brothers' political fortunes. Although she remained in Washington, the advantage of family connection was nullified and she was confronted with the barriers that stood before every woman. Her return to power and influence would depend on her brothers. Until then she was forced to perform her job within narrowed confines, find other outlets for her unflagging energy, and wait for new opportunities.

The new opportunity arrived in December 1952 following the election of Dwight Eisenhower. Eleanor was working at the Commerce Department when she was approached by James Riddleberger, head of the Office of German Affairs at the State Department. Riddleberger, who knew Eleanor from her days in Austria, wanted to find someone to direct economic policy toward Berlin. He offered her a position as special assistant to the director of the German Bureau and she immediately accepted.

In nearly every respect, Berlin represented the anomalies of the Cold War. The image of "an island in the middle of a Communist sea" was freqeuntly invoked: Berlin was symbolic of East-West struggle. Leaders consistently utilized the vocabulary of war while stating that there could be no victories. Yet, in the Berlin Blockade of 1948–49, the West had come closest to just such a victory. Here was overt struggle in an identifiable sense, and the West won. Victory was measured in the number of flights per day, the quantifiable tonnage of goods flown into the city, the ultimate lifting of the blockade. A retreat from those 186 square miles would have considerable consequence in the balance of world affairs: Berlin could never be abandoned.

Nevertheless, there were several dilemmas central to the continued occupation of the city. First, Berlin was a badly battered city, its young people were leaving and it was increasingly expensive to support. Symbolic or not, the city was dying. Second, there were monumental political complexities associated with Berlin. As Phillip Windsor notes, "the maintenance of the city, depends, in fact, on upholding an ambiguous position."[21] Berlin's political and economic survival depended upon the closest possible integration with the Federal Republic of Germany. However, buried deep within East Germany, and in the absence of a final Allied agreement, Berlin remained an occupied area albeit with a relatively independent city administration. As a result the Adenauer administration tended to view Berlin as solely an American concern.

Berlin and Bonn were also divided by partisan and ideological differences. Konrad Adenauer and Ludwig Erhard, Federal Minister of economic affairs, established a program of *Soziale Marktwirtschaft*, a "social free economy," as the centerpiece of their blueprint for a new Germany. This policy, which maximized private initiative and investment and moved Germany away from a tradition of a rigidly controlled economy, met strong opposition from socialists.[22] Berlin was traditionally a stronghold of Social Democratic support and, during the fifties, the SPD maintained the majority in the city administration. Although strongly anticommunist and anti-Soviet, the SPD opposed much of Adenauer's program. They favored welfare plans and liberal spending for social programs, which constituted "an unwelcome object of expenditure for the *Soziale Markt-*

wirtschaft policies of the CDU coalition in Bonn."[23] Naturally as the dispenser of ERP funds and an occupying force, Washington was forced to deal with these conflicting priorities.

Whereas these domestic, economic differences were significant, the international implications of the city were not only more crucial to divisions between Bonn and Berlin, but also the thorniest problem for Washington. Adenauer was determined to build the economic, political, and military strength of the Federal Republic to a point of equal partnership within the western alliance. Although he recognized that German reunification would be accomplished through Four-Power negotiation, he wanted assurance that Bonn would have a strong role in the reunification process. Berlin's special status symbolized commitment to a reunified Germany. Yet the chancellor viewed the very existence of the city, outside Bonn's jurisdiction and with leaders who had direct access to Allied authorities, as a continuing challenge to his leadership and ability to represent Germany to the West. Daniel Margolies, director of the office of German economic affairs within the State Department, put it succinctly: "Adenauer was no enthusiast about Berlin. After all, Berlin raised real questions about the legitimacy of Bonn. Bonn is so artificial—like having Painesville, Ohio capital of the United States."[24]

Washington was equally concerned about this contradiction. No one could publicly admit less than total commitment to a peace treaty and the ultimate reunification of Germany. However, United States policy was integrally linked to the development of an economically and militarily revitalized West Germany. Reunification resulting in an neutralized Germany, or one outside the western sphere, was unthinkable. Dulles's position, a special "desk" within the German Bureau, an attention granted no other city in the world, reflects these contradictions.

Eleanor's colleagues within the German Bureau candidly admit to the special advantage of her appointment. As one member pointed out:

The real problem was somehow to indicate that although we were focusing on the solution to the German problem, Berlin was not going to be forgotten. However, we did not have anyone in our organization that had the time to do that. After all, *we* were getting the complex issues of West Germany sorted out, within the European complex. Berlin was really quite a unique and peculiar situation. There was a complex of economic, political and social issues involved. Part of it was, do we take it seriously enough?

But the fact that *she* was associated with Berlin made the Germans think we attached importance to it. Why else would the Secretary of State have his sister on it? Of course the Secretary of State did not have his sister on it. But he did not take her off. And they knew, or thought, that if they saw her and she gave them an answer, chances were she might have talked to her brother.[25]

The appointment was brilliant: everyone won and the male-dominated bastion was safe. As Margolies noted, "*We* were getting the complex issues sorted out, no one had time for Berlin." But with Eleanor Dulles "bustling in and out of the city,'' Berlin got reassurance, the German Bureau got a direct line to the secretary of state, and a woman with reemployment rights in the State Department got a postition that kept her occupied but on the periphery.

Eleanor's first trip to Berlin fulfilled her colleagues' hidden expectations about the magic of the Dulles name. In December 1952 she left Washington to begin a round of meetings in Bonn and Berlin. Upon arrival, she was greeted and entertained by Chancellor Adenauer. It is unlikely that he would have met personally with an official of her rank had she not been the future secretary's sister. In retrospect, Eleanor recalls that Adenauer questioned her at length about Foster's attitude toward Germany and about his relationship with Eisenhower. She notes that she ''found great curiosity and . . . an anxiety to express enthusiasm for all Dulleses.''[26]

Within six months of her initial visit events focused world attention on Berlin, when on June 17, 1953, clashes occurred between East German workers and Soviet troops. The Central Committee of the ruling Socialist Unity Party (SED) had announced that individual production quotas would be increased by 10 percent and angry East Berlin workers staged a protest march on the German House of Ministries. The protest ultimately spread to 250 towns in the eastern zone and lasted for two weeks. One bystander in East Berlin was killed, 10,000 workers were arrested and 16 leaders executed.

Dulles was in Berlin near the sector border when the protests began. She maintains that, from the outset, the U.S. military commandants and their political advisers favored restraint; there was no overt attempt to aid the East Berliners. Eleanor spoke with Foster and Allen, then director of the Central Intelligence Agency, and cites Foster's moderation as proof that he never supported a policy of ''rollback'' for Eastern Europe. The three Dulleses agreed that the United States response should be to use the uprising for propaganda purposes and to initiate an East German Food Program, which involved borrowing food from the West Berlin stockpile, packaging it and giving it to anyone with an East German identity card.[27] The program was carried out from July 27 through October 10, 1953, and distributed over 5.5 million food parcels. Official estimates indicate that one-sixth of the population of the Soviet zone took advantage of the opportunity.[28]

The uprisings and the success of the food program Dulles initiated had a significant impact on policy. A National Security Council policy statement (NSC 132), issued just prior to the protests, stressed the need for a stockpile and the promotion of economic stability so that Berlin could survive another blockade. Later reports, however, indicated a shift in priority. These NSC analyses reported that the uprisings and success of the food program were significant. The possibility of a Soviet attack on West Berlin now appeared remote. Therefore NSC 132/1, issued while the food program operated, stated that ''the disruptive and irritating influence of the Western presence in Berlin upon the implementation of Soviet policy in the Soviet zone has been more fully demonstrated.'' A second report (NSC 173) dated December 1, 1953, noted that Berliners had made ''a

gradual adjustment, economic and psychological, to isolation and self-sufficiency." United States policy henceforth would be aimed at strengthening that
adjustment and giving priority to programs that went beyond defense of the city.
As long as a Soviet attack on the city was a remote possibility, the Eisenhower
administration intended to augment the "disruptive and irritating quality of West
Berlin."[29]

As a result of the new emphasis, Dulles received additional funds for Berlin
projects. Monies for the stockpile increased dramatically ($4.2 million in 1951,
$3 million in 1952, $15.5 million in 1953, and $38 million in 1954). Her focus
on this program and her ability to wrest allocations from the larger German
budget meant that by 1959, when she left the Berlin "desk," the original goal
of stockpile supplies to provision the city for a minimum of twelve months had
been not just reached but surpassed.[30]

More important, the years 1952–59 saw significant growth in the Berlin economy. The problems of unemployment and lack of investment, although not
eradicated, were less acute. With new tax incentives and a 10 percent reduction
in wage and income taxes, Berlin began to prosper. Eleanor's colleagues credit
her with the success of these programs. She paid special attention to light industry
and consumer goods, as opposed to the build-up of heavy industry that immediately followed the blockade. Her focus on the garment industry stimulated
growth to the point that it not only provided for the needs of Berliners, but also
provided 30 percent of all exports from the city as well.

Unemployment remained a problem for some time, and Dulles was willing
to get support for any project that created jobs. She arranged funding, both public
and private, for the construction of a number of hotels (including the Berlin
Hilton) to stimulate tourism and the construction industry. Although these priorities infuriated Berlin's Social Democratic leadership, they did result in benefits.
In the summer of 1952 unemployment stood at 300,000. By the summer of
1955, 100,000 people were unemployed. In 1959 the figure had dropped to
40,000, and by 1961 Berlin had a shortage of labor.[31]

Once Berlin's economy was strengthened, a new phase, use of the impact
project, began. Planning for this was part of the new priorities following the
June uprisings. The NSC progress report of September 1953 stated that there
was a new "psychological strategy plan for Berlin" in which attention would
be devoted to bolstering morale and improving the city's image.

From 1954 through 1958 Dulles directed a number of these projects. Building
the Benjamin Franklin Congress Hall (a conference center on the East-West
Berlin sector border where cultural events and the annual Berlin meeting of the
FRG Bundestag could be held), the Berlin Medical Center, and the Student
Village housing project for the Free University, all fell within the scope of the
impact project. Eleanor summed up the intent of these projects when she said
that the Student Village "illustrated the kind of thing we were trying to do. We
tried to introduce a new element, something that people could talk about, . . .

help their morale, . . . make them proud of Berlin, and make other people say, "Well, look what they have . . . right there on Khrushchev's doorstep."[32]

In large measure the success of the programs she directed was ultimately reflected in the Berlin crisis of 1958. In November, Soviet Premier Nikita Khrushchev delivered an ultimatum: the West had six months to negotiate a settlement ending four-power occupation of Berlin. At the end of that period, in the absence of an agreement, the Soviet Union would withdraw and leave the East German government in control of the city.

The origins of the crisis lie in the larger European issues of nuclear arms for West Germany, the Rapacki Plan, and recognition of the permanent division of Germany and legitimacy of the Adenauer and Ulbricht regimes. Khrushchev attempted to force these issues by holding West Berlin hostage. When Dulles took over in 1952, she was charged with creating a showcase from a dying city and with "increasing the disrupting and irritating influence of the Western presence" there. In November 1958 Khrushchev contended that Berlin had become "a state within a state," that it was the base for subversion against the German Democratic Republic. What better proof that she had done her job well?[33]

The months following the ultimatum were difficult ones. In February 1959, Foster entered Walter Reed Hospital for a hernia operation. Doctors discovered a return of cancer originally diagnosed and treated in 1956, and told the family that Foster had only months to live. He resigned his position on April 15, 1959, and was replaced by Under Secretary of State Christian Herter.

Following Foster's resignation Eleanor found herself progressively excluded from the decision-making process. As members of the Department discussed a policy for the Geneva talks scheduled to deal with the crisis, she was increasingly limited in her ability to advance opinion, openly or behind the scenes. Christian Herter supported a policy of negotiation and compromise that included agreement to liquidate those agencies and activities involved in subversion and hostile activity against the Soviet zone.[34] This was a policy considerably less firm than that advocated by Foster Dulles.[35]

Eleanor recognized that she would not be among the Geneva delegation. Although she continued to work on the position papers she was excluded from many of the preparatory meetings in which they were discussed. Her declining influence was based on real policy differences, a circumstance that confronts many State department officials when changes in leadership occur. However, the means of her exclusion point to, in her words, "the subtle yet considerable ability of men to insinuate and make dubious the accomplishments of women." In an interview, she reported:

Following Khrushchev's ultimatum, the department was constantly receiving telegrams on the situation. Someone had to be there at night to evaluate these telegrams—whether immediate attention was needed or whether it could wait until morning. I was willing and able to do this. Despite the fact that I had an underground parking space in the building, the Division Chief declared it unsafe for me to undertake night duty, and that it was a job which could be handled by someone with a lower rank than mine. A young man was assigned. Then when it came time to go to Geneva, the young man handling the telegrams was assigned to go.[36]

Eleanor Dulles left the German Bureau in October 1959, aware that her effectiveness had come to an end: the double-edged nature of family connection was clear. Despite the fact that she had proven herself capable, creative, and energetic in dealing with the Berlin situation, her influence even behind the scenes was ultimately based on her brothers. Foster was gone and Eleanor's links to Allen were politically embarrassing at Geneva as Washington admitted to hostile and subversive activity.

Eleanor was reassigned to the Bureau of Intelligence and Research, where she stayed until January 1962 when she formally retired from the federal bureaucracy. Although she was reluctant to leave, officials in the State Department made it clear that Dulleses were not welcome in the Kennedy administration. Unwilling to retire completely, Eleanor returned to teaching at Duke and Georgetown universities.

Talking to Eleanor Dulles, one is aware of her vitality, intelligence, and quick wit. Despite failing eyesight and hearing, even in her nineties she remains a proud, aggressive, competent woman. When asked about feminism she replied that she "was never a feminist. Women's power or credit was never my major goal. It was more important to me to be a good political scientist and economist."[37]

By nearly any standard Eleanor Dulles was successful in that pursuit. She proved herself an able academic and scholar, a respected economist and capable bureaucrat. She exerted influence within various government agencies achieving particular success in Austria and Berlin. Though some colleagues call her arrogant and "bossy," all characterize her as creative, energetic and, extremely able.

Certainly her attitudes reflect the prevailing Cold War ideology of the Truman-Eisenhower administrations regarding Soviet expansionism and the necessity of the Marshall Plan to stabilize Europe and prevent the spread of communism. Her efforts in Austria reflect those convictions.

Nor should her influence in Berlin be overlooked. Following the July 1953 uprisings the focus of U.S. policy changed. The former emphasis on defense against blockade gave way to a more aggressive policy. Eleanor Dulles concurred with this change and actively and creatively implemented it. She candidly, indeed proudly, admits that "the very success of the efforts led Khrushchev to his determination to smash the 'Berlin showcase' in 1958."[38] Unsuccessful at that, she implies that the building of the Berlin Wall in 1961 was a logical and necessary step for the Soviet Union and Ulbricht regime.

This somewhat unorthodox opinion is, however, inconsistent with Dulles's overall analysis. She remains too much a product of her time, a defender of

Eisenhower administration policy, too much a Dulles to criticize or question American foreign policy. She has written extensively about Berlin, "the greatest testing ground of Western resolve." She asserts that "Berlin has not been a *cause* of tension, but a consequence of alternating Communist calculations and tactics."[39] This analysis denies any provocative or obstructionist policy on Washington's part and maintains an image of United States policy that is largely reactive to Soviet aggression.

Eleanor was an "insider" in American foreign policy because of the Dulles connection, but she is noteworthy in her own right and not merely because she was "Foster's sister." What is significant is that she sprang from the same circumstances as he and then attempted, as a woman, to succeed in an environment created, run, and designed for men. She states with pride that she "never engaged in outright warfare with the male-dominated Department. I decided that if I were not promoted, I would act as if I had been."[40]

In this attitude, Eleanor Dulles is representative of many professional women of her generation. They necessarily believed in the individual; that they would and could succeed if they were capable. Merit would be recognized and rewarded. Eleanor Dulles developed tactics for overcoming barriers in her path and thus achieved what few women of her time were able to: she gained entry into what remained a boys' club.

NOTES

1. Author interview with Elwood Williams, Washington, D.C., January 9, 1980.

2. Eleanor Lansing Dulles, *Chances of a Lifetime: A Memoir* (Englewood Cliffs, N.J., Prentice-Hall, Inc., 1980), p. 3 See also Michael J. Devine, *John W. Foster: Politics and Diplomacy in the Imperial Era, 1873–1917* (Athens, Ohio, Ohio University Press, 1981).

3. The Reminiscences of Eleanor Lansing Dulles, Oral History Research Office, Columbia University. Interview conducted by John T. Mason, Jr., for the Oral History Research Office from 1962 to 1967, p. 6.

4. Townsend Hoopes, *The Devil and John Foster Dulles* (Boston, Atlantic Monthly Press, 1973), p. 13. See also Leonard Mosely, *Dulles: A Biography of Eleanor, Allen and John Foster Dulles and Their Family Network* (New York, The Dial Press, 1978), pp. 18–19.

5. Columbia Oral History, p. 17.

6. Dulles, *Chances*, p. 78.

7. Ibid., p. 189.

8. For Moscow Declaration, see Protocols of the Conference, November 1, 1943, U.S., Department of State, *Foreign Relations of the United States 1943* (Washington D.C.: Government Printing Office, 1960), 1:761. Hereafter cited as *FRUS*.

9. Eleanor Lansing Dulles to Margaret Dulles Edwards, July 3, 1945, Eleanor Lansing Dulles Papers, Dwight D. Eisenhower Library, Box 5, Correspondence from Austria, 1945–46. Hereafter cited as *ELD Papers*.

10. Eleanor Lansing Dulles to Margaret Dulles Edwards, July 20, 1945, *ELD Papers*.

11. For discussion of Soviet occupation activity and Austrian response, see William

Bader, *Austria Between East and West, 1945–1955* (Stanford: Stanford University Press, 1966). For Eleanor Lansing Dulles's views, see *Chances*, p. 202.

12. Eleanor Lansing Dulles, *Berlin—The Wall Is Not Forever* (Chapel Hill: The University of North Carolina Press, 1967), pp. 25–26.

13. For discussion, see Bader, pp. 45–46.

14. Eleanor Lansing Dulles, Speech to Unknown Group, February 12, 1957, *ELD Papers*, Box 12, Speeches and Trips.

15. Mark Clark, *Calculated Risk* (New York: Harper & Bros., 1950), pp. 470–471.

16. Eleanor Lansing Dulles to Margaret Dulles Edwards, April 17, 1946, *ELD Papers*.

17. Eleanor Lansing Dulles to Margaret Dulles Edwards and Nataline Dulles Seymour, May 26, 1946; Eleanor Lansing Dulles to unnamed correspondent, October 20, 1946, *ELD Papers*.

18. For discussion of Austrian reconstruction and economic needs, see Franz Heissenberger, *The Economic Reconstruction of Austria, 1945–1952* (Washington, D.C., Library of Congress, European Affairs Division, 1953); William B. Bader, *Austria Between East and West 1945–1955* (Stanford, Stanford University Press, 1966); United States Allied Commission Austria, *The Reconstruction of Austria, 1945–46* (Washington, D.C., Government Printing Office, 1947).

19. Eleanor Dulles's accounts of these conversations can be found in the *ELD Papers*, Correspondence from Austria file.

20. Dulles, *Chances*, p. 228.

21. Phillip Windsor, *City on Leave: A History of Berlin 1945–1962* (New York, Frederick A. Praeger, 1963), p. 133. For discussion of the special relationship between Berlin, the Federal Republic, and the United States, see U.S. Congress, Senate, *Documents on Germany, 1944–1959*, Committee on Foreign Relations, 86th Congress, 1st Session (Washington, D.C., Government Printing Office, 1959).

22. Windsor, p. 133.

23. Ibid., p. 134. See also, Kurt Becker, "The Developments in Domestic Politics," in *The Politics of Post-War Germany*, ed., Walter Stahl (New York: Frederick A. Praeger, 1963), pp. 57–64.

24. Author interview with Daniel Margolies, director, office of German economic affairs, Washington, D.C., January 16, 1980.

25. Ibid.

26. Columbia Oral History, p. 529.

27. Dulles, *Chances*, pp. 253–256. On the issue of rollback, see Eleanor Lansing Dulles, "No Policy of Rollback," *Washington Post*, September 16, 1984.

28. Foreign Service Dispatch—Subject: The East German Food Program, November 3, 1953. Dwight D. Eisenhower Papers, White House Central File, 1953–61, Official File Series, Box 865.

29. National Security Council Progress Report on the Implementation of United States Policy and Courses of Action to Counter Possible Soviet or Satellite Action Against Berlin (NSC 132/1), September 10, 1953 (Box 37); and NSC 173-A, Report to the National Security Council by the NSC Planning Board on United States Policy and Courses of Action to Counter Possible Soviet or Satellite Action Against Berlin, December 1, 1953. Dwight D. Eisenhower Papers, NSC Series, Policy Papers Subseries.

30. For statistics on the stockpile through 1955, see *Ibid.*, NSC 5404/1. For 1959

statistics, see James C. Sherrell to Major John Eisenhower, Feb. 3, 1959, *ELD Papers*, Berlin, Box 6.

31. For official statistics, see "News from the German Embassy" and "What We Have Done in Berlin," *ELD Papers*, Berlin, Box 13.

32. Columbia Oral History, p. 561.

33. Note from the Soviet Foreign Ministry to the American Ambassador at Moscow (Thompson), regarding Berlin, Nov. 27, 1958, *Documents on Germany 1944–1959*, pp. 330–31.

34. For discussion, see Jean Edward Smith, *In Defense of Berlin* (Baltimore: The Johns Hopkins Press, 1969).

35. Author interview with Eleanor Lansing Dulles, June 18, 1980, and December 15, 1981.

36. Author interview with Eleanor Lansing Dulles, December 15, 1981.

37. Ibid.

38. Dulles, *Berlin—The Wall Is Not Forever*, p. 157.

39. Eleanor Lansing Dulles, "Berlin—Barometer of Tension," in *Detente: Cold War Strategies in Transition*, eds., Eleanor Lansing Dulles and Robert Dickson Crane (New York: Frederick A. Praeger, 1965), p. 124.

40. Columbia Oral History, p. 566.

7

Speaking Out, Selling Out, Working Out: The Changing Politics of Jane Fonda

Jeanne Zeidler

Jane Fonda was a highly visible opponent of the United States involvement in the Vietnam War. Jane Fonda is also an award-winning actress, a social activist, a best-selling author, and self-proclaimed pioneer in women's health and fitness. Since the end of the Vietnam War, she has consciously worked to moderate her image as a strident radical. Once she called herself a "revolutionary woman,"[1] but she has come to favor the term "progressive," and has been quoted as saying that she is "much more middle-of-the-road than most people realize."[2] Her accomplishments since the end of the war in both her primary profession (film) and her more recent avocation (fitness) are very impressive. Despite these accomplishments, however, Fonda's anti-Vietnam War activism continues to shade and shape the public's perception of her. Although more than a decade after the end of the war she ranks as one of the ten "most admired"[3] women in the United States, for some she remains a symbol of radical politics and un-American activities. For others she was and is a shallow and opportunistic, if talented, movie star, clever enough to have become "a lightning rod for a generation"[4] in her successful self-promotion. In fact, Fonda is more complex than either characterization admits. She is at once less ideological than the first view implies, while also having a genuine commitment to working for what can only be described as an amorphous and somewhat romantic vision of an improved world.

If Fonda is destined to be forever defined by her anti-Vietnam War activities, it is also true that the social and political climate of the Vietnam years stimulated the development of her political consciousness and continues to provide the framework within which she operates. In an interview by Erica Jong published in April 1984, Fonda put it this way: "I think we changed the consciousness of the '50s. Basically we're the beneficiaries of two great social changes that occurred in our times: the women's movement and the Vietnam War . . . the women's movement made it possible to go out and achieve without too much guilt, and the Vietnam War made us ask basic questions about our values and our society."[5] There is an abundance of evidence that the political climate produced by the Vietnam War did, indeed, stimulate Fonda to "ask basic questions about our values and our society." Coming from a family with a liberal political tradition, her politics were moved further to the left, at least for a brief time. There is also substantial evidence that she was influenced by the women's movement. However, the impact of this movement upon her thinking and activism was somewhat broader than her comments about career achievement suggest.

Jane Fonda, a college dropout, is not particularly well-educated, nor is she an intellectual. Her politics are emotional and based upon the belief that valid political action emerges from an understanding of personal circumstances. This concept of personal politics helped shape her actions during the Vietnam era, and it became increasingly important as the radical movement lost momentum after the war and as broader political action was frustrated. If her politics became increasingly self-centered, however, they did not become selfish. In her 1984 book, *Women Coming of Age*, she lists "the things that really matter—my children, my husband, my friends, my community, my hopes for our country and for world peace."[6] Possibly the most succinct summary of Fonda's philosophy appears in the final sentences in *Jane Fonda's Workout Book for Pregnancy, Birth and Recovery* authored by her associate Femmy DeLyser. DeLyser writes, "Parenthood starts at home as a very private relationship. But as the child matures . . . you will realize that caring for your child means caring about the world."[7] Fonda's own workout books put forth the corollary notion that caring for yourself means caring about the world. These simple statements are the basis of Fonda's current political thinking at a time when her work in film and her role in the fitness movement have boosted her popularity to unprecedented heights.

In early 1985, a *Washington Post* reporter wrote about Jane Fonda that, "Fonda isn't just part of the movement. She is the movement. If you want to trace the changes in American culture over the last 20 years, all you have to do is look at her."[8] During these twenty years, Fonda first gained fame as a sex symbol movie star, then she attracted notoriety as a radical critic of American foreign and domestic policy, and finally she achieved renown as a progressive celebrity in the film industry and as a vocal activist in behalf of health and environmental causes. She has been a public personality of international proportions, enjoying extraordinary access to the media, to publicity, to powerful people, and to great wealth. Yet in her work for social change her popularity and her direct influence have expanded as her goals have become less concerned with foreign policy, less immediate, and arguably more limited. Her goals have also become more centered on certain kinds of women's issues, or on issues seen as traditionally within the woman's sphere. It is a shift in political style and emphasis that Fonda explained to Erica Jong by saying, "in the last ten years I've grown up."[9] Fonda, in fact, explicitly expressed regret over her militant antiwar activism, because she doubted that she was effective in winning converts to the cause. Her current politics, therefore, were born directly out of her experience as a radical critic of American foreign policy and the fact that the radical movement was unable to sustain political influence once the Vietnam War ended. She now seeks success defined as mainstream political credibility. However, the real measure of Fonda's effectiveness as an antiwar activist is not numbers of converts, for her major contributions to the protest movement were in other areas.

Jane Fonda was already a celebrity in 1970 when she joined the antiwar movement. Not only was she the daughter of Henry Fonda, one of America's most famous actors, but she had sixteen films to her credit and had already achieved recognition as an accomplished actress. In spring of 1970 Fonda set off on a three-month car trip to enhance her political education by personally visiting military bases, G.I. coffee houses, Indian reservations, and black urban ghettos. It quickly became apparent during this trip that her presence would bring major media attention to any event or to any cause. This, she learned, was one of the unique and important contributions that she could make to the movement and thereafter she was generous with her time in support of numerous causes. She was in such demand as a publicist, in fact, that her critics accused her of being "a hitchhiker on the highway of causes,"[10] while her friends were concerned that she was being exploited. Had she been "used for promotional purposes . . . manipulated by the movements that attracted you?" an interviewer asked in 1974. Fonda responded, "It's true to a degree. But I kept coming upon people who were living life-and-death experiences . . . The people weren't getting their stories out . . . I found it difficult to say no."[11]

While Fonda was still on her car trip, news of the American invasion of Cambodia inflamed the antiwar movement and inspired massive demonstrations across the United States. On May 4, four students at Kent State University in Ohio were killed by National Guard troops during a demonstration and these deaths further escalated the protests and the violence on college campuses. Provoked to increased action by these events, Fonda made her first appearance before a huge rally to speak against the war at the University of New Mexico. From that time until the end of the war, she made countless speeches at rallies and demonstrations, maintaining an exhausting schedule crisscrossing the country. Although she was much in demand by rally organizers as an attraction and a crowd pleaser, Fonda also drew much criticism for her speeches both from within and without the antiwar movement. Ironically, the criticism of her from both the right and the left focused on the same two themes. First her motives and sincerity were questioned. "Very few people believe me," she said. "They think it's a phase I am going through, a psychic trauma. Others think that I'm trying to be important, or that I do it for publicity. It seems kind of strange to them to see someone like me, someone who had everything, suddenly surfacing on the left and making speeches in the universities and preaching revolution."[12]

Second, Fonda's critics continually attacked her knowledge and grasp of the issues. Typical were the comments of William F. Buckley, who wrote that "a lack of information [has] plagued Miss Fonda much of her life.'' From his conservative perspective, however, he added that "She thinks like a calliope programmed at the Lenin Institute."[13] In retrospect Fonda, herself, expressed dissatisfaction with her role as a speaker. As early as a 1971 interview, an interview given during one of her extended speaking trips, Fonda commented "But I can't go on speaking in the universities forever. I hate to speak in public. I was so worried the first few times. And what I say in my speeches does not satisfy me because it doesn't come from my original ideas. I just tell what I heard, the experiences of others. There are so many people more qualified than I am, and I would rather stay at home reading a book."[14] Several years later when the war was over, when her approach to politics had changed and mellowed, Fonda was even more critical of herself. "You know how sometimes, when you don't know much about something, you try to sound superauthoritative? That's what I did," she said. "I came on like a Big Expert. I was defensive and unsure of myself. I spoke all over the country; I went on TV and said things that sounded too pompous and inflammatory. And it was all because I had all this emotion but I didn't know enough."[15]

Fonda, like her critics, was too hard on herself. She was certainly no scholar nor was she an expert on the causes she supported, but neither was she ignorant. With her characteristic intensity she sought to educate herself on the issues through reading, listening, observing, and reflecting on her own experience. Years later even she admitted that, " . . . in the end I *was* an expert in many areas about the war, but in the beginning, I was strident."[16] The tremendous criticism leveled against Fonda probably had less to do with the fact that she was ignorant or strident, than that she was a beautiful, successful movie star, who was very visibly active in radical causes. She disappointed and confused people, according to her own analysis. When she "stopped dressing to look sexy," she remarked, "people now say in disappointment: 'Are you really Jane Fonda?' And they almost refuse to accept this flat chest, this plain suit, this face that is nothing special."[17] Reflecting on this phenomenon in the Erica Jong interview, Fonda added, "I was on soapboxes, and *Barbarella* was playing down the street. People must have been given terribly mixed messages."[18] This disappointment and confusion translated into criticism. Yet, her job as a speaker and as an activist was not to formulate theory or policy, but to draw attention to the issues and to generate financial support for various causes. Thus, when journalist Oriana Fallaci asked her why she continued to make speeches if she was uncomfortable with it, Fonda replied, "I had to raise funds . . . "[19]

Fonda's financial support of radical causes was considerable, both through generous giving of her personal wealth and through various fund-raising activities. The Secret Service noted, for example, that she was paid $1250 for one university speech.[20] While traveling she walked up the aisle on commercial airline flights introducing herself and soliciting contributions. In the early stages of her activism, Fonda directed her support to a number of groups, perhaps most notably the Black Panthers. Although she never abandoned her multi-cause approach, in the aftermath of the Cambodian invasion and the Kent State killings, her attention increasingly became focused on issues surrounding the Vietnam War and G.I. rights. Through Fred Gardner, Fonda had been introduced to the United States Servicemen's Fund, an organization that sought to build an antiwar movement within the military. The Servicemen's Fund established coffee houses for G.I.s near military bases and staffed them with left-wing political organizers. Fonda visited a number of coffee houses in the spring and summer of 1970, encouraging the staff and talking to G.I.s. She devoted part of the summer to raising money for the Servicemen's Fund.

During the summer of 1970, Fonda also became involved with two other projects related to sevicemen. With a group of other activists, including Mark Lane, she participated in establishing a G.I. office in Washington. Fonda was convinced of the persecution and mistreatment of American soldiers, and thus the purpose of the office was, "to collect their statements, document them, coordinate them, verify them, and get them to the Congress and to the Senate for investigation."[21] To ensure the existence of the office, Fonda, in fact, pledged to subsidize the cost of operating the office for one year. Additionally, she became associated with the Vietnam Veterans Against the War, which was actively planning a series of public hearings designed to gather data on, and draw attention to, atrocities that had been committed by American military personnel in Vietnam. The Winter Soldier Investigation, as the hearings were called, was scheduled to take place in Detroit in January and February of 1971. In late fall of 1970, she set off on an ambitious speaking tour to raise money for the Winter Soldier Investigation. It was an incident that occurred during this speaking tour that probably completed the radicalization of Jane Fonda.

On November 2, Fonda spoke at a Canadian college. Traveling back to the United States to continue her speaking tour, Fonda's plane landed shortly after midnight, November 3, at the Cleveland International Airport. While going through U.S. Customs, she was harassed by Customs officials. Singled out of the line, her bags were thoroughly searched and in the process, "The customs men reported that they had found a supply of amphetamines and tranquilizers in her shoulder bag and 105 plastic vials of capsules in the suitcases she was carrying. . . . "[22] Additionally, she was detained for three and a half hours and denied permission to use the restroom even though she had her monthly period. Fonda, in anger and discomfort, finally attempted to force her way into the restroom. The result was that she was arrested, handcuffed and spent ten hours in the Cuyahoga County Jail on charges of assault and drug smuggling.[23]

After several months of legal action, all charges against Fonda were dropped. The "drugs" were found to be mainly vitamins, and small amounts of Dexedrin and a tranquilizer to help her maintain the demanding schedule that she was keeping. However, the incident had an important impact on Fonda. She experienced for the first time the violation of her own rights and she was convinced that the entire incident was a plot by the United States government to discredit her. Interviewer Oriana Fallaci asked Fonda if she believed " . . . that what happened at the Cleveland Airport was premeditated?'' Fonda responded, ''Of course.''[24]

Subsequently, Fonda's suspicions were proven to be correct. Her ability to attract attention to radical causes and to raise large amounts of money made her a person of interest to Richard Nixon's Washington. For nearly three years, beginning in May of 1970, agents from the F.B.I., the C.I.A. and the counter-intelligence branch of the Defense Intelligence Agency monitored her actions and built a file of over 500 pages. The existence of the confidential government dossier on Fonda became public in the revelations surrounding the dissipation of the Nixon administration. However, it was not until 1975 that it became known that transcripts of Fonda's 1970 long distance telephone calls were made by the National Security Agency and distributed to highly placed government officials including Nixon and National Security Adviser, Henry Kissinger.[25] Fonda, who received a partial copy of her dossier from newspaper columnist Jack Anderson, described its contents, in part, as follows:

They copied my entire address book, which was taken from me at the Cleveland Airport . . . They Xeroxed it and it appears as part of the dossier. Also, two banks, the Morgan Guaranty Trust Company of New York and the City National Bank of Los Angeles, turned over—without subpoena—my bank accounts . . . Other appalling things appear. There's a whole section devoted to my daughter . . . So, according to this file, the F.B.I. has people spying on kindergarten! It goes from that kind of thing to transcripts of speeches I've made . . . ''[26]

The government surveillance and harassment of Fonda did not stop, in fact, until after the fall of 1973 when she brought a suit against the U.S. Department of Justice naming officials of the Nixon administration including the president. The government, involved in covering up the Watergate affair, settled with Fonda out of court.[27] Nixon and his associates simply could not tolerate opposition to their policies, and as a critic of the administration, Fonda possessed certain characteristics that might have made her a formidable opponent. She had unusual access to wealth for support of political activities, to media attention to publicize her views, and to powerful people to lobby for causes. However, despite her privileged position in American society, it seems apparent that she exercised little or no direct influence on those public officials who made American foreign policy. They did not take seriously the views of a rich female film star who had recently appeared nude in films, but now preached revolutionary politics in what was considered to be a shrill and strident manner.

Additionally, the Nixon administration was probably worried about Fonda's potential to influence public opinion and build opposition to the war in Vietnam. As with the public officials, however, it is doubtful that her numerous speeches and public pronouncements converted many people to oppose the war. Asked, for example, what the controversial radio broadcasts she made from Hanoi accomplished, she responded, ''What speaking out always accomplishes. It may instill an idea, a new thought in the minds of even a few people . . . if there was one pilot who was already having second thoughts about it, it would be useful.''[28] In short, Fonda's important contributions to the antiwar movement were neither directly influencing policy-makers, nor directly attracting large numbers of people to the cause. Rather, her positive impact was indirect, and was a function of her celebrity status. She was a very significant fund raiser who generated money for critical movement activities. Through some of these activities, such as the G.I. office in Washington and the Winter Soldier Investigation, facts and information were gathered and disseminated—a process essential to changing public opinion about the war. Additionally, she was significant as a highly visible, outspoken opponent of the war. She encouraged and inspired other activists to continue their work, while she also attracted attention to their causes.

Jane Fonda, however, was not just a publicist and a fund raiser for other people's projects. She also developed her own area of work for the movement that was uniquely suited to her own abilities and interests—acting. In 1969 Fonda made *They Shoot Horses Don't They*. The movie, set in the Depression of the 1930s, took on contemporary political importance for Fonda. Although not yet an activist, by 1969 she opposed American involvement in the Vietnam War. During filming she drew parallels between the war and the ''agonizing experience'' of the Depression, speculating that audiences might come away from the movie with the feeling ''that if we could pull out of the Depression, we can pull out of the mess we're in now. . . . ''[29] She became preoccupied with the political implications of the film and the opportunity it offered her to ''become involved in a bigger statement.''[30] Thereafter she sought to make only movies that offered more than entertainment, and to use her acting ability, whether in commercially made films or in independent projects, for political purposes.

In early 1971, after her transformation to radical activist was completed, Fonda embarked on an acting project in which she explicitly attempted to combine her politics and her profession. The project was known as FTA, which at various times was translated as either ''Free the Army'' or ''Fuck the Army.'' Suggested by one of Fonda's associates, the concept was to create a high quality show that would tour military bases, entertaining troops in a fashion similar to Bob Hope's long-lived U.S.O. show. FTA, however, was built on material generated by leftist and antiwar writers. The cast included prominent antiwar entertainers such as Donald Sutherland, ''Country Joe'' McDonald, Dick Gregory, and Holly Near. Fonda put the show together under the auspices of the Servicemen's Fund. In mid-February, she held a press conference to announce the beginning of a tour to military bases.

The FTA opened near Fort Bragg, North Carolina, in March and then toured for about eighteen months. The show ''focuses on the dehumanization of G.I. life and links it to the military's sexism and racism'' according to a contemporary account.[31] The idea was to build a G.I. movement by raising the servicemen's consciousness of their situation. Reportedly the Fort Bragg audience was enthusiastic, but as the tour continued, internal politics disrupted the show and audiences declined. There were several criticisms made of FTA, all focusing in some way on Fonda. First, it was said that the effect of the show on the G.I.s was softened because of the men's fascination with her. Many only came to the performances to see her and even though she had stopped "dressing to look sexy" they were distracted from the political message by her personality and attractiveness. Other critics of FTA, especially Joe McDonald, who ultimately left the tour, accused Fonda of not being able to work collectively, of being manipulative, and of attempting to exercise too much power and influence. Finally, another critic simply stated that there was nothing revolutionary about the show. It served only two groups of people, "career radicals and film land opportunists, both of which felt they could advance their fortunes through their association with Jane."[32] There was probably some truth in each of these criticisms, a fact that gives some substance to the claim that through FTA Fonda hurt the G.I. movement more than she helped it.

The evidence suggests that overall, Fonda's active participation in the antiwar movement indirectly did more good than harm for the causes she supported. However, the facts also show quite clearly that her impact on the movement was both positive and negative. Her public actions and pronouncements, in fact, often served to polarize society rather than to coalesce public opinion against the war. The outstanding example of this is her first trip to Hanoi. Fonda first made arrangements to go to Hanoi in February of 1971. She planned to investigate the effects of the saturation bombing that had been carried out in and around the North Vietnamese capital city the previous December. A week before her intended trip, however, the government canceled all travel visas to North Vietnam, suggesting that official Washington learned of her plans and thought her significant enough to thwart her travel.[33] It was more than one year later when Fonda finally went to Hanoi.

Jane Fonda's arrival in North Vietnam in July of 1972 received worldwide attention from the press. The Nixon administration was claiming to be winding-down the war effort. One of the purposes of Fonda's visit was to call attention to the fact that on the contrary, the U.S. was escalating the air war. In Vietnam, Fonda visited schools, hospitals, dikes, and other civilian sites that had received extensive damage to demonstrate the effects of the bombing on the population. She took slides for use later in lectures, and shot home movies to further document her case. The fact that Fonda visited a country that the United States was at (undeclared) war with, and offered that kind of moral support to the enemy, incensed many Americans. She positively outraged people, however, even giving pause to many of her defenders, by making radio broadcasts from Hanoi. The broadcasts were directed at American servicemen in South Vietnam and were designed, in Fonda's words, to provide pilots access "to new information about the war." Her hope was that when the soldiers understood the devastation they were causing, they would refuse to continue bombing.[34]

In Hanoi, Fonda once again became a publicist for a cause, this time on behalf of the North Vietnamese. In keeping with the pattern of her activism, she used her celebrity status to draw world attention to the North Vietnamese cause. In turn, the actions of Hanoi officials were in keeping with the pattern of other individuals in causes Fonda supported: they exploited her generosity and commitment, and violated her trust. Much of what Fonda learned in Vietnam about the war was based upon her personal observations and experiences as she visited civilian bombing targets. This data served to further her political education and her effectiveness as a spokesperson against the war. However, in some other areas the North Vietnamese government misguided or misinformed Fonda to promote their cause. From her first ventures in political activism, Fonda maintained an almost blind loyalty to causes she adopted, and consequently, she accepted the North Vietnamese position uncritically.

Fonda returned to the Untied States more committed to antiwar activism than ever before. She was prepared to give eyewitness accounts of what she saw, and spoke freely and forcefully against American involvement in the war. Her reception was very hostile from many quarters. The ten or more radio broadcasts that she made in Hanoi were interpreted as attempts to undermine the morale of U.S. troops and to encourage rebellion and desertion. For those broadcasts she was branded a traitor by some. An editorial in the Manchester *Union Leader*, for example, stated that she should "be tried for treason. She should be shot if a verdict of guilty comes in."[35] Members of Congress actually enlisted the assistance of the Department of Justice to bring charges against her and a Maryland state legislator suggested that appropriate punishment would be to cut out her tongue. The charges against her ultimately were dropped because the undeclared war, itself, was technically illegal and not a sound basis for litigation. However, a segment of Americans, many of them veterans, would never forgive Fonda for her radio broadcasts, and upon her return she further inflamed people with her statements about prisoners of war in North Vietnam. Fonda met a few carefully selected POWs while in southeast Asia. From this controlled exposure and from information supplied by Hanoi officials, Fonda repeatedly and forcefully made a series of public statements about the condition—physical, mental, and political—of the POWs, which many Americans found outrageous. With this subject and with the Hanoi trip, she touched issues so sensitive that even twelve years after her first visit to Vietnam, an author could accurately continue to say that, "Jane Fonda remains the point-woman for the wrath of many veterans."[36]

The very intense several months after her return from Hanoi probably represent the apex of Fonda's antiwar activity and her radicalism. Together with Tom Hayden, a nationally known antiwar activist, Fonda formed the Indochina Peace Campaign (IPC) and spent the fall on a cross-country tour working to defeat Richard Nixon in the November election. Nixon was reelected, but in January of 1973 a cease-fire agreement was signed, and all American combat troops were out of Vietnam within two months. Fonda rightfully claimed that, "The only thing that forced the negotiations to take place, and forced an end to the killing, besides the Vietnamese resistance, was pressure by the antiwar movement . . .

it made it impossible for Nixon to continue. . . . ''[37] In this way Fonda's activities, especially in helping to publicize the escalation of the bombing, were instrumental in ending the Vietnam War. The most visible of any antiwar leader, she was courageous and tireless and made an important contribution to creating the climate in this country that forced the end of American military involvement in that conflict.

Fonda and Hayden, who married in January of 1973, did not abandon their Indochina Peace Campaign with the cease-fire agreement. However, once the killing of United States servicemen stopped the issues were less compelling to an American public who sought to put the war behind them. IPC's goals continued to be concerned with foreign policy; they included helping provide medical aid in North Vietnam and lobbying Congress to stop aid to the Thieu government in South Vietnam.[38] Fonda, continuing to seek ways to incorporate her politics with her profession, also established a film company under the auspices of IPC. IPC Productions initially served as a vehicle to create the slide shows and films that supported the political education goals of the Indochina Peace Campaign. *Introduction to the Enemy*, a very sympathetic portrayal of the North Vietnamese, which was made by Fonda and Hayden during an extended visit to that country in 1974, was, in fact, distributed by IPC Productions.[39] This film, like other IPC activities during 1973–74, never received much attention from the American public. The unfolding revelations surrounding the Watergate incident focused attention on domestic issues and leadership. Although the Watergate investigations in many ways vindicated Fonda by exposing the criminal actions of the administration, the ultimate effect of the affair was to mitigate the impact of the radical critique of American society. Richard Nixon's resignation from the presidency symbolized proof that the system worked. Frustrated by the inability of the left to build a mass movement after the cease-fire, and stung by the strong and continuing personal criticism, Fonda changed her politics.

Jane Fonda has no well-developed political ideology. "She always had this thing about the underdog," explained one of her associates.[40] This basic humanitarianism combined with a strong reaction to events taking place in the world around her to form her political beliefs. Fonda admitted that her transformation into a radical activist "was not an intellectual process."[41] It was an emotional response to a set of circumstances that were to her clearly unjust, unfair, and simply wrong. No explanation, for example, could justify such governmental actions as bombing civilian targets in Vietnam or beating peace marchers in Chicago. It appears that as much as any other factor, Fonda's activism was motivated by her outrage and frustration that these kinds of injustices were perpetuated against innocent people. In 1971 she called herself "a revolutionary woman." She claimed she was ready for armed struggle if it came, and defined herself as a socialist, "but without a theory, without an ideology."[42] By 1974, Fonda had mellowed. She announced that even "participatory democracy would be revolutionary" in the United States, and agreed with Tom Hayden that "if you want change, you have to be part of the mainstream. . . . ''[43] It may be somewhat unfair to say, as some did, that Jane Fonda "sold out" to the establishment after 1974, since she had no ideology, she had no particular plan for the future. However, it is clear that Fonda consciously sought to change her radical image, and that she pursued goals that were much more limited in scope than at the height of her revolutionary fervor. First through the Campaign for Economic Democracy and through political campaigns Fonda began focusing most of her attention on domestic issues that, at least to some degree, were achievable.

In 1975, Tom Hayden announced that he would run for the U.S. Senate. As Fonda continued to do into the mid–1980s, she worked for her husband's election and was a major financial supporter of his campaign. Some observers suggested that Hayden actually muzzled Fonda's radicalism to broaden support for his political ambitions and to enable her to increase her earnings in support of their political projects.[44] This interpretation of Fonda is characteristic of much that has been written about her. The majority of published accounts of Fonda's life and career develop her story through an unbroken series of relationships with men. Beginning with her father, ending with Hayden, and highlighted in between by her former husband Roger Vadim, Fonda is seen as being molded by and reflecting the interests of over a half dozen different men. Each of these men is credited with exercising critical influence during the various stages of her life. Fonda, it appears, had a series of "mentors" from whom she learned about acting, about politics, and about activism. The striking characteristic of each of these relationships, however, is not her dependency upon the individuals, nor is it their manipulation of her. It is the simple and undeniable fact that Fonda is an intelligent and contemplative student, a complex and independent person, who at every stage outgrew her teacher. She repeatedly surpassed the achievements of those from whom she learned, and then sought new challenges and formed new associations. This is as true in her relationship with Hayden as with earlier men.

By 1976 America saw a Jane Fonda who was concerned about such issues as day-care centers, rent control, sexism, heating bills, and the environment.[45] Although she did not abandon interest in national political issues, and issues of foreign policy, increasingly she focused her activity and attention on feminist issues, and issues relating to quality of life, consumerism, and health, which can be seen to fall within the traditional "sphere" of women. The women's liberation movement was one of the causes Fonda embraced in the early 1970s. While working on the film *Klute* she became a confirmed advocate of the women's movement. "Well," she said, "my whole thought and thinking changed. . . . I began to realize that this particular revolution is not only their [other women's] revolution, it's my revolution, too."[46] Fonda claimed that her 1968 pregnancy and the birth of her daughter played a significant role in transforming her into an activist.[47] During her 1972 trip to Vietnam she was inspired by the women who "were not only fighting with their hands, they were fighting with their bellies, having babies."[48] Despite these rather romantic notions, Fonda's foreign policy stance has no distinct feminist perspective and differed little from that of her male antiwar colleagues. With the exception of the treatment of sexism in the FTA show, Fonda's feminism did not appear in her politics until she withdrew from radicalism.

It is noteworthy that while Fonda acknowledged her feminism, she denied having had any female mentors. "She could not name a single woman," wrote Erica Jong, "who inspired her as an actress, and activist or a mother."[49] Clearly individual women were much less visible influences on Fonda's life than were specific men. However, despite Fonda's denial, she was not without female influence. For example, there is considerable evidence that Elisabeth Vailland served as a teacher and a friend during Fonda's period of transformation into a radical activist. Vailland, an intellectual and an experienced member of the French left, guided and facilitated Fonda's education on the issues and accompanied her on the 1970 car trip.[50] Additionally, actress Vanessa Redgrave apparently served as an inspiration and a model for Fonda during this same period when she plunged into activism. By the mid–1970s and the filming of *Julia*, however, Redgrave, who clung to uncompromising and radical politics, became for Fonda a model of what not to do. Fonda, it seems, related to strong women as readily as she related to strong men; she learned from them and then made her own choices, eventually going her own way.

The path Fonda created for herself was one of activism on issues that have a direct, sometimes immediate effect on her life. Her actions echo Hayden's words when he said, "I've felt from the beginning of my political activity that I was really just reacting to things in this society that were interfering with my life and the lives of millions of others."[51] Fonda has "sold out" in the sense that she no longer seeks a fundamental, or revolutionary change in society. Far from remaining outside, the determined critic rejecting the benefits of the establishment, she joined it and achieved her own power and wealth. Through her commercially successful IPC Productions, she has been able to control the films she has made in ways that were not previously available to women. High on entertainment value, IPC's feature films for a mass audience promote a political message as well. *Coming Home* (1978) even dealt with issues surrounding the Vietnam War. More commonly these films had feminist messages such as did *Nine to Five* (1980); always they had strong female characters.

Essentially, Fonda has channeled some of her political energy into career achievement for women in the film industry, and into making box-office hits that carry a sugar-coated, soft political message. Additionally, Fonda moved to a focus on causes arising from her immediate surroundings. Living in a very polluted Santa Monica, California, she worked on environmental and health issues. She began a summer camp for underprivileged children and became active in various consumer causes. It is not that she came to totally ignore national issues. In the usual pattern of her activism, she donated her time, energy, and money to a variety of causes such as the antinuclear power movement and the farm movement. However, her primary concerns moved to be those of children, health, family, and equal opportunity for women.

In terms of foreign policy, Jane Fonda has sold out in that she no longer speaks out. As an important part of her campaign to rehabilitate her image—to establish and maintain credibility—she has attempted to obscure and in some ways to belittle her past actions as a radical. In 1979, when she was forced to take a public position on the Boat People, the refugees from the new unified Vietnam, she maintained the lowest possible profile. Refusing to condemn the government she once so actively supported, she contributed to raising relief funds.[52] One of Fonda's few involvements with foreign policy implications that has continued into the 1980s has been her support through Amnesty International of an elderly Russian woman.[53] This activity, however, seems more a function of her "thing about the underdog" than any statement on foreign policy.

Fonda's workout books and best-selling workout video tapes stand out as symbols and examples of her politics. The books are based in her analysis of her experience and the needs of her own body. She generalized from this analysis to develop a program for America. Throughout the books is the message that the organization of this society and its economy has been working to the detriment of the personal health of all its citizens. Through her program—by at least three workouts each week, proper eating habits, and wise consumerism—people can change America. If Fonda's political ideology has not become much more sophisticated in her nearly twenty years of activism, her goals have certainly changed. "I don't think of myself as a leader. I'm a woman who's changing," Fonda said of herself.[54] Indeed, her life and career are full of ironies, contradictions, and changes. For example, she began her professional life as a model and an actress, relying for success in part on her personal appearance. Two decades later, despite what her intentions may be, the tremendous success of her workout business has little to do with the political implications of the program, and much to do with the implications for physical appearance. An additional irony of her life has to do directly with her activism on foreign policy issues. Fonda failed to exercise direct influence on American foreign policy-makers in part because they did not take her views seriously. She was not only a woman, untrained in diplomatic and historical matters, but she was, in their view, a frivolous, somewhat amoral movie star. However, her contribution to the antiwar movement was precisely because she could attract attention and money through her power as a beautiful, female film star. Finally, beginning in 1976, Fonda has been among the most admired women in America according to a number of annual polls.[55] In a relatively short period of time she overcame the stigma of being one of America's most intensely despised activists to become one of the nation's female role models. She did this as she left the male-dominated sphere of foreign policy and moved into issues more traditionally associated with women.

NOTES

1. *Time*, 3 October, 1977, p. 90.
2. Leo Janos, "Jane Fonda: Finding Her Golden Pond," *Cosmopolitan*, January, 1985, p. 171.

3. Katherine Barrett and Richard Greene, "America's Favorite Women," *Ladies' Home Journal*, November, 1985, p. 62.

4. Jane Leavy, "Jane Fonda, Good as Old," *Washington Post*, 26 January, 1985, section C, p. 1.

5. Erica Jong, "Jane Fonda: An Interview," *Ladies' Home Journal*, April, 1984, p. 35.

6. Jane Fonda with Mignon McCarthy, *Women Coming of Age* (New York: Simon & Schuster, 1984), p. 14.

7. Femmy DeLyser, *Jane Fonda's Workout Book for Pregnancy, Birth, and Recovery* (New York: Simon & Schuster, 1982), p. 234.

8. Leavy, section C, p. 1.

9. Jong, p. 36.

10. Thomas Kiernan, *Jane Fonda: Heroine for Our Times* (New York: Delilah Books, 1982), p. 268.

11. "*Playboy* Interview: Jane Fonda and Tom Hayden," *Playboy*, April, 1974, p. 90.

12. Oriana Fallaci, "Jane Fonda: 'I'm Coming into Focus,' " *McCall's*, February, 1971, p. 123.

13. William F. Buckley, Jr., "Secretary Fonda," *National Review*, 18 August, 1972, p. 919.

14. Fallaci, p. 152.

15. Martha Weinman Lear, "Jane Fonda: A Long Way from Yesterday," *Redbook*, June, 1976, p. 148.

16. Jong, p. 36.

17. Fallaci, p. 151.

18. Jong, p. 36.

19. Fallaci, p. 152.

20. Fred Lawrence Guiles, *Jane Fonda: The Actress in Her Time* (Garden City, New York: Doubleday and Company, 1982), p. 177.

21. Fallaci, p. 152.

22. "The Cause Celeb," *Newsweek*, 16 November, 1970, p. 65.

23. Fallaci, p. 140; Kiernan, pp. 239–65; Guiles, pp. 179–80.

24. Fallaci, p. 140.

25. Guiles, p. 165.

26. *Playboy*, pp. 77–78.

27. Guiles, p. 223.

28. *Playboy*, p. 78.

29. Kiernan, p. 190.

30. Jong, p. 144.

31. "The Show the Pentagon Couldn't Stop," *Ramparts*, September, 1972, p. 32.

32. Kiernan, p. 273.

33. Guiles, pp. 183–84.

34. *Playboy*, p. 78.

35. Ibid., p. 80.

36. Myra MacPherson, *Long Time Passing: Vietnam and the Haunted Generation* (Garden City, New York: Doubleday and Company, Inc., 1984), p. 466.

37. *Playboy*, p. 37.

38. Guiles, pp. 225–26.

39. Ibid., pp. 234–37.

40. Kiernan, p. 107.

41. Fallaci, p. 148.

42. Ibid., p. 151.

43. *Playboy*, p. 184.

44. Kiernan, p. 292; Guiles, p. 239.

45. Kiernan, p. 298.

46. Guiles, p. 172.

47. Fallaci, p. 148.

48. *Playboy*, p. 180.

49. Jong, p. 35.

50. See Kiernan, Fallaci, and Guiles for more detail on Vailland and her relationship with Fonda.

51. *Playboy*, p. 184.

52. Guiles, p. 52.

53. Janos, p. 171.

54. *Playboy*, p. 90.

55. Guiles, p. 298; Chuck Conconi, "Personalities," *Washington Post*, 11 December 1985, section C, p. 3.

8

Barely in the Inner Circle: Jeane Kirkpatrick

Judith Ewell

Jeane Kirkpatrick mused recently at the end of her United Nations term:

> I was the only woman in our history, I think, who ever sat in regularly at top-level foreign policy-making meetings. Those arenas have always been closed to women, not only here but in most other countries. And it matters a great deal. It's terribly important, maybe even to the future of the world, for women to take part in making the decisions that shape our destiny.[1]

How will historians evaluate the tenure of the first woman to participate in the inner circle of U.S. foreign policy-making? Neither Kirkpatrick nor her critics would claim that she brought a uniquely female perspective to U.S. foreign policy. Nor did she pull much weight within the cabinet or National Security Council in day-to-day decision-making on specific issues. From the time of Ronald Reagan's 1980 campaign, Kirkpatrick had considerable visibility as part of his foreign policy team, and she was perceived as a standard-bearer for the hard-line policies that conservatives found so attractive. Her role clearly was an important one in helping to publicize the general outlines of Reagan's foreign policy and ensuring that neoconservative, anticommunist views received serious consideration.

Analysts recently have fallen upon the term public diplomacy to describe the role that people like Kirkpatrick play. Although the phrase more frequently denotes activities undertaken by the United States Information Agency or Voice

An earlier version of this article was given as a paper at the annual meeting of the Society for Historians of American Foreign Relations at Stanford University on June 25–28, 1985. I should like to thank the following people for their helpful criticism of the earlier draft: Barton Bernstein, Edward Crapol, David Dessler, Joan Hoff-Wilson.

of America, it is a term that Kirkpatrick has used to describe her work at the United Nations.[2] By law, the VOA and USIA are prohibited from disseminating their message to the U.S. domestic audience, but such restrictions cannot apply to the United Nations Ambassador. Kirkpatrick's deputy on the United Nations staff, Kenneth Adelman, elaborated on the distinction between public and traditional diplomacy in a 1981 *Foreign Affairs* article:

Traditional diplomacy is formal and official; public diplomacy is usually informal and engages non-officials. Traditional diplomacy is private and quiet, while public diplomacy is open and can be noisy. Traditional diplomacy seeks to avoid controversy, to smooth out differences, whereas public diplomacy tends to expose and stimulate controversy, whether artistic or intellectual or political. The most fervent proponents of traditional diplomacy, such as Henry Kissinger, are among those least inclined toward public diplomacy.[3]

Adleman accurately predicted that public diplomacy would be a "growth industry" in the Reagan administration. In January, 1983, President Reagan established the Special Planning Group on Public Diplomacy to oversee and coordinate the administration's foreign policy messages.

Kirkpatrick's career and training had prepared her well to play a public diplomacy role, although little in her background qualified her to be what she claimed to be: an expert in foreign policy. Kirkpatrick was born Jeane Jordan in 1926 in Oklahoma. Her father, Welcher Jordan, was a prosperous oil wildcatter, who held rather traditional views of women's roles. Her mother, Leona, had attended secretarial school and was an accountant in her husband's business. She encouraged the young girl in her zest for reading and education.[4] A love for words at an early age—she claims that she taught herself to read by age four—prompted Kirkpatrick to use her allowance money to buy a thesaurus at age ten.[5] In her Illinois high school, she showed a flair for acting in school plays and also was an editor of the high school paper. She first followed her father's advice and attended Stephens College in Columbia, Missouri, which she characterized as little more than a women's finishing school. After two years of study in Missouri, she took what she recalls as her "first clear-cut decision"[6] and transferred to Barnard College, where she received a B.A. in political science in 1948. She earned a Master's Degree in 1950 and wrote her thesis on Oswald Mosley and the British Union of Fascists.[7]

Kirkpatrick's years at Columbia University coincided with public denunciations of atrocities in Stalin's Russia and the Holocaust in Germany. At the university she had been influenced by liberal professors such as Franz L. Neumann, who directed her M.A. thesis, Robert MacIver, and Harold Lasswell, and she also met a number of German and Russian refugees. From this experience, she dates her conviction that abstract ideological systems ran counter to human tradition and destroyed human freedom. Hannah Arendt, Lionel Trilling, William Barrett, and Norman Podhoretz led the New York intellectual world in exploring these same issues in the 1950s. Kirkpatrick, however, apparently was not associated with the active network of New York literary intellectuals during her student days. Podhoretz does not mention her in *Making It*, and she later says that she shares many views with the *Commentary* set, but "I wasn't born to that group."[8]

Armed with introductions from Neumann, Kirkpatrick headed to Washington to work with former OSS analyst Evron Kirkpatrick at the State Department. She liked Kirkpatrick, but she found the bureaucratic job tedious.[9] She escaped to a French government fellowship at the University of Paris's Institute of Political Science in 1952–53. Evron Kirkpatrick found reasons to travel to France to maintain his relationship with his young associate. Fifteen years her senior, Evron had taught political science at the University of Minnesota before coming to the OSS in 1945 and then to various positions in the State Department. In 1954, he left his State Department job to become the Executive Director of the American Political Science Association, a position he kept until his retirement in 1981. He continued to develop many ties in Washington, helped considerably by his close association with Hubert Humphrey, whom he had taught at the University of Minnesota and whose political campaigns he helped to manage.[10]

Jeane Jordan returned to the U.S. from France in 1953 and began to work on a Defense Department study on refugees from the People's Republic of China. In 1955, she and Evron Kirkpatrick were married. Kirkpatrick became her mentor and closest adviser, encouraging her to write when she was at home to rear their three young sons (1957 to 1962). Of her marriage, she says, "I never gave up anything. I had intellectual interests. I married one of the best libraries in the world. . . ."[11] In another interview, Jeane Kirkpatrick mused: "I've never had a career goal in my life. . . . I've never felt a drive to pursue a specific career— I guess you could say I'm an experience collector. My goal is living to the hilt."[12] In nearly all of her interviews, Kirkpatrick has expressed satisfaction with her life as a wife, mother, teacher, and writer.

In spite of avowing no specific career goals, Kirkpatrick's transit over the hurdles of an academic career seemed fairly rapid. As an assistant professor, she taught at Trinity College in Washington from 1962 until 1967 when she moved to Georgetown University as an associate professor. She had lacked only the dissertation to receive a Ph.D. from Columbia University, and in 1965 she began work on a study of Juan Peron's followers in Argentina. The study was based on a survey questionnaire, which Kirkpatrick designed. International Research Associates conducted the interviews, and Kirkpatrick analyzed the results without spending time in Argentina. In 1968, she received her Ph.D., and in 1971 a revised version of the dissertation was published by MIT Press. In 1973 she was promoted to full professor at Georgetown, and in 1974 her second book appeared: a study of women in politics in the U.S., again an analysis of questionnaire responses. After her third book appeared—*The New Presidential Elite*, deriving from a survey distributed to delegates to the presidential nominating conventions in 1972—she was named to the Leavey Professorship in the Foundations of American Freedom at Georgetown in 1978. Her research and teaching fields in the 1973 APSA *Directory* were listed as foreign and cross national political institutions and behavior and "Mediterranean political systems, including Latin America."

If Jeane Kirkpatrick had married a mentor and a library when she married Evron, she recognized that she had also "married into Humphrey circles."[13] She became active in local and national Democratic politics and was elected to the 1972 Democratic Convention as a Humphrey delegate. Her distress at the Democratic divisions in 1968 and 1972 must have been personal as well as political. Any hopes that she and Evron had had of becoming government insiders on the coattails of a Humphrey victory were dashed. She blamed the national crisis on the young idealists and, by her terms, elitists who had scorned and reviled Humphrey in favor of George McGovern. Subsequently Kirkpatrick decided that the Vietnam War had to end because it was tearing apart the society of the United States. Perhaps, she acknowledged, her views on the war had also softened because her eldest son was approaching draft age. Significantly, she did not conclude that such foreign forays were necessarily ill-advised, but rather that they could not be conducted in the face of such internal dissent.[14]

In 1972 she and Evron joined Daniel Patrick Moynihan, Norman Podhoretz, Midge Decter, Henry Jackson, Michael Novak, and other disheartened Democrats to form the Coalition for a Democratic Majority. The Coalition advocated an aggressive, anticommunist foreign policy coupled with progressive domestic social policies. Later Jeane Kirkpatrick also joined the Committee on the Present Danger, which lobbied for a stronger national defense. In 1977 she became a resident scholar at the American Enterprise Institute for Public Policy. Although she now says that she quietly voted for Gerald Ford in 1976, her neoconservative group tried to bring President Jimmy Carter around to their way of thinking. Kirkpatrick accompanied a delegation to visit the president in January, 1980, to plead for a harder line against the Soviets. Carter apparently was not persuaded or even hospitable. Kirkpatrick said, "They have treated us like pariahs. . . . We have acted like good Democrats for a long time. Meanwhile the Republican Party keeps telling us they like what we say."[15]

By 1980 her writings and philosophy were well in the mainstream of the new conservatism. She was not nationally or widely known as an original scholar, or an intellectual groundbreaker. Her research had not focused on international or inter-American politics, although she later claimed expertise in Latin America.[16] Yet she had a respectable publishing record of monographs and well-written essays, a prestigious university professorship, resident scholar status at a nationally recognized think tank, valuable contacts in Washington, in the political world, and in the political science network. Her friends, acquaintances, and students knew her as an articulate and assertive speaker.

By 1980, what were the main themes of Kirkpatrick's writing? Quite simply, she stresses the primacy of culture and tradition over abstract ideas, ideologies, or "rationalism." Political culture changes slowly and can not be altered by political elites, except through unacceptable intrusions on the personal liberties and desires of the majority of the citizens. Stable political systems usually have competitive political parties, which are inspired by interests, rather than ideas, for interests can be compromised, but morals and ideas can not be and contribute to rigid and inflexible systems. There are no inevitable movements or forces in history. Communism had achieved victories in the world only when it was imposed by a skillful elite. Communists often concealed their true aims and either lured or forced people into compliance. Gradual change and reform were to be lauded, but rapid change, which alienated people from their traditional values, left the field open to the machinations of communists. Although Kirkpatrick does not always link her abhorrence of new left politics in the United States in the 1960s with the erosion of U.S. power in the world, she clearly would perceive a connection between the idealistic U.S. left, which challenged traditional U.S. culture and values and a national inability to project those values abroad. In the 1960s and 1970s, communists had skillfully competed in the third world for influence. The United States had not competed, and had thus lost influence.

How to reverse this alarming trend? One of the major tools, Kirkpatrick asserted, is words. Words depict reality, words have consequences, and the U.S. could use words to combat the evil and doublespeak of the Communists. Other actions must be taken as well, but words are actions and are an important weapon in the arsenal of democracy. At home, word/actions can be internalized and provide a means of reinforcing traditional values and culture.

This is the theoretical world of an intellectual who deals with and exaggerates the power of words. It is also a world dominated by a new class of "symbol specialists" in politics whose task is "formulating and transmitting opinions about the nature and meaning of events."[17] In spite of her stated commitment to welfare state policies, Kirkpatrick's philosophical world is one in which status prevails over economic class and economic factors receive short shrift as salient variables.

Kirkpatrick's theories, along with her more concrete attack on Jimmy Carter's foreign policy, reinforced Ronald Reagan's view of the world and his nostrums for the loss of American power. He too was fond of attributing the U.S. "decline" to a loss of will. He too wished to evangelize for democracy and American values. As an actor, he too had a faith that words could move people, could change things. Perhaps as an actor he also recognized that a varied set of roles would make more successful theater. State Department career professionals and White House staff could practice traditional diplomacy. The U.S. ambassador to the United Nations could play a major public diplomacy role.

Richard Allen, a Washington insider who became Reagan's first national security advisor, called Reagan's attention to Kirkpatrick's article "Dictatorships and Double Standards" during the 1980 electoral campaign. The article, which had appeared in *Commentary*, criticized President Carter's foreign policy. Alliance with people who called for radical change in traditional societies had contributed to a loss of prestige and allies for the United States, Kirkpatrick had argued. U.S. interests were best served by supporting traditional, if authoritarian, leaders such as Anastasio Somoza and the Shah of Iran because they were secure friends of the United States and could encourage an evolution toward more democratic institutions. Human freedom and human rights had suffered since the victories of the Sandinistas in Nicaragua and the Ayatollah in Iran, as they do under any abstract and totalitarian philosophy of government.[18]

Ronald Reagan liked the article, Allen arranged a meeting with Kirkpatrick, and she was signed up for an adviser's role on foreign policy during the campaign. She prepared Reagan for the presidential debates, and she won a place on the foreign policy transition team after the election. Her ability to articulate the interests that Reagan favored, her symbolic value as a woman, a Democrat, and a neoconservative with influential contacts inspired Reagan to name her to the United Nations post. Norman Podhoretz referred to Kirkpatrick's rapid rise as a "Cinderella story."[19] The *Washington Post* remarked on the parallels with the career of fellow neoconservative Daniel Patrick Moynihan and predicted that if the parallel held, Kirkpatrick would be "more of a preacher than a diplomat in the job, using it as a pulpit from which to rail against critics of the United States."[20]

Kirkpatrick's testimony in her confirmation hearing before the U.S. Senate indicated that she understood both the limitations and the possibilities of the post:

I think the United Nations Ambassador does not and should not devise her own foreign policy in New York. . . . I also believe that the United Nations Ambassador should not be merely a passive reflector—a ventriloquist's dummy, if you will—for policies which she had no role in formulating. . . . I think the United Nations Ambassador also does not ever undermine administration policy, either publicy or privately. I take a firm strict constructionist view of an ambassador's role. . . . Finally, I think the United Nations Ambassador should neither seek confrontation with other delegates nor shrink from confrontation when that is necessary to defend American values or national integrity.[21]

Kirkpatrick also saw the post as an important one for developing domestic support for a more aggressive foreign policy. At her confirmation hearing, she spoke about her public role at the UN:

I expect that public communication with Americans will be an important part of my job, and it is one I have already thought quite a bit about, in fact. It is the one that fits my background best, I might add, too.[22]

Although she recognized that the UN post primarily called for a spokesperson rather than a formulator of policy, Kirkpatrick may have been chagrined at how little influence she had in the cabinet and National Security Council. The ambassador to the United Nations must report to the secretary of state even though there is also direct access to the president through the cabinet. If the UN ambassador is at odds with the secretary of state, policy influence is minimized. It is difficult for the ambassador to attend all cabinet and National Security Council meetings while also presiding over the U.S. mission in New York. When she first came to the United Nations, Kirkpatrick was criticized by other delegates for her frequent absences to attend cabinet meetings in Washington. By mid–1981 she was spending more time in New York, usually Tuesday through Friday, even though that schedule meant that she had to miss some cabinet meetings.[23] Kirkpatrick's colleagues in the cabinet could and sometimes did schedule meetings when she could not attend.[24]

Kirkpatrick's further ability to affect policy was limited because her sometimes extreme positions and her inexperience put her at a disadvantage in the cabinet. Her ideas had the greatest currency when she had a strong ally or mentor who could press them on Reagan or the rest of the cabinet. For instance, Reagan's foreign policy team was in relative disarray from January, 1981, until the appointment of William Clark as national security adviser (January 1982) and the resignation of Alexander Haig as secretary of state (June 1982).[25] Haig, in his desire to be the "vicar" of foreign policy, constantly warred with White House aides Edwin Meese, James A. Baker, Jr., and Michael Deaver as well as with Kirkpatrick. Kirkpatrick's first mentor, Richard Allen, had relatively little influence as national security adviser since he reported to Meese rather than directly to the president. Moreover his staff was deemed weak, and his own management style was ineffectual.[26] It is doubtful that he would have been a strong ally for Kirkpatrick even if he had not been forced out at the end of 1981 because of his having accepted a cash payment from a Japanese journalist who had interviewed Nancy Reagan. His replacement by Judge William Clark provided Kirkpatrick with her most reliable ally, but she still had to contend with Haig and the White House staff.

Various accounts have reported that Meese, Baker, and Deaver had little patience with Kirkpatrick. Haig's edginess over Kirkpatrick's claims to expertise in foreign policy and her independence of the State Department are legendary. The slight attention given to the feuds with the UN ambassador in Haig's book *Caveat* suggests that he did not consider her of great importance. Yet the comments he does permit himself are rather snide.

Mrs. Kirkpatrick called on me to complain about the inadequacy of her office, her limousine, her personal staff, and her security detail. She made a very strong first impression with her determined stride, her obvious intelligence, and her crackling personality and manner of speech.[27]

Haig's memory of the first cabinet meeting on January 7 was no more flattering: "The meeting, as I remember it, was largely taken up with an interesting if somewhat discursive lecture on the nature of conservatism by Mrs. Kirkpatrick."[28] Although Kirkpatrick later said that the press had blown her confrontations with Haig out of proportion, several accounts in 1981 and 1982 reported that she had considered resigning and that she hated the constant tension. In 1983, she confessed to an interviewer:

I hated it, you know. I didn't really know how to deal with it. It created an intensely difficult situation for me, both personally and professionally. I had never encountered anything remotely like it. I had never been in a professional situation in which there was a contentious relationship between me and a superior or a significant colleague even. All I can say is that I hated it. [29]

In this context, it must be assumed that Kirkpatrick had minimal influence in the cabinet in the first year and a half even with her access to President Reagan.

From mid–1982 until Ocotber 1983, Kirkpatrick's opinions received fuller attention in the cabinet. Alexander Haig's replacement as secretary of state, George Shultz, also wanted to centralize decision-making in the State Department and he too specifically wished to keep Kirkpatrick on the fringes of the policy discussions. [30] Kirkpatrick had found an ally in NSC adviser William Clark, however, for he endorsed many of her conservative views, especially on Central America, and he had the confidence of President Reagan. Even so, Kirkpatrick herself disclaims any major credit or blame for Reagan administration policies.

I have not been an architect of our Central American policy. I have had a substantial influence on two issues. One was U.S. support for the Contadora group. The other was the formation of the bipartisan commission on Central America—a concept [the late Sen. Henry] Scoop Jackson and I conceived with Sen. Charles Mathias' help. [31]

Both of these initiatives might be seen as image-conscious efforts to portray U.S. Central American policies as balanced and reasonable. Kirkpatrick had not been present at the meeting that decided to launch the Grenada invasion in October 1983. [32]

The White House staff and Secretary of State Shultz further indicated their unwillingness to include Jeane Kirkpatrick in the inner circle of substantive foreign policy-making when they blocked or ignored her bid to succeed William Clark as national security adviser in October, 1983, and as NSC adviser or secretary of state in early 1985. Even her ally Clark apparently did not press her case strongly, although some of her other conservative supporters lobbied the White House on her behalf. On both of these occasions, Kirkpatrick allegedly was offered the posts of director of the Agency for International Development (AID), the deputy to the national security adviser, and counselor to the president. None of those positions gave her significant policy-making responsibilities, all would have stripped her of cabinet rank, and none would have allowed her the same leeway to address the U.S. and foreign publics as the UN job did. Kirkpatrick in 1983 believed that the administration moderates had encouraged Clark's resignation and were also trying to humiliate her or to edge her out of the administration. If that was the intention, she weathered the challenge but was unable to secure a more powerful office either then or at the outset of Reagan's second term.[33]

From October 1983 until her departure from the United Nations job in April 1985, Kirkpatrick probably had somewhat less influence in Washington than she had while Clark was NSC adviser. She had no White House mentor—except Reagan himself who remained above the fray; she had been somewhat humiliated by the media accounts of her lusting after a job that she had not secured; she had no one to facilitate end runs around a hostile secretary of state; and the White House staff preferred a less aggressive foreign policy image for the up-coming presidential election. Judged by what we know of intra-cabinet politics, Jeane Kirkpatrick seems not to have been a leader or opinion setter. Yet, even so, she reassured the conservatives, who feared that Reagan was surrounded by and advised by moderates. Her conservative posturing was more visible in the United Nations and in her public speaking and writing than it was in the cabinet. Arguably, had she been more self-confident and experienced she might more frequently have leaked news of her differences with the cabinet majority. Both a loyal team player and one who was struggling to master a new job, Kirkpatrick only rarely aired her differences in public.

Positions that she is known to have supported in the cabinet and National Security Council are generally consistent with her writing and speaking before she came to office. She favored a strong and hard line against the Soviets, even if that position should be impractical in terms of domestic political pressures. She unsuccessfully opposed the lifting of the grain embargo to the Soviet Union in 1981, and she, also unsuccessfully, advocated consideration of forcing the Polish government into bankruptcy after the military crackdown in December 1981. The economic interests of U.S. grain farmers or of U.S. bankers who had loans out to Poland did not outweigh to her the merits of a strongly principled stand.[34]

The Reagan government did encourage closer relations with authoritarian governments, in harmony with Kirkpatrick's argument in "Dictatorships and Double Standards." Kirkpatrick probably did not initiate the new tilt toward South Africa, but she did inadvertently call attention to the warming trend when she met with South African military intelligence officers in March 1981. That meeting caused the U.S. Black Congressional Caucus to call for her resignation. Kirkpatrick avowed that she had not known who the men were and that she had an academic's willingness to listen to anyone. She speculated that she had been "set up" in order to force Reagan's hand on South Africa.[35]

The most public battle over policy toward authoritarian governments that arose during Reagan's first term involved U.S. actions during the Falklands/Malvinas war between Argentina and Great Britain. Kirkpatrick advocated strict neutrality so that the U.S. would not alienate Latin American allies, especially ones like the Argentines, who had provided aid in the struggle against the guerrilla left in Central America. Haig and most of the rest of the foreign policy team accorded primacy to and gave logistical support to the British. Even after the U.S. decision was taken, Kirkpatrick continued to meet with high-ranking Argentines. Haig believed that her public sympathy for Argentina sent erroneous signals to the Argentinean junta and perhaps prolonged the war, and he pressed for Kirkpatrick's resignation. Kirkpatrick pleaded her case with Reagan, and she received no public censure for her actions.[36] The White House asked for Haig's resignation shortly thereafter. Kirkpatrick gained by Haig's departure, but her own reputation within the administration was not enhanced by her support of the Argentines.

Kirkpatrick's Argentine thesis failed, but her writings inspired a change in U.S. rhetoric on human rights. Public denunciations of human rights abuses ceased, although Congress continued to insist on some progress before awarding increased military aid. Kirkpatrick had argued that Carter's definition of human rights had been too broad and utopian and that a more realistic definition would focus on "fundamental political freedoms—free speech, free press, rule of law, due process."[37] Undersecretary of State Richard Kennedy, in October 1981, suggested adopting the more narrow definition of political rights as administration policy. The presence of democratic forms could then be used to take the offensive against Congressional and public critics of Reagan's policy.[38] Pressure on Latin American nations to hold demonstration elections met with some success, but "double standards" in the U.S. official assessment of these elections cast doubt upon the administration's credibility in the new human rights emphasis.[39] Uruguay's and Guatemala's elections in 1984 were ballyhooed as real advances, while Nicaragua's presidential election in November 1984, more meaningful and open than most in the region, was entirely ignored and characterized as illegitimate.

Kirkpatrick frequently asserted that she was not the hard-liner that the media considered her to be.[40] If her statements may be taken at face value, her "toughness" toward Central America remained primarily at the symbolic level, although she did endorse increased military aid to El Salvador and aid to the *contras*, who were fighting against the Sandinistas in Nicaragua. She did not advocate direct U.S. military intervention in the region, and she said that she was "incredulous" at Haig's proposal in the National Security Planning Group to use force to go to the "source"—Cuba—in the Caribbean. The mining of Nicaragua's harbors had not been discussed in her presence, but she says she would also have opposed that action.[41] If Kirkpatrick opposed the hardest line—that of direct U.S. military intervention—she also opposed negotiation with the Nicaraguan Sandinistas or the guerilla FMLN in El Salvador.

Clark and she were instrumental in wresting control of the Central American policy from Thomas Enders, assistant secretary of state for Latin America, in February 1983. Enders had advocated a moderate two-track strategy toward the Sandinistas: continuing to pursue diplomatic negotiations at the same time that pressure was maintained by aid to the *contras*. Kirkpatrick and the hard-liners had concluded that negotiation with the Sandinista government was neither possible nor desirable. The covert aid that had begun as a means for the C.I.A. to collect intelligence about the Sandinistas' alleged shipment of arms to the guerrillas in El Salvador had evolved into the effort actually to overthrow the Nicaraguan government. In that strategy, there was no room for negotiation, and Clark and Kirkpatrick saw that Enders was replaced by H. Langhorne Motley.

In Ronald Reagan's cabinet then, Jeane Kirkpatrick contributed to setting a general tone and, in alliance with William Clark, occasionally had a more direct impact on specific policies and personnel. What can be said about her contribution as ambassador to the United Nations? Among her specific goals, she hoped to encourage UN moderates to vote with the U.S. more consistently; to defend Israel and South Africa from what she considered unrelenting attacks; to combat Soviet propaganda initiatives, which had too often gone unchallenged; to limit the inflated budgets of the UN and to look carefully at administrative agencies that took political or social viewpoints that were inconsistent with U.S. policy or did not employ a sufficient number of U.S. citizens. Despite her criticism of the UN, Kirkparick frequently stated that she did not think that the U.S. should withdraw from the forum.

The United States has seldom appointed professional diplomats to head the UN mission. Kirkpatrick as the first U.S. female head of mission was highly visible and compounded her own inexperience by her decision to dismiss most of the professional staff in favor of her own team of hard-liners. She received considerable criticism in her first months in office.[42] The heavy security that surrounded her and her difficulty in keeping to an office schedule provoked unfavorable comments. UN diplomats and other observers also remarked that she had little patience with the informal, but necessary, exercise of diplomacy in the corridors and the delegates' lounge. She was considered stand-offish, cool, unfriendly, and not "one of the boys."[43] Relatively few women hold high positions in the United Nations, and they usually remain in the "ghettos" of committees that relate to women's interests.[44] Kirkpatrick commented that even her choice of wardrobe was a problem. Although it was acceptable for men to go from business sessions to evening receptions in business suits, her own suits and "sensible low-heeled shoes" were out of place when she had no opportunity to change.[45] Feeling uncomfortable in this "very exclusive male preserve," and by some accounts shy, Kirkpatrick did not commence her job with the exuberance of a Daniel Patrick Moynihan.[46]

Her colleagues most frequently complained about her professorial tone and attitude. One journalist who perhaps had not frequently been in a classroom wrote: "She was accustomed to having dutiful students take notes on her every word. . . . "[47] She liked to lecture the delegates and, particularly with third world issues, she could appear quite condescending. The other delegates naturally resented it, and Latin American representatives also noted that her well-touted expertise on Latin America had some amazing gaps.[48] The criticism, however, valid, became cliché as the U.S. media frequently described her as "schoolmarmish."[49]

Kirkpatrick, however, probably earned approval from some U.S. conservatives by her "amateur " actions. When the delegates from the nonaligned movement met and issued a statement that criticized the U.S. for the firing on Libyan planes in the Gulf of Sidra in September 1981, Kirkpatrick immediately dispatched harsh and chastising letters to many of those delegates, calling them to account for their action. The letter was probably counterproductive. Some moderates who had intended later to back away from the memorandum then refused to do so for fear of appearing to bow to the U.S. One recipient of the letter characterized it as the action of "the absent parent who scolds her child for misbehavior committed in her absence."[50] But her stern response played well in Peoria.

Two other incidents that put her in the center of a storm of controversy appeared to have reflected Haig's awkwardness and ambitions rather than Kirkpatrick's. While Haig was in the Far East and Australia in June 1981, a UN resolution to censure Israel for its attack on the Iraqi nuclear reactor was being discussed in the Security Council. Most reliable reports confirm that Kirkpatrick did a skillful job of negotiating a resolution that criticized Israel rather mildly but called for no sanctions. Yet some of Haig's aides in New Zealand claimed that Kirkpatrick would have voted for an unacceptable version of the resolution if Haig himself had not gotten on the phone to arrange a compromise. The leak had the effect of minimizing Kirkpatrick's achievement and undermining her reputation as a professional. If taken seriously, it could also have weakened Kirkpatrick's credit with the strong pro-Israel lobby in the U.S. The aides may have taken the action on their own in order to bolster Haig's reputation, but the episode became the first in the series of public Haig/Kirkpatrick confrontations.[51]

The squabbles over U.S. policy during the Falklands war have already been alluded to. Public conflicts between Haig and Kirkpatrick came to a head again over the Security Council resolution for a proposed cease-fire in the Falklands War. Haig, the president, and most of the White House staff were in Europe when the resolution came up in the Security Council. Kirkpatrick received orders from the State Department to vote against the resolution, which she did. Minutes later, Haig, believing that the vote would be an error, informed his State Department contact by telephone that she should abstain. The order passed through the State Department and reached her too late. UN votes, once cast, cannot be withdrawn. Kirkpatrick then announced that if she could withdraw the vote, she would have changed it to an abstention. Again, she—and the entire administration team—were made to look like amateurs. A few days later, Kirkpatrick spoke to the Heritage Foundation on the United States' "persistent ineptitude in international relations" over several administrations. White House aides in Europe were not amused at more negative publicity.[52]

In terms of her own objectives for the United Nations while she was there, Kirkpatrick had some success in forcing a zero budget growth. She admitted that her principal ally in that campaign was the Soviet Union.[53] Her other major goal—to limit the invective and insults toward the U.S. in the United Nations—might be considered successful or not, depending on how attitudes toward the U.S. in the institution were measured. Once when confronted with a public-opinion survey whose outcome she did not approve of, she commented that if she had framed the questions, the results would have been different. "If I could put the questions in the polls, why I'd get a majority."[54] Her way of measuring her influence in controlling attacks on the U.S. was to define ten important votes in the year and then to show the percentage of nations that had voted with the United States on those issues. Her office also compiled a list of the percentage of times that each country had voted with the U.S. throughout the year.

In testimony to Congress Kirkpatrick stressed the victories on the important votes. Yet, a *New York Times* accounting in 1985 found that the United States had voted with the majority only 14 percent of the time in 1984 as compared with 21 percent in 1983. The State Department confirmed the *New York Times* findings, but lamely added that "even though the numbers are down, it's quite fair to say we've done better this year."[55] Kirkpatrick also asserted that U.S. influence was stronger, as measured by the

decline in harsh language used against the United States during debates, the fact that a number of resolutions opposed by the United States never come to a vote, a decline in criticism of the United States by name in resolutions, increased support on issues that are particularly important for the United States and moderation in the language of a number of resolutions.[56]

Kirkpatrick's influence then in two of her three major arenas—the cabinet and the UN—seems to have been a general one of tone setting rather than one of concrete policy achievements. What of her role as a public advocate for the Reagan policies? A difficult, if not impossible, influence to track. Her appearances or announced appearances on college and university campuses (Barnard, Smith, University of California, University of Minnesota) caused an uproar especially in 1983. It is quite possible that those who supported her outnumbered the protesters, but the campus upheavals drew unwelcome attention to Reagan's unpopular policies, especially in Central America. She did well in preaching to the converted—Heritage Foundation, American Enterprise Institute, the Hadassah Women's Zionist Organization, the Republican National Convention. As a persuader of Congress, she met with mixed success on issues relating to El Salvador or Nicaragua.

She wrote frequently and produced two compilations of her speeches and earlier writings while she was in office: *Dictatorships and Double Standards* (1982) and *The Reagan Phenomenon* (1983). Numerous speeches were reprinted in the *Department of State Bulletin*. She also wrote occasional newspaper editorials and letters to the editor. Her husband, Evron, practically turned the journal that he edited, *World Affairs*, into an exclusive forum for her articles and speeches. Given the continuing public and Congressional resistance to the administration's policies, one might speculate that Kirkpatrick gained personal reknown as an advocate for those views but that—again in the short run—she was not particularly effective in changing people's minds or in contributing to a renewal of an American consensus.

She and other neoconservatives may have misread the mandate that Reagan received in the 1980 election. Polls found more support for President Carter's foreign policy, but for Reagan's economic policies. "Standing tall" had an emotional appeal, but actual involvement in military encounters had less appeal. A strong defense establishment met initial approval, but the public also had a limited tolerance for military spending and waste in the face of rising national deficits. The 1979–1981 hostage crisis probably represented the height of aggressive nationalism in recent years.[57] Polls also reported that women were more tentative than men toward the Reagan military build-up and Central American policies.[58] Kirkpatrick would present an ambivalent symbol to women voters in 1984. She did not fit well into the campaign strategy of trying to soften Reagan's foreign policy image at the end of 1983.

Because of her wide public recognition and conservative views then, Kirkpatrick had a public constituency that admired and defended her. She did not break through to a larger constituency, and she did not wield a great deal of personal influence within the administration. There were five major reasons. First, the position of U.S. ambassador to the UN had never been considered a high level policy-making job. Kirkpatrick did not come to the job with a major reputation as a foreign policy theorist, which could have given her more influence. Second, Kirkpatrick's own lack of practical experience put her at an initial disadvantage both in Washington and in New York. She apparently overcame that to be an effective ambassador in New York. In Washington, however, she remained relatively helpless to influence policy when she did not have a powerful ally such as Clark. Third, Reagan's "overwhelming" mandate in 1980 did not include a deep and continuing popular desire for a hard-line and expensive foreign policy. Since Kirkpatrick represented that hard-line policy, she was useful and influential politically only to a minority of voters—admittedly a significant minority, but one that continued to be offered symbolic and rhetorical victories rather than real ones.

A fourth reason for her relative lack of direct influence deserves some more elaboration. She claimed that her strongest reason to belittle Jimmy Carter's foreign policy was that it did not work. The same criticism might be made of her views. Toughness at the United Nations arguably did not restore U.S. dominance in that institution. Failure to support Argentina in the Falklands war did not lead either to a communist sweep of the hemisphere or any measurable lessening of U.S. power and influence. The tilt toward South Africa may have caused more domestic and Congressional criticism than it was worth and may have contributed to the tragic recalcitrance of President Pieter Botha. At least in the short run, the covert strategy in Nicaragua has been largely ineffective, expensive, and has pushed the Sandinistas closer to the Soviet Union. Moreover, it has distanced the U.S. from its European allies, who correctly reject the exaggerated versions of Nicaraguan reality that are beamed from Washington. Kirkpatrick's advocacy of the grain embargo overlooked the economic interests of U.S. farmers. Similarly, her view that Poland should have been pushed to bankruptcy overlooked the economic interests of U.S. banks and suppliers and European allies.

In short, her advocacy of cultural factors as the primary driving ones for foreign and domestic policy seems exceedingly weak. Her view that audiences can be won by rhetoric alone seems naive and misbegotten. She has overlooked the strength of economic factors in driving and influencing foreign policy. While rhetoric and hard-line policies may be practical when the economic cost is slight, a policy consistently based on ideology rather than interests (as she notes herself in her condemnation of the McGovern delegates in 1972) can not be compromised and can not make incremental gains. Moreover, she oversimplifies the views of the American public on foreign policy. Indeed, she may frame questions in whatever way she chooses to make the "polls come out right." But she can not alter a general distaste for expensive—in lives and in money—and interventionist foreign policies. Although she frequently qualifies her views and claims that she has been misquoted and unfairly characterized as a hard-liner, her anticommunist rhetoric and lack of sympathy toward the Third World nurture and encourage those who are most interventionist.

Aggressive rhetoric and projection of values have a place in the general arsenal of foreign policy weapons. That place is the place reserved for public diplomacy, but public diplomacy can not replace traditional diplomacy based on interests— both those of other nations and those within the U.S. Perhaps in fairness, it might be said that it cannot be measured by the same yardsticks either. If Kirkpatrick's contributions are judged by the standards of traditional diplomacy, they generally fail to advance U.S. interests; if judged by the standards of conservatives who wish to build a new consensus and to press an unceasing battle against the communists, Kirkpatrick's visible advocacy of that position may have contributed to make such a course more acceptable.

The fifth and final reason that Kirkpatrick has not been any more effective may be related to her gender. Both the United Nations and the White House Situation Room remain male bastions. Kirkpatrick was very aware of that when she noticed a mouse in the room during a meeting of the National Security Planning Group. In words reminiscent of Lydia Maria Child, Dr. Kirkpatrick thought, "That mouse is no more surprising a creature to see in the Situation Room than I am—no stranger a presence here, really, than I am."[59]

In public, Kirkpatrick projected great forcefulness and authority, but she did not have that same authority with her male colleagues. Meese, Deaver, Baker, Haig, Shultz—all power players—were acknowledged to dislike her. They might have been annoyed solely at her views, although it is more likely that her personality quirks were deemed unacceptable for a woman. Haig commented on the "discursive" nature of her first speech in the cabinet. Kirkpatrick has several times spoken of her affection for Reagan because he is not one of those men "whose eyes glaze over" when a woman speaks.[60] We may assume from that that there were some other White House men whose eyes did glaze over when Kirkpatrick, and some other women, were around.[61]

Reactions to her speech and personality seldom if ever openly mentioned her gender. One White House aide noted that some women "suffer because they are cantankerous."[62] Kirkpatrick said frequently, however, that she is not confrontational, does not seek confrontation, does not like nor seek bureaucratic infighting. How does that reconcile with the public image of her as "tough" and "cantankerous"? Kirkpatrick speculates that some people mistake adherence to ideas for personal toughness.[63] Certainly, one who is inflexible in adhering to a minority position within a group might be termed "cantankerous."

Kirkpatrick's gender may be relevant to this discussion only in that she had a double strike against her: she as a woman and an academic had much to prove to the pragmatic, and experienced, men with whom she dealt. They found her articulate and forceful but with inadequate public backing or experience to earn credibility in the group. A person who came with a highly respected academic reputation might also have commanded more respect than Kirkpatrick's relatively modest credentials in foreign policy scholarship.

To conclude, what future for Kirkpatrick? She says "I have more self-confidence now than I have ever had in my life."[64] She says, however, that she has no interest in an elected position such as senator from Maryland or vice president. She prefers to write, to influence policy from the classroom and the editorial barricades. She still is practicing public diplomacy, by her trip to El Salvador in April 1985, her heading up the *Washington Times* campaign to gain private contributions for the Nicaraguan *contras*, her highly visible membership in organizations such as friends of the Democratic Center in Central America (PRODEMCA), her speaking, her newspaper writing. With the experience of the White House and the UN behind her, she may now have more influence than ever.

She has also bought herself a measure of economic and intellectual independence with her "costly" four years. She has a contract for $900,000 for the book she began to prepare after leaving the UN. Her lecture fee is said to be $20,000.[65] A nationally syndicated newspaper column will add more to her coffers. As a consultant, or visiting professor at prestigious universities, she will no doubt command much higher fees than previously. Why is this important? Her husband, Evron, is now seventy-four while she is fifty-nine. She told one interviewer that the UN experience had been good because she had learned to live alone "which is an important thing for a woman to learn to do."[66] She now independently has an assured income, an assured, and prestigious career, and immeasurably widened options.

She speaks for herself, and perhaps for the future of women in such powerful positions, when she says:

I think the price for participation in high-level politics in our society is very, very high— for both men and women. One lives under continual scrutiny and criticism, much of it unfair. It is a very harsh game, and I do not think women want whatever it is at the end of that particular rainbow badly enough to pursue it. There are already more opportunities for women in politics than there are women ready to pay the price. . . . We are making the price of power much too high in this society. I worry that we are making the conditions of public life so tough that nobody except people really obsessed with power would be willing finally to pay that price. That would be tragic from the point of view of public well-being.[67]

Perhaps, after all, the lobbyist on the outside has more latitude than the mouse on the floor of the Situation Room. Arguably, the lobbyist on the outside—with the credentials and experience and contacts to confer authority upon her—may even have more impact on foreign policy, on building a public consensus for a different direction for foreign policy, than the mouse in the inner circle.

NOTES

1. Jane Rosen, "The Kirkpatrick Factor," The *New York Times Magazine*, 28 April, 1985, pp. 48–50.

2. Marie Brenner, "The Blooming of Jeane Kirkpatrick," *Vanity Fair*, July 1985, p. 34.

3. Kenneth Adelman, "Speaking of America: Public Diplomacy in Our Time," *Foreign Affairs 59* (Spring, 1981): 934.

4. Bernard D. Nossiter, "Questioning the Value of the UN," *New York Times Magazine*, 11 April, 1982, p. 17.

5. The memory of using her allowance for books may be a bit idealized, since she also told Senator Hayakawa at her confirmation hearing that she had used "my own allowance money" while at Barnard to purchase his book (p. 29); see also James Conaway, "Jeane Kirkpatrick, the Ambassador from *Commentary*," *Washington Post Magazine* 11 November 1981, p. 11.

6. Nossiter, p. 17.

7. George Urban, "American Foreign Policy in a Cold Climate" (Interview, *Encounter* 61 (November 1983): 16.

8. Nossiter, p. 18.

9. Ibid., p. 17; Maureen Orth, "Woman Capable of Reason," *Vogue* 171 (July 1981): 180.

10. Conaway, p. 12; American Political Science Association, *Biographical Directory 1973* (Washington: APSA, 1973), p. 258.

11. Nossiter, p. 17.

12. Orth, p. 181.

13. Nossiter, p. 17.

14. *Newsweek*, 3 January, 1983, p. 19.

15. The *Washington Post*, 23 December, 1980.

16. Eldon Kenworthy, "Our Colleague Kirkpatrick," *LASA Forum* 14 (Winter, 1984): 23–24.

17. Jeane Kirkpatrick, *The New Presidential Elite: Men and Women in National Politics* (New York: Russell Sage Foundation and the Twentieth Century Fund, 1976), p. 246.

18. Jeane Kirkpatrick, "Dictatorships and Double Standards," *Commentary* 65 (November 1979).

19. Conaway, p. 17.

20. The *Washington Post*, 23 December, 1980.

21. U.S. Senate, Committee on Foreign Relations, *Hearing on the Nomination of Jeane J. Kirkpatrick to be Representative to the United Nations*, 97th Congress, 1st Session, 15 January, 1981, pp. 6–7.

22. Ibid., p. 25.

23. The *New York Times*, 24 June, 1981.

24. *Newsweek*, 3 January, 1983, p. 16.

25. For example, see I. M. Destler, "The Evolution of Reagan Foreign Policy," in *The Reagan Presidency: An Early Assessment*, ed., Fred I. Greenstein (Baltimore: The Johns Hopkins Press, 1983), pp. 117–28.

26. Ibid., p. 121.

27. Alexander Haig, Jr., *Caveat: Realism, Reagan, and Foreign Policy* (New York: Macmillan Publishing Co., 1984), p. 69.

28. Ibid., p. 76.

29. Anne Tremblay, "Jeane Kirkpatrick," *Working Woman* 8 (May 1983): 109.

30. *Newsweek*, 3 January, 1983, p. 16.

31. The *Washington Post*, 2 December, 1984.

32. Ibid.

33. *Time*, 31 October, 1983, pp. 29–30; *The Washington Post*, 23 October 1983.

34. Haig, p. 81; Lou Cannon, *Reagan* (New York: G. P. Putnam's Sons, 1982), p. 313; Miles Kahler, "The United States and Western Europe: The Diplomatic Consequences of Mr. Reagan," in *Eagle Defiant: United States Foreign Policy in the 1980s*, ed., Kenneth A. Oye, et al. (Boston: Little, Brown, & Co., 1983), pp. 293–94.

35. The *Washington Post*, 1 April, 1981.

36. Haig, pp. 269–70; *Time*, 14 June, 1982, p. 36.

37. Charles Maechling, Jr., "Human Rights Dehumanized," *Foreign Policy* 52 (Fall, 1981), pp. 123–24.

38. Ibid., p. 121.

39. U.S. Department of State, Bureau of Public Affairs, "Democracy in Latin America and the Caribbean," Current Policy No. 605 (August 1984), p. 1; for a discussion of the notion of demonstration elections, see Edward S. Herman and Frank Brodhead, *Demonstration Elections: U.S.-Staged Elections in the Dominican Republic, Vietnam, and El Salvador* (Boston: South End Press, 1984).

40. Jeane Kirkpatrick, "Pardon Me, But Am I That 'Hard-Liner' the Anonymous Sources Are Talking About?", The *Washington Post*, 20 June, 1983.

41. Rosen, pp. 69, 72.

42. Dom Bonafede, "Tensions over U.N. Ambassador's Role Will Outlast the Haig Resignation," *National Journal*, 10 July, 1982, p. 1212.

43. Bonafede, p. 1213; Conaway, pp. 12, 14–15; Nossiter, p. 20; *Time*, 21 June, 1982, p. 36; Tremblay, p. 107.

44. Betsy Thom, "Women in International Organizations: Room at the Top," in *Access to Power: Cross-National Studies of Women and Elites*, ed., Cynthia Fuchs Epstein and Rose Laub Coser (London: George Allen & Unwin, 1981), pp. 171–72.

45. The *Washington Post*, 27 December, 1982; Nossiter, p. 16.

46. Conaway, p. 16; Tremblay, p. 107.

47. Nossiter, p. 16.

48. *The Christian Science Monitor*, 26 November, 1984.

49. *Time*, 26 October, 1981; 31 December, 1984.

50. *Time*, 26 October, 1981, p. 24.

51. *Time*, 6 July, 1981, p. 11; The *New York Times*, 24 June, 1981; The *Washington Post*, 25 June, 1981.

52. The *Washington Post*, 7 June, 1982; *Time*, 21 June, 1982, p. 36.

53. U.S. Sentate, Committee on Appropriations, *Foreign Assistance and Related Programs for Fiscal Year 1984. Statement of Hon. J. J. Kirkpatrick, Permanent Representative to the United Nations*, 7 March, 1983, p. 556.

54. *New York Times*, 30 June, 1983.

55. *New York Times*, 15 February, 1985.

56. Ibid.

57. William Schneider, "Conservatism, Not Interventionism: Trends in Foreign Policy Opinion, 1974–1982," in *Eagle Defiant*, ed., Kennedy A. Oye, et al., pp. 33–64.

58. *U.S. News & World Report*, 8 November, 1982, pp. 52–53; Alice Rossi, "Beyond the Gender Gap: Women's Bid for Political Power," *Social Science Quarterly* 64 (December, 1983), p. 718.

59. Rosen, p. 68.

60. *New York Times*, 21 August, 1984; *Washington Post*, 15 November, 1980.

61. A *U.S. News & World Report* article noted that Anne Gorsuch was perceived by White House circles as "too aggressive," and Elizabeth Dole was sometimes not involved in the decision-making process because they thought she talked too much. (8 November, 1982, pp. 52–53). Secretary of Health and Human Services Margaret Heckler later saw her job threatened because she was considered too "weak." The *Washington Post*, 17 August, 1985.

62. *Time*, 31 December, 1984.

63. Orth, p. 228.

64. *New York Times*, 1 February, 1985.

65. Rosen, p. 73.

66. Tremblay, p. 109.

67. *Time*, 3 September, 1984, p. 18.

9

Conclusion: Of Mice and Men

Joan Hoff-Wilson

Although the careers of Jeane Kirkpatrick and Lydia Maria Child were separated by over a century, both compared their attempts to influence U.S. foreign policy to that of being mice in a man's world—out of place and usually out of positions of real power. When Child wrote to Senator Charles Sumner in 1870 that she perceived herself as "the little mouse" working behind the scenes and only occasionally savoring success, it was not unlike the words uttered by Kirkpatrick several times in the spring of 1985, describing a mouse she once saw scurry across the Situation Room floor. "That mouse is no more surprising a creature to see in the Situation Room than I am—no stranger a presence here, really, than I am," she said, adding on another occasion: "I don't think there had ever been a woman in that room before [because] the male monopoly of foreign policy had been so complete."[1]

Likewise, the sporadic diplomatic influence of such women as Jane M. Cazneau and Eleanor Roosevelt, whose far-flung domestic and foreign activities also occurred over one hundred years apart, was limited despite their wealth and connections in high places. Indeed, for obvious reasons, all the essays in this collection attest to the marginality of women (even to one who was a First Lady like Roosevelt) in the formulation of U.S. foreign policy from the first half of the nineteenth century to the last half of the twentieth. Most operated as critics *outside* the system; only a few ever occupied even low-level policy-making positions *inside* the Foreign Service of the State Department; and fewer still were appointed ambassadors or deputy chiefs of mission—none at major diplomatic posts. In any case, even as more women follow in the footsteps of Frances E. Willis, who held three minor ambassadorial positions following World War II, and Jeane Kirkpatrick, head of the United States delegation to the United Nations in the first Reagan administration, it must be remembered that such posts are not ones of policy formulation, but of policy implementation.[2]

Most simply stated, women have played, and continue to play, insignificant roles in determining U.S. diplomacy because they were (and are) not present in top policy-making circles. This fact has been documented from 1800 to 1981 in two major studies.[3] Probably Abigail Adams was the first woman to have an unofficial, but a direct, impact on the foreign relations of the United States. She decisively influenced the terms of a new loan with the Dutch, which her husband negotiated in 1799.[4] Moreover, until the Civil War, fewer women were employed by the government than by industry. While women provided the Department of State with a variety of goods and services throughout the nineteenth century, between 1800 and 1874, none had anything to do with policy formulation. For example, Homer L. Calkin pointed out that the department employed its first female employee in 1804 "to fold, stitch, and cover with cartridge paper and blue paper 3,467 copies of the laws enacted by the 8th Congress, 1st Session." She was paid six cents a copy—the same as men hired to do the same work.[5]

Although most women performed clerical duties for the State Department in the first half of the nineteenth century, some were also hired as janitors. In 1874 five women constituted 9.4 percent of all full-time department employees. From 1884 to 1909 the percentage of full-time females employed ranged between 15 and 20 percent, or from eleven to seventeen full-time women. It took the department thirty-five years after it hired its first full-time female to appoint one to a professional or semi-professional position. After employing Anne H. Short-ridge in 1909 as a law clerk, women lawyers and scholars appeared in ever greater numbers in legal and intelligence positions, particularly during the First and Second World wars.[6] By 1918 they made up almost one third of the total State Department personnel, which remained small by today's standards—only 177 men and 81 women.

During the Great Depression years, however, the ranks of married women working for the State Department were decimated by compliance with Section 213 of the "Economy Act" of 1932 aimed at preventing husbands and wives from both working for the government. Despite increased discrimination stemming from New Deal legislation, by the time the U.S. entered World War II women made up 49.6 percent of the total number of State Department employees. While they were mainly clustered in the lowest paying clerical ranks, thirty-six women held professional positions, four semi-professional ones, with others scattered in administrative and fiscal positions.[7]

Growth in the number of females employed by the Civil and Foreign services did not always correspond with dramatic increases in the overall size of the department. Between 1904 and 1909 a 100 percent expansion of State personnel occurred with corresponding increases in female employees; however, between 1909 and 1918 women increased 142.5 percent while there was scarcely any increase in male employees because of the war. Then between 1918 and 1934 when the size of the department burgeoned once again, so did the number of women hired, until Section 213 resulted in the firing of married women because of the Depression. During World War II women employees increased so rapidly that by 1945 they made up over 50 percent of all State Department personnel. Female employees have remained more than half of all the department's personnel since that time, most of them clustered in the Civil Service, not Foreign Service.[8]

Not surprisingly, discrmination against women working in the Foreign Service continued unabated from the decades of the 1920s to the 1950s when attempts were made to upgrade the quality of appointments and increase regional specialization. Rationalizations for this continued discrimination became more subtle during these years. In the 1920s, for example, general prejudices against women focused explicitly on the cultural difficulties they would face as public figures in certain countries and implicitly on the problems of fulfilling entertainment functions without a "wife"; on the assumption that if a female foreign service officer married a foreigner (or even another U.S. national), this would ultimately lead her to abandon her career to be with her husband;[9] and on the difficulty of female career officers (but apparently not female secretaries or administrators) to cope with inclement weather in various parts of the world.

By the 1950s and 1960s the collective of such overtly sexist attitudes became more covert but continued to contribute to a negative demographic profile of female Foreign Service officers. Among other things, they were older than their male counterparts because they were not promoted so rapidly. Instead of being recruited to take the Foreign Service examination as men routinely were, most often women entered the State Department by making a lateral switch from long-term service in other government personnel systems under the so-called Wriston program beginning in 1962. Moreover, by the end of the 1960s, only 40 percent of the women had earned bachelor degrees, compared to almost 55 percent of the men. In the 1970s and 1980s this educational differential disappeared and women were actively encouraged to take the examinations. As a result, the ratio of women taking and passing both the written and the oral exams began to equal or exceed that of men, but, the percentage of women taking both kinds of exams fluctuated from 12 to 28 precent in the first half of the 1970s.[10] A report issued on May 23, 1984, by the Women's Research and Education Institute (WREI) of the Congressional Caucus for Women's Issues confirmed that despite a concerted effort in the last fifteen years (especially since 1977 when Cyrus Vance took a personal interest in increasing the number of women and minorities in the Foreign Service), there has been only minimal improvement in the status and number of nonclerical females employed by the State Department.[11]

As of January 31, 1981, women constituted 68.8 percent of the total Civil Service workforce of the State Department, but only 25.8 percent of the Foreign Service workforce. While the number of State Department women employees increased by more than 800 between 1970 and 1981, there has been little change in their employment pattern over the last decade. Women continued to be markedly underrepresented at the senior levels, particularly in the Foreign Service, where they are still rare—contributing only around 3 percent by early 1981.

Moreover, no Foreign Service career woman has ever been appointed as ambassador or deputy chief of mission at a major diplomatic post. Only one woman had ever been appointed head (assistant secretary) of one of the State Department's five geographic bureaus and this did not occur until 1985. No woman has ever been appointed assistant secretary of the Bureau of International Organization Affairs or of the Bureau of Economic and Business Affairs.

Below the senior level, however, there have been some gains in the last decade. The proportion of women increased at the middle level, most notably at GS–12, in the Civil Service. Women accounted for nearly 36 percent of the Civil Service mid-level workforce in early 1981, up from about 27 percent in 1970. Among junior-level Foreign Service Officers, the proportion of women increased from less than 10 percent in 1970 to almost 25 percent by early 1981. Such gains as there have been largely involved white women. Minority women's representation in the Foreign Service increased by only one half percent over the decade—to 2.5 percent in early 1981. Most of these gains, however, were at the support level known informally as the Foreign Service Staff (FSS) Corps, not the Foreign Service Officer (FSO) Corps. Women have never accounted for more than a small fraction of the FSO Corps (and by 1981 the FSO Corps represented less than 40 percent of the total personnel of the Foreign Service). Statistics starting in 1957 indicate that a high of 9 percent was reached in 1959 and sustained in 1960. In the following decade, however, the proportion of women among FSOs dropped steadily until it reached a low of 4.8 percent in 1970. The previous "high" of 9 percent was restored by 1975, and by 1981 the proportion had reached 10.5 percent (14 percent when officer candidates are added to the tenured officers). Minority women in the FSO Corps were almost invisible—0.5 percent in 1975. By early 1981, the proportion of tenured minority women in the FSO Corps had increased to 0.8 percent (seven percent of FSO candidates).

Moreover, women have never accounted for more than 10 percent of the thousands of delegates chosen annually to represent the United States at international conferences, despite Eleanor Roosevelt's strong 1952 plea (one that many women have reiterated) to the UN General Assembly:

I believe we will have better government in our countries when men and women discuss public issues together and make their decisions on the basis of their differing areas of experience and their comon concern for the welfare of their families and their world . . . Too often the great decisions are originated and given form in bodies made up wholly of men, or so completely dominated by them that whatever of special value women have to offer is shunted aside without expression. . . .

The State Department's Office of Equal Employment Opportunity and Civil Rights (EEOCR) has frequently lacked leaders with relevant knowledge and experience, and has suffered both from prolonged personnel vacancies and from the assignment of personnel apparently indifferent to its mission. The Federal

Women's Program has seen a steady reduction in its status within EEOCR. As late as the early 1980s, the State Department's computerized personnel data base could not provide the information needed for effective EEO monitoring (e.g., whether women and minorities are remaining in the Foreign Service and being promoted at the same rates as men). EEOCR has also failed to give sufficient emphasis to monitoring EEO progress.

According to this 1984 WREI report, the single most important factor in achieving equal employment opportunity in the Department of State is the degree of commitment demonstrated by the secretary of state and the under secretary for management. Top-level commitment to the principles of equal employment opportunity *has never been strong enough for a period long enough* to break through the general apathy on the subject that appears to prevail thoroughout the Department of State, especially under the Reagan administration, which was the only two-term presidency in which gains for female career officers could have been achieved since the Eisenhower decade of the 1950s.

Given these kinds of statistics and findings, it was to be expected that a class action suit[12] would be brought against the State Department. It alleged sex discrimination under Title VII of the Civil Rights Act of 1964, as amended, in all aspects of the employment process: hiring, cone (i.e., functional field of specialization) assignments, job assignments, promotions, performance evaluations, awards, and class at hire. Certain applicant and hiring claims involving junior and mid-level women were settled prior to trial with two consent decrees on October 12, 1983, and March 5, 1985. These decrees required the State Department to appoint before the end of 1986 a specified number of women at each level who were parties to the class action suit.

Testimony in the trial on the remaining claims took place between May 6 and June 5, 1985, before a U.S. District Court Judge in Washington, D.C., with the plaintiffs arguing, among other things, that women had been "disproportionately overassigned to the consular cone and disproportionately underassigned to the political cone" from 1976 to 1983. On this point the defendant replied that "more females than males historically preferred . . . the consular cone" (which traditionally had been considered a less prestigious function within the Foreign Service). On September 13, 1985, the court found that the female Foreign Service Officers "failed to show by a preponderance of evidence any sexual discrimination by the State Department." This decision rested as much on the flawed statistical evidence presented by the male attorney for the women as it did on the judge's interpretation of previous Title VII case law defining "disparate treatment" and "disparate impact."

The time-period under review in *Palmer v. Shultz* was 1976 to 1983 (the last year for which either side had conclusive figures in 1985) and so the statistical data in this suit is two years more current than the 1984 WREI report. The defendants were greatly aided by the fact that since 1975 the State Department had initiated both a Mid-Level Affirmative Action Program and a Junior Officer Affirmative Action Program designed to increase the women and minority Foreign Service Officers. Under these programs it was estimated that by 1986 so many women would have been appointed that the programs would then be phased out in order not to "affect the opportunities of those entering the bottom levels." In general, the U.S. district judge concluded that since 1976 the "Department of State had made sincere efforts . . . to improve the status of women in the Foreign Service and has successfully responded to many individual and class-wide grievances of female Foreign Service Officers."

Despite this legal finding that the State Department does not discriminate against women, the essays in this collection demonstrate how easy it is to document their marginality in the foreign policy establishment of the United States. The essays also show the general potential women have for influencing American diplomacy. It is now possible to assess such studies about women who attempted to change the course of U.S. foreign policy not only in terms of their contribution to the field of diplomacy, but also in terms of their contribution to one of the most important and rapidly expanding subfields of U.S. history; namely, women's history.

Women's history has passed through several phases in the course of this century, but particularly in the last fifteen years. There is a natural tendency for initial work on women to exhibit what are called compensatory or remedial characteristics. This refers to historical works that concentrate on outstanding or notable women, often portraying them as both exceptional and yet victimized or exploited in some way. All of the articles in this book exhibit some of these first-stage characteristics in the writing of women's history. But some of them also exhibit characteristics of what I call the second stage of writing about women. By this I mean that while these essays obviously concentrate on notables, as they must, in a field such as foreign policy, where so few women have succeeded, there is also critical analysis of these individuals as people and as professionals. Many authors attempt to place these women in the context of their time, rather than simply to describe their virtues or defects in a historical or a gender vacuum.

Since the mid–1960s a third phase or school in the writing of women's history has emerged simultaneously with the appearance of the so-called new social history. Such historians of women's history often abandon traditional method-ological approaches; attempt interdisciplinary analysis; and try to present collective, rather than individual portraits of women by concentrating on a particular class, profession, or some other grouping where females played a significant role.[13] Most of the essays in this collection do not fall into this latest development in the writing of women's history primarily because too little research has been conducted on the few women who have obtained some prominence in, and influence over, U.S. foreign policy. Basic biographical data has to be collected and evaluated before we can begin to talk about other than raw statistics, such as I have just summarized for the 1970s and early 1980s both from the 1984 report of the Women's Research and Education Institute and the decision in *Palmer v. Shultz*, and which Homer L. Calkin summarized in 1977 for the entire nineteenth century and first half of the twentieth. In addition, there have been two in-house State Department Studies on the Status of Women and Minorities— one in 1977, the "Executive Level Task Force on Affirmative Action," and the "Habib Committee" in 1979.

Despite the existence of such reports, collective biographical and career patterns, especially of middle-level women in the State Department and of those participating in various twentieth century peace movements, have yet to be analyzed using the methodology of the new social history. Until this is done, historians and political scientists cannot move beyond the statement over statistical methodology in *Palmer v. Shultz* or remedial narratives on the few women who have managed to rise in the Foreign Service branch of the State Department, such as the following sketches of Frances Willis and Jeannette Rankin.

Willis emerged during the administrations of presidents Truman and Eisenhower as the first U.S. woman to obtain the rank of Class One as a career diplomat and as a senior officer in the Foreign Service. Although two other women had previously become ambassadors under Truman: Pearl Mesta to Norway in 1949 and Eugenia Moore Anderson to Denmark in 1949, Willis's appointment as Ambassador to Switzerland in 1953 marked the first time a female career officer rose through the ranks to such a position. Born in Illinois in 1899, Willis received a Ph.D. from Stanford in 1923. Like other female Ph.D.s in the 1920s, she discovered she could only teach at private women's colleges, which she did, until 1927. Then she joined the Foreign Service. Despite remaining unmarried, her promotion record lagged behind and was less prestigious than that of her male colleagues. From the 1953 Swiss appointment she went on to serve as ambassador to Luxembourg in 1957 and ambassador to Ceylon in 1961. Willis retired in 1964 and her papers have been deposited at Stanford University.

Interestingly, there is some indication that Willis was one of the first female "mentors" in the Foreign Service, influencing and encouraging the career of Marjorie Jay Tibbets, who became ambassador to Norway in 1964. Tibbets, in turn, may have "mentored" Rozanne L. Ridgway, who served as ambassador to Finland and East Germany before becoming the first assistant secretary of state for European Affairs. It was Ridgway who drafted the summary statement for the 1985 Reagan-Gorbachev summit meeting.[14] Yet, until biographies of Willis, Tibbets, Ridgway, and others like them are written, statistical data cannot be made personally relevant and meaningful through what has been called the use of "anecdotal evidence" to bring "cold numbers convincingly to life." The decision in *Palmer v. Shultz* noted several times that this type of personal evidence was singularly lacking in the plaintiff's case against the State Department.

Likewise, until many more individual and collective biographies of twentieth century women pacifists are completed, we will continue to speculate about their influence and common characteristics without adequate documentation.[15] For example, Jeannette Rankin (1880–1973) was the first woman elected to the House of Representatives and the only member of Congress to oppose entry of the United States into both world wars. Jeannette Rankin's pacifism originated in connection with her suffragist activities in the states of Washington and Montana. In particular, her association with a transplanted eastern pacifist, Minnie J. Reynolds, convinced Rankin by 1910 that the quest for peace should be incorporated into the suffrage movement, but like Mead, she steadfastly refused to put women's rights before peace because they both believed that peace was a "woman's job";[16] that is, a specifically female or gender-induced pursuit. Like so many of her female contemporaries, Rankin's participation in the social justice wing of the Progressive movement also reinforced her pacifistic views. Finally, books by the English sociologist Benjamin Kidd led her to the singular and powerful conclusion that women were the primary source of "power" for all future peace activities in the United States and the world.

After helping win the vote for women in Montana in 1914, Rankin became the first woman elected to the House of Representaives in 1916. Within four days after assuming her seat in Congress she voted, along with fifty-six others, against United States entrance into World War I. Later, in 1941, while serving a second term in the House, she became the only Congressional opponent of entry into World War II. In the intervening years she continued her pacifist activities in a variety of official capacities. As early as 1915 Rankin joined the Woman's Peace Party. She subsequently belonged to the National Committee on the Cause and Cure of War, the Women's Peace Union, the Women's International League for Peace and Freedom (WILPF), and finally the National Council for Prevention of War (NCPW). With the exception of the Georgia Peace Society, which she founded in 1928, none of these organizations subsequently lived up to Rankin's idealistic or organizational standards.

Often she opposed their political tactics or they refused to finance her grassroots plans for organizing. For example, Rankin left her position as field secretary with the WILPF in 1925 after it proved impossible to finance her elaborate plans for gaining western members. In 1929, in a dispute over tactics, she resigned as a lobbyist for the Women's Peace Union, whose sole purpose was to outlaw war through a constitutional amendment. Similarly, after a ten-year association with the NCPW, in 1939 Rankin ended this affiliation primarily because she had become much more critical of the international policies of both Secretary of State Cordell Hull and President Franklin D. Roosevelt than had the NCPW.

Rankin's difficulties with the NCPW were due, in part, to her particular foreign policy views. In the interwar years she remained a "nationalist," or one who supported very limited American commitments around the world. She was not, however, an isolationist. Unlike most isolationists of the 1920s and 1930s, she did not support isolation from European affairs while accepting the use of force in the Far East or Latin America. Instead, Rankin remained true to her pacifist ideals: she objected to the use of American military force anywhere in the world, except for the defense of the continental United States. Consequently, she supported international cooperation, and opposed American interventionism.

Economic views conditioned Rankin's brand of pacifism between the two world wars, as they had earlier for Child and Mead. As America became an urban and consumer nation, those who first experienced mass consumerism in the 1920s tended to be more interventionist than those who did not. Rankin increasingly turned away from the consumer society and led a spartan life outside Athens, Georgia, without telephone, electricity, or running water until after 1943. Although she continued to vote and own property in Montana, Georgia became her "home" and the Georgia Peace Society remained her base for pacifist activities from the late 1920s until its demise on the eve of World War II. From Georgia she pursued a lifestyle without modern conveniences, organized "sunshine" clubs for local boys and girls to teach them "peace habits," established a foreign policy study group for adults, and transformed the Georgia Peace Society into one of the first peace action groups in the country with perennial attempts to defeat the naval appropriations bills of Congressman Carl Vinson. The Atlanta American Legion Post labeled Rankin a "communist" for these efforts and prevented Brenau College in Gainesville from establishing a "Chair of Peace" for her.

Senator Gerald Nye's investigation from 1934 to 1936 of the role played by the munitions industry in America's entrance into World War I confirmed Rankin's worst suspicions about the economic origins of modern warfare. After World War II, her economic argument became an attack on the military industrial complex and its relationship to the monetary system. Accordingly, Rankin revived an idea she had espoused during both world wars that called for the creation of special "profit removing" currency in time of military hostilities. Like Fonda several decades later, she also championed other domestic reforms she thought would correct the defects she saw in the American capitalist system.

Although she never lived to see any of her peace reforms enacted, she was a consistent critic of the Cold War, including the Korean and the Vietnam conflicts. Unlike Cazneau and Carroll in the nineteenth century, Rankin increasingly associated American expansionism with deficiencies in the country's political economy and with the power of a conspiratorial military-industrial complex. As the war in Indochina escalated, she gave serious consideration, at the age of eighty-eight, to running for the House of Representatives again in order "to vote against a third war." Although Rankin had been out of the national limelight for over two decades, the Vietnamese conflict revitalized both her spirits and her career. Her final protest against war would not be as a congresswoman, however, but as an antiwar demonstrator and titular head of the Jeannette Rankin Brigade, organized in 1967. Thus her long pacifist career ended as it had begun, amidst a flurry of travel, public appearances, and exhortations against the war.

But how representative, for example, was either Lucia True Ames Mead or Jeannette Rankin as female leaders of the U.S. peace movement from the late nineteenth century down to the present? For that matter, how representative was Lydia Maria Child, Eleanor Roosevelt or Jane Fonda of the individual U.S. women who have attempted to influence the country's foreign policy? Are women who take an active interest in diplomatic affairs predisposed by their socialization as females in American society to favor peaceful negotiated, rather than bellicose military solutions to international problems? Using only these eight essays, and the careers of Rankin and Willis, such questions, and others like them, can begin to be answered.

First, the traditional gender stereotype about women being more pacifistic than men seems to apply only to those (Child, Mead, Rankin, and Fonda) who agitated for peace without holding any official or semiofficial government job. Women working in formal capacities (Dulles, Willis, and Kirkpatrick) did not generally fit the stereotype. Second, one of the reasons for this deviation is that professional women in official diplomatic jobs seem to be *inside* the establishment by family connections and/or ideology; therefore, they act more like men. Those who operate *outside* the establishment as pacifists or critics of U.S. foreign policy appear not to break out of their female socialization. In addition, some like Cazneau, Carroll, Roosevelt, and Kirkpatrick tried to have it both ways by being both *insiders/outsiders* and, with the possible exception of Roosevelt, the authors in this collection indicate that this dual role has usually produced not only ambivalent results, but also confusing, if not actually contradictory, positions on U.S. diplomacy.

In many respects Roosevelt is the exception to all these generalizations I am making about women and foreign policy because of her extraordinary position in American life and politics from the 1920s to the early 1960s. As both gadfly and galvanizer on many domestic and foreign policy initiatives, her vision of a better world, based on individual rights, came to triumphant fruition in the 1948 U.N. Declaration of Human Rights. In contrast, when someone like Kirkpatrick tried to work both sides of the fence—as academic outsider and well-connected Democratic insider—her achievements were far less impressive than those of Roosevelt, but far more impressive than those of Cazneau and Carroll.

Third, despite the claims of most of the women in these essays that their success owed little to their gender and much to their ability to become "one of the boys," almost all have expressed frustration with their male colleagues and exhibited what Carol Gilligan and Carroll Smith-Rosenberg have described as typically a female or feminine "behind-the-scenes" *modus operandi.*[17] This is particularly true of nineteenth century women because they had neither the franchise nor the option of obtaining official government positions. But well into the middle of the twentieth century, it is particularly obvious that Eleanor Dulles resorted to formal and informal entertaining when working with Austrian officials after World War II, in order to both circumvent and enhance her position within the "old boy" network of the U.S. Foreign Service. "This place is a real man's world—if there ever was one. It's riddled with prejudices!" Dulles ruefully concluded in 1958, four years before she retired: "If you are a woman in government service you just have to work ten times as hard—and even then it takes much skill to paddle around the various taboos. But it is fun to see how far you *can* get *in spite* of being a woman."[18]

In contrast, Kirkpatrick openly asserted that she did not like participating in bureaucratic infighting, while at a semiofficial level Cazneau, Carroll, and Roosevelt seemed to thrive on it. Ewell notes that Kirkpatrick exhibited a typical female professional career pattern; that is, one interrupted by marriage and children, and therefore, did not obtain experience or training necessary for participating in power struggles. Given her slim scholarly qualifications, Kirkpatrick's meteoric academic career could only have been achieved with considerable bureaucratic know-how and hardball tactics. (Granted, infighting and power plays in academe are for relatively low stakes compared with similar games played by top government officials.)

That Kirkpatrick claimed to dislike bureaucratic infighting at top levels reflects, I think, more the fact that she lost so many of these battles than that she was an inexperienced infighter. She had been one of the boys for some time. Kirkpatrick's remark about university life being a more comfortable setting for women than top government circles if probably true, but is also represents the classical lament of the academic outsider (male or female) who tried to be a government insider and did not succeed to the degree that Henry Kissinger, the ultimate model or standard for this type of endeavor, did. Thus, my third point is that gender socialization made women foreign policy specialists sensitive to sexism; at the same time they had no choice but to rely on stereotypic female skills to rise professionally.

Fourth, the role of male mentors appears as essential for women who rise in the Foreign Service as it has been traditionally for men. It is also characteristic of those like Cazneau, Carroll, and Roosevelt, who spent most of their lives in semiofficial positions contacting influential men in government and politics about foreign affairs. It is not surprising that both of these particular groups of women insiders would have had male mentors on the subject of U.S. diplomacy, but the same is largely true of the most critical outsiders who agitated for peace far removed from official positions of power. They, too, were tutored in foreign policy by a series of male acquaintances. Fonda probably provides the most striking example, as Zeidler notes, of a woman who "at every stage outgrew her [male] teacher" and went on to a new mentor, which, in Fonda's case, often included a sexual as well as intellectual relationship. However, it should be remembered that Child, Cazneau, Mead, and Kirkpatrick (not simply Fonda) all married their mentors and so also mingled the intimate with the international. Only Carroll, Rankin, and Roosevelt did not cohabit with their male mentors. (Once again, Roosevelt is the exception because she appears to have pushed and prodded her husband on foreign policy matters, while he did not influence her views so much as women and a few other men did.) Of these three, Jeannette Rankin and Eleanor Roosevelt stand out from all the other women in this collection, since they appear to have been influenced more by a series of women, rather than men, when developing their own views on U.S. diplomacy.

Fifth, I believe gender not only accounted for the fact that State Department women so often operated in typically female fashion, but also that gender, while endorsing male foreign policy views, nonetheless distinguished their general

intellectual or conceptual approaches to foreign policy. Whether trained as econ-
omists or political scientists, teachers, social workers, or film stars, many stressed
cultural values, rhetoric, and persuasion through candid negotiation, not reliance
on abstract theories or ideology, in preference to the use of military or economic
force in foreign relations. Ultimately, however, they accepted various forms of
force when it was adopted as official U.S. policy; but female pacifists in the
1920s and 1930s, as well as their successors in the 1960s and 1980s, always
remained truer to their original female way of thinking about U.S. diplomacy.

My sixth point is the most obvious emerging pattern that can be deduced from
these essays. Almost every woman was held to a double standard when she tried
as a female to operate inside the "old boy" network or outside of it as a critic.
In all instances these women faced the possibility of being singled out for behavior
unbecoming women, *but not men*, in carrying out their foreign policy jobs, and
for acting or talking outside their areas of expertise. Being held to such a double
standard led to criticisms of amateurism or abrasiveness, which would not have
been applied to men holding similar positions or participating in peace and antiwar
movements.

Seventh, most of these women were strongly male identified, often trying to
steer a middle course between warring factions of men or simply adopting views
of various male mentors. Few became leaders of women's rights groups, in either
the nineteenth or twentieth centuries, or made connection between women's
rights and peace, although most appear to have passively supported the goals of
such groups. Typically, Child commented to Elizabeth Cady Stanton that women
"should go right ahead and do whatever they can do well, without talking about
it." Both Rankin and Fonda, however, made much stronger statements about
women's rights the longer they struggled for peace. "This women's lib movement
is such a delightful surprise to me," Rankin said in a 1972 interview at the age
of ninety-two, "because I have followed them [sic] inch by inch and it has been
only so so, but now it is bursting." Fonda is atypical of women in this collection
because she became so engrossed in the Second Women's Movement in the
1970s that she actually appeared to abandon her work for peace and lose interest
in foreign policy issues in general. To a lesser degree, the same is true of Carroll
who also ended up focusing on domestic issues, albeit from a decidedly non-
feminist stance.

In addition to placing these essays in the context of the new social and new
women's history, it is possible to go beyond the marginality most of these
individual women exhibited in the area of foreign policy formulation and look
at the potential impact women qua women have had and may have on U.S.
diplomacy. As "squeaking" mice, thousands of women acting collectively pos-
sess, at least theoretically, the power to counter the "macho factor" in U.S.
foreign policy. Women will not soon replace men as formulators of diplomatic
policy, but they can and have contributed to movements aimed at altering the
climate or atmosphere in which male policy-makers operate. For example,
throughout World War II women expressed more dovish sentiments than men

even though the amount of indifference or actual antiwar sentiment varied among them depending on income, age, and marital status. Moreover, like female abolitionists of the nineteenth-century antislavery movement, women constituted the backbone of the peace movement before the First and Second World wars, in the 1960s and again in the 1980s.[19]

Despite the fact that since the 1930s national polls have demonstrated the existence of a "gender gap" on foreign policy that crosses class and race lines, one should not rush to the conclusion that the existence of a different climate of opinion among women will significantly change U.S. diplomacy in the future any more than it has in the past. Some women (and men) are too quick to reach this conclusion, forgetting that unorganized (as well as organized) sentiments about diplomacy stand little chance of influencing foreign policy formulation because the process remains essentially undemocratic at top government levels. They also forget that most of the women who reach high level positions within the Foreign Service have, to date, thought more like their male colleagues at State than they have like women peace advocates—at least in this century.

Abigail Adams noted as early as 1782 that "patriotism in the Female Sex is the most disinterested of all virtues." The vast majority of women continue to personally experience war largely, as she said over two hundred years ago, in terms of surviving the loss of "those whom we Love most."[20] Women must oppose war in intellectual as well as emotional and personal ways, if their distinctly female approach (however socially conditioned it may be) to world affairs is to be effective. Otherwise, to talk about "global feminism" as a countervailing force in the decisions governing relations between nations, as *Ms* magazine did in 1985, is to distort the decision-making process and to delude ourselves about the effectiveness of gender-gap politics.[21] Women's different attitudes on war and peace will remain marginal as long as the most feminist among them remain excluded from top level, decision-making positions of authority in business, religion, health care, the military, the media, and politics.

This does not mean that the mice inside and outside the foreign policy establishment cannot begin to do more than individually or collectively "squeak" at the men in charge of the country's diplomacy. Since for security reasons foreign policy formulation is, and will remain, inherently undemocratic, women must begin to become more knowledgeable about foreign affairs in general and weapons systems in particular, to infiltrate the decision-making structure in greater numbers, and to organize more practically, using their collective clout as consumers to organize economic boycotts (for example, between Thanksgiving and the end-of-the-year buying season) when dissatisfied with certain diplomatic actions. The establishment responds primarily to power—whether it be economic or political. Despite Geraldine Ferraro's vice presidential candidacy in 1984 and the increasing number of women in politics at the local, state, and national levels, in the shortrun, women have more potential for exercising significant economic pressure to change U.S. foreign policy than they do political pressure, inside or outside of government circles.

In the final analysis, however, until there is a generation of women foreign policy formulators who are feminists, the diplomacy of the United States will not fundamentally change. Likewise, without the presence of a significant number of feminists in top policy-making positions, macho bellicosity will continue to characterize foreign policy here and abroad, regardless of the ideology or political economy of the individual countries. It is discouraging to think that Child, Mead, Rankin, Roosevelt, Fonda, and the numerous anonymous women who have led and participated in the various nineteenth and twentieth century peace movements were probably more feminist in their thinking and actions than those who rose in the ranks of the Foreign Service. The gender gap in domestic and foreign policy will remain a myth (as was so embarrassingly proven in the 1984 election) until women in top policy-making positions stop thinking like men. This probably means until they develop their own female support networks and until they constitute a critical mass of Senior Foreign Service Officers.

NOTES

1. Child to Sumner, Wayland, 1870, in John Greenleaf Whittier, ed., *Letters of Lydia Maria Child* (Boston, 1883), p. 208; Jane Rosen, "The Kirkpatrick Factor," *New York Times Magazine*, April 28, 1985, p. 68, and *Washington Post*, February 28, 1985, p. D9.

2. See forthcoming composite biography of forty-five U.S. women appointed as Chiefs of diplomatic missions since 1933, by Jean Wilkowski and Ann Morin, entitled, *Madam Ambassador*. Of the forty-five only 17 or 37 percent were career officers; the majority were political appointments.

3. Homer L. Calkin, *Women in American Foreign Affairs* (Washington, D.C.: Department of State, 1977), and Mary S. Olmsted, Bernice Baer, Jean Joyce, and Georgiana M. Prince, *Women at State: An Inquiry into the Status of Women in the United States Department of State* (Washington, D.C.: Women's Research and Education Institute of the Congressional Caucus for Women's Issues, 1984).

4. Joan Hoff-Wilson, "The Illusion of Change: Women and the American Revolution," in Alfred F. Young, ed., *The American Revolution: Explorations in the History of American Radicalism* (DeKalb: Northern Illinois University Press, 1976), p. 444, footnote 119.

5. Calkin, *Women in American Foreign Affairs*, p.20.

6. *Ibid.*, pp. 28, 46.

7. *Ibid.*, p. 41–42, 46.

8. *Ibid.*, pp. 45–46.

9. As late at 1974 Gladys P. Rogers, Special Assistant to the deputy under-secretary for management, said it was almost impossible to be married and in the Foreign Service if you were a woman. The exception, she said, occurred when the husband accompanied the woman and these were "very few indeed . . . [basically,] you did have to be single." Interview with Gladys Rogers, Schlesinger Library, Radcliffe College.

10. Calkin, pp. 135, 141.

11. The following figures are from the report by Olmsted, et al., *Women at State*, pp. v-vi, 1–20.

12. *Palmer v. Shultz*, 616 Federal Supplement 1540.

13. For more details about the phases and changing interpretations in women's history see Joan Hoff-Wilson review essay in *Signs: Journal of Women in Culture and Society*, 7 (Summer 1982): 880–86; *idem*, review essay in *The Women's Review of Books*, 3, no. 2 (November 1985): 17–19; and *idem*, Joan Hartman and Ellen Messer-Davidow, eds., "From Patriarchy to Feminism: Sources, Stages and Significant Schools in U.S. Women's History," *Critical Issues in Feminist Inquiry* (forthcoming).

14. Wilkowski's and Morin's *Madam Ambassador* (forthcoming) will contain the first extensive biographical account of Willis based in part on interviews with her. For brief sketches of her career, see *Current Biography*, 1954, pp. 650–51, and *Who's Who of American Women*, Sixth Edition, 1970–71, p. 1340.

15. Harold Josephson, ed., *Biographical Dictionary of Modern Peace Leaders* (Westport, Conn.: Greenwood Press, 1985). Despite their prominence in and dominance of most peace movements, women pacifists constitute a small minority in most reference books. For example, the latest dictionary of peace leaders cites 133 for the United States but only 26 or approximately 20 percent of these are women. A total of 699 peace leaders are cited in the appendix of this collection, of whom 120 or 17 percent are women. According to my calculations from this listing, the percentages of female peace leaders by country are:

Sweden 69%	India 8%;
Chile 50%	Germany 7%
Denmark 50%	Argentina 0%
Hungary 43%	Brazil 0%
Australia 40%	Bulgaria 0%
Norway 25%	Central African Republic 0%
Switzerland 24%	Costa Rica 0%
Canada 21%	Czechoslovakia 0%
Japan 21%	Ecuador 0%
Belgium 20%	Ethiopia 0%
Netherlands 20%	Ghana 0%
United States 20%	Greece 0%
France 19%	Guatemala 0%
Italy 19%	Liberia 0%
Austria 17%	New Zealand 0%
USSR 17%	Paraguay 0%
Poland 16%	Portugal 0%
Finland 14%	South Africa 0%
Great Britain 14%	Spain 0%
China 12%	Venezuela 0%

16. Joan Hoff-Wilson, " 'Peace Is a Woman's Job . . . ' Jeannette Rankin's Foreign Policy," two-part essay in *Montana: The Magazine of Western History*, 20, nos. 1, 2 (January and April 1980): 28–41, 38–53. The following details about Rankin's life can be found in this article and in my biographical sketches of her in Josephson, *Biographical Dictionary of Modern Peace Leaders*, pp. 790–93; and Barbara Sicherman, et al., ed., *Notable American Women* (Cambridge: Harvard University, 1980), pp. 566–68.

17. Carol Gilligan, *In a Different Voice: Psychological Theory and Women's De-*

velopment (Cambridge: Harvard University Press, 1982); Carroll Smith-Rosenberg, *Disorderly Conduct: Visions of Gender in Victorian America* (New York: Knopf, 1985).

18. *Current Biography*, 1962, p. 117.

19. Lawrence S. Witner, *Rebels Against War: The American Peace Movement, 1933–1983* (Philadelphia: Temple University Press, 1984); Pam McAllister, ed., *Reweaving the Web of Life: Feminism and Nonviolence* (Philadelphia: New Society Publishers, 1982); Karen Sue Anderson, *Wartime Women* (Westport, Conn: Greenwood Press, 1981); Susan Hartmann, *The Home Front and Beyond: American Women in the 1940's* (Boston, 1982); and D'Ann Campbell, *Women at War with America: Private Lives in a Patriotic Era* (Cambridge: Harvard University Press, 1984).

20. Joan Hoff-Wilson, "Illusion of Change," p. 390.

21. *Ms magazine forum*, "Women—A New Superpower?" March 1985, p. 41ff.

Selected Bibliography

Scholarly works dealing directly with women and their influence on American foreign policy scarcely exist. With the exception of two studies that concentrate on women in the Foreign Service—Homer L. Calkin's *Women in American Foreign Affairs* (1977) and Mary S. Olmstead, et al., *Women at State* (1984)—there are no major studies detailing women's role in American diplomacy. The following bibliography is necessarily eclectic. It covers a 150-year time period as well as a diverse group of women. It reflects the fact that when the activities of these women were reported, frequently it was in sources not usually examined by historians of American foreign policy. Given these parameters, the bibliography suggests a number of sources covering selected aspects of American foreign policy and also provides some of the works considered most important for an understanding of the individuals included in this collection.

BOOKS

Barrett, Lawrence. *Gambling with History: Ronald Reagan in the White House*. Garden City, New York: Doubleday & Co., 1983.

Boneparth, Ellen, ed. *Women, Power and Policy*. New York: Pergamon Press, 1982.

Brown, Charles H. *Agents of Manifest Destiny: The Lives and Times of The Filibusters*. Chapel Hill: University of North Carolina Press, 1980.

Brownstein, Ronald, and Nina Easton. *Reagan's Ruling Class*. Washington: The Presidential Accountability Group, 1982.

Calkin, Homer L. *Women in American Foreign Affairs*. Washington: Department of State, 1977.

Carroll, Anna Ella. *The Great American Battle; or, The Contest Between Christianity and Political Romanism*. New York: Miller, Orton & Mulligan, 1856.

———. *Review of Pierce's Administration; Showing Its Only Popular Measures to Have*

Originated with the Executive of Millard Fillmore. Boston: James French & Co., 1856.

————. *The Star of the West; or, National Men and National Measures.* Boston: James French & Co., 1856.

Cazneau, Mrs. William Leslie. *Our Winter Eden: Pen Pictures of the Tropics.* New York: Author's Publishing Co., 1878.

Child, Lydia Maria. *An Appeal in Favor of That Class of Americans Called Africans.* Boston: Allen and Ticknor, 1833.

————. *Anti-Slavery Catechism.* Newburyport, Massachusetts: Charles Whipple, 1836.

————. Letters from New York. 2 vols. 3rd ed. New York: C. S. Francis & Co., 1845.

Conrad, Susan P. *Perish the Thought: Intellectual Women in Romantic America, 1830–1860.* New York: Oxford University Press, 1976.

Curti, Merle. *Peace or War: The American Struggle, 1636–1936.* New York: W. W. Norton and Co., 1936.

DeBenedetti, Charles. *The Peace Reform in American History.* Bloomington: Indiana University Press, 1980.

Dulles, Eleanor Lansing. *Berlin—The Wall Is Not Forever.* Chapel Hill: The University of North Carolina Press, 1967.

————. *Chances of a Lifetime: A Memoir.* Englewood Cliffs, New Jersey: Prentice-Hall, Inc., 1980.

Gilligan, Carol. *In a Different Voice: Psychological Theory and Women's Development.* Cambridge: Harvard University Press, 1982.

Ginzberg, Eli, and Alice M. Yohalem. *Educated American Women: Self-Portraits.* New York: Columbia University Press, 1966.

Greenbie, Sydney, and Marjorie Barstow. *Anna Ella Carroll and Abraham Lincoln.* Manchester, Maine: University of Tampa Press in cooperation with Falmouth Publishing House, 1952.

Guiles, Fred Lawrence. *Jane Fonda: The Actress in Her Time.* Garden City, New York: Doubleday and Co., 1982.

Haig, Alexander M., Jr. *Caveat: Realism, Reagan, and Foreign Policy.* New York: Macmillan Publishing Co., 1984.

Hoff-Wilson, Joan, and Marjorie Lightman, eds., *Without Precedent: The Life and Career of Eleanor Roosevelt.* Bloomington: Indiana University Press, 1984.

James, Edward T., ed. *Notable American Women 1607–1950: A Biographical Dictionary.* 3 vols. Cambridge: Harvard University Press, 1971.

Josephson, Harold, ed. *Biographical Dictionary of Modern Peace Leaders.* Westport, Conn.: Greenwood Press, 1985.

Kiernan, Thomas. *Jane Fonda: Heroine for Our Times.* New York: Delilah Books, 1982.

Kirkpatrick, Jeane, ed. *The Strategy of Deception: A Study of World-Wide Communist Tactics.* New York: Farrar, Straus & Co., 1963.

————. *Leader and Vanguard in Mass Society: A Study of Peronist Argentina.* Cambridge, Mass.: The MIT Press, 1971.

————. *Political Woman.* New York: Basic Books, Inc., 1974.

————. *The New Presidential Elite: Men and Women in National Politics.* New York: Russell Sage Foundation and the Twentieth Century Fund, 1976.

————. *Dictatorship and Double Standards: Rationalism and Reason in Politics.* New York: American Enterprise Institute and Simon & Schuster, Inc., 1982.

———. *The Reagan Phenomenon and Other Speeches on Foreign Policy*. Washington: American Enterprise Institute, 1983.

Lash, Joseph P. *Eleanor and Franklin*. New York: W. W. Norton, 1971.

———. *Eleanor: The Years Alone*. New York: W. W. Norton, 1972.

Lerner, Gerda. *The Majority Finds Its Past: Placing Women in History*. New York: Oxford University Press, 1979.

LeVeness, Frank P., and Jane P. Sweeney, eds. *Women Leaders in Contemporary U.S. Politics*. Boulder, Colo.: Lynne Rienner Publishers, Inc., 1986.

May, Robert E. *The Southern Dream of a Caribbean Empire, 1854–1861*. Baton Rouge, Louisiana: Louisiana State University Press, 1973.

Mead, Lucia Ames. *Swords and Ploughshares, or the Supplanting of the System of Law*. New York: G. P. Putnam, 1912.

———. *Law or War*. New York: Doubleday, Doran and Co., 1928.

Meltzer, Milton, and Patricia Holland, eds., *Lydia Maria Child, Selected Letters, 1817–1880*. Amherst: University of Massachusetts Press, 1982.

Montgomery, Cora. *Eagle Pass; or Life on the Border*. New York: Putnam, 1852.

Mosley, Leonard. *Dulles: A Biography of Eleanor, Allen and John Foster Dulles and Their Family Network*. New York: The Dial Press, 1978.

Olmstead, Mary S., and Bernice Baer, Jean Joyce, Georgiana M. Prince. *Women at State: An Inquiry into the Status of Women in the United States Department of State*. Washington: Women's Research and Education Institute of the Congressional Caucus for Women's Issues, 1984.

O'Neill, Lois Decker. *The Women's Book of World Records and Achievements*. Garden City, New York: Anchor Press/Doubleday, 1979.

Osborne, William S. *Lydia Maria Child*. Boston: Twayne Publishers, 1980.

Patterson, David S. *Towards a Warless World: The Travail of the American Peace Movement, 1887–1914*. Bloomington, Indiana: Indiana University Press, 1976.

Roosevelt, Eleanor. *This Is My Story*. New York: Harper and Brothers, 1937.

———. *This I Remember*. New York: Harper, 1949.

———. *Autobiography*. New York: Harper, 1961.

Steinson, Barbara J. *American Women's Activism in World War I*. New York: Garland Publishing, 1982.

Wallace, Edward S. *Destiny and Glory*. New York: Coward-McCann, 1957.

Whittier, John Greenleaf, ed., *Letters of Lydia Maria Child*. Boston: Houghton Mifflin Co., 1883.

Woloch, Nancy. *Women and the American Experience*. New York: Alfred A. Knopf, 1984.

Articles

Brauer, Kinley J. "1821–1860: Economics and the Diplomacy of American Expansionism," in William H. Becker and Samuel F. Wells, Jr., eds. *Economics and World Power: An Assessment of American Diplomacy Since 1789*. New York: Columbia University Press, 1984, pp. 55–118.

Brenner, Marie. "The Blooming of Jeane Kirkpatrick," *Vanity Fair* 48 (July 1985): 30–35+.

Cheney, Lynn. "The Decline of the Dutiful Wife." *The Washingtonian*, April 1985, pp. 138–49.

Conaway, James. "Jeane Kirkpatrick, the Ambassador from *Commentary* Magazine." *Washington Post Magazine*, 11 November, 1981, pp. 11+.

Crapol, Edward P. "The Foreign Policy of Antislavery, 1833–1846," in Lloyd Gardner, ed. *Redefining the Past, Essays in Diplomatic History in Honor of William A. Williams.* Corvallis: Oregon State University Press, 1986.

Dulles, Eleanor Lansing. "Berlin—Barometer of Tension," in Eleanor L. Dulles and Robert Dickson Crane, eds. *Detente: Cold War Strategies in Transition.* New York: Frederick A. Praeger, 1965.

Fallaci, Oriana. "Jane Fonda: 'I'm Coming into Focus.' " *McCall's*, February 1971, p. 123+.

Grenier, Jeannine E. "Women in U.S. Foreign Policy," *American Politics* (June 1986): 12–13+.

Hales, Jean Gould. " 'Co-laborers in the Cause': Women in the Ante-bellum Nativist Movement," *Civil War History* 25 (June 1979):119–63.

Hoff-Wilson, Joan. "Foreign Policy Trends Since 1920," *SHAFR Newsletter* (September 1977):1–17.

Jong, Erica. "Jane Fonda: An Interview," *Ladies' Home Journal*, April 1984, p. 32+.

Kenworthy, Eldon. "Our Colleague Kirkpatrick." *LASA Forum* 14 (Winter 1984):23–24.

Kirkpatrick, Jeane. "Dictatorships and Double Standards," *Commentary* 65 (November 1979):34–45.

———. "U.S. Security and Latin America," *Commentary* 71 (January 1981):29–40.

———. "Establishing a Viable Human Rights Policy," *World Affairs* 143 (Spring 1981):323–24.

Kraft, Barbara. "Peacemaking in the Progressive Era: A Prestigious and Proper Calling," *Maryland Historian* 1 (Fall 1970):121+.

Laurino, Maria. "Political Woman: Is Jeane Kirkpatrick a Feminist?" *The Village Voice*, 9 July 1985, pp. 19–22+.

Marcum, John. "The Kirkpatrick Era: The U.S. at the U.N." *Worldview* 24 (June 1981):19–21.

May, Robert E. "Lobbyists for Commercial Empire: Jane Cazneau, William Cazneau, and U.S. Caribbean Policy, 1846–1878," *Pacific Historical Review* (August 1979):383–412.

Rosen, Jane, "The Kirkpatrick Factor," *New York Times Magazine*, 28 April 1985, pp. 48–51+.

Rossi, Alice S. "Beyond the Gender Gap: Women's Bid for Political Power," *Social Science Quarterly* 64 (December 1983):718–33.

Rubin, Barry. "Reagan Administration Policymaking and Central America," in Robert S. Leiken, ed. *Central America: Anatomy of Conflict.* New York: Pergamon Press, 1984.

Ruddick, Sara. "Pacifying the Forces: Drafting Women in the Interests of Peace," *Signs: Journal of Women in Culture and Society* 8 (Spring 1983): 479–80.

Smith, Hilda L. "Women's History and Social History: An Untimely Alliance," *OAH Newsletter* (November 1984):4–6.

Snyder, Charles McCool. "Anna Ella Carroll, Political Strategist and Gadfly to President Fillmore," *Maryland Historical Magazine* 68 (Spring 1973):119–38.

Index

About the Contributors

BLANCHE WIESEN COOK is Professor of History at John Jay College of Criminal Justice, City University of New York. She is the author of *The Declassified Eisenhower: A Divided Legacy of Peace and Political Warfare* and editor of *Crystal Eastman on Women and Revolution*. At present she is completing a biography of Eleanor Roosevelt.

JANET L. CORYELL, Assistant Professor of History at Western Michigan University, is the author of *Neither Heroine nor Fool: Anna Ella Carroll of Maryland* and coeditor of the forthcoming *Surgeon with the 121st: The Civil War Letters and Diary of Dr. Daniel M. Holt*. She is at work on a biography of Maria Mitchell.

JOHN M. CRAIG teaches history at Slippery Rock University and is the author of *Lucia Ames Mead (1856–1936) and the American Peace Movement*.

EDWARD P. CRAPOL, Professor of History at the College of William and Mary, is the author of *America for Americans: Economic Nationalism and Anglophobia in the Late Nineteenth Century* and "The Foreign Policy of Antislavery, 1833–1846" in *Redefining the Past*, edited by Lloyd Gardner.

LYNNE K. DUNN is an Assistant Professor of History at Winthrop College. She has completed a biography focusing on Eleanor Lansing Dulles's career and influence upon U.S.-Austrian and U.S.-Berlin relations. Her current work is on internationalists and the United States from 1920 to 1941.

JUDITH EWELL, Newton Professor of History at the College of William and Mary, is author of *The Indictment of a Dictator: The Extradition and Trial of Marcos Pérez Jiménez, Venezuela: A Century of Change* and coeditor (with William Beezley) of *The Human Tradition in Latin America: The Nineteenth Century*. She is working on a history of U.S.-Venezuelan relations from 1800 to the present.

JOAN HOFF-WILSON is Professor of History at Indiana University. She is the author of several books on twentieth-century American foreign policy and politics, has taught courses in women's studies, and published articles in the field of women's history. Her current research is on the Nixon presidency. Her most recent book is *Law, Gender, and Injustice: A Legal History of U.S. Women*.

ROBERT E. MAY is a Professor of History at Purdue University. He is the author of *The Southern Dream of a Caribbean Empire, 1854–1861* and *John A. Quitman: Old South Crusader*, which won the McLemore Prize of the Mississippi Historical Society.

JEANNE ZEIDLER is Director of the Hampton University Museum. She is coauthor of " 'Things African Prove to be a Favorite Theme': The African Collection at Hampton University," in *Art/Artifact: African Art in Anthropology Collections*, edited by Susan Vogel. She is also the publisher of the *International Review of African American Art*.

flipped learning

GATEWAY TO STUDENT ENGAGEMENT

JONATHAN BERGMANN
AARON SAMS

International Society for Technology in Education
EUGENE, OREGON • WASHINGTON, DC

Flipped Learning: Gateway to Student Engagement
Jonathan Bergmann and Aaron Sams

Editor: *Lynda Gansel*
Production Coordinator: *Emily Reed*
Copy Editor: *Cecelia Hagen*
Proofreader: *Ann Skaugset*
Cover Design: *Tamra Holmes*
Book Design and Production: *Kim McGovern*

First Edition
ISBN: 978-1-56484-344-9 (paperback)
ISBN: 978-1-56484-489-7 (e-book)

Printed in the United States of America

ISTE® is a registered trademark of the International Society for
Technology in Education.

About ISTE

The International Society for Technology in Education is the premier membership association for educators and education leaders committed to empowering connected learners in a connected world. Home to the ISTE Conference and Expo and the widely adopted ISTE Standards for learning, teaching, and leading in the digital age, the association represents more than 100,000 professionals worldwide.

We support our members with professional development, networking opportunities, advocacy, and ed tech resources to help advance the transformation of education. To find out more about these and other ISTE initiatives, visit iste.org.

As part of our mission, ISTE works with experienced educators to develop and publish practical resources for classroom teachers, teacher educators, and technology leaders. Every manuscript we select for publication is carefully peer reviewed and professionally edited.

Also by Jonathan Bergmann and Aaron Sams

Flip Your Classroom: Reach Every Student in Every Class Every Day

Also from ISTE

Differentiating Instruction with Technology in K–5 Classrooms
Differentiating Instruction with Technology in Middle School Classrooms
Grace E. Smith and Stephanie Throne

Intelligence Quest: Project-Based Learning and Multiple Intelligences
Walter McKenzie

Reinventing Project-Based Learning: Your Field Guide to
Real-World Projects in the Digital Age
Suzie Boss and Jane Krauss

To see all ISTE titles, please visit iste.org/bookstore

About the Authors

Jon Bergmann is a teacher who used to love being the center of the classroom. But he gave it up when he saw how engaged his students became in the learning process when he began flipping his instruction. Flipped learning allowed him to know his students better which brought him back to the reason he became a teacher in the first place. He is considered one of pioneers of the flipped learning movement and now shares his passion for learner-centered classrooms with educators around the globe. He is currently chief learning officer of TurnAbout Learning. He received the Presidential Award for Excellence in Math and Science Teaching in 2002, and was named a semi-finalist for Colorado Teacher of the Year in 2010. Jon serves on the advisory board of TED Education, and hosts "The Flip Side," a radio show which tells the stories of Flipped educators. Additionally, he is a founding board member and the treasurer of the Flipped Learning Network, the only not-for-profit organization run by and for flipped educators.

Aaron Sams has been an educator since 2000. He received the Presidential Award for Excellence in Math and Science Teaching in 2009 and co-chaired the committee to revise the Colorado Science Academic Standards. He is a founding member of the Flipped Learning Network, adjunct instructor at Saint Vincent College, director of digital learning at the Reformed Presbyterian Theological Seminary, advisor to TED-Ed, and as taught chemistry in California and Colorado. Aaron holds a BS in Biochemistry and an MAEd, both from Biola University.

Acknowledgments

Thank you to Kari Arfstrom for her tireless work as the executive director of the Flipped Leaning Network.

Dedication

For the amazing teachers who have embraced flipped learning around the world. We are humbled by your dedication and commitment to kids.

Contributing Authors

Brian Bennett is a customer solutions engineer for TechSmith, and a former chemistry teacher. His primary goal is to help teachers effectively leverage technology to enhance student learning.

Delia Bush is a fifth grade teacher at Kenowa Hills Public Schools, Grand Rapids, Michigan. Bush has a bachelor's degree in elementary education, a master's degree in education administration, and an educational specialist degree with a focus on curriculum and instruction.

Kristin Daniels is a technology and innovation coach for Stillwater Area Public Schools, Stillwater, Minnesota. In 2011, she helped develop and implement flipped professional development for the Stillwater elementary schools. Daniels trained teachers for a fifth grade flipped classroom pilot and currently supports a growing number of elementary flipped classrooms in Stillwater. She conducts flipped learning workshops nationally and sits on the board of directors for the Flipped Learning Network.

Thomas Driscoll is a social studies teacher at Putnam High School, Putnam, Connecticut. Driscoll's teaching and scholarship involve curriculum design and instructional technology.

Mike Dronen is the the executive director of technology for the Minnetonka Public Schools, Minnesota. He helped to design and implement the flipped learning professional development model for teachers and school administrators. Dronen initiated Minnesota's first bring your own device program, and in 2011 received the TIES Minnesota Technology Leader Award.

Carolyn Durley is a high school biology teacher at Okanagan Mission Secondary School, Kelowna, B.C., Canada. Durley received her Bachelor of Science from McGill University and a Bachelor of Education from the University of British Columbia.

April Gudenrath is a high school English teacher both in the classroom and online for Discovery Canyon Campus, Colorado Springs, Colorado. She has collaborated with many flipped pioneers on presentations and webinars. She has also created several videos for TED-Education.

Jason Hahnstadt is a physical education teacher at The Joseph Sears School, Kenilworth, Illinois and an assistant football and track coach at New Trier High School, Winnetka, Illinois. Hahnstadt's teaching and coaching involve large group activities and on-field instruction. He was selected as one of the Top 40 Innovators in Education 2013 by the Center for Digital Education.

Steve Kelly has been teaching high school math and science in St. Louis, Michigan, since 1990. Kelly became a National Board Certified Teacher of secondary mathematics in 2010.

Crystal Kirch is a high school math teacher at Segerstrom Fundamental High School in Santa Ana, California. Kirch holds a Bachelor of Science in Kinesiology and a Master of Arts in Education with a focus in Curriculum and Instruction.

Contents

Contents

Preface

As the first days of school began in 2006–07, we—Aaron Sams and Jonathan Bergmann—arrived to teach science at Woodland Park High School in Woodland Park, Colorado. Jon came from the Denver metropolitan area and settled into Room 313; Aaron came from the greater Los Angeles area to occupy Room 314.

We both had taught chemistry at our previous schools, Jon for eighteen years and Aaron for six. Since we represented the entire chemistry team, we decided to work together to develop a strong chemistry program at Woodland Park High School. Though we were very different in our approaches to teaching, we had similar philosophies: we both wanted to put our students first so they could develop both cognitively and affectively. Our decision to work together created a culture of collaboration and reflection that helped us as we explored ways to use technology to enhance learning.

During the 2006–07 school year we taught traditionally, using a great deal of direct instruction in an engaging lecture style. As part of our collaboration, we decided to use common assessments and experiments so that our students would have a similar experience regardless of which chemistry teacher they were assigned. We met on a regular basis to reflect about best practices and about how to integrate technology into our classes. These voluntary meetings grew out of the fact that we worked together well and realized that two heads are better than one.

One frustration we encountered while teaching at this small school was the large number of absent students caused by school activities. Woodland Park is situated 20 miles and 2500 feet above Colorado Springs. The road to Woodland Park is a winding mountain pass, which made travel to school activities a time-consuming challenge: it took 45 minutes to reach the nearest school of comparable size. This commute to events caused students to frequently miss the last class of the day, and missing a difficult subject such as chemistry set those students back.

In the spring of 2007, Aaron discovered a review of a computer program that recorded PowerPoint lectures, including digital "ink" with which a lecturer could write on the screen as well as an audio component. At this point we were ready to dive into the world of teacher-created video. Ken Boyer, chairman of the Woodland Park High School science department, agreed to contribute $100 for two copies of the software. As they say, "The rest is history."

First we used the software to record live lectures. The assistant superintendent in charge of curriculum and instruction in the Woodland Park School District took note and came down for a chat. Her daughter was attending university, and one of her daughter's professors was recording the audio of his lectures. She told us that her daughter loved this model because "she didn't have to go to class anymore." Later that week, a lunchtime conversation about that interaction ensued, and we asked ourselves: "What is the value of class time if a student can access all the content while not attending class?" Then we asked: "What do students *really* need a physically present teacher for?"

As the conversation continued, Aaron said, "What if we stopped lecturing in class and pre-recorded all of our lessons? Then, in class, students would do the stuff that they used to do at home?" Jon said, "OK, let's do it!" After this exchange, neither of us ever used direct instruction as a whole-group, in-class teaching tool again.

During this time of development, we shared what we were doing with a group of teachers online. We had been active on the AP Chemistry listserv for many years, using it to connect and learn from other AP Chemistry teachers from around the world. This group became our sounding board as the concept of the flipped classroom grew. Other teachers who were also experimenting with video as an instructional tool began to emerge, and an informal professional network began to form. The flipped classroom was not born in a vacuum; it was not developed only in Rooms 313 and 314 at Woodland Park High School. Though we were pioneers in developing the flipped classroom, it would have never happened without this broader network of amazing teachers. Eventually, with the partnership of Jerry Overmeyer at the University of Northern Colorado, an online community for educators interested in the flipped classroom was born. This community, the Flipped Learning Network (flippedclassroom. org), has grown exponentially in recent years. As of this writing, it has a membership of over 20,000.

The idea of the flipped classroom is really quite simple: direct instruction is done through video, or some other learning object that students can use individually prior to coming to class. This time shift then allows the teacher to use class time for work that is either better done as a large group, or that requires individualized teacher attention. That's the flipped classroom in a nutshell: direct instruction delivered to the individual outside of class, and more strategic use of in-class time for group work and individualized attention. We soon found that we had stumbled onto something that could radically transform our classrooms into something we had never dreamed they could become.

Much of this is chronicled in our first book, *Flip Your Classroom: Reach Every Student in Every Class Every Day,* (Bergmann & Sams, 2012). In the first half of that book, we explained the flipped classroom. The second half tells how we were able to implement a mastery model called the "flipped mastery model." In the flipped mastery model, students work asynchronously through objectives (competencies) as they master content.

Since the publication of *Flip Your Classroom,* we have continued to refine the flipped classroom process, along with thousands of educators in the flipped class community. The original flipped classroom concept changed how teachers delivered content, but it was a strategy that was narrowly focused on delivering content efficiently. A flipped classroom didn't ensure a student-centered classroom. Learning in a flipped classroom was still very much teacher-centric. Even the flipped mastery model was still quite teacher-centric, albeit student-paced.

This book will take you to the logical next step in the evolution of the flipped classroom—flipped learning—a path toward powerful learning and teaching strategies that can transform learning by engaging each student and taking their learning deeper and further.

Introduction

a challenge
and
the one question

JOHN TAGUE IS a 20-year veteran mathematics teacher from Fairfax, Vermont. Three years ago, a student came to John at the end of class to get some help. She didn't have time to get a complete explanation, so she said, in exasperation, "I will just find a YouTube video to explain it." At that moment, John realized he had to do something different to meet the needs of his students.

John understood that the traditional model, where he stood up and talked *at* 30 students every day, needed to change. He then scoured Twitter and started looking for answers. Through Twitter, John was able to connect with some flipped classroom advocates. From there, he implemented flipped learning in both his AP Calculus and his ninth-grade math course. Today his students are more actively engaged in their learning. By working with students individually, John was able to make a difference in their learning. Whenever he has a chance to share his experience as a flipped classroom teacher, he says: "No one is left behind, no one is held back."

Amber Mueller is a second-year fifth grade teacher at Lily Lake Elementary School in Stillwater, Minnesota. As a first-year teacher, she arrived with energy and enthusiasm. Unfortunately, she quickly got discouraged, especially with teaching math. She had so many topics to cover and felt like the program she was developing overemphasized the filling in of worksheets. After six months of frustration, she was introduced to flipped learning. Her district started a professional development program centered on flipped learning principles, and she jumped in with both feet. Before Amber implemented flipped learning, her students dreaded math; now they beg to do more. Her students not only watch instructional videos, they are also given a choice in how they demonstrate their understanding of a topic. Amber has even incorporated elements of her flipped math classroom into her literacy course.

Even though these two teachers have pronounced differences in age and experience, they both concluded that something needed to change in education and, more specifically, something needed to change in their classrooms. They aren't alone. More and more teachers are asking themselves: Do I need to rethink the way I'm teaching my classes? Is there a better learning model than lecture-discussion? Is there a better way to engage students? And they are finding the answers are yes, yes, and yes.

John and Amber each concluded that they needed a personal transformation, and they needed to transform their classrooms into centers of learning and inquiry. Flipped learning gave them a framework with which to accomplish this.

A Challenge to Teachers

This book is about transformation: teachers transforming classrooms and schools from the bottom up to meet the needs of each individual student. This is not an overly academic tome, but rather a book of stories that describe the personal transformations that various teachers have experienced as they follow the path of flipped learning. We invite our readers to join them in this transformation.

Flipped learning is a grassroots movement, not a top-down approach to change. It is changing one teacher at a time, one class at a time, and one school at a time. Teachers need to be the change agents in education. We challenge our readers to be these change agents, to not wait for administrators or reformers to tell you how to change, but to act based on what is best for your students. We challenge teachers to not only consider flipping their classrooms, but to consider moving deeper and further, to flipped learning.

The One Question

How, then, do teachers bring about this change? How do teachers become the transformational change agents in their own school settings? We think there is a fundamental question all teachers need to ask, and at the risk of sounding overly dramatic, we will refer to this question as the One Question. This One Question will be a common thread throughout this book:

What is the best use of face-to-face time with students?

The most valuable assets teachers have are those minutes spent each day with students. Teachers need to leverage those precious minutes to maximize learning. Talking at students each day is not the best use of class time! Students need teachers most when they are stuck on a difficult concept or problem that, in a traditional classroom, often happens at home, when the teacher is unavailable. The best use of class time incorporates enriching learning activities and relevant experiences.

What is the answer? What is the best use of your face-to-face class time? Is it problem-based learning? Is it inquiry? Is it discussion? Is it direct instruction? Is it guided practice? If you are looking for one answer for all your students, you will be frustrated with this book. We will propose many possible answers, and each of the educators featured in these pages will share with you how they answered the One Question for themselves. We do not believe there is only one answer to this question: there are many. In fact, we believe that maybe the greatest power in flipped learning is the ability to individualize the learning for each child. There are many different answers, because each student is different and comes to you with a different set of gifts, abilities, passions, and interests.

We want all educators to ask themselves the One Question, and we believe that answering this question honestly will forever change the way educators teach and interact with students.

Chapter 1

the flipped learning model

WITH THE EDUCATIONAL media outlets full of articles, blog posts, webinars, and interviews about flipped classrooms and flipped learning, many educators are left wondering: What exactly is the flipped classroom? We have hesitated to answer this question because we strongly believe that what we originally called the flipped classroom is just a stage leading to what we were really promoting—flipped learning. This may seem like mincing words, but we want to be clear that what has popularly become known as the flipped classroom is only one basic form of the flipped learning model.

Defining Flipped Learning

The commonly known definition of a flipped classroom is when students watch instructional videos at home and do the typical homework (worksheets, problem sets, back-of-the-chapter exercises) in class. We are calling this version "Flipped Class 101." This is the entry point, but it is not the goal or a place to stop. Moving direct instruction out of the group learning space and into the individual learning space is a great place to begin your journey, but it is not the destination itself.

In our first book, *Flip Your Classroom* (Bergmann & Sams, 2012), we wrote about the first year we flipped using Flipped Class 101. That year we focused primarily on producing high-quality videos for our students. However, as the year progressed, we realized we could use elements of the flipped classroom to move students to mastery. So we moved through Flipped Class 101 and developed the flipped mastery model. Even that wasn't the ending point. We moved further, into flipped learning.

But what exactly is flipped learning? We like the definition that the Flipped Learning Network (www.flippedlearning.org) adapted from the work of Ramsey Musallam (www.cyclesoflearning.com):

> Flipped learning is a pedagogical approach in which direct instruction moves from the group learning space to the individual learning space, and the resulting group space is transformed into a dynamic, interactive learning environment where the educator guides students as they apply concepts and engage creatively in the subject matter.

The basic premise is that direct instruction, which is often referred to as lecture (though it is not necessarily the same thing), is not conducted in large groups. In flipped learning, the direct instruction is delivered individually, usually—though not exclusively—through teacher-created videos. This time shift then frees up the face-to-face time for richer, more meaningful learning experiences for students.

If a teacher is not using direct instruction in class, what does she do instead? You can get to the answer to that question by answering the One Question: What is the best use of face-to-face time with students?

Flipped learning, at its core, is individualized learning. There are many methods, variations, and types of student-centered learning—differentiated instruction, problem/project-based learning, inquiry-based study, and many others. When combined with the flipped learning concept, these strategies become practical to implement. Flipped learning is fundamentally learner-centric.

Flipped learning isn't a set process; it allows for many expressions of the model. There is no single strategy that works in every class-room, for every teacher, and for each student. However, flipped learning is adaptable to your style, methods, and circumstances. Each teacher can personalize their version of flipped learning for their students. It also allows teachers to play to their individual strengths as educators. However, there are some key components of all successful flipped learning environments.

Components of Successful Flipped Learning Environments

As we have interacted with many teachers, we have noticed some key reasons they have been successful with flipped learning.

Collaboration

It is very difficult to incorporate flipped learning alone. When we implemented flipped learning, our rooms were right next to each other. As we were developing our versions of flipped learning, we were constantly talking with each other about how we could tweak and overhaul our teaching practice. Neither of us could have done this alone. And as others have discovered flipped learning, many of the most successful teachers have done so within a community.

A great example of collaboration involves English teachers Andrew Thomasson (found on Twitter at @thomasson_engl) and Cheryl Morris (@guster4lovers). Andrew teaches in North Carolina and Cheryl teaches in California. They met while attending the 2012 Flipped Class Virtual Conference, realized they had similar teaching philosophies, and began to collaborate. They are now making instructional videos together, even though they are three time zones apart. Their success is primarily due to how well they networked and connected with each other. They are also connected to the larger flipped learning community via Twitter and other social networking sites.

Student-Centered Learning

Too often, classrooms are centered around the teacher. The teacher is "teaching" by standing up and giving a presentation of some sort to their students. Even when this is done well, there are often students who are disengaged from the learning process. We observe that when the teacher steps off the stage and becomes a facilitator of learning, rather than a presenter of content, the classroom becomes a center for learning where the focus of the classroom is on the student.

Optimized Learning Spaces

The physical design of most classrooms is based on the idea that the teacher and the presentation of content should be the focus. Twenty years ago, this meant the blackboard and a teacher desk were the focus of the room. As technology changed, the blackboard became a whiteboard, the whiteboard was replaced with a screen and LCD projector, and many schools invested great amounts of money in interactive whiteboards. Unfortunately these changes did little to change the teacher-centered classroom dynamic. The teacher remained the center of attention of the class, and students still sat in nice neat rows while passively being exposed to content.

As teachers implement flipped learning and find that they are not consistently presenting content to all the students at one time, many also make changes to their physical space. Sometimes this is not possible due to the permanence of some school furniture. Others have to share their rooms with other educators who may not want to alter the structure of the room. But those teachers who have the flexibility to do so can creatively alter their spaces.

As there is no one way to flip a class, there is also no one way to configure learning spaces for students. However, there are a few general principles that we want to highlight:

Create collaborative spaces. Flipped learning is inherently a collaborative endeavor, and we encourage flipped learning teachers to arrange furniture in ways that encourage collaboration.

Create individual spaces. Not all work should be done in groups. There should also be places in the room where students can work individually with fewer distractions. This is often difficult in a room that emphasizes collaboration. One possible way is to acquire a few sets of noise-canceling headphones for student use.

Emphasize student-centeredness of the class. The class is now student-centered, thus the room layout should take the focus off the teacher. We know of teachers who have gone so far as to get rid of their teacher desk. This has forced them to be up and about, working with students.

Emphasize learning, not teaching. Rearrangement of the room should emphasize that this space is designed for learning, not teaching. Often schools think direct instruction should be the priority and that the classroom ought to be arranged accordingly. We argue that learning should be the number one priority of a school, and that the learning space should reflect that priority.

Adequate Time for Implementation

A great deal of time is required to fully implement any new teaching strategy, and flipped learning is no exception. There will be a steep learning curve as teachers not only rethink how their classes should operate, but also learn new technologies and implement new procedures. In 2010, we had an opportunity to help the school district in Sioux Falls, South Dakota, implement a mastery system. They were planning on using elements of the flipped mastery model in their implementation. This district applied for and received a grant to develop this program. The leadership realized that the limiting factor in implementation of this model was time. So they designed the grant to pay teachers extra money for overtime work as they developed the necessary learning objects to implement the flipped learning curriculum. Honoring teachers in this way produced great results. We encourage schools and districts to think of ways of compensating teachers for the extra time it takes to truly implement the flipped learning methodology.

Support from Administrators

Flipping a class, or even just a lesson, is a different way to teach. Administrators need to support their staff as teachers lead the way in innovation and change. We have seen the most remarkable change happen when the school leadership, whether at the school level or the district level, embraces the flipped classroom concept and provides professional development, resources, and a willingness to embrace change for the sake of their students.

Support from the IT Department

One of the big questions that each school and district needs to answer is: Where do I put my videos? We have found that there is no one right way to answer this question. Different schools will have their students access the videos from different places. But for adequate access to effectively occur, the IT department must be supportive of flipped learning. It is best that the IT experts develop simple workflows for their teachers that make it easy to create, post, and share videos and other learning objects.

Thoughtful Reflection

The teachers who are most effective at using flipped learning are thoughtful and reflective about their teaching practice in general. They are constantly looking for ways to improve their craft. They realize that there is not just one way to flip a class, and they are constantly modifying and tweaking their practice to meet the needs of their learners. These teachers evaluate every aspect of their classrooms to determine if it is helping to achieve learning goals. This metacognitive process ultimately benefits all their students.

One teacher who attended a past Flipped Class Conference went back to his school and implemented the Bergmann-Sams version of the flipped classroom model, and it was an utter failure. He reflected on why it didn't work and came to the conclusion that he needed to customize the model for his own setting rather than emulate Bergmann and Sams. Once he did this, he experienced great success.

Many Paths to Flipped Learning

We have met a great number of amazing educators around the globe who have moved through Flipped Class 101, just as we did. They usually spend about one or two years teaching via Flipped Class 101, but then realize the flipped class is only a gateway to flipped learning. Not all teachers gravitated to the flipped mastery model like we did. Many have gone from Flipped Class 101 directly to flipped learning. We want to encourage our readers to move through the Flipped Class 101 stage to "deeper and further" learning experiences for their students. These learning strategies are discussed in Chapters 3 and 4.

For example, Justyna Kalinowska is a seventh-grade math teacher at the Joseph Sears School in Kenilworth, Illinois. During her first year of Flipped Class 101, she focused on making instructional videos. In the spring of that year she had the opportunity to attend the National Council of Teachers of Mathematics conference in Philadelphia. While there, Justyna attended presentations about better ways to engage students in math. She came to realize that the heart of good math education isn't memorizing how to complete mathematical processes: students needed to be able to think mathematically. With this insight, she came back energized and began to implement deeper learning strategies. Justyna was a fast learner. She didn't need a whole year like we did. She had recovered valuable class time with Flipped Class 101, and moved through that model of instruction over the course of one year. Later in this book you will hear from several teachers as they explain how they moved through the flipped class to their own classrooms of deeper learning.

Transformational Versus Revolutionary Change

Some educators might ask: Why isn't this book about a top-down revolution in education? It might be helpful to understand the difference between revolutionary and transformational change. Recently, on a widely syndicated radio show, the host was interviewing a guest about this topic. The guest made some very salient points about the nature of revolutions:

- Revolutions are change from the outside in.

- Revolutions target the head of a government.

- Revolutions typically replace the "leader" of an organization/country.

- When a revolution occurs, change happens from the top down.

- Often revolutions replace one despot for another, which doesn't change the plight of the people very much, if any.

The guest then went on to contrast revolutionary change with transformational change. In transformational change:

- Change happens from the inside out.

- Change happens virally, as one person at a time is "converted."

- Transformational change happens via multiplication, meaning that as each person changes, they share what they have learned with others who in turn become change agents.

- Change happens from the bottom up.

And lastly, the guest argued that transformational change is a far superior model to revolutionary change. This is not to say that all revolutions are all bad, but rather that transformational change is a better and more lasting change model.

In our experience, too many of the change ideas in the educational world come as top-down revolutions that often left teachers out of the dialogue about how schools should function. Unsurprisingly, these revolutions have done little to change individual classes. These educational initiatives come and go, and though many were, and are, great pedagogies with solid research background, they have not significantly changed schools for the better because of the limited adoption by individual teachers. We must confess that we have seen many of these changes come and go throughout our careers, and we have responded in the same way as many of our colleagues: we simply ignored the dictate, closed our doors, and did what we thought was best for our students in our classes. We often gave lip service to the flavor of the day, filled out all of the forms required by our superiors, and happily went back to our rooms to do what we had always done.

Flipped learning might seem like just the latest fad, destined to go away when something else captures the attention of the educational community, but we believe that flipped learning has staying power because it is transformative change. It is spreading virally across the globe as more and more educators adopt this model.

Flipped learning is a grassroots movement, not a top-down approach to change, and it seems that the grassroots nature of this change has resonated with teachers in the trenches. They too have been "subjected" to professional development that was irrelevant to their daily practice. Flipped learning is professional development they have chosen for themselves.

Consider the way we pioneered our flipped classroom model in 2007—we were just two teachers trying to do what was best for our students. It was not an idea we got from a book or an article.

As we went down this road we were quick to share our successes and failures with others. As other educators got interested in this model, we began to conduct workshops and teach others.

This led to more teachers starting to flip their classes, who, in turn, taught others. The beauty of this is that now we had a growing community of flippers with whom to bounce ideas off of. We did not operate in a vacuum. We had help from other educators who helped us refine our practice, and the idea spread. We see the flipped learning model continuing to evolve as more and more minds grab hold of it.

Chapter 2

misconceptions about the flipped classroom

OVER THE PAST FEW YEARS there has been some criticism of the flipped classroom approach from bloggers and educators. We think many of the concerns are valid if you're considering just Flipped Class 101. However, as teachers move beyond Flipped Class 101 to flipped learning, their teaching practice is transformed from a teacher-centered learning environment to a student-centered one, and many of these concerns become moot. Nevertheless, we would like to address some of the misconceptions and explain how flipped learning resolves these concerns about the flipped classroom.

The flipped class is all about videos

Much of the press surrounding the flipped classroom has centered around the videos and what they provide—or fail to provide—to students. Websites such as the Khan Academy have received much attention because they provide access, through video, to content that was at one point available only in text-books and in the minds of instructors. Though we certainly see video as important, it is not the most critical element to flipped learning. The most essential aspect in a flipped learning environment is the reclamation of in-class time that occurs because direct instruction is not being delivered to a large group—taking up everyone's class time—but to individuals at the time they are ready for it. Although video is an important aspect to flipped learning, it is not the most important. Video should be used as an entry point to flipped learning from which deeper and further learning can occur.

Flipped classrooms disenfranchise students without adequate access to technology

Probably the most common misconception about flipped class-rooms is that students who have limited access to technology cannot participate, and therefore, a flipped classroom ought not be implemented. When we started flipping our classrooms in 2007, about 25% of our students could not access the internet at home, and we had to provide these students with access to the video content by other means. We took a multifaceted approach to helping students with limited access.

Some students had computers at home, but had either dial-up internet or no internet at all. We had these students bring in flash drives and we downloaded the videos onto the drives. For students without a computer or the internet, we burned our videos onto DVDs that we handed out. Students then watched the videos on their home DVD player. We found that all of our students had at least this technology at home. If not, we were ready to purchase a few DVD players for these students.

Though we recognize that this is an important issue, we believe that with a little creativity, this issue can be resolved for all students. And although the means of providing access described above addressed our issues, each setting is unique. The good news is that since 2007, technology has advanced and many more students have access to a personal device, such as an iPod or cell phone, that allows them to access the video content outside of school time.

Jon has recently been working with Havana High School in Havana, Illinois. Havana High School has decided to implement Flipped Class 101 throughout their entire school. Fifty percent of the students in this school qualify for free and reduced-price lunch. Knowing this, the administrators anticipated that many students would lack adequate access to technology, making it hard for them to view video content at home. In preparation for implementing flipped classrooms throughout the school, Superintendent Mark Twomey purchased several DVD players that students could take home and use if needed. As of yet, no students have had to check out the DVD players. Twomey reports that his students have sufficient technology in their possession to gain access to the content. Although this example represents only one school with potentially less than ideal access to technology, it does demonstrate that bridging any actual digital divide may not be as big of a hurdle as anticipated.

These approaches resolve issues of access in a flipped classroom, but how does a flipped learning approach address the issues of access? In a Flipped Class 101 environment, all students are expected to access content on the same night, prior to the next day's class. If any teacher requires anything to be completed outside the class time, the teacher must also provide access. But what if the expectation is not that all students will view content prior to class, but rather, that students will access the content when most appropriate? In a flipped learning context, content is made available to the students when they are ready for it. This may be in class, out of class, or both—but regardless, the student does not necessarily need to access content at home, and the issue of access becomes diminished. Adequate access becomes a class-room concern rather than an individual student concern.

Flipped classrooms propagate bad pedagogy

Many critics feel that the flipped classroom method is a poor method of instruction. They contend that simply turning lectures into videos propagates bad pedagogy. If the flipped classroom was simply about replacing lectures with videos and keeping everything else the same, then we would agree with these critics. However, most teachers do not stay at Flipped Class 101. Most of them transition to what our friend and fellow educator Troy Cockrum calls the "second iteration." As all good teachers do, they reflect on their practice, keep what works, and fix what does not work, moving from Flipped Class 101 to something better: flipped learning.

What many of the critics—who are also amazing teachers—seem to have forgotten is that they have gone through their own transitions, and change takes time. A lecturer of 20 years cannot be told that tomorrow he must now teach using only project-based learning. A teacher cannot make such a significant transition overnight. Those making a change need a desired destination, a roadmap to guide them, and time to travel. Change is a process, and it takes different people different amounts of time. Freeing teachers from old patterns is the key. We are often asked: "What is the biggest hurdle in implementing flipped classrooms?" To that we answer: "Flipping the minds of the teachers." Change is not easy for anybody. But we have observed that Flipped Class 101 has been a great entry point for so many teachers. These teachers eventually arrive at flipped learning, and that is where we see the greatest gains. We encourage teachers to start with Flipped Class 101 because it is a familiar strategy that is tangible for most, but we hope teachers do not stop at Flipped Class 101, but transition to flipped learning.

Flipped classrooms cause unnecessary homework

Both students and teachers have told us that students report spending less time viewing assigned videos than they do completing traditional homework. Stacey Roshan, a high school mathematics teacher at the Bullis School in Potomac, Maryland, reports that since she flipped her AP Calculus classes, her students have less anxiety, spend less time doing homework, and that her AP Calculus scores are better than ever. (You can watch her in action in "Ditching Anxiety" at www.youtube.com/watch?v=8IvjH4aiCeY.)

Flipped learning has contributed in a positive way to the broader homework conversation. When students can spend a fixed amount of time watching a video, they are better able to anticipate their homework load. Often, students get home and are lost because they didn't understand what happened in class. In the flipped classroom, students are simply building a learning foundation by watching the videos; when they come to class they can go deeper and further into learning.

Parents also report that they can help their children complete their homework. Many parents claim that they learn alongside their children and appreciate the videos. Well-meaning parents often try to help their children only to become frustrated that they are unable to do so, or fear that they will teach their kids in a way that is different from how their kids are taught at school. With the flipped classroom approach, parents can watch, learn, and then help; or they can simply encourage their children to view the videos if the subject is beyond the parents' areas of expertise. And this is just in a Flipped Class 101 approach. It gets even better when teachers move to flipped learning.

Chapter 3

content, curiosity, and relationship

A MAJOR THEME in our presentations to educational audiences is that good teaching has always been about relationship. No computer or video can replace a real, live teacher. The relationship that a teacher develops with his or her students is what makes teaching good regardless of whether or not a teacher flips a class.

Jon was participating in a Twitter chat with Kwame M. Brown (@drkmbrown), a psychology professor at Hampton University in Hampton, Virginia. They were discussing what defines good teaching. Jon argued that good teaching has always been about building relationships between teachers and students. Brown pushed back, tweeting, "How about we acknowledge #edu is the *intersection* of content, curiosity, and relationship?" That tweet helped to hone what flipped learning is all about. Good teaching happens in the context of good relational connections, but curiosity and content are also essential components of a good education. We fear that current educational systems overemphasize content at the expense of the more existential aspects of learning. Standardized tests and standardized curricula do not leave much room for connections and curiosity.

Today's educational landscape looks too much like the pie chart in Figure 3.1:

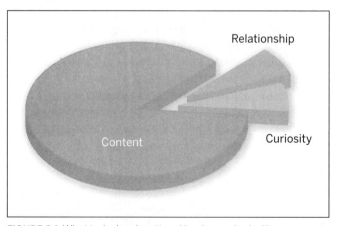

FIGURE 3.1 What today's educational landscape looks like.

Instead, it needs to look more like the pie chart in Figure 3.2:

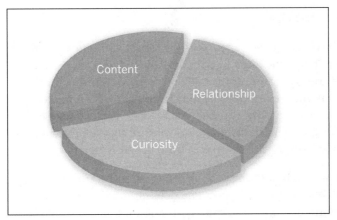

FIGURE 3.2 What today's educational landscape *should* look like.

Let's break this down a bit and take a closer look at content, curiosity, and relationship in education.

Content

Content is central to learning, and we are not in any way dismissing its importance. We realize that students often "don't know what they don't know." There are certain areas of study and skills that all students should master. For example, a child who cannot read cannot plumb the depths of learning.

We are certainly not saying that we need to dismantle all the carefully crafted courses that have been developed. However, we are saying that many curricula are too large, too specific, and offer too little flexibility. We want educators to be intentional about *what* we expect all students to know, and we hope that in making these important choices, educators will use content as a conduit to teach the process of learning and to instill a passion for knowledge.

Curiosity

Young students enter school with an innate curiosity about the world. They come ready to learn and ask all kinds of questions. This curiosity is a fundamental component of learning. However, we think the opportunity for students to follow their interests may be missing in today's school climate. Teachers simply have too much content to cover. Because of this, they are reluctant to allow students choice in what to learn or how to learn.

What we teach has been determined for years by groups of adults who sit on committees and determine what information is important and what information is not. If it makes it into the textbooks, the curriculum guides, and the standards, then it gets taught. If it doesn't get in, then it doesn't get taught. Which, by implication, means it is not important.

We have both been one of those adults who helped determine state content standards. Jon served on the Colorado Oversight committee that rewrote the state standards in 2009, and Aaron was chairman of the Colorado Science Standards committee during the same time. When we did this, we gathered content experts from all fields and asked them to tell us what was important so that we could fashion the standards. A major challenge with this approach was that all the experts thought that their fields were the most important and had to be included in the standards. What often emerges from this approach is a bloated curriculum with too much content that is impossible to teach within a school year. Yet, even with the numerous and highly specific content standards that exist in many educational settings, what we teach addresses only a sliver of all there is to know about the world. We think of it much like the pie chart in Figure 3.3.

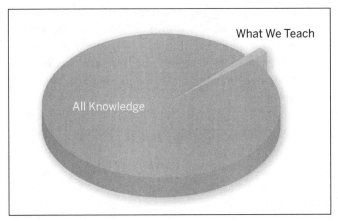

FIGURE 3.3 What we teach versus what there is to know.

Given the sum total of human knowledge, the narrow portion of that knowledge addressed in specific educational standards, and the limited amount of class time, what ought to be taught? Teachers can rely on traditional fields of study, teacher pet topics, or state standards, but regardless, students have very little input as to what they learn and how they learn it. The curiosity component is where we allow students choices in what and how they learn. Students are allowed to choose things they are passionate about and can explore topics on their own. We should note that giving students absolute autonomy and control over their learning may not be the best option; frankly, very few students would choose to learn their 7s when learning to multiply. However, giving students a portion of their learning time to explore their interests is important.

Because of the extra time in the classroom that flipped learning affords, several teachers have been able to implement what some are calling the "Genius Hour," or the "20% time." These ideas to boost creativity began in the business world and are discussed in Daniel Pink's book *Drive* (2009). Examples include Google, which allows its engineers to devote 20% of their work time to their own projects, and companies that conduct "FedEx Days," where employees work on a project separate from their regular job and must deliver something out of it within 24 hours. In education, teachers are giving students between 10–20% of their in-class time to conduct passion-based projects and research. Students are required to demonstrate their learning in a variety of ways. The key is that students get to pick what they want to learn. Regardless of how we bring in student choice, we teachers must be the ones who foster an environment that encourages these choices for our students.

Relationship

When we think about our time in school as students, we realize it was those teachers who cared about us who left the most profound impression on us. It is no accident that Jon became a high school chemistry teacher; he had a high school chemistry teacher, Edie Anderson, who took notice of a geeky kid who was trying to fit in. She mentored him and helped him find a passion for chemistry. He then turned that passion into a 25-year teaching career. And he has been able to work personally with about 3000 students in his career as a teacher, where he noticed not only the geeky out-of-place kids, but many others as well. Edie Anderson never flipped her class, but her impact on Jon's life touched many others. Aaron had a similar experience in college under the instructional care of Professor David Johnson.

Clearly, Ms. Anderson and Professor Johnson had lasting impacts on Jon and Aaron, but what makes relationship so important to the educational process? It is possible that someone could learn the same amount of calculus looking at Wikipedia on the computer in his basement as another could learn from a teacher in a classroom? Although their content knowledge may be equivalent, these students have not shared an equivalent educational experience. When done well, teaching is fundamentally a human interaction in which the passions and interests of the students are fanned to a flame. Students realize that they need more from their teachers than mere content. They need passionate, caring professionals who encourage them to pursue excellence.

Regardless of whether a student learns from a person in the same room, from a teacher on a video, or from an author in a book, the student learns from a person. However, although these situations are similar, they are not the same. A face-to-face interaction between two people is more multifaceted and multidimensional than the interaction between a person and a recording or document. Face-to-face interactions build a relationship that cannot be reproduced in an online, printed, or isolated environment. So we encourage teachers to cultivate positive relationships with their students and to take advantage of their class time to enrich learning through face-to-face interactions.

As leadership expert John Maxwell (2001) points out, "People don't care how much you know until they know how much you care." So, is good teaching just about relationship? No, but it is a fundamental component of learning.

What does all this have to do with flipped learning?

Teachers should teach within the context of content, curiosity, and relationship, which allows them to take their students deeper and further in their learning than they have ever been before. And yes, teachers need to move beyond the flipped classroom to what we are now calling flipped learning. In the next chapter we will go into more depth about content, curiosity, and relationship.

Chapter 4

take learning deeper and further and make connections

IN CHAPTER 3, we discussed the tweet in which Kwame Brown stated, "How about we acknowledge #edu is the *intersection* of content, curiosity, and relationship?" Each of those elements is critical to learning. As we have thought about how this intersection of ideas is connected specifically to flipped learning, we have expanded the concept to express how each category—content, curiosity, and relationship—benefits students. Some of our critics have argued that flipped learning is just a repackaging of what good educators have always practiced, with a new name attached to it. To some extent they are right, as there is little new under the sun. However, research continues to emerge that helps explain how people learn, and we will use these three categories to help frame the discussion of how flipped learning can dramatically help teachers teach and students learn.

We have defined each category as follows:

Content Taking learning *deeper*

Curiosity Taking learning *further*

Relationship Making *connections* with students

Content: Taking Learning Deeper

Bloom's taxonomy is one instructional framework that is often used to discuss teaching and learning. Though it is not the only way to understand the way people learn, it is a good framework for discussing how individuals go through the process of learning.

One way to look at the revised version of Bloom's taxonomy is to start at the bottom, lay the groundwork for learning, and move students up the pyramid toward higher-order thinking skills (Figure 4.1). Implicit in the pyramid representation of Bloom's taxonomy is that class time should be allotted accordingly, with lower-order skills taking up the most class time and higher-order skills taking up the least. This is in fact what usually happens in the classroom: teachers spend the bulk of their time focusing on Remembering and Understanding, and barely get to Applying. Teachers may hope to get to higher-order thinking skills, but very little time is allotted for Analyzing, Evaluating, or Creating.

We believe that teacher-created videos are best used as content-delivery tools in the bottom two tiers of Bloom's taxonomy: Remembering and Understanding. This then allows teachers to spend their valuable class time with students as they engage in activities that require skills in the upper regions of Bloom's taxonomy, which facilitate deeper learning.

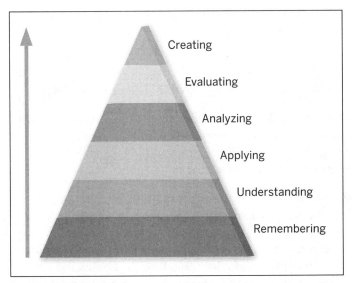

FIGURE 4.1 Bloom's taxonomy, a useful framework for understanding how people learn.

What do we mean by taking the flipped class *deeper*? When teachers go deeper using flipped learning, they drill down deeply into a given topic, allowing students a more comprehensive and thorough understanding of content. In a more traditional approach this is done by carefully building the cognitive framework from the bottom of Bloom's taxonomy up, and much time is spent on the mastery of content. Students learn a prescribed curriculum, which most likely is determined from Common Core objectives, state standards, and the teacher's professional judgment. Students must then demonstrate mastery of content on a summative assessment. What is new in the flipped learning model is how the content is delivered. Teachers are able to leverage asynchronous instruction through video and can take their students deeper using flipped learning.

Students not only learn the required curriculum but, because of the higher-level learning enabled by flipped learning, are able to demonstrate mastery of topics, apply their new knowledge to unique situations, and create learning objects that demonstrate the depth of their learning.

Curiosity: Taking Learning Further

Having explored how flipped learning can be used to drill down deeply into content knowledge, we can now explore how flipped learning can be used to foster curiosity and take students and teachers further into educational experiences.

How does "further" learning differ from "deeper" learning? If deeper is a more comprehensive and thorough understanding of content, further takes a broader look at content. Content mastery does not come at the beginning of the learning cycle, but within the context of meaningful learning. Teachers can use flipped learning to foster student curiosity, to launch out from prescribed content, and to give students opportunities to go through the messy process of learning before intervening with instruction—all ways to go "further." Taking learning further often entails engaging in the inquiry process, incorporating project-based learning (PBL), or allowing students to pursue their passions and exercise their creativity. But why would flipped learning need to be incorporated in order to engage with these types of classroom practices? Can a teacher simply use PBL or inquiry without any elements of flipped learning? Yes, of course!

However, many teachers report that flipped learning is a bridge from traditional teaching methods, which are heavily dependent on content, to more engaging learning methods that focus primarily on the acts of thinking and learning. Without sacrificing the quality of instruction or the value of content, teachers have found a way to move from content-driven, teacher-directed classrooms to student-centered classrooms. Content is important, but it does not necessarily need to be the driving force behind instruction. Teachers making the transition through flipped learning into PBL or inquiry are doing so gradually, and giving students access to instruction when they need it. We have noted that this transition takes time. Many have experienced a progression like this:

Year 1. Create an archive of on-demand video content.

Year 2. Provide students opportunities to move through curriculum at their own pace, accessing content as they move through a curriculum.

Year 3. Give students teacher-created projects, guiding students to content when appropriate.

Year 4. Let students generate problems and projects on their own and provide support by directing students to archived content when they need it.

Other teachers are finding a place for video within the inquiry cycle. Some use video at the beginning of the inquiry cycle, to cause students to generate questions for which they will explore possible answers. Others use video in the middle of the inquiry cycle, after the process of concept development has occurred, to help reinforce learning or correct misunderstanding. The inquiry process is not devoid of direct instruction, it is just not driven by it.

In the previous section on "deeper" learning, we discussed the idea of using Bloom's taxonomy as a framework to understand where flipped learning fits into a bottom-up learning cycle. We found that off-loading the lower end of Bloom's taxonomy from class time allows more class time to delve into the higher end of Bloom's taxonomy. Now that we are discussing "further" learning, we will look at Bloom's taxonomy from the top down. We will use Bloom's taxonomy as a framework again, but this time we will look at it as an inverted pyramid (Figure 4.2).

Bloom's taxonomy has been expressed in many shapes recently, and this inverted pyramid is just one of the many permutations. This top-down approach to the learning pyramid is the way in which both PBL and inquiry strategies approach content. Students spend the majority of their time Creating and

Evaluating, and when they hit a content-dependent roadblock, they tap down into the lower tiers of the taxonomy, acquire the information they need, then pop back up to the top where their project lies.

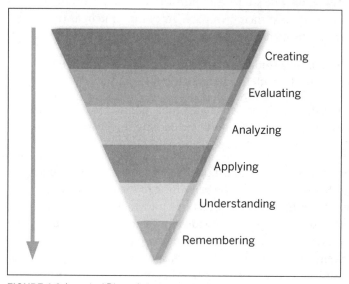

FIGURE 4.2 Inverted Bloom's taxonomy.

For example, one of Aaron's students wanted to design and develop a device that could charge a cell phone using solar power at night. This student embarked on her project and eventually was able to use energy from the sun to split water into hydrogen and oxygen. At this point, she was confused about why she always ended up with twice as much hydrogen as oxygen. Aaron saw that she needed some assistance with the concept of balancing chemical equations and directed her to two short videos that explained the concept. She was operating in the upper portion of Bloom's taxonomy, she got stuck, so she tapped down to the lower tiers in order to move on. Once she had the appropriate information, she went back up to the top, creating and evaluating her project.

Another example is when Aaron's snowblower broke. Aaron began to diagnose and repair his snowblower and realized that he did not have the requisite knowledge to complete his task. So, what did he do? He did what anyone might do: he searched the model number of his snowblower on YouTube and found a video series that taught him how to diagnose and repair the snow-blower. This is how many of us naturally learn, and yet we seem to think that more-prescribed systems of learning are more effective for our students. Flipped learning provides a viable method to escape from the tyranny of content-driven instruction to the land of projects and inquiry, without completely abandoning the value of appropriately used direct instruction. So, how does this take students further into learning? In this model, PBL and inquiry rely on directed instruction to supplement learning within a larger context. This type of learning is more organic and values the passions and interests of the students without denying the value of content knowledge. It also does not require content mastery prior to embarking on the creative or evaluative process, but allows access to content whenever it becomes necessary during the process.

Relationship: Making Connections with Students

Flipped learning is neither a pedagogy nor an educational philosophy. Flipped learning is a flexible technique to be used when appropriate to maximize face-to-face time with students. And students are what matter most. Content is important, and we encourage teachers to use flipped learning to drill down deep into the content that students must learn. We desire all students to have a solid foundation in a variety of subjects from which they can build future knowledge. Curiosity is also important, and we encourage teachers to allow students to explore their interests, work on projects, and engage in inquiry. All students should have rich learning experiences that provide relevance for their learning, and choice and autonomy in the learning process. But we believe that relational connections are just as important, and that they are indispensable components of learning. The connections between individuals make learning social and beneficial for more than just the sake of learning.

This is why teachers matter! And as teachers move to a flipped learning environment, they are able to spend more one-on-one time with their students and foster strong relationships. These relationships have a lasting impact in the lives of students. Recently, we were invited to speak to a group of policy makers about the flipped classroom. After our session, one of the legislators asked us if the flipped classroom model allowed schools to have larger class sizes. He proposed that with the videos doing much of the basic instruction, the class would be easier to teach and need less supervision from qualified teachers. Frankly, this statement scared us. We answered with a resounding "No!" A major point of the flipped classroom, and more importantly flipped learning, is to maximize the relationships between teacher and students. Increasing class sizes would only diminish the amount of time the teacher has to interact with each student.

Why Relationships in Video Are Important

We are often asked if it is OK to use videos created by other people rather than creating one's own. When we started making instructional videos for our students, we made our own. We did this out of necessity, because few free, online chemistry videos existed. That was 2007. Now there are many videos online, made by amazing teachers and available for free. So why should teachers make their own videos? We typically frame this discussion in the context of creation versus curation, and view this as a continuum (Figure 4.3).

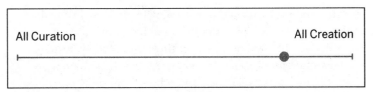

FIGURE 4.3 Creation-versus-curation continuum showing the "sweet spot."

A number of students have told us that they prefer content that their own teacher created over content created by someone else. Teachers also say that they prefer making their own videos. Early on in the flipped class, Brett Wilie, a chemistry teacher in Texas, started using our videos to flip his class. He then started making his own videos. We chatted and he told us, "Jon and Aaron, your videos are better than mine, but my kids like my videos better because I am their teacher." His story reflects the stories we continue to hear. We feel that the best place to be is in the sweet spot marked on the figure above. A colleague recently commented to us that when teachers make videos, they are making a social contract with their students: the teacher trades content they have made in exchange for the students' effort in learning that content.

Teacher-student relationships are genuinely important, and students don't just connect with content, they connect with people. If students have an inspiring teacher who loves Shakespeare, they will be more likely to love Shakespeare. The connections made with students are at the heart of great teaching.

Tying It All Together

As teachers pass through Flipped Class 101 to flipped learning, they will discover that a focus on deeper learning and further learning can vastly change the way their classes operate. Teachers can take students deeper or they can take students further, and both occur within the context of the relationships between students and their teacher. In the following chapters you will read personal stories from teachers who have gone through Flipped Class 101 and on to something better. Some of these teachers share more about deeper learning, others share more about taking learning further, and others focus more on the relational aspect of learning. But all of these authors share the common theme of landing in the intersection of content, curiosity, and relationship, and they got there by moving through Flipped Class 101 to flipped learning.

Chapter 5

deeper learning
through a
student-centered classroom

CRYSTAL KIRCH'S STORY

Crystal Kirch is a high school math teacher at Segerstrom Fundamental High School in Santa Ana, California. She connected with the flipped learning community through her widely read blog, in which she writes transparently about her teaching, sharing her triumphs and struggles as she works in an economically disadvantaged school. She has a lot to say about the flipped classroom approach and eventually began writing blog entries about flipped learning. She is best known for developing a tool students use to interact with and learn from the videos. This technique, Watch-Summarize-Question (WSQ), has become so much a part of the flipped learning culture that people are adopting and adapting her model worldwide. Crystal describes the WSQ technique in this chapter.

JUST PICTURE IT: Forty students, one teacher. A well-planned learning activity that just didn't work. Students went home to work on homework problems confused, frustrated, and feeling hopeless. Some understood the point of the lesson. Most didn't. Students were expected to return to class having mastered the lesson from the previous day, ready to move on.

This described too many of my days. It all came to a head one day in the fall of 2011. In exasperation I thought to myself: I'm tired of living bell to bell. I'm tired of forcing all students to learn at the exact same pace. I'm tired of rushing through content just to "cover" it while my students miss the deeper meaning of what they are learning and how it is connected to the world around them. I'm tired of having students stare at me, sometimes focused and sometimes completely spacing out. I'm tired of "teaching to the middle," not challenging my higher-achieving students yet still not serving my struggling learners. I'm tired of passive learners, students who expect to be spoon-fed and just spit it back out on a test. I'm tired of it all.

I wanted to see my students take an active role in their learning so that I could see their passion come alive. But I didn't know how.

That night I sat down and made a video. In five short minutes, I explained to my students the concept that our activity that day had failed to convey. After uploading the video to SchoolTube, I sent out the URL on our course site, Edmodo, and hoped it might help alleviate some of the stress and frustration I knew my students were feeling as they attempted to do their homework.

Little did I know that this small step was the first in a huge transformation of not only my classroom, but also my entire educational philosophy and mindset. This step led to asking the bigger questions: Why was I spending class time—the only time I had all my students together in my presence—trying to deliver content? Why was I spending the majority of my time working on the very basic skills of remembering and understanding content rather than applying, analyzing, evaluating, or creating? My brain began to turn.

I tried making another video, this time with an intentional goal in mind. Students went home and watched a lesson that introduced what they would be practicing in class the next day. The feedback from students was great, so I continued to research the use of video as an instructional tool. Through my research, I found there were hundreds of teachers attempting the same model I had stumbled upon. Through much trial and error, a lot of teacher-student discussion and feedback, and daily reflections on this new way of teaching and learning, I was on my way to having what is known as a flipped classroom. My journey didn't end there, however. I have continued to refine and tweak my educational practice, transforming my classroom into one that fosters deeper learning, higher-order thinking, and active (rather than passive) learners. I have made the transition from the flipped classroom to flipped learning.

My Students

I teach two different levels of math classes in a school where 71.7% of the students are of low socioeconomic status and not all of them have consistent access to internet or technology at home. My Math Analysis Honors (Pre-Calculus) course consists of juniors and seniors who are preparing to take AP Calculus and head to a four-year university. These are students who know how to make good grades but may not have been challenged to achieve true deeper learning. My Algebra 1 course, on the other hand, consists of struggling freshmen and sophomores, many of whom are in the course for the second or third time. They struggle with basic mathematical concepts, but also struggle to believe in themselves and persevere when learning gets tough. Despite the large differences in my two classes, both groups of students had a similar need for flipped learning.

Before I Flipped My Classroom

I began to think about why I wasn't fully satisfied with my students' level of engagement or their ownership of their learning. It was more than just a single failure of a lesson activity; my dissatisfaction grew out of years spent searching for ways to engage and motivate my students, going to workshops to learn new strategies, and trying to find something that worked. I knew that learning was happening in my classroom, but also knew that there had to be something better. Something deeper. Something more enjoyable and more effective for true and deep learning. Something more engaging for my students.

I realized my classroom structures were failing in areas that I felt were most important for my students. Three key areas stuck out to me:

1. My class was teacher-centered. Students were all taught the same way. I was not differentiating the learning for each student.

2. My class did not foster deep learning. It didn't go beyond rote memorization and didn't allow time in class for connections, inquiry, and other Higher-Order Thinking (HOT) activities.

3. My class was filled with passive learners. I did not create an environment where students could be active learners on a daily basis.

Teacher Centered

Living in the 54-minute bubble of a traditional classroom, class time was very teacher-driven and teacher-focused. What *I thought* my students needed. What questions *I thought* my students had. What parts of the lesson *I thought* were most interesting. I wanted to make my classroom more student-centered, but I constantly struggled with a lack of time to allow students to demonstrate true Thinking, Writing, Interacting, Reading, Listening, and Speaking (TWIRLS) in my class.

I first heard the phrase "TWRLS" at a Pearson Sheltered Instruction Observation Protocol (SIOP) workshop several years ago, and after some discussions with colleagues, I later added the "I." This acronym clearly laid out what I wanted my students to demonstrate on a daily basis. I came to realize there were a lot of TWIRLS going on in my classroom—but I was the one demonstrating them, not my students:

Thinking. I was the one doing most of the thinking in class— students were comfortable sitting back and watching me work my magic, engaging when required but completely satisfied being passive.

Writing. Despite my constant efforts, I wasn't finding consistent opportunities for students to write in my math class.

Interacting. Students were given opportunities to interact, but they were minimal and often surface-level. Students had no accountability for participation.

Reading. Reading for students in my math class was nonexistent.

Listening. Students were listening, but really only to me, not to their peers.

Speaking. Speaking and practicing academic language was forced, sporadic, and subject to teacher instruction, not student interest or creativity.

Because the direct-instruction piece was still occurring within the group learning space, there was not enough time during class to focus on individual students and their needs after the lesson was taught. Students weren't able to demonstrate TWIRLS, nor drive the discussion, the questioning, and the interactions within class.

Surface-Level Learning

I could see that my students were not reaching the point of true, deep learning. Every day students worked from bell to bell and we were able to cover a lot of content; however, they did so while taking notes, engaging in surface-level academic conversations with little to no accountability, and practicing in isolation. None of these activities led to deeper learning. The group learning space was focused on the low end of Bloom's taxonomy (remembering and understanding) and gave little time for higher-level activities such as applying, analyzing, evaluating, and creating. If even attempted, those activities were assigned for students to struggle with independently, outside of class time. My students did an excellent job of rotely memorizing operations and processes, but the classroom structure did nothing to foster their ability to make connections among concepts and across disciplines.

> The flipped classroom has allowed me to not just do math, but to actually understand it. Some students go by learning how to do the math and memorizing the formulas, but really never understanding the subject in its entirety. What the classroom has done for me is extend the borders of learning to not just retaining information, but understanding and applying said information.
>
> —Kaylen, 11th-grade Math Analysis student

Passive Learners

I had a classroom full of very bright—but very passive—learners. I came to realize that I had assumed all the responsibility for learning and had not been encouraging my students to take responsibility for their own learning. Class time was micro-managed, needlessly busy, and devoid of both questioning and reflection. I had created an environment where students were expected to stay focused by passively sitting at a desk for

54 minutes. They had become spoon-fed learners who learned enough to pass my tests but saw no incentive to take ownership of their learning.

After I Flipped My Classroom

As I continued to explore flipped learning, I realized that changing my mindset about teaching and learning would allow me to create the type of classroom environment I had always wanted but could never seem to foster.

I began by asking the question, "What if?" What if...

- I took all direct instruction outside of the group learning space? I realized I could create video lessons my students could watch asynchronously, at their own pace, at just the time they needed it.

- I flipped the use and purpose of the 54 minutes of face-to-face time I had with my students, so that when students needed me the most (for deeper learning), I was there to support and guide them?

- the group learning space was reserved for differentiation, enabling me to meet the needs of each student?

With the ultimate goal of making the time in class more enjoyable, effective, and engaging, I pursued flipped learning full-force. I wanted to move my class from teacher-centered to learner-centered; from surface thinking to deeper thinking; and from passive learners to active learners.

Learner Centered

My classroom became learner-centered, where students (instead of the teacher) demonstrate TWIRLS. I have a student, Arlene, who comes to class every day with great questions. She really enjoys the class, because in her learning she needs to interact with others as she thinks through difficult content. For her, the "I" (Interacting) and the "T" (Thinking) in TWIRLS help the most.

In the flipped classroom, there is not a day that goes by where a student does not interact with another student in a conversation. When you think you understand a concept, it is put to the test the next day, because there might be someone who doesn't understand. Not everyone is able to grasp math concepts at the same pace, so even if one student gets the concept, there might be others that do not and so they will ask their teammates for help. In the conversation it's either you asking the questions or you being the one that is teaching someone else.

—*Sayra, 11th-grade Math Analysis student*

Deeper Learning

I am now fostering higher-level, connected thinking where my students are applying, analyzing, evaluating, and creating. Students are making connections among concepts they have learned in math, and also making connections to other subjects, such as science and history. In addition, time is freed up to explore and discover concepts in an inquiry-based fashion. For example, when students learned the unit circle (a circle with the radius of 1) I didn't spoon-feed them the steps, even in the video. Instead, they used prior knowledge of right triangles and trigonometric relationships to construct the unit circle collaboratively. The unit circle became more than just a memorized fact, but something that had meaning and allowed students to see the relationship that existed among all the trigonometric concepts.

I like the whole "work-together" environment that it creates. It simply engages us (students) in the learning.

—*Ben, 12th-grade Math Analysis student*

Active Learners

My classroom became full of active rather than passive learners, who are taking responsibility for their learning and are freed up to explore, connect, and question. This changed the whole culture of my classroom. One student, Michael, came to class and was comfortable with being a passive learner. At first he struggled with the new format, but in about two months he became passionate about math and began to lead group discussions.

In a traditional classroom, students spend the precious time they have with the teacher listening, as opposed to interacting. The flipped classroom flips the focus of the teacher to the student. I believe it offers students more down time to really practice, learn new concepts, and later on master them. I've gotten much more individual attention with the flipped classroom. Instead of waiting until the end of a lecture to ask the teacher questions that I was too afraid to voice during class, I have been given a whole 45–50 minutes to really reach out to not just my teacher but my peers as well. This class has taught me not just math but life lessons. Throughout this year, I've learned how to manage my time more efficiently. To go above and beyond and not to settle for the bare minimum when so much more can be accomplished.

—*Kaylen, 11th-grade Math Analysis student*

The WSQ Tool

When I first started flipping my classroom, I found that my students were watching the videos but not necessarily learning from them. They knew how to watch videos for entertainment, but not for education. I needed to find a better way to engage them with the video so the learning goals for class time could be met. I developed a tool that I named Watch-Summarize-Question, more commonly known as WSQ (pronounced "wisk") to help guide my students in becoming more active in watching and learning from a video lesson. In addition, the WSQ tool also helps to structure class time so it is learner-centered, focused on deeper learning, and open to having students be active in their learning. Further details and examples of the use and purpose of the WSQ technique can be found at my blog: http://flippingwith-kirch.blogspot.com/p/wsqing.html.

> Homework feels like learning instead of a grind.
>
> —*Brian, 12th-grade Math Analysis student*

The WSQ process for students is as follows:

Watch. Students are given video lessons to watch. While watching or researching the content, they take guided notes in packets I have created for them (Figure 5.1). Students are expected to pause, rewind, and rewatch the lesson as needed so they understand the key points before coming to the group learning environment.

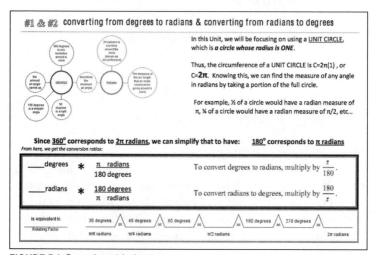

FIGURE 5.1 Sample guided notes.

Summarize. After students watch the video, they are asked to summarize, in writing, what they learned. Not only does this help them retain what they learned, it also helps them grow in their use of academic language. At first I just had them write a summary, but I found that many of my students needed more structure in this step. I am now providing guiding questions or sentence starters to help them process what they learned from the videos (Figure 5.2).

Summary Questions

Concept 1

1. How can you find the leading coefficient?
   "You will find the leading coefficient by..."
2. What does standard form of a polynomial look like?
   "Standard form means that you..."
3. What are the four options (in order) for "number of terms"?
   "The four options for number of terms are..."
4. What are the six options (in order) for "degree"? What happens if it has a biggest exponent of 6 or higher? "The six options for degree are..."
   "If there is a biggest exponent of 6 or higher, it is called..."

Concept 2

1. What do you do with the negative in between the sets of parentheses?
   "Whenever there is a negative in front of a set of parentheses, you..."
2. How do you know how to color code the problems?
3. In what order do we write our answers?
4. Write out the proper sentence frame for this problem: $5x^4-3x^2-3x$
   (see SSS for sample sentence frame)

Concepts 3–4

1. In what ways is the "box" method better than simple distributing (C3) or FOILing (C4)? "The box method is better because..."
2. When multiplying, you _____ the coefficients and _____ the exponents. (Write out the sentence and fill in the blanks.)
3. What does Mrs. Kirch mean when she says to draw a "1 by 3" box or a "2 by 2" box?
4. Explain what a "square of a binomial" means and what you need to do in order to solve it correctly.

Concept 5

1. What mistake did Mrs. Kirch make in the video? What did she do wrong? What should she have done instead?
2. How do you know what you can combine together?
3. What is the "normal pattern" that we notice about combining terms from the box.
4. Write the answer to #61 in the sentence frame for the chapter.

FIGURE 5.2 Sample guiding questions.

Question. After summarizing, students are prompted to ask about what they didn't understand in the video, ask a higher-level (HOT) question about the concept that would lead to good group discussion, or create their own example problem similar to the ones in the video. Students write this question or problem right underneath their notes so it is easily accessible the next day in class. I use the questions in class to guide discussion, and the example problems to challenge other students who might need extra practice or extensions.

Using WSQ in the Group Learning Space

When students come to the group learning space, several structured activities help them deepen their learning. Two of these activities are group discussion and practice time.

Structured Small-Group Discussion

The purpose of this "talk time," which I call a "WSQ chat," is to give each student the opportunity to demonstrate TWIRLS, to clarify confusions or misconceptions from the video lesson, and to deepen understanding through hands-on activities. Through the WSQ chat, I can easily tell if we need to have a whole-group mini-lesson or go over something that wasn't taught clearly in the video. I vary each WSQ chat based on the questions and needs I have been able to identify from the students' WSQ responses, which they submit on a Google form the night before class (Figure 5.3). One thing I have struggled with is coming up with new ways to engage students in the group discussion; I find that my students get tired of the WSQ chats if I don't change up the structure occasionally.

"SUMMARY" questions

Answer these questions in full, complete, detailed sentences. You should notice that these questions cover the most important aspects of the lesson. If you have trouble answering any of these questions, go back and rewatch the video.

1. **What is the direct substitution method? ***

2. **What are the 4 types of answers you can get when doing direct substitution and what do they mean/indicate? ***

3. **What is indeterminate form and what does it mean? ***

FIGURE 5.3 A typical Google form.

Practice Time in Small Groups

In a math class, students need time to practice solving problems. Since I have collected data in the WSQ Google form, I can then make an informed decision about the individual needs of each student. Some need to be placed in peer groups: students in these groups are ready to work with each other and practice the current learning objective. Others need to be retaught; I usually have between five and eight students out of an average class of forty who need to be retaught. These students receive individualized support, and I present the content in a new and fresh way. I think one of the reasons flipped learning has been so successful is that the right students are getting the help they need at the right time.

Assessments

I still give unit tests. Students can take them as many times as they need until they have mastered the content. Along the way I have many formative assessments, so that when they take the summative assessment, most are successful the first time. Students are formatively assessed on each concept when they are ready to demonstrate mastery, the timing of which is different for every student. The formative assessments I use include:

- Mini-quizzes for individual concepts.

- Student-created problems. Students create short videos where they verbally explain their thought process.

- Analyzing mistakes made in other student problems.

- Answering a "Big Question," which is an overarching theme of the unit.

- Explaining real-world connections to the math concept involved.

- Inquiry activities that allow students to form their own understanding of a key concept.

With the exception of the mini-quizzes, students post these formative assessments on their blogs, where they must also reflect on their learning in writing. For most concepts or activities, only one type of formative assessment is used. Ideally, students would be able to choose from a broader menu of assessments for each concept.

Classroom Transformation

Transitioning to a flipped learning model transformed my classroom in a significant manner. Class is now an enjoyable place where students can come to learn, interact, and challenge themselves. It is an engaging environment where students can have their needs met daily. My students don't feel pressured to get everything right the first time. It is an effective place where deep learning happens on a daily basis and student learning has increased.

If I had to describe my transformed classroom in three phrases, they would be those same three phrases that I used as the goals I struggled to achieve so many years ago: a learner-centered environment; a place for deeper learning and higher-level thinking; and a community of active learners. While every year brings a new batch of students and new mindsets, the processes I have established in my classroom help me engage students quicker and meet their individual needs.

Unplanned Successes

While many of the outcomes from adopting flipped learning were ones I had hoped and planned for, there were some surprises.

First, my classroom has transformed to a community of learners in which I have an individual relationship with every student. Because of the structure of the class, I am able to talk with every one of them every day. Though I had good relationships with my students in the past, I now have deeper and more meaningful relationships with each of them.

Second, I have been able to participate in a phenomenal community of teachers who are all exploring ways to transform and deepen the learning in their classrooms. I discovered the flipped learning community through blogs, Twitter, and other social media. Great places to connect include the Flipped Learning Network Ning (http://flippedclassroom.org) and several Edmodo teacher groups. My personal learning network has helped me to reflect, probe, question, explore, and challenge both myself and my students to go deeper in our understanding of math.

Why Flipped Learning?

Our students need to play an active role in their education. They need to be challenged to think more deeply and to make connections. The short time that teachers have with their students should be focused on them, and structured to best support their learning needs. Flipped learning has enabled me to do this. By simply moving direct instruction—where everyone has to learn at the same time and at the same pace—from the group learning space to the individual learning space, I am now able to make more effective use of face-to-face time with my students.

The transition to flipped learning has been huge not only for me, but also for my students, their parents, and my administrators. Flipped learning has transformed the way they see teaching and learning. No longer is a classroom a place full of passive, surface-level learning. Rather, it is an active and engaging environment where all students can receive personalized support and be held accountable for their learning.

My transition has taken place over a period of three years. It takes time, understanding, and experience to see all the benefits flipped learning holds for creating a truly student-centered classroom.

Chapter 6

shifting to student-centered learning

BRIAN BENNETT'S STORY

Brian Bennett is a customer solutions engineer for TechSmith and a former chemistry and biology teacher. A thoughtful and reflective educator, Brian's widely read blog (www.brianbennett.org/blog) often deals with the topic of his reflective educational practice. Brian was inspired to change his teaching practice and adopt flipped learning through careful consideration of the needs and interests of his students. In doing so, Brian flipped the attention in his class away from himself and to his students, and more specifically, to his students' learning. Brian is a board member of the Flipped Learning Network and a frequent contributor to the global conversation around flipped learning.

On Teaching Chemistry

My first year of teaching chemistry was hard; everyone's is.
We are warned about that from the time we enter our college's
education program until we actually begin that first day. Lesson
plans, worksheets, grading, parent meetings—the list of pitfalls
goes on and on. Somewhere in there, we also have to teach, learn
school protocols, manage a class, and then, finally, get to know
some kids. Now, imagine all of that on top of getting married and
moving to South Korea for your first teaching job. Needless to say,
it was a lot to take in and process for my first year. I say all this
not to solicit sympathy, but to set the stage for moving into year
two, when I essentially relearned how to teach.

Noticing Problems

In the spring of 2010, when I finally felt comfortable managing
my life as a teacher, some patterns emerged that began to gnaw at
the pit of my stomach.

I didn't know my students nearly as well as I wanted to. I wanted
to know what motivated and moved them, but I didn't know how
to find the time to do that. After all, I had standards to meet,
and my precious class time didn't allow for too much discussion
outside of chemistry.

Some of my students failed chemistry. That really bothered me,
although at the time, I naively chalked up the failures to the bell
curve. Most of my students would fall in the middle, some would
be higher, others would be lower. I thought that's just the way
it was. But as I continued to look at the curve, I felt like I had
cheated some students. I saw their failures as a failure on my part
to engage them effectively. I decided then and there that I didn't
want my classes to fit bell curves. My students are individuals,
not normalized data.

The truth was, my students were bored and so was I. Teaching
chemistry for the first time, I relied on lecture as a primary source
of content delivery. After all, it was how I had learned chemistry

from the 10th grade all the way through college. I could communicate well, but communication alone wasn't adequate when I wanted my students to build a deep understanding of the material. I wanted my classroom to be a place of consistent engagement and discussion. If I was the center of attention every day, those qualities would be difficult to manifest. I had to find a way to maintain student access to information while reinforcing active learning behaviors in class.

Conditioning Our Students

B.F. Skinner (1938) is widely recognized as the father of operant conditioning, even though his work was based on that of another researcher, Edward Thorndike (1905). Basically, Skinner believed that the behaviors of a subject that were reinforced would become stronger, and those that weren't reinforced would die out. His experiments are well-documented, and the implications of this belief tie directly into the classroom.

Our system of education is built on a teacher commanding the attention of his or her pupils. Year after year, students are conditioned to sit quietly, taking notes while the teacher lectures (communicates) on a given topic. The student is then expected to regurgitate that information on an assessment, with the positive reinforcement being a passing mark.

Essentially, we have dehumanized the classroom. Instead of being an active and collaborative process, learning has been turned into a system of reward and punishment. Students don't see the teacher as a person, and the teachers don't treat students as the elastic, dynamic learners that they are. The conditioning pattern begins at a young age and continues throughout their school careers. By the time students are in high school, we've conditioned them to act in certain ways that may not help them learn.

Benjamin Bloom's (1956) taxonomy of learning can be tied to Skinner's work. Most educators are familiar with the cognitive levels of Bloom's taxonomy, which is typically shown as a pyramid (Figure 6.1):

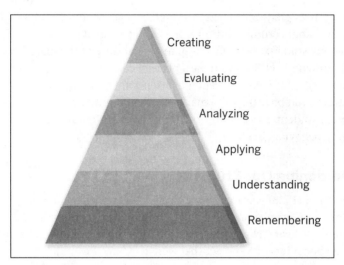

FIGURE 6.1 Bloom's taxonomy.

By looking at the relationship between mode of instruction and Bloom's taxonomy through the lens of Skinner's reinforcing behaviors, it becomes clear that by relying on lecture as the primary mode of instruction, with reinforcement of student behaviors related to lectures (being quiet and taking notes), students will learn only at the Remembering and Understanding levels. Switching to active and collaborative modes of instruction, with reinforcement of active behaviors (engagement and discussion), leads to students learning at the higher cognitive levels.

Looking for Resources

As I was looking for ways to address my concerns, I was receiving emails from the AP Chemistry listserv, managed by the College Board. One contributor in particular stood out. This was a typical conversation:

Teacher 1   My students are having a very hard time understanding chemical kinetics. Does anyone have suggestions about how to help them with homework?

Teacher 2   My teaching partner and I have seen the same
thing. We recorded ourselves giving homework
keys and extra examples that kids could watch at
home on Google Video. They can watch the video
as often as they want and wherever they want.

Teacher 2 was Jon Bergmann, at that time a Colorado-based
chemistry teacher. Jon was my introduction to the flipped
classroom. I remember writing that first email to Jon. It said
something to the effect of, "I saw your email on the listserv.
Can you tell me more?" Jon was gracious enough to send an
email outlining the basics of a flipped classroom, and invited me
to join Aaron Sams and himself in Colorado for their conference.
The conference helped me think about collaborative learning
using video as a means of instruction based on Jon and Aaron's
example. I was able to kickstart a total redesign of my curriculum
based on my learning that summer.

Implementing Changes

Fast forward to year two. The difficulty of learning to teach
during my first year had been significant. When I decided to flip
the instruction, I once again had to completely relearn how to
teach, making year two just as difficult. It began with recording
video lessons for my students to watch as homework. I used the
software I had received at the conference in Colorado and began
recording presentations I had already created. They were close
to what I would have done in class, which is to say, nothing out
of this world in terms of teaching methods. But having students
watch the video lessons at home allowed me to focus class time
on activities that would help students understand the material
in the videos.

Facing Challenges

The first big problem I faced when I flipped my classroom was
what to do with all the in-class time. I realized that I needed

to do some serious planning in order to have engaged, active learning take place on a daily basis. I had created activities here and there, but I never really had been asked to prepare those kinds of tasks for students on a regular basis. So I started to do some research. I looked for other science teachers' materials on the internet and began to pull those into my own instruction. At the beginning, it was very basic—things like worksheets or small labs. As time went by, though, I began to create my own materials that pushed critical thinking, reasoning, and questioning.

Right around the time I was solving the problem of how to plan meaningful in-class activities, the next one came along: what happens if students don't watch the videos at home? The first answer I turned to was the obvious one: they would lose class time and have to watch the video before they could move on. This tactic, again, proved to be naive and shortsighted: I quickly discovered that my content was not the only thing students could learn from. At times, students would come in and ask if it was okay to just read the text or use a different website to learn the concepts. The realization that my content was essentially an option produced a strange feeling, but at the same time a liberating one. I then approached the problem from two angles: one, what content do I, personally, need to teach my students? And two, do they really have to watch the videos at home, or at all?

From the Flipped Classroom to Flipped Learning

What I had stumbled upon was student-centered learning. I had transitioned from Flipped Class 101, where videos were used at home to focus on practice during class, to flipped learning, where learning is encouraged any time, and technology supports the learning. The game changer was that I realized it didn't matter if students watched my videos, or watched any particular presentation of content. What mattered was that they could do the science—that they could learn with or without my specific instruction.

I wanted students to be resourceful enough to be able to find help when they needed it. I wanted my students asking questions and drawing connections between ideas. I wanted them problem-solving and working together to learn. The content was important at times, but it wasn't always the most important idea. I'd much rather see students problem solving together than sitting and listening to an instructional video. As a young teacher, this was a hard, but timely, lesson. I also began receiving more-useful feedback from students when they chose to use class time to find information. These questions would help me see things I could change about how I taught, which led to improved lessons as the term progressed.

The nice thing about the [videos] was that we could watch them over and over again, even the ones all the way from Chapter 1. Also, you handed us worksheets that we had to do during and after watching the videos. So we weren't just blankly staring at the video, but were thinking and doing activities. The podcasts were concise and it was clear that you really took your time to make them. (I remember you telling us that you were always talking to your computer at home—haha.) Also, you gave us our class time to ask questions, watch the podcasts, and do whatever we needed to do for that class. So we were interacting with you in class, not just through our computers.

—*Susanna, 11th-grade Chemistry student*

Great. Students were learning, ideas were being shared, and I felt like I was growing as a teacher. But now what? Here's where the changes to my teaching really got deep.

What Is It about Flipped Learning That Helps Students Grow?

Short answer: Interaction. The time spent discussing material and working one-on-one with students makes the biggest difference. This is something any teacher can tell you, but it is the most elusive part of teaching. The fact of the matter is that if we try to do it all ourselves, we just don't have enough time to fit in content instruction, practice, and assessment. Flipped learning is simply using technology to remove a component of a traditionally taught class, which allows us to focus on the more important things during the day.

At the end of the 2011–12 school year, I had my students write letters to my next year's students. I asked them to give advice on how to be successful in a flipped classroom. To be honest, when I gave the assignment, I was worried too many kids would focus on the videos. Rather than reading 120 responses, I copied the text and made a word cloud (Figure 6.2).

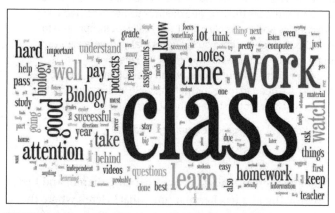

FIGURE 6.2 Word cloud for students' advice for success.

I was pleasantly surprised. At times, the mode of instruction can speak louder than the message, but that wasn't the case here. An overwhelming majority of my students saw the value in the connections they had made during the class time. I'm convinced that the class time would not have been nearly as meaningful had I not incorporated video in 2010. Other teachers have told me that the change was due to my maturation as a teacher, and I don't deny that was a contributing factor. But I can tell you that the growth I've experienced would not have been as significant if I were still a teach-from-the-front science teacher.

The experiences I've had with flipped learning are significant. I feel lucky to have found it at the end of my first year of teaching. The transitions I've made and the lessons I've learned from flipped learning are an integral part of who I am as a person and as a teacher.

Chapter 7

the flipped classroom in physical education

JASON HAHNSTADT'S STORY

What is the best use of your face-to-face class time? This question has probably been asked as many times as a flipped classroom has been created. Most teachers who have flipped their classrooms have done so in academic courses. When Jason Hahnstadt, a K–8 physical education teacher in Kenilworth, Illinois, first heard the One Question, he realized that he wanted to flip his class as well. Learn from him as he shares his experiences of flipping his physical education course.

MANAGING TIME ISSUES in class is not unique to teachers of core subject areas. Teachers of special subjects, including physical education (PE), must also analyze their use of time to ensure that both fitness and instructional goals are met. PE teachers are challenged by the need to use valuable class time explaining activities, teaching rules to games, setting up units, and grouping procedures. Flipping PE can help overcome the need to use class time for these tasks, providing more class time for activities.

Of course, there are obstacles to flipping PE, one of which is that PE teachers do not traditionally give out homework the same way that teachers for most other subjects do. Because of this, students often view PE class as less academically rigorous than their core classes. The Flipped Class 101 model offers opportunities for students to participate outside of class, thereby making the curriculum richer and more challenging.

Traditionally, PE teachers have students sit down in class for instruction and give in-class quizzes for assessment. Flipped learning allows teachers to move instruction and assessment outside of class time. Teachers can create instructional videos, and students can record their comments and complete quizzes online. In addition, adding fun and meaningful opportunities to get involved in the curriculum outside of class—such as voting on dances created during class for a "So You Think You Can Dance" unit—gets students invested and motivated to increase their level of participation. PE teachers can also take advantage of other virtual opportunities, such as posting class results and updates on web pages or social networks. And for those students who have a greater interest in PE, teachers can more easily develop resources for advanced work by using collaborative creation tools such as Google Docs, Sheets, Slides, Drawings, and Forms.

Why Should a Physical Educator Consider Flipped Learning?

Activity time is precious at all grade levels. For PE, the heavy emphasis on core standards and testing has led to reductions in class time. At the same time, the American Heart Association recommends children engage in at least 30 minutes of physical activity daily for healthy-heart living. I am blessed to work at a school that has daily PE for all grade levels, with a minimum of 30 minutes of activity time for every class. Many schools today may have students engage in physical activity only one to three times a week for as little as 15 minutes at a time.

My experience with students is that when they reach middle-school age, most want to be actively participating in a game or activity as soon as possible. When I request that they pay attention to my presentation on a game or activity, they seem to tune out quickly. They don't expect to have to listen to a "sage on the stage" giving them material to learn, as they do in other classes, and it's easy to see that this method of instruction doesn't challenge them (Bergmann & Sams, 2012). This is where the flipped classroom model can help. By prepping students before they enter the classroom, a PE teacher can maximize their activity and exercise time.

What Levels of Physical Education Should Be Flipped?

I see flipped PE classrooms possible at nearly all levels, from first grade forward. Flipping will look very different at each grade level, but the benefit of creating videos for students is universal. Younger students enjoy seeing themselves and their teachers on video, so I have created examples of myself and students practicing basic skills, such as throwing and catching. I have also created videos of games that we commonly play, because it helps students to see the game being played before they participate. For students in fourth and fifth grade, I transition into an instructional format of higher-level games such as badminton, with skills mixed into each video. At the middle school or junior high level (typically Grades 6–8), the videos I create are exclusively instructional, with the content primarily based on rules. At the high school level, I recommend PE teachers combine video instruction with instruction on how to do advanced-skill breakdown and game analysis. Students at this level can even create their own instructional videos or demonstrate their knowledge and growth by analyzing game strategy or by assessing their own or their peers' skill levels.

How the Flip Happened in Physical Education

Two years ago, at our first faculty meeting of the year, we were introduced to Jon Bergmann as our new Lead Technology Facilitator. Jon's presentation to us was the first time I had been challenged to reexamine my use of class time since my master's coursework. The question Jon asked that most struck me was: "What do you say or do, that you find yourself repeating all the time?" I have learned that the things you repeat are the things that can be presented in a video. Students can watch it outside of class, which adds valuable time to your classroom for whatever activity you deem is more important. In the gym, our highest priority is quality activity time that gets students moving and participating. As I analyzed my daily class organization, I saw that I spent many minutes per day repeating instructions to games or setting up units. Once the unit was rolling, we were able to have great use of activity time. Unfortunately, if students were absent for that time, I had to find a way to reteach the material without distracting or holding up the class that was already in progress.

With these thoughts in mind, I began the process of flipping my gym. The first unit I decided to flip was going to be Pickleball. To make the video, I did a Google search and downloaded several pictures that would be helpful to my Pickleball presentation. Using a free source for pictures, I found a funny picture of a grandma with a Pickleball racket glaring down an opponent. I also found pictures of Pickleball courts to use and inserted these pictures into presentation software in which I described the history and rules of the game. Using screencapture software, I pressed Record and began capturing everything I was doing, both on the screen and in front of my webcam. Then I gave my presentation, as I would normally do to the class. As I recorded my presentation, I didn't worry about making mistakes because they can always be edited out later. When I was done I edited the video. The editing took a while, but got easier and faster each time I did it. After saving the completed video to my computer, I uploaded it to our school's video-storage site for students' viewing, as well as to YouTube. (The video can be viewed at www.youtube.com/watch?v=P_hk5UgC-og.)

Once the video was complete, it was time to flip the assessment.

Flipping Assessment in Physical Education

Just because I had a video ready to go, with all the information for the unit I needed the students to know, didn't mean I was done. I now had to find a way to make sure my students knew the material; only then could I be certain that we could begin that unit without me giving my traditional lecture. Remember, without a clear way to assess the content you have created, you have no way of knowing if students have even watched your video. When I first began flipping in physical education, I was slow to create these assessments. Because of this slowness, students were not taking the importance of the content seriously. I found myself back at square one, giving lectures instead of using our in-class hours for activity time. This taught me that everything has to be ready and completed before a unit begins, so students can complete the prerequisite work and participate in all the activities that I set up for them. You will find that if your activities are sufficiently engaging, they will motivate students to get their work done so they can participate instead of doing some alternate activity, such as having to watch the video and take the quiz during class!

I have found that an online quiz is the best way to measure students' comprehension of a video. I have experimented with a number of such programs, and will review the ones I found most useful. The first type is an online form creator. These can be easily created and shared with a link on a web page. Questions can typically be created in various formats, including multiple choice, short answer, long answer, check boxes, choosing from a list, rating scales, and grids. Online form creators are easy to use and flexible. I can even embed Google forms on the same pages where I post my videos. Questions can be set as either mandatory or optional, and results can usually be viewed in a time-stamped spreadsheet. In my experience, an online form creator is best used for gathering information and surveying students.

Another online assessment tool I've found useful is a computer-based quiz program. Many of these programs are relatively inexpensive but can give you a highly developed quiz system that is very teacher-friendly. You can add pictures, sounds, videos, text, and web links to questions, and your questions can be multiple choice, multiple select, fill in the blank, short answer, true or false, matching, numeric, essay, or survey. Once the quiz is created it can be shared with a direct link for taking it. Quizzes are scored automatically. Make sure that the tool you use lets you randomize the questions and answers, to prevent students from cheating. Each quiz can also be set up with a time limit. The only negatives to this type of program are that they are often for single users only. While quiz files may be transferred among users, the cost of each software license adds up for multiple teachers and prohibits sharing quiz results.

The assessment tool that I currently use is part of our school's learning management system. It allows classes, pages, and assessments to be built and shared with all other faculty and students. Secure online quizzes are available with the following question options: fill in the blank, matching, multiple choice, true/false, and short answer. All questions are stored in a quiz bank, which is handy when you're looking to add variety. Quizzes are timed and scored automatically, and results can be exported. Google docs, files, text, links and pictures can also all be added to questions. Because of this tool's flexibility and its integration with our students' individual Google accounts, I've found this to be a great option for my classes.

Outcomes from Flipping in Physical Education

Flipping physical education has been an experience steeped in some trial and error. Once I had worked through the challenges, I saw the growth and development of both student interest and knowledge in our curriculum. I have also successfully gained more in-class time for fitness, games, and activities. Students have adjusted well to these changes, and I've had few complaints. Students enjoy having the freedom to take a quiz outside of class, on their own and at a time of their own choosing. If a student is absent, I can still easily hold him or her accountable for completing the work. My quiz scores have increased because I set up the online quizzes so that they can be taken multiple times for higher scores. This, in turn, has increased students' overall grades. The level of preparedness for class games and activities has also increased. With students adjusting to the flipped classroom, I have also been able to introduce new games that students have never seen before, and get great participation from the onset.

I do not require that all my videos be watched outside of class. Sometimes, because of the inconsistent nature of flipping in PE, getting students to watch videos is easier if the videos are shown in class. The benefits of this strategy are many: for one, I am able to convey a very consistent message that is performed perfectly every time. I never go over the allotted time, and I can generally keep these rules presentations to an appropriate length. I am also able to use the video to project images, diagrams, and demonstrations of many of the skills and strategies I am instructing students about.

The fascinating aspect of having students watch my videos in class is that I can manage their attention better because I have the freedom to focus solely on the learning environment. Also, because of students' experience with video technology or television, they pay better attention to me on the screen than they do in person. My ego gets a little boost every time students clap after watching one of my videos, too; they never clap after I give a rules presentation in person! I find that video presentations allow me to end up refreshed as a teacher and leave me with more energy to direct to the remainder of the class.

Conclusion

As I reflect back, a few common themes and questions have resurfaced that I would like to address. First, how often do I use videos to teach? In PE it may work best to flip a class only at the beginning of a unit, when students need to learn a large amount of new information. After students know the rules and procedures, I find that I can manage the class well through the end of the unit without much interruption.

Another common question I get is, "Do I make all my own videos or do I show other videos I have found?" I answer this one with simply, "It depends." The videos I have made are the most specific to what I am instructing, and I will use only those to create a quiz. I find that the relationship I have with students is also positively impacted when they are watching their teacher as the presenter. In class, however, I occasionally use other videos, especially ones that give clear skill demonstrations for students.

Access to iPods or iPads that have video capability gives PE teachers a great opportunity to have students record their own video instructions. Not only do students really enjoy doing this, but it also can be used as an assessment to demonstrate knowledge and skill proficiency. The highest level of learning is to use analysis and create a reflection. We have used an app for this sort of assessment: students first record themselves practicing a skill or game, and then they can watch the recording frame-by-frame or in slow motion. The app, Coach's Eye, also features telestration (drawing lines) over the video and can then record these telestrations and comments live, in an analysis video that can be both exported and shared. This kind of approach to a sport is commonly seen in most high schools' competitive sports, where the coach reviews a video with the athlete and offers comments for improvement. To have PE students be able to do the same process so easily opens up great possibilities for assessment and student growth. As a further bonus, these reflections often make great flipped videos for students to watch and learn from in future classes.

Chapter 8

flipped classroom
transitions to
deep learning

CAROLYN DURLEY'S STORY

Carolyn Durley, a biology teacher in Kelowna, British Columbia, Canada, burst onto the flipped learning scene when she wrote a blog post entitled, "Excuse Me: I Think I'm Having a Revolution." In that blog she stated: "I *knew* the world was changing. I knew it ... but no one, *no one,* told me how to move from here to there." Through flipped learning, she found a way to move her students to deeper learning. She has continued to add to the conversation by training other teachers to implement flipped learning. She and her colleague Graham Johnson have started a Canadian conference on flipped learning. Enjoy her transformative story.

IF YOU HAD ASKED ME five years ago to describe what student-centered learning looked like, I would have struggled to come up with a description. I wouldn't have been able to describe "deep learning" (see Table 8.1) at all. With over 20 years in the classroom, my expertise was teaching and my focus was there, not on student learning. I had believed that if I organized, planned, and delivered the curriculum to students in their seats, learning would occur. I now see that I was encouraging what I call "shallow learning." At the time, I felt a strong sense of responsibility to deliver the curriculum; from my perspective, this meant teaching *to* students. The action part of the class was owned and operated by me, the teacher. This mindset had kept my classroom in the shallow end of student learning and prevented deep learning from developing and flourishing.

Teaching Changes from a Revolving Door to an Evolving Door

Each September, I found myself trying to solve the same problems—again. I would enter the classroom and, as if it were a revolving door, find myself facing the exact same problems as the previous year, with no significant growth to my teaching practice. Despite my annually renewed commitment to organization, preparation, and new practices, the same challenges would surface and produce little lasting or impactful change to student learning. The time and energy needed to evolve my teaching practice threatened my ability to cover the curriculum for my Grade 12 students, many of whom required a specific grade point average to get into a post-secondary program.

TABLE 8.1 Comparison of Shallow and Deep Learning

Shallow Learning	Deep Learning
Students do activities out of habit rather than from self-knowledge.	Students can articulate and identify what learning activities best suit their learning goals.
Students are highly dependent on the teacher for specific instructions.	Students are interdependent and work peer-to-peer as well as with the teacher.
Students dislike trying new activities, as lack of success may negatively impact their success.	Students see value in taking risks in their learning, are able to learn from their mistakes, and reflect and take appropriate action.
Students are disconnected from the learning process; learning seems impersonal and irrelevant.	Students take pride and ownership of the learning process.
Students focus on strategies to acquire points (marks).	Students focus on strategies and habits to improve their learning.
Students are passive and compliant.	Students are active and engaged.
Students find it difficult to explain or find connections between topics or units.	Students can explain connections between units and explain how topics relate to the big picture of the course.
Students view evidence for learning as a grade or mark.	Students view learning as an ongoing process.
Students lack self-knowledge or awareness on specific areas that they find challenging.	Students are able to articulate specific areas of both strength and weakness in a course.
Students see topics as lists of facts to be memorized and quickly forgotten.	Students can relate topics to the bigger picture of the topic (why and how does this relate).

I was investing increasing amounts of time and energy towards developing "better" school and departmental policies that maximized the time students spent in their seats. Misguidedly, I thought that if my students were in their seats, the rest of the learning equation would be easy. These policies did not focus directly on improving student learning, but instead on superficial managerial procedures involving matters such as writing tests on time, students leaving class early, and excused or unexcused absences.

This narrow focus kept my teaching practice and perspective of student learning superficial and shallow. My teacher skill set was built around content organization, behavior modification, class control, entertainment, and engagement. While well-suited to test preparation for high-stakes exams, these skills did not facilitate deep student learning. And yet I had a rewarding teaching practice, excellent rapport with students, and positive feedback from students, parents, and administration; I felt proud of my work in the classroom. This success had reinforced my definition of student learning: that students gain the ability to move at my predetermined pace, follow instructions closely, and process large amounts of content quickly without discussion or reflection. I could not imagine exploring inquiry, metacognition, or any new teaching or learning strategies—such as Understanding by Design (UBD), problem-based learning (PBL), Universal Design for Learning (UDL)—until I had more time. After all, there wasn't time to complete what I was already doing, much less time to explore or add anything else.

This lack of time is what got me in the flipped classroom door. My initial motivation for using the flipped classroom was the increased time it would make available in class. I started with Flipped Class 101, creating and archiving screencasts of my lectures for my students to watch at home (see Table 8.2 for tips on successful screencasting). The newly created class time allowed me to do justice to the curriculum. I was now able to incorporate labs, do science rather than just talk about science, talk to every student every day, help students who needed help, and challenge students who had previously been bored. As I started with Flipped Class 101, I admit my goal was simply to create more time for my students to be in their seats, delving into the curriculum. Flipped Class 101 quickly solved my superficial problems, but just as quickly, it produced new ones.

TABLE 8.2 Screencasting Smarts

Time	Maximum 10–12 minutes in length.
Format	Create a screencast template and use the template for each subsequent screencast.
Instructions	Provide direct instruction on how to watch educational screencasts.
Note Organizer	Provide note organizers for students so they know what they are watching for.
Cooperative Watching	Encourage students to watch screencasts with a partner or in groups.
Flex Time	Provide time during class where students can choose to watch videos.
Teacher-made	Videos made by teacher demonstrate that teacher is committed to student success and establishes trust.
Download Videos	If you have computers in your room, download screencasts to hard drive of each computer to avoid lack of access on days when connection is slow or unavailable.
Provide Alternatives	Have an alternative ready in the event students say they don't want to watch videos or videos don't work for their learning.
Earphones	Have earphones available in the classroom and encourage students to bring their own.

Flipped Class 101
Reveals Paradigm Deficiencies

The archived screencasts, which I produced over the course of the first year, provoked a shift in my focus away from my teaching and onto student learning. Using the screencasts provided "white space" in terms of time and energy both inside and outside of the school day. Most significantly for me, using the screencasts lifted the mental responsibility I had felt to deliver and cover content—a responsibility that had inadvertently promoted shallow learning. However, this white space provided unforeseen insights and new challenges in regards to student learning.

As content delivery moved out of the face-to-face time, I now interacted with my students on a daily basis; I was able to have meaningful conversations with each student in every class. Although this in itself was rewarding, I became aware that many students lacked basic skills that prevented them from becoming independent learners. Students were well trained at "playing school," but did not have the skills to "play learning." Before we were able to move to deep learning, we needed to purposely develop habits and skills that would facilitate students' success in a different classroom dynamic than the one they had been programmed to exist in previously.

I also came to the realization that students were not ready for drastic overhauls to classroom practices: they needed time to adapt. Many students initially felt resentful and angry at me for "not being their teacher anymore." Their reaction was hard for me, as I was used to strong positive relationships with students. I recognized I needed to find a way to maintain student trust by using a graduated introduction of new activities. I also observed that students needed targeted support to map out action plans to overcome areas of challenge, whether it was with work habits or specific content topics. Students wanted to learn and had their own personal long-term goals in place, but they struggled with time-management skills and connecting their day-to-day habits to these goals. The timeline for student ownership to develop was longer than what I had anticipated. However, when students did make choices for themselves, it was with stronger commitment than when I had made the choices for them. Given time and space, students could learn to make appropriate choices for themselves and their success.

Learning is not linear, and students can self-pace. Talking with my students every day about what they were learning and thinking about, I quickly discovered they were self-pacing regardless of the pace I set for them. More amazing to me, I discovered students could accurately identify areas where they struggled, especially when learning targets or standards were made clear to them on a regular basis. I used to think some students were not learning because they went for long periods of time with little or no apparent growth. In flipped learning, however, I have observed many students experience rapid periods of growth and change. This observation helped me to realize that many students can be responsible for their own learning. For students to self-regulate, they need targeted support to map out a plan of action to overcome their specific areas of difficulty, whether with work habits or content areas. Some students struggled with time-management skills and aligning work habits to long-term goals. Because of the time I had available for each student, I was able to individually target their challenges and provide them the responsive assistance they needed.

Another issue I discovered is that many students were unfamiliar and uncomfortable with the self-reflection and self-direction skills they needed to support their learning. Metacognition (thinking about thinking) was, from their perspective, not valuable as a key component to enhance their learning. These students viewed any activity that was not done for points as extraneous and a waste of their energy.

From Flipped Class 101 to Flipped Learning

Flipped Class 101 revealed cracks in my old paradigm and helped me imagine a learner-centered education. I had two main goals when working towards flipped learning: to create a self-sustaining learning community in the classroom (see Table 8.3) and to empower students to become self-regulating. Therefore, the transition to a new classroom dynamic required building a strong sense of community among the students and helping students develop skills that fostered self-regulation rather than external regulation. In a self-sustaining community students worked together both cooperatively and collaboratively. Both these ways of learning enhanced the sense of belonging and team approach in our classroom. Collaborative learning was especially important because it made students feel valued regardless of their skill set or ability level.

TABLE 8.3 Key Components of Class Community

Collaborative Learning	Cooperative Learning
Commitment to co-create with others a tangible project where each learner has a specific and interdependent role in the creation of the project.	Commitment to co-learn with others and be part of a community that is trying to make sense of a topic.

Creating a Self-Sustaining Learning Community in the Classroom

I identified actions I could employ to help students become successful and active members of a classroom learning community:

Create policies together. I actively involved students in developing class routines and policies. For example, we created our personal electronic device policy as a class and all signed the document.

Arrange the physical space. I arranged classroom furniture to facilitate both group and individual work. I wanted to reduce the focus on the teacher as the center of the class. One way I did this was to set up three small conversation areas, each with comfortable seating for group discussions.

Normalize group work. I spent the first several weeks of each semester establishing classroom routines that required and built teamwork and skill differentiation.

Make groups responsible. I assigned regular and repeated group tasks to develop ownership and independence. For example, I gave each group a weekly task and rotated these tasks through the groups over the course of the school year.

Develop class culture. In the past, the culture of the class was derived from my personality and energy. Class culture derived from students is not as immediately obvious in a class that is student-centered. A student-driven culture takes longer to develop and requires a more purposeful creation. Once it is established, a class culture is self-sustaining and extends beyond the classroom walls. An example of something I did to encourage a student-created class culture was to use a class Facebook group where students could interact and ask each other questions.

Solicit student feedback. I asked for student feedback on a regular and ongoing basis. I then responded openly to their feedback and their constructive criticisms. I tried to implement their suggestions wherever I could and explained why if I could not.

Students as Self-Regulating Learners

Because my students were used to being externally regulated, I needed to activate the following in order for self-regulation to be an integral part of the class culture:

Promote regular guided metacognition. Students needed regular and guided practice to think about their thinking. Many, at first, saw this activity as pointless. "Why are we doing this?" was a common question. With time, students did become better at this process and began to self-select this activity without prompting. Student comments included "Reflection helped me sort out what I needed to do" and "When I was overwhelmed and stressed reflection helped me to break down what I needed to do into smaller chunks." Students used soft-cover, inexpensive copy books as learning journals. They could leave these in class and easily access them at any point during the day. See Table 8.4 for further activities to promote class culture and self-regulation.

Model metacognition. Students need to see the teacher as the chief learner in the room. To this end, I would write my own reflections about our classroom on my blog during classroom reflection time. I wanted to model that I am a learner who is thinking about my learning and that it is a valuable and important activity.

Set goals on a regular basis. Students were asked to set both short-term and long-term goals on a regular basis and record them in their learning journals. For some students these goals were as simple as asking for help or completing a small project. Some students already had this skill internalized; for others this was helpful in allowing them to develop ownership of their time and learning. For certain students this quickly became an authentic habit they began to use without prompting.

Make goals visible. At the start of the year we developed class goals together and students made personal goals. We publicly displayed these goals in the classroom for the duration of the semester.

Make goals public. Students would share goals in their groups and with me as well during "hot seat" (described in Table 8.4). I found that verbalizing and talking about goals worked to reinforce student ownership of their day-to-day choices as learners.

Provide choice. I gave students physical space and time in class to complete work as needed. Students have off days and we need to honor them when they say they need personal space. I provided what I term "flex time" every class, and during this time students could self-select what they needed to get done to best meet their personal learning goals.

Introduce new activities repeatedly. I encouraged students to try new activities (see Table 8.4 for possible activities) but ultimately I trusted them to choose to be involved in a new activity when they were comfortable and ready to do so. When students saw a new activity as "fun" they would choose to give it a try the next time we did it in class. Tweeting in class to answer questions or using Poll Everywhere are examples of such choice activities.

Respect personality differences. Some students are introverted and prefer to contribute in less publicly visible ways, such as online. Providing a choice of how to contribute allowed students to feel comfortable and valued. Whenever possible I would give students a choice of how they could best contribute. For example, some students are comfortable contributing in an online forum, such as our Facebook group, but not publicly in front of the entire class.

Trust students. In the past I had always put pressure on students to keep up, get their work done, and come in for help. After much discussion with students I realized that students do not enjoy being micromanaged. Moreover, for some students it has the reverse effect and shuts them down. Although this was a hard habit for me to break, I made every attempt to trust students when they said: I can do it alone.

Allow for supported failure. I found some students respond more quickly and positively to change if they experience supported failure first. This does not imply you let a student fail. Rather it means that you provide opportunities for them to show their learning when they are ready to. I accomplished this by providing opportunities for retests and for alternative assessments. For example, I used both exit interviews and portfolios.

TABLE 8.4 Possible Activities in the Flipped Classroom

Learning journals	An inexpensive copy book that remains in the classroom to provide opportunities for metacognition, goal setting, and private communication with the teacher.
Learning packets	A handout made up of the possible learning activities for each unit with the optimal unit deadline, along with note organizers for screencasts and the learning standards (or targets) for the unit.
Hot seat	Time in class before a test where each student has an interview with the teacher. The student presents his or her evidence for learning, and student and teacher have a conversation about what is going well and where the student is struggling.
Redo application	An application that students complete and submit if they wish to apply for a redo (retest). Parameters are set for specific criteria students must meet before they are eligible for a redo.
Flex time	Time provided in class during which students can select the activity they need to best suit their individual situation. At the start of the semester, time provided is 10 to 20 minutes. The amount of time is slowly increased related to the specific personality of the class. During this time many students watch the screencasts.
Traditional activities	At the start of the semester I do a small stand-and-deliver lecture component every day to put students at ease and to prove to them I am still their teacher. As students become more comfortable and familiar with the flipped classroom structures, I extinguish this whole-class lecture portion but may still do small group review sessions or mini-lectures to smaller groups as needed.
Community time	This is time where the whole class works on the same project. In Biology this is usually a lab activity that the entire class does at the same time. However, if a student has fallen behind, they may forgo the group activity to catch up. This is negotiated on a student-by-student basis.

Fail Fast, Fail Frequently, and Fail Forward

To change means to try something new, whether it is going to the gym, cooking new recipes, or working with a new phone. Mistakes will be made. Changing a learning environment, as I now know, involves failure—specifically, making mistakes in front of 30 teenagers.

Being ready and willing to embrace failure was the hardest part for me. As an "older" teacher, I was used to my classroom running smoothly, without any hiccups or fuss. The transition from a stable predictable environment to making small mistakes every day for the first several months was very uncomfortable. I felt stressed because it was not perfect; it was messy and chaotic. I had to embrace failure, learn from it, and move on to the next mistake, which was waiting right around the corner. So my words of wisdom would be: fail fast, fail frequently, and those failures will propel you forward! Failure is not an ending but a new beginning. If we don't learn to fail we fail to learn. Flipped Class 101 allowed me to fail, but to fail safely and slowly forward, in a direction that helped me design a classroom centered on students and their deep learning.

Ending Up at Flipped Learning

My flipped classroom journey began with making videos. I was able to use the lecture and organizational skills I had developed over the course of my 20-year teaching career to be a successful Flipped Class 101 teacher. Once the screencasts were made and archived, I was freed from repeating the content explanation; my time was repurposed. Wear and tear on me was diminished and my time was now focused on how to differentiate the classroom and develop a student-focused classroom. This happened slowly over the course of several months, with daily reflection and discussions with other teachers who had flipped their classrooms. Throughout this time of transition, my focus shifted to working with students where they were at, allowing students to drive their learning, make choices, and take ownership of both their successes and failures. This design evolved over the course of the first year.

When I started with Flipped Class 101, I could not have imagined how it would shift my classroom so dramatically and irrevocably. I was not aware of the possibilities that would emerge when I began with my initial desire to have more time in class to do justice to the curriculum and prepare students for post-secondary education. Flipped Class 101 caused me to shift from a highly teacher-driven and externally regulated model to one that was student-focused and student-centered. I had become a flipped learning teacher. Though I have room to grow, I would never go back to the old way. My teaching, my students, and their learning are all forever changed.

Chapter 9

democratize learning
through the
flipped classroom

TOM DRISCOLL'S STORY

When the flipped classroom is discussed in the press, the academic subjects most often cited are math and science courses. Teachers in the humanities often feel their courses can't be flipped. Tom Driscoll, a social studies teacher in Putnam, Connecticut, has not only flipped his history classroom, he has used flipped learning to increase the number of interactions in class, personalize learning for each student, and democratize education for the whole class. Enjoy his story of transformation.

Why can't we vote on what topic we will learn next? Why are you going so fast, can you slow down? Where is my freedom of speech? Can I petition this grade?

QUESTIONS SIMILAR TO these would sporadically arise during my first four years teaching American Government. Many educators, including myself at the time, would brush these remarks off as a student strategy for work avoidance. My response typically drifted into an argument that I had repeated over the years: "Well, this class may be about democracy, but in fact it is closer to a dictatorship. A benevolent dictator I may be, but it is a dictatorship nonetheless." I am not sure exactly where I heard this, but for some reason I thought it was great idea.

It was not until the summer of 2011 that I started to truly reevaluate the nature of my teaching. Did these students have a point? As a social studies teacher who truly believes in the guiding principles of our nation, was my teaching style really that hypocritical? In a course that extols the virtues of democracy, did our own class fail to resemble one? That simply could not be. Group dialogue and discussion were cornerstones of my class, particularly during the Center for Civic Education's "We the People" mock-congressional hearings. My students engaged in the Project Citizen program, in which they collaborated to solve real-world problems in the community. I also leveraged technology in countless ways to improve engagement and help build students' 21st-century skills.

Upon further reflection, however, it was evident where the problems lay. First, my instructional practices were significantly dependent on direct instruction via lecture. I also maintained firm control regarding what students were learning and how they would be assessed. Beyond this, I was at times stringing together assignments and projects without conveying any greater sense of purpose. Students may have been demonstrating mastery of the designated learning objectives, but there was little sense that what they were learning applied to their lives and the world beyond high school. In the end, students had little choice or control over their learning. It is no wonder, then, that despite my best efforts, many students were disengaged and lacked the passion and drive to learn. It is also no surprise that they found little amusement in my "benevolent dictatorship" speech.

A New Start

I changed districts for the 2011–12 school year and began teaching at Putnam High School (PHS) in Putnam, Connecticut. This small public school of about 350 students serves a predominantly working-class community in Connecticut's northeastern "Quiet Corner." Although I was teaching three subjects, the bulk of my assignment was a mixed-level World History course. Putnam's student population represented a wide range of abilities, at times varying from second- to eleventh-grade reading levels in the same class. In sum, it was a challenging start to the new school year. My lectures were too fast for many, yet frustratingly slow for others. Some students were chronically absent, falling further and further behind. Several students simply did not complete assignments, citing a wide variety of reasons. I had experienced similar issues in my previous teaching position, but now they were exacerbated. The major concern, however, was not with this new student population; instead, it was with my instructional practices and the learning environment that they promoted.

After much soul-searching and reflection on my performance and role as an educator, I came to the following conclusion: I needed to transform my class into a more democratic learning experience for all students. This would help push their thinking further by embedding them in learning environments based on problem solving in real-world contexts. Content and skill mastery would remain essential, but learning would also be grounded in a greater sense of purpose. The goal was to create a learning environment that both mirrored and prepared students for the dynamic, democratic world of which we are all a part.

There are, of course, many different visions of democratic education and of what one actually looks like in practice. My interpretation is influenced by a wide range of sources, including John Dewey (1916), Joseph Kahne and Joel Westheimer (2003, 2004), Howard Budin (2010, 2011), and the Partnership for 21st Century Skills (2011). After conducting preliminary research through a master's program at Columbia University, I developed the following framework regarding democratic education:

A democratic education:

- ensures equitable access to intellectual opportunities

- ensures access to diversity of knowledge and opinions

- develops personal initiative and adaptability

- develops knowledge and skills necessary to engage in civic life

- values various modes of student expression

- values student choice and control

Students in a democratic classroom regularly engage in:

- collaborative decision making

- critical thinking

- inquiry-based problem solving

- social interactions and cooperative pursuits

- active and experiential learning opportunities

- critical examination of social issues

The elements of this framework are not, of course, exclusive to democratic education; these are the building blocks of all effective teaching. My own classroom, however, was not always conducive to this type of teaching and student learning. I had to ask myself, "How could my instructional strategies and curriculum design evolve in a way that shifts towards a more democratic learning experience for students?"

Starting the Transformation

Flipped Class 101

In October of 2011, a colleague introduced me to the flipped classroom concept. After conducting some initial research, I began experimenting with what many term Flipped Class 101. I shifted my in-class lectures into online, screencast videos. I assigned these videos for homework, and designated class time for every other type of learning activity. Although there was a positive student response and modest improvement in achievement, several issues persisted. First, I had to develop a system that assessed whether these videos helped students learn the material. I therefore created guided viewing questions and online quizzes for each. This strategy certainly helped, but learning gaps persisted.

It seems obvious in hindsight, but a major concern that presented itself early on in this process was pacing. Since most class time was now devoted to student activity, it became increasingly evident that students learn at different rates. Some students demonstrated mastery of the day's objectives more quickly than others, leaving them with little to do for the remainder of class. This issue had always existed, but it was now glaring. How could I address this problem, yet still incorporate elements of flipped learning?

Flipped Mastery

Starting in January of 2012, we transitioned to the flipped mastery model (Bergmann & Sams, 2012). I designed each unit around four learning goals, and each goal had three to four corresponding learning objectives. Each objective then had one to six associated learning tasks. Students progressed through the unit once their learning-task performance demonstrated mastery of each objective. Students used the instructional videos as resources, but they were just one of many tools that they used throughout the learning process. Flipped mastery proved a substantial improvement over the previous semester's traditional flipped approach. There was still much work to be done, however, to further democratize the learning environment.

Adopting a Learning Management System

To assist with organizing and managing our online content, I began searching for an effective learning management system (LMS). For the remainder of the 2011–12 year, I relied on the Edmodo platform. The following year I migrated my resources and assessments over to EDUonGO (see Figure 9.1), a more advanced and collaborative LMS. This new learning platform serves as a space for students to access instructional videos and other course materials. The discussion stream, interactive e-reader, and video notation tools also promote student interaction and collaboration. As for assessments, Google forms are linked or embedded into the LMS, while the Flubaroo grading script provides response analytics. Although there are multiple options regarding assessment programs and learning management systems, those mentioned above have proven most effective.

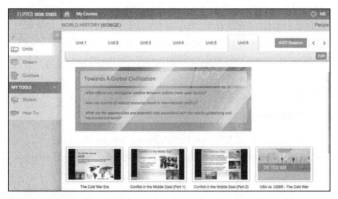

FIGURE 9.1 The EDUonGO learning management system.

Toward a More
Democratic Classroom

As our class evolved, it was increasingly evident that learning was becoming more democratic in nature. Although the foundation of my instructional practice remained rooted in flipped mastery, I incorporated principles of inquiry-based learning while preserving time and space for group dialogue and discussion. More specifically, flipped learning democratized our class by individualizing instruction, increasing opportunities for interaction and expression, promoting active and experiential activities, offering equitable access to intellectual experiences, encouraging ownership of learning, and valuing critical thinking and collaborative problem solving. In other words, our class successfully developed the aforementioned characteristics of democratic learning. What follows describes how I believe this process unfolded.

I really like our flipped social studies class because it gives me more control over how I learn. First, I have more choice over when and where I complete each assignment and learn the material. I also like that it is a lot easier to access the lectures and assignments online and that they will always be there. It helps that I can stop and replay the videos when I'm taking notes. Sometimes I will watch them a few times to really understand them. The best part is that I have the time I need to accomplish the tasks. I focus well in class and am usually ahead of other students. It is great how, in this class, I can move ahead even if not everyone has finished with the unit.

—*Ethan Bruso, Putnam High School student*

Individualization

Many educators see a tradeoff between whole-class direct instruction and addressing the needs of individuals. For instance, if teachers lecture, they are not working with individual students.

If they are helping individual students, they may be seen as neglecting the group direct instruction that most educators consider essential. Flipped learning, however, transformed the nature of my class: I now had more time to work with students without sacrificing valuable direct-instruction time. The direct instruction I do find necessary remains available to students, whether it be during the first few minutes of class or through video readily available online through our LMS.

Flipped learning has also personalized our class by enabling greater differentiation. Students can learn at their own pace and are granted more choice and control over their learning. In fact, when I asked PHS student Mike LaRochelle to describe flipped learning, he mentioned nothing of the video lectures. The first thing he referenced was that "you can go at your own pace and you are not limited from learning faster than others." Noah Mailoux, another PHS student enrolled in our World History course, provided similar feedback. Noah said that "the flipped classroom concept clearly lets me know what the expectations are and lets me jump right into the unit. This gives a much less restricted feeling in the classroom because I get help when I need it and no one is holding me back."

Within each of our units, students advance through a series of learning objectives. Once the student demonstrates proficiency in the learning objective, they move on. Based on their performance on the aligned assessments, I determine whether they are ready to progress or if they need remediation. Therefore, students who learn at a quicker pace are not held back, while slower learners are not rushed through without truly grasping the concept or skill. This approach not only grants students more control over their learning, but it highlights the fact that our focus is not on assignment completion, but on learning.

Flipped learning continued to personalize our class by promoting student choice and control. Since our goal is to demonstrate proficiency in learning objectives, there is greater freedom to differentiate assignments. I have attempted to incorporate principles of Universal Design for Learning (UDL) into my course by providing multiple means of demonstrating mastery. For example, I will often offer a choice of assessments for each learning objective. I also provide the students with the opportunity to develop their own assessment, as long as they discuss with me beforehand how this will in fact demonstrate mastery.

In my opinion, flipped learning makes you more motivated to do well in the course. Instead of the teacher just telling you what to do each day, you can choose what assignment you want to work on for each objective. If you think one assignment might not be as interesting, you can just choose a different one that is linked to that objective. Also, if none of them looks good to you, you can make your own as long as you can show how it demonstrates the objective.

—*Joshua Allard, Putnam High School student*

Social Interaction and Student Expression

Our class has increasingly emphasized social interaction and student expression, two elements central to democratic education. Flipped learning increases the number and improves the quality of student-teacher interactions. I now spend most of each class having conversations with individuals and small groups. Students do not often get the chance to actually sit down and talk with their teacher on a regular basis. Mykaela Taylor, a World History student at PHS, recently claimed that she "learns a lot more by having these conversations, which I seldom get to do in some classes." This ability to engage in dialogue not only aids instruction, but also creates a more open and trusting learning environment.

Beyond student-teacher interactions, flipped learning emphasizes the value of discussion among peers. My students often create small study groups on their own as they tackle the unit objectives. In these groups, I have witnessed a dramatic increase in the number of times I observe students teaching other students. I also encourage students to work individually if that is their learning preference. No two students learn exactly the same way, and I respect the fact that many prefer to complete the learning tasks on their own. This is yet another example of student choice and control in the classroom.

In the flipped class I have a lot more time to work and collaborate with other students. Sometimes I would actually watch the screencast videos with other students to help understand them better.

—*Joshua Allard, Putnam High School student*

Another way that flipped learning promotes interaction and expression is that it incorporates modern communication technologies, which are second nature to most students. Interaction through digital media is not the exception for today's students, but the norm. For those who are not fluent in the use of today's digital technologies, their immersion in these practices will help them develop the skills that are certainly needed in today's world. One example of this is our ability to conduct asynchronous discussions with our online instructional videos. A concern that many teachers express with videos is fear of losing much of the in-class discussion that accompanies lectures. There is a way, however, to compensate for this perceived loss in discussion time: when I embed a video into our LMS, students can post comments and questions at specific points in the video using video noting (see Figure 9.2). When any user reaches that point in the video, the comments will appear. If the video is paused, viewers can reply to the comment or question, leading to a conversation based on that video segment. A second example is the discussion forums regularly conducted through the course "Stream" module (see Figure 9.3). These are effective online tools that enable students to engage in academic discourse beyond the walls of the classroom.

FIGURE 9.2 Video noting lets students ask questions and engage in asynchronous discussion while viewing instructional videos.

FIGURE 9.3 Online discussion forums allow students to engage in discussion through our learning management system.

Active and Experiential Learning

As repeatedly stressed by Dewey (1916) and countless reformers since, democratic education requires an active and experiential learning environment. Flipped learning, particularly when paired with mastery and inquiry, enables students to engage in experiential learning in a more meaningful way. For example, two students recently proposed researching the origin of muscle cars. They also asked if they could present their research via a screencast video, similar to those I create for instructional purposes. Up until this point, these students were regularly disengaged regarding our World History curriculum. I could tell, however, that they were motivated to do this assignment. By choosing a topic that they have real-world experience with, they made the project relevant to them. By choosing the screencasting performance task, they were able to present their findings in a way that was meaningful to them as well. Travis Stringer, one of the two students, said it best when he asserted, "See what happens when we can learn about things we care about?"

Equitable Access to Intellectual Experiences

As a society, our democratic ideals require that all students be provided with equitable access to high-quality educational experiences. Flipped learning helps create a more equitable learning environment. For example, the ability to differentiate instruction while spending more time individually with students provides opportunities for learners who may fall behind in traditional settings. The instructional videos themselves also provide more access to instruction for students who are absent for a variety of reasons.

Sometimes I get distracted during class lectures, so the instructional videos help me stay focused. I also like how you can stop and replay them as much as you need to, especially before we take the quiz. The other great thing is that they are always there to review, where if you miss a lecture in class it is gone.

—*Cody Lascola, Putnam High School student*

There are other practical reasons why flipped learning has made learning more equitable. Typical daily interruptions that disrupt in-class lectures are reduced. Anyone who has spent time in a classroom understands that announcements, fire drills, phone calls, or the restless student can easily derail even your most engaging lecture. Regardless of the cause, this is a real dilemma regarding equity. Each interruption to group direct instruction takes valuable learning time away from students. It is simply unfair for students to miss out on educational opportunities due to these disruptions. The archiving of direct instruction online, as well as the asynchronous nature of mastery learning, helps address this concern.

> The part of flipped learning that I like the most is that there are so many options for where I can get information. In some classes, I just have the book and the lectures to go off of. In our flipped class it is not like that at all. I can find information from the instructional videos and tutorials, the handouts, the text-book, and we are also allowed to look up things on the internet any time we need to.
>
> —*Mykaela Taylor, Putnam High School student*

Personal Initiative and Ownership of Learning

Theories of democratic citizenship, particularly those that focus on the personally responsible citizen, emphasize the development of individual initiative. Since our flipped learning environment is more student-centered, personal initiative and self-regulated learning are requirements. Many educators avoid granting students more control because they believe their students could not handle the freedom and are not responsible enough to work efficiently. In response to this view, if students do not have the necessary skills to learn in this environment, it is our role to help students build these skills. I have incorporated metacognitive learning objectives into each unit to accentuate the point that these skills are absolutely essential for everyone. Students are required to set goals, monitor progress, and reflect on both a short- and long-term basis. Daily learning journals (see Figure 9.4) and unit-objective grids help students manage their daily progress, while wikis enable them to reflect and set goals for each unit. In the end, students will never develop these skills unless they are provided with opportunities to improve them, along with guidance from educators.

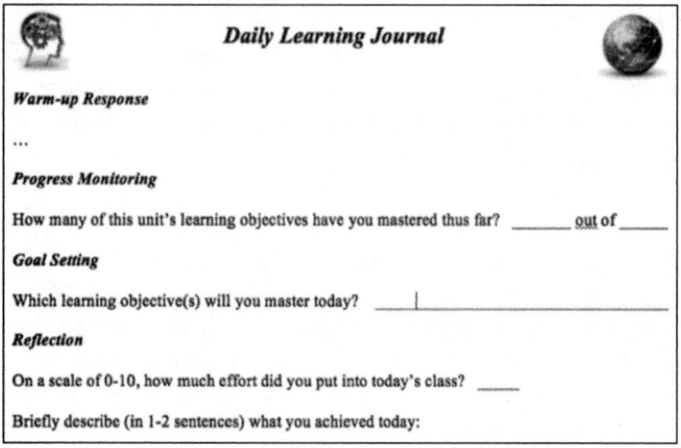

Daily Learning Journal

Warm-up Response

...

Progress Monitoring

How many of this unit's learning objectives have you mastered thus far? _______ out of ______

Goal Setting

Which learning objective(s) will you master today? ______________________

Reflection

On a scale of 0-10, how much effort did you put into today's class? _____

Briefly describe (in 1-2 sentences) what you achieved today:

FIGURE 9.4 Daily learning journals improve students' ability to set goals, monitor progress, and reflect on their learning.

Critical Thinking and Collaborative Problem Solving

The very nature of democracy requires its citizenry to think critically and solve problems collaboratively. Our class promotes this by increasing opportunities for student collaboration and shifting towards an inquiry-based learning environment. In a traditional class setting, the teacher is viewed as someone who owns all of the knowledge. That may have been the case a century ago, but in today's world, information is everywhere. A teacher's content knowledge serves as an invaluable resource, but just one of many. Flipped learning allows students to use each other as resources and to work collaboratively in learning tasks. One example of this has been students' utilization of Google Docs and Google Hangouts to collaborate in real time while engaging in inquiry-based activities. I am certain that as these technologies continue to evolve, students will have more opportunities to collaborate through these rich online experiences.

Another example of our increasing focus on critical thinking has been the incorporation of "20% Time." This relatively new concept is based on research that stresses how substantial a role intrinsic motivation plays in students' ability to think critically and creatively (Pink, 2009). Without going into great detail, this project grants students the freedom to spend 20% of their class time developing a project that they are individually passionate about. Although we are in the initial stages of 20% Time implementation, the concept complements both flipped learning principles and the increasingly democratic nature of our classroom.

I think the flipped classroom gets students excited about learning while shifting the responsibility to learn onto the student. The standards-based learning approach affords the students the opportunity to obtain subject mastery while having the independence to work at their own pace and to more fully investigate topics or themes that pique their interests. Therefore, each student has his/her own unique learning experience. Finally, it lets the students decide how to display their knowledge through various independent authentic assessments. As someone who will be entering the teaching field very soon, I'm excited about utilizing the flipped learning approach in my classroom.

—*Jeffrey Lueth, former co-teacher in PHS World History course*

Flipped Learning and Democratic Education Survey

Although I had witnessed this transformation in my own classes, I wanted to know if similar changes were occurring in other flipped classrooms across the country. As part of my graduate research, I conducted a survey of students and educators that gauged the extent to which flipped learning democratized the classroom in diverse settings. Responses came from 228 students from eight school districts. Twenty-eight teachers from various parts of the nation completed the educator survey.

As illustrated in the survey results listed below, responses demonstrate overwhelming support for the claim that flipped learning democratizes education in many ways. Since the concept of democratic education itself is rather ambiguous, participants were never posed with the question directly. Their responses, however, clearly align with the common elements of democratic education.

Student Survey Results: Flipped Learning and Democratic Education

77%   have more frequent and positive interactions with the teacher during class

79%   have more frequent and positive interactions with peers during class

80%   have greater access to course materials and instruction

80%   have greater opportunity to work at their own pace

70%   are more likely to have choice regarding what learning tasks they engage in

77%   have more choice regarding how to demonstrate their learning

66%   are more likely to engage in collaborative decision making with other classmates

70%   are more likely to engage in critical thinking and problem solving

69%   believe their teacher is more likely to take into account their abilities and interests

82%   believe learning is more active and experiential

(Results compiled from 228 students from 8 school districts.)

Educator Survey Results:
Flipped Learning and Democratic Education

96%   reported an increase in positive interactions with students

86%   reported an increase in positive interactions between
        students

93%   reported that students have greater access to course
        materials and instruction

96%   reported that students are more likely to have choice
        regarding their learning tasks

75%   reported that students are more likely to have choice
        regarding their modes of representation

83%   reported that students are more likely to engage in
        collaborative decision-making

92%   reported that students are more likely to engage in
        critical thinking/problem solving

96%   reported that instruction has become more differentiated
        and personalized

100%   reported that learning is more active and experiential

*(Results compiled from 28 educators from school districts across the
Unites States.)*

An Evolving Approach

I am encouraged by the increasingly democratic nature of
learning in our class, yet there are still some things I must
consider as my instructional approach evolves. First, since our
class offers students more control over their learning, I must place
even more effort into building students' self-regulated learning
skills. To do so, I must regularly provide effective guidance,
structure, and feedback. Second, I must ensure students have
significant opportunities to engage in large-group dialogue about
big ideas and controversial issues. Even though personalizing the

learning experience is important, I must not lose sight of the vital need to develop citizens' abilities to effectively engage in civil discourse.

What is my role as an educator? What knowledge and skills do my students need for success in today's world? What particular qualities do I as an educator bring to the table? Where do we go from here? These are questions that all of us ask ourselves and reflect on regularly. Fortunately, flipped learning has enabled me to join a vast network of passionate educators who continuously attempt to answer these big questions. Although there are guiding principles to the flipped learning concept, we all tailor it to suit our particular interests, skills, and goals. This is one aspect of the movement that is so exciting. Educators from around the world are leveraging technology to experiment with pedagogical approaches and classroom practices that were never possible in a traditional setting.

Personally, I aim to prepare students for success in our modern, interconnected world while trying to create a learning environment that mirrors the 21st-century democracy we live in. The very nature of education as we know it is undergoing profound changes. As a teacher and a father of two beautiful children, I am a stakeholder in this transformation on two fronts. It is therefore my duty to make the most of the promise and potential that these times have to offer. It is an honor to be joined in this effort by the vast number of passionate educators out there who share this goal.

Chapter 10

english was made to flip

APRIL GUDENRATH'S STORY

Many curious teachers ask how to begin using a flipped learning approach. April, a high school English teacher in Colorado Springs, Colorado, began with a visit to observe a flipped classroom in action and then took the plunge. In this chapter, April lays out some basic principles for why a teacher might want to use flipped learning, and some basic instructions for how to get started. She masterfully and reflectively changed the way in which she used her class time with her students.

MY LIFE CHANGED with a field trip. I know this sounds kind of cliché, but it is the truth. As part of a technology cadre in my school district, I was asked if I wanted to sojourn up the mountain pass to Woodland Park and talk to some guys who were looking at education a little differently by doing something they called the "flipped learning model." Initially, the thought of creating sub plans to cover my classes made me want to say no— but I am so glad that I went. I have no memory of the lesson I left for the sub, but the lesson I learned on the field trip started me down a path of innovation that shifted my educational pedagogy forever.

As a fairly new public school teacher (three years), I was already facing the challenges that so many of us face: lack of student motivation, absence of student accountability, and too much curriculum to cover in too little time with too many students. Coming from a background in industry and college-level instruction, I saw these hurdles as frustrating, but also as a personal challenge for me to overcome. Jon Bergmann and Aaron Sams, the Woodland Park teachers, shared with us a simple question that I still use and that has become my educational mantra: "What is the best use of your face-to-face class time?" The answer to that question propelled my amazing journey.

I walked into Jon's and Aaron's classroom and I was astounded. I saw a room of chaos that I instantly fell in love with. Students were doing their own investigations and were engaged in learning at their own level. The instructors were able to walk around the classroom and have individualized conversations with each student, free to ask as well as to answer questions. Students were motivated to learn because they were able to do so at their own pace, in a manner that was native to them. Because the teachers were able to walk around and interact with every student, there was inherent student accountability. This model provided me with a flash of hope that I had found a way to energize my teaching.

Why Flip?

After visiting Jon and Aaron, I did what they told everyone not to do—I jumped in with both feet and changed my whole classroom overnight. I went back and started to reexamine my use of class time, immediately applying the concept of mastery in my classroom. To be honest, I am surprised that I survived that year! The change was a massive undertaking, and to flip and to attempt any type of master or standards-based grading at once is more than ambitious, it is insane. But by making this pedagogical shift, I was able to further a movement in my district that has allowed our high school to implement a standards-based grading system for secondary levels, as well as to consistently have one of the highest reading and writing scores for high schools in the entire district (Colorado Department of Education, 2012).

After year two, I felt like I needed more specific direction. I did some reflection and realized that I needed data to help guide my decisions. That is when I started doing research to help answer the One Question. I was fortunate enough to find three resources to help direct me and give me a specific focus. This, in turn, allowed me to radically change my classroom and instruction.

Visible Learning

The first resource was John Hattie's *Visible Learning* (2009), which single-handedly confirmed my instinct that the flipped classroom provides the best learning environment for my students. Hattie's research on the influences on students' achievement in school-aged children is based on more than 800 meta-analyses, 500,000 studies, and over 200 million students.

His initial findings state that in order to make an impact on student learning, a teaching strategy has to increase student achievement by 40% (an effect size of .4) (Hattie, 1999).

The sources of variance in achievement are shown in Table 10.1 in order of their effect on achievement.

TABLE 10.1 Sources of Variance in Student Achievement

Source of Variance	Effect on Student Achievement (%)
Students	50
Teachers	30
Home	5–10
Schools	5–10
Peer Effects	5–10
Principals	Negligible due to being incorporated in schools

(Source of data: Hattie, 2003)

As you can see, the biggest impact on student achievement comes from the students themselves, whether the cause is intrinsic or external. Hattie then went even further: he isolated the influences that had the strongest effect on student achievement and tied them to the source (Table 10.2).

As Table 10.2 clearly shows, out of the top 20 influences, all but four fall under the influence of the teacher. What does all this mean? It means that, as educators, we need to work smarter, not harder. If we focus on what makes the biggest impact on student achievement, then we are doing what is best for kids. Looking at the top 20, I saw that I needed more class time to do these things well and to help my students succeed. To have more time, I needed to make time, which meant examining my instructional methods and pedagogy.

TABLE 10.2 Influences on Student Achievement
and Sizes of Their Effect

Influence on Student Achievement	Effect Size	Source of Influence
Feedback	1.13	Teacher
Student's prior cognitive ability	1.04	Student
Instruction quality	1.00	Teacher
Direct instruction	.82	Teacher
Remediation/feedback	.65	Teacher
Student's disposition to learn	.61	Student
Class environment	.56	Teacher
Challenge of goals	.52	Teacher
Peer tutoring	.50	Teacher
Mastery learning	.50	Teacher
Parent involvement	.46	Home
Homework	.43	Teacher
Teacher style	.42	Teacher
Questioning	.41	Teacher
Peer effects	.38	Peers
Advance organisers	.37	Teacher
Simulation and games	.34	Teacher
Computer-assisted instruction	.31	Teacher
Testing	.30	Teacher
Instructional media	.30	Teacher

(Source of data: Hattie, 2003)

Writing Next

The second resource that helped focus my changing instructional method was the "Writing Next" report (Graham & Perin, 2007). "Writing Next" provided me with more data to support the concept of the flipped classroom. The report states that for students to become better writers, they need to see writing as a process that involves strategies at writing's various stages. They need to use inquiry skills to develop content, and they need the opportunity to study models. All of these require focused instruction and time in the classroom in order to succeed. This data was another support for the need to refocus my instructional time and purpose.

Reading Next

The third resource that helped guide me was the "Reading Next" report (Biancarosa & Snow, 2006). This focuses on reading instead of writing, and lists 15 recommendations to raise middle and high school literacy. The six recommendations listed below are the ones from "Reading Next" that have proven to be most powerful to my classroom instruction:

Direct, explicit comprehension instruction, which is instruction in the strategies and processes that proficient readers use to understand what they read, including summarizing, keeping track of one's own understanding, and a host of other practices

Motivation and self-directed learning, which includes building motivation to read and learn and providing students with the instruction and supports needed for the independent learning tasks they will face after graduation

Strategic tutoring, which provides students with intense individualized reading, writing, and content instruction as needed

Intensive writing, including instruction connected to the kinds of writing tasks students will have to perform well in high school and beyond

A technology component, which includes technology as a tool for and a topic of literacy instruction

Ongoing formative assessment of students, which is informal, often daily assessment of how students are progressing under current instructional practices

Any one of these three resources, by itself, would have made me do some serious evaluation, but putting all three together created something that I could not ignore, something I felt I had to immediately act upon. Of course there were times when the magnitude of the changes I was facing seemed overwhelming, maybe enough to make many just want to walk away. But I would encourage you to start small and remember the Chinese proverb: the longest journey begins with a single step.

Where to Start? Three Steps

As I mentioned before, I was a fairly new public school teacher when I was introduced to the flipped model. Teaching high school English is my dream job, but I did not start there. I started in technology, so I was already well-versed in the technological aspects of the flipped learning model. I have never had any trouble playing with and exploring new technologies; in fact, it seems that I am wired for it (please excuse the English teacher's pun). For many, however, the technological hurdle is the highest to overcome. So I want to acknowledge the elephant in the room and talk about it before I move on.

It seems to me that many English teachers are reluctant to use technology in the classroom. We are still holding on to the print, while our students are playing with the digital. I think that this is true because of the nature of our field: we are accustomed to holding our text in front of us and reading from it, writing in the margins to annotate, and composing our thoughts in composition books for manual editing. When we think of English class, we think of the hard assets—that is how we were instructed and how we learned as students. However, this is not how our students view the classroom. While to some this shift to a higher integration of technology in the classroom may seem overwhelming, for our students it is a welcome change. So, where to start? I suggest three steps that will help inspire small and manageable changes while allowing time to explore and get used to technology before sharing it with students.

Step 1: Eliminate Redundancies

The easiest and most effective way to start is to eliminate redundancy. I am going to walk through two redundancies that I experience in my classroom and explain how I used the flipped model to address them to gain valuable instructional time.

Redundancy 1: MLA Formatting Expectations

As an English teacher, I spend much time each day, week, month, and year teaching and reteaching students how to properly format a paper. I can guarantee that I have wasted approximately five minutes per class per week on this single concept. Not to mention all the "late" papers that students turn in, papers whose only reason for being late was that students didn't know the formatting requirements. This was the very first thing that I flipped. I created a simple video that walked students through the MLA formatting expectations and then how to set up this formatting in a word-processing document. Then I published the video on my website.

Now, I go over the MLA expectations in class. From then on, I refer students to the video. If students consistently get the format incorrect, I can redirect them to the video and have them give me a concise summary of the expectations and create a template that they can use for all of their papers going forward. Students now have 24/7 access to a resource that will provide them accurate information. By taking this simple step, I gained back 180 minutes (5 minutes times 36 weeks) for quality instruction. I am now holding the students accountable for learning and retaining the information.

Redundancy 2: Classroom Procedures and Expectations

Constantly reviewing and talking about procedures and expectations was the second source of redundancy in my classroom. Although I would send home classroom expectations and have both students and parents sign them, inevitably I spent a huge amount of time discussing things that had been laid out since the start of the year, such as my late-work policy, due dates, and expectations for written assignments. Students would interrupt the instruction in the middle of class and ask about late-work information (what did I miss, when is this work due for me, etc.) more times than I can count. This might just be a personal issue, but I have a feeling that many other teachers may also experience this. So I recorded several themed videos on different classroom components. Now I not only send home the sheet, I also ask both the student and parents to watch the video and sign off on it electronically. Students then must take a quiz on it, and the quiz is graded. By doing all of this, I am transferring the responsibility of learning from myself to the students, where it belongs.

Step 2: Examine Your Use of Class Time

One of the biggest flipped learning hurdles for many humanities teachers is that we don't see how it could work for our subjects. But I didn't see this hurdle as a barrier—I saw it as a challenge to make flipped learning work for me and my students.

I began, as all teachers should, with the One Question: "What is the best use of your class time?" I teach Literature of the Americas to high school sophomores, and when I examined how I used class time, I found that I spent a large portion of my time providing background information on historical time period, author biography, and authorial style. Transferring my lectures to video provided students with a way to learn the information at their own pace—whether it was a first-time pass or a review. Having access to the lecture in video format allowed students to go back and listen to it again if they needed to. I researched and created a video series for every new author/genre. For example, one of our books was *The Old Man and the Sea* by Ernest Hemingway. My video series for this book/author included:

- historical background of the time period in which the author wrote

- a biography that focused on issues and themes in this particular work

- author technique and style

- themes and motifs found in the work

I found that this format worked well with each new topic we covered. Students were able to learn at their own pace and at the most convenient time for them. Since implementing this across other classes, I have added a video on close reading and annotating. Watching a video before class also provides students with a framework that helps them approach a piece of literature. They were able come to class with focused questions that shaped the discussion and learning in the classroom.

Recently, I became even more ambitious. Our school is now using a new grammar program, so I created grammar videos on concepts and definitions. This way, when we work on grammar in the classroom, it is a brief definition followed by an in-depth application of grammar to our writing.

Step 3: Evaluate Your Feedback Methods

Providing timely and effective feedback can make a substantial impact on student achievement. Feedback was the second thing that I flipped in my classroom, and it is the piece from which I get the most positive comments and advice for improvement from my students. We all know the heartache of watching a paper that we spent 30 minutes editing and making thoughtful comments on being placed in the recycling bin or, even worse, the trash can. Going back to the recommendations from "Writing Next" (Graham & Perin, 2007), I decided to break the writing process down into steps that students would follow for every formal paper.

10 Steps for Writing

1. Review your notes and come up with a defendable and interesting thesis statement and ask yourself, "Is the thesis statement appropriate for the prompt?"

2. Is there evidence that clearly and strongly supports your limiting ideas?

3. Write a skeleton outline and turn it in as requested by your teacher.

4. Write a reflection on the skeleton outline and turn it in as requested by your teacher.

5. Write a full-sentence outline.

6. Write a reflection on the full-sentence outline and turn it in as requested by your teacher.

7. Write a rough draft, run it through SAS Curriculum Pathways (this is a free resource that has a writing reviser for your students to use), and email the results to your teacher.

8. Write a reflection on the teacher and/or peer edits and turn it in as requested by your teacher.

9. Record your final draft and share it with your teacher.

10. Write a reflection on the recording and turn it in as requested by your teacher.

Students soon learn that in this process, they will receive detailed feedback from their instructor that they not only have read, but also reflect upon. In my classroom, each step of the process holds equal weight in the grade book.

But to do this, I had to flip feedback. I started using a screen-capture program to record my feedback and commenting. Now, I give students a detailed recording of me discussing their paper in real-time rather than a few static comments on paper. After a short learning curve, I find it easier to record meaningful comments as verbal feedback than to write them on the students' papers. And each step I take is followed by a step by the student, which keeps the responsibility of learning still on them. They can see that I am a willing partner who wants to help them succeed.

This process may seem daunting and time consuming—and to be honest, at first it is. You have to give yourself permission and time to make mistakes and try out what works best for you and your students. And if the whole process seems too much, don't start with the entire process. Pick one paper and do one of the things listed above. Even if you only give students oral and visual feedback on one paper, it will make a difference.

Benefits of Flipped Learning

There are many benefits to applying some form of the flipped classroom to a class. Remember that there is no one right way to flip, or only one model to apply—teachers have to go back to their answers to the essential question and individualize their approach from there. Here I will share some of the benefits I have experienced in my classroom and with my students, in hopes that my words might spark an inspiration for you to forge a new trail.

Engagement

I have flipped each of my classes—from Grades 9 through 12 and at all levels—and every grade and every level has shown increased engagement. The biggest gain that I experienced was with a semester-long class this year. Students in semester classes have opted not to take any honors English classes and often have struggled in English and other classes. These particular students can perform well, but often choose not to do so. To date, those students have completed the video tasks as well as the writing process at around a 75% rate. These are students who normally would not go home and do any written homework, but they will go home and watch a video and then come back to class and talk about it. When given an authentic reason to do an assignment, they not only meet but exceed expectations.

Growth

Giving a good teacher more time to provide quality instruction in the classroom will always lead to good things. I have seen my students grow, not only by improving their grades, but by increasing their critical thinking and writing skills.

To illustrate this growth, I include an example from one of my students' work on crafting a thesis statement on the novel *Perfume* by Patrick Suskind:

> Grenouille's point of view gives the reader a new perspective on how people are viewed, providing a new entity in which to understand relationships within life.

After going through the writing process and having more time to do one-on-one writer's conferences, either in the classroom or via video, the student submitted this as her final thesis:

> Suskind's point of view constructs the journey of Genouille moving from the outside of a social paradigm up to the point where he becomes the center of a newly created one. The twist in the journey allows the author to show mankind's inability to achieve perfection.

Now, I know that this example is not perfect, but it definitely shows growth for that student. And it was the best thesis statement that I had ever seen from her over the past two years. This could only have happened after flipping my class, which gave me more time to interact, provide students with formative as well as summative feedback, and create a relationship of trust.

Performance

I intentionally left the discussion of test scores until the end of this chapter, because I do not feel that scores should be the main focus of teaching. Rather, improved scores are a natural by-product of good teaching. But to answer the question, "Does flipping make a difference in test scores?" My answer is an enthusiastic yes. I am more excited to be in the classroom than ever. I get to do what I love—to teach—and that is clear to my students. My students' ACT averages are up, and my International Baccalaureate overall Language A score is one level higher than international averages. But the biggest performance gain is when my students come back from college and tell me how easy English is for them because I took the time to show them not only how to write, but how to think and reflect.

Chapter 11

my road to becoming a modern educator

STEVE KELLY'S STORY

Steve Kelly, a high school math and science teacher in St. Louis, Michigan, came on the radar of flipped learning after he presented his journey toward modern education to the Michigan Board of Education. His presentation was recorded and placed on YouTube (www.youtube.com/watch?v=bXlh8wOazXs). In that recording he said: "This is the creative generation...my students are now creating." Since that time he has presented at numerous conferences and shared his knowledge and expertise about how teachers can bring creative projects and activities into the classroom.

I WOKE UP in late 2009 to the realization that I had not made any significant changes in the way I had been teaching since the mid 1990s. My students were beginning to show a rapid decline in productivity and classroom engagement. I had always thought I was a really good teacher until December 2009, when I was invited to be a part of the Network of Michigan Educators. There I met outstanding educators who made me rethink everything I had been doing as a teacher. On the drive home from the conference, I made a personal commitment to become a modern educator. I committed to learning about what motivates this current generation of students and what skills they will need to take with them as they enter the larger world.

How does a teacher in a solitary classroom learn how to "get better"? I started by doing several things:

- I got out of the classroom during my conference period and into other teachers' classrooms.

- I asked other teachers what they were doing that I was not.

- I started reading every modern book on education I could get my hands on.

- I started to collaborate with other teachers and humble myself to ask for help with new technology that I was too inept to figure out on my own.

- I started creating a list of all the things I wanted to change in my classroom to make it more modern.

The list started to get obnoxiously long and I had no idea how to accomplish all of it within our current bell and calendar schedule. I needed a new way of managing my class time. Luckily, three months into my transformation, I ran across an email for a flipped classroom conference in Colorado. I didn't know much about the flipped classroom, but I knew the direct instruction was recorded on video and traditional homework was done in class. It sounded intriguing, so I went.

There were two things from the conference that truly sold me on using the flipped classroom to help reinvent myself as an educator. The first was a quote from Jon Bergmann: "The flipped class is not about the videos, but rather the quality curriculum that can be offered during class time." The second powerful motivator came from a student panel. The students were asked what subjects they would like taught in the flipped style and all of them answered, "Math!" At that point I decided to steal everything Jon and Aaron were doing and make it fit my little school. After spending three days with outstanding educators and a handful of Woodland Park students, I was off and running—or so I thought!

I worked over the summer so I could be prepared to offer my students a flipped classroom experience in the fall. It took over a month of thinking and planning before I created a screencast of my first official video lesson. I first had to reorganize my curriculum according to the newly released Common Core State Standards (CCSS). I took the time to separate all of the CCSS topics for Algebra II into 10 units to be covered over one school year. Within each unit, I included:

- outlines for students to take notes from the screencast

- practice problems

- second-chance assignments in case mastery was not obtained on the first practice

- small projects/application problems for each topic

- one culminating project to be used as an alternative form of assessment

At the Flipped Classroom conference, all attendees were given a copy of Camtasia—a screencasting and video-editing program—and trained in its use. As a cross-country coach, I had been editing highlight videos for my team for over a decade, so the transition to editing with a new program was quite smooth. The software allowed me to easily record a lesson with my classroom's interactive projector along with a video of myself on the screen at the same time. I am a strong believer in my students seeing me teaching while the presentation is happening, because I want my students to see facial expressions and body gestures, just like they would with a live lesson.

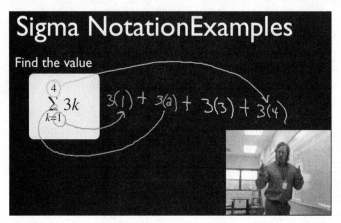

FIGURE 11.1 Screencasting software allows both the lesson and the teacher to be seen simultaneously.

Originally I thought I could store my videos on my school's server or website, but storage space and bandwidth became an issue. I thought about using free web-hosting sites like YouTube, but most are blocked by our school district. If something is blocked at school, how could I rationalize students using it out of school for educational purposes? I ended up hosting all of my videos at Screencast.com because of its reputation of reliability and ease of use with Camtasia. With the daunting task of creating over 90 videos in one school year, ease of use was a huge factor in my decision. Later I learned how easy it was for my students to use Screencast.com to watch my videos and even download them from the site onto their mobile devices when internet access was not available.

As summer ended and my first year of flipped classroom drew near, I was still very concerned about all of my students having access to my lessons outside of school. I was pleasantly surprised to have all access issues resolved within two school days. Over 80% of my students had internet access at home or on a mobile device. Some of my students without access watched the videos on the school computers, and the rest borrowed a DVD of my videos to watch at home. I was also able to burn a data DVD of the entire semester's worth of my instructional videos for students to take home. This has proven very valuable to students who have a computer at home but have slow or no internet access.

> The flip classroom will work just as much as the teacher is willing to put in the time needed.
>
> —*Chris, senior Calculus student*

During my first year as a Flipped Class 101 teacher, I was very pleased with my newfound class time. I had a chance to attack the items on my observation and book-study list. As I talked to other flipped classroom educators, I began to realize that I could take the flipped classroom and go much further. I then made the transition from the flipped classroom to flipped learning.

Assessment of Student Work

As I thought through how to assess students in flipped learning, I saw three key elements:

1. Projects and activities

2. "Check-out" conversations (formative assessments)

3. Traditional summative assessments

Projects and Activities

Because I have flipped my classroom, I have been able to reintroduce higher-level thinking skills and digital-age projects that I had to let go of in the past in order to "make it through the curriculum." I now have my students creating things and applying their new knowledge. Sample projects include student-created videos (both instructional and entertaining), Glogs, blogs, Geogebra worksheets, Excel discovery activities, collaborative essays and presentations on Google Drive, cell-phone pictures used for student-generated problems, Prezi presentations, and some differentiated projects that are student-chosen. I have been trying to expose my students to a wide variety of technology for motivational purposes and to create new paths of learning that many students have not been exposed to prior to my class. If students can apply what they have learned in new situations, then deeper learning and long-term retention has occurred.

I have observed tremendous student growth with simple video projects. Most of my students have a video camera (cell phone) in their pockets at all times. We use these cameras and a few school-provided Flip video cameras to create short projects to show mastery, release creativity, and clarify key concepts. Most of our projects are one-shot takes with no editing allowed. Students must prepare more than they would for an edited video, since they get only one chance to get it right. Some of the videos are generated to instruct other students on how to understand the topic being studied, in a process very similar to the way teachers create content in order to flip their classroom.

I like making movies in stats class explaining what we are studying. I get a lot more out of it than book work.

—*Chase, senior math student*

Other videos are meant to tap into student creativity. We make infomercials about mean, median, and mode; we make news broadcasts, rap videos, and videos where students appear with messages written on whiteboards timed to music. We frequently copy videos that are trending on the internet, modifying them to show student knowledge of mathematics. For example, we are currently copying the YouTube sensation "How Animals Eat Their Food" into "How Z-Scores Work."

Not only are my students more creative on video projects, they also produce better-quality work when we post them on the web (where they are accessible to the general public). I require most projects to be posted to the web, with their associated URL and Quick Response (QR) code displayed on the wall of our class-room. The simple addition of a QR code dramatically increased the quality of my students' work, because students are motivated by having an authentic audience outside of the classroom. In the future, I am going to require each student to create a blog post with photographs of their projects, including any low-tech projects. I am hoping that both the public nature of blogging and the opportunity to reflect on their work will help students make improvements in their learning.

"Check-Out" Conversations (Formative Assessments)

Flipped learning has given me time to interact one-on-one or in small groups with all of my students every day. I have been able to reintroduce mastery learning and online testing. My students are now able to work at their own pace through Algebra II while taking assessments only when they are truly ready. I use a short "check-out" system within each unit of study for assessing mastery prior to students moving on to the next topic. To "check-out" of a topic and move on to the next, all students must have an individual conversation with me. Sometimes I will simply ask students to show me how they completed part of the homework and other times I try to ask questions that will lead to deeper learning. My Algebra II student population is very diverse in their mathematical abilities, so individual differentiation is a must. These "check-out" conversations are differentiated by student, allowing me to ask for basic knowledge of a topic from some students, and asking others more-probing questions that lead to a deeper understanding of the topic.

I believe our mastery "check-out" conversations have led to more student growth than any other thing I have implemented while becoming a modern educator. Students rarely try to "check out" with me prior to having a firm grasp of the topic. This is a *huge* change from the way I taught mathematics in the past; before switching to the mastery system, I assigned homework each night that did not have teacher support, was only completed by students motivated by grades, or was copied from other students. Traditional homework had very little impact on student learning and very little impact on my personal decisions about where to lead the class. By implementing the new "check-out" conversations, I have the ability to lead individual students through a differentiated experience in learning mathematics.

> After having mastered 100% of Algebra II for the first nine units, I am obsessed with perfection on the last two tests this year.
>
> —Jonathan, junior math student

Traditional Summative Assessments

I developed a set of online, traditional multiple-choice tests for final assessments at the end of each unit of study. The tests are only ten questions, so we do not use up entire class periods on testing. I have a database full of questions for each CCSS that I use to generate new tests for each student.

In my new flip class, 90% of the students are working 90% of the time and they are fully engaged.

—*Kevin Stedman, St. Louis High School math teacher*

Does Flipped Learning Work?

The class average for Algebra II in the two years prior to flipping was an appalling 62%. This was one of the key reasons I chose to flip Algebra II before any of my other courses. At the end of our first year with the flip, our class average was 83%, and 80% at the end of the second year. I realize these are not standardized test scores being compared, but they are my scores. Flipped learning has given me class time to observe student growth on an individual basis. I am confident that my students now have a deeper understanding of the concepts of Algebra II as well as a new appreciation for the beauty of mathematics. Over 90% of my students have shown mastery, through the "check-out" conversations, in over 85% of the CCSS for Algebra II. Fifteen percent of my students mastered all of the CCSS two to four weeks prior to the end of the school year. These students earned the right to dig into differentiated projects outside of the CCSS curriculum. Example projects included TI-84 (graphic calculator) programming, logic and truth tables, proof by induction, and matrix algebra. These projects were so successful that I have decided to incorporate more student-chosen differentiated projects into my class as I move forward.

Next Steps

As I continued to develop flipped learning in my classroom, I began to reach out to other educators. I collaborated with Zach Cresswell, a former student-athlete of mine and a second-year teacher at Mt. Pleasant High School in Mt. Pleasant, Michigan. It is our goal to reinvent pre-calculus for our students. We are essentially co-teaching our pre-calculus classes, even though our schools are 20 miles apart. Zach and I have had lengthy discussions about the structure of our new course. Both of us have had success with flipping our classes previously and wanted to use flipped learning concepts as the backbone of our new course. We have created most of our instructional videos together. For two or three weeks we work separately, with frequent video chats online. Two times per month we meet in person on a Saturday morning to produce our videos or to brainstorm new ideas.

Neither of us has much experience with project-based learning (PBL), but we want our version of PBL to enhance student discovery and inquiry. We want our projects to be relevant to pre-calculus students. Our intent is to have our students working on projects that inspire them to expand their knowledge of mathematics beyond the classroom. The goal of our projects is to take advantage of the strengths of both inductive and deductive reasoning.

Our version of PBL involves one video story or question at the beginning of each major topic, followed by numerous small projects throughout the unit. Our video story-problems are presented in goofy videos where Zach and I complete multiple "extreme sports" spoofs. These "Cress and Little" videos are quite popular with our students: our goofy videos get watched hundreds of times more than our instructional videos. Each video ends with a question or activity that is used to guide students through the learning process. We ask questions about college loans when studying exponential and logarithmic equations, create video mathematical models when studying functions, predict weather when studying trigonometry, and calculate incomes when studying sequences and series.

The discovery activities are hard. I like to be told exactly what to do. Out-of-the-box thinking is a little scary.

—*Taylor, senior math student*

As our class evolves, we are incorporating more inquiry activities. Zach is a genius at finding other teachers' activities and tweaking them to fit our needs. My students exhibit a greater understanding of a topic if they discover it on their own, so I often use an inquiry activity that leads my students to discover the same topic they watched in the previous night's instructional video homework. In the past I used inquiry-learning activities prior to the direct instruction, but I am finding my students have many more *ah-ha* moments by discovering the same thing they were taught the day before. My students have yet to catch on to the fact that they are discovering the same topics that are covered in the videos.

We have also added a student-inspired (differentiated) culminating project after each unit. We want the students to dig deeper into topics that were of interest to them within each unit. The students are responsible for generating something of value from their research. We help guide the students in picking topics, but then step back and let them create their own projects. Letting go of my "teacher control" felt a little strange, but the end products were well worth the discomfort. Our students' work is some of the best I have seen in my 23 years in education. We have had students create presentations, videos, websites, digital books, and even an iPhone app.

I feel very blessed to have been given the opportunity to use flipped learning to help me transition to being a modern educator. I do not know if flipped learning is the answer to all of the issues in our education system, but it has been my road map for personal growth as well as the growth of my students. The members of the Flipped Learning Network and the #flipclass educators on Twitter have given me the professional development I needed. I use my social network as "on-demand professional development" numerous times each day. Also, collaborating with Zach Cresswell has prompted me to develop more collaborative projects. There are teachers all over the globe creating similar projects in isolation. With the ease of modern communication, it is time to start working together to offer a quality educational experience in all classrooms. I truly believe we can use the grassroots flipped learning movement to help us transition all classrooms into modern learning environments.

My journey toward being a modern educator has reinvigorated my love for teaching. I challenge teachers to take a risk and flip one unit of study to witness for themselves how flipped learning can transform their classes. Taking risks, collaborating, communicating, networking, entrepreneurial thinking, and continuous learning are all valuable skills our students need in order to thrive in this creative world. I, for one, am working hard to model these skills to my students. Though I have not arrived yet, I feel I am well on the way to becoming a modern educator.

Chapter 12

getting to really know my students

DELIA BUSH'S STORY

Some have argued that the flipped classroom works only for older students. Delia Bush is a fifth grade teacher in Grand Rapids, Michigan. She writes a popular blog about how flipped learning is transforming her class. Her blog is authentic and candid; she shares her triumphs and her struggles. You can find her blog at: http://flippedclassroom.blogspot.com. Enjoy as Delia shares her story.

Where It All Began

Delia,

Have you heard of a flipped classroom before? I learned about it in one of my Administrative meetings...take a look at this video.

Jason

This was an email I received from my principal in July 2011. Attached to his email was a link to a video about a flipped classroom. It showed two guys (Jon Bergmann and Aaron Sams) talking about using video lectures as homework, which enabled them to have more face-to-face time with the students in their classes. I had one of those moments when I thought to myself, How could I have not thought of this before?

To clue you in on why the flipped classroom resonated with me, I want to talk a bit about my educational philosophy. In my 10 years as a teacher, I have become passionate about the idea that every child can learn. Finding out how each child learns is one of the favorite parts of my job. I refuse to quit on children just because they struggle or behave poorly. I work in a school that has a large at-risk population (78% free and reduced-price lunch). These kids are coming to me from a variety of home-life situations where learning is often a low priority.

I am willing to try anything that will potentially help my students. I am optimistic to a fault, and when I hear about something that is going to benefit my students, I quickly jump on board. So you can imagine my excitement when I watched the video. That evening I was talking with my husband about the flipped classroom, and he asked me, "Why? Why in the world would you want to go to all the trouble of making all those videos? Isn't your time better spent on other things?"

That evening, I thought deeply about my husband's concerns and realized that I was not happy with the way school was going. Bottom line: I was frustrated. Frustrated with an educational system that pushes kids on when they aren't ready. Frustrated that I was not meeting the needs of every student (highs, lows, and in-betweens). Frustrated that I didn't know my students as well as I wanted to. Frustration, frustration, frustration! So much so, that I was applying for administrative positions rather than staying in teaching. I still loved teaching, and I was good at it... but not good enough. Teaching is too important of a job to just be good. I feel as though you have to always strive to be amazing. So when my husband asked if it would be worth it, my answer was 100% *yes*.

Where It Went Next

Walking into my classroom at our small rural school before this revelation, you would see desks arranged in groups, student work on the walls, and comfortable spaces for reading. You would see students working together with a reasonable amount of noise. If I am being honest, though, working together in the past often included one student doing most the work, a few students helping out here and there, and probably one student who was happy to sit back and let the others do the work. Typically the students were working on exactly the same thing at the same time, unless they finished early and were reading.

Since I am an elementary teacher, I am charged with teaching all subject areas. And I am expected to be able to differentiate instruction for all students in every subject. This is not an easy task, but I do my best. One way my fellow fifth grade teacher, Mikie McVey, and I have tried to accomplish this is by dividing instruction based on our areas of expertise. Since I love math, it seemed like a natural fit for me to teach math while Mikie taught science and social studies. Thus, I teach all the fifth grade math. In addition to math, I also teach language arts to my class only.

A Story of Two Students—Mitchell and Nelly

Last fall at our school's open house, I met many of my upcoming students. One that I remember quite vividly was Mitchell. He was polite as can be, and was excited about the prospect of helping with our school webpage (which my class runs). He was also quick to inform me that he "can't do math." I was curious to see how flipped math would work with a kid like him.

Mitchell was one of my most consistent students at watching the videos and coming to class prepared. His parents were very supportive of the whole flipped process. At the beginning of the year, his mom would watch the videos with him so she could help if he got stuck. As the year progressed, he needed her less and less. His scores in math were consistently in the 80%–90% range. This shocked him. By the end of the year, he was one of my go-to students when others were stuck. On our last day of school, I got the nicest card from him. On one side was a letter from him; on the other, a letter from his mom. As I read it, it brought tears to my eyes, and I am not a sappy person. My favorite line: "Mrs. Bush, you taught me that I can do math."

Nelly was a fifth grade ELL student who struggled in school. Her parents spoke only Spanish. In previous years, she almost never did her homework, and math in particular was difficult. She started her year in a traditional manner, and again she turned in almost no homework. Then her class got flipped...

Nelly became much more consistent at returning the notes that she took while watching her math videos. Slowly, she started gaining some confidence in her abilities. I was pleased with how flipped math was working for Nelly. I was surprised at the parent-teacher conferences when I found out it was working for her mom, too. Her mother watched each video with Nelly, but not to learn math—she was watching the videos to learn English. Was my intent of flipping to help people learn English? Nope. Is it still pretty awesome? Absolutely!

During math, I usually started the lesson by getting everyone pulled together to do a quick review of the day before. Then we moved into the meat of the lesson. Basically I would stand at the board, or use my document camera to present the information. The students all had their own dry-erase boards to do practice problems, or they worked with manipulatives. I would explain and show examples, then have students practice. Meanwhile, the lesson was often interrupted by questions and students being off-task. While the students were practicing, I would move around checking work. I would get to a handful of students who were raising their hands for help before it was time to move on. Students who did not raise their hands often did not get the help they probably needed because time was limited. By the time the lesson was over, there was very little, if any, time to discuss how they might actually use this knowledge in the real world.

At assessment time, I thought I had a pretty good handle on which students were struggling with different concepts. Unfortunately, I always had a handful of surprises when I was grading. I thought the students understood, but I was wrong. The fact that I had not caught their confusion was difficult for me. It became a pattern: me thinking the students understood more than they really did, and the students not speaking up when they were confused. I quickly became tired of moving on when many of my students were not ready. Thus, I realized I needed to change.

> The flipped classroom helped me a lot because when I brought the homework home I didn't understand it. But with flipped class my teacher could help me understand it better. Every night I watched a video that the teacher posted on a school website. Then all I had to do was write notes about the lesson in a notebook while I watched the math video. This helped me understand the lesson better.
>
> —*McKenzie, fifth grade student*

The Transformation Begins

After getting the "all clear" from my principal and superinten-dent, I realized I needed to figure out this whole flipping thing, fast! The first hurdle was making the videos. I won't go into the how-tos, as there are abundant resources out there that tell you different ways to make the videos. What I will say is that you can do it with limited technology and it is a learning process.

When I first started making videos, I did not have a document camera. I had a projector and my computer. Each time I made a video, I wheeled my computer into the middle of the room, pointed my webcam at the screen, and pressed record. These videos were not going to win me any Oscars, that is for sure. But they did what they were supposed to do, which was teach the lesson.

I am not going to lie and tell you that it was a fast process. At first, it was not. Every planning period I had was dedicated to making videos. I was lucky to stay one video ahead of the kids. After I got my document camera, life got a little easier. I no longer had to drag my computer to the middle of the room: I now had the capability to record my screen.

For the majority of the year, I taught the same lessons that the other teachers in the district were teaching, but I prerecorded mine. I kept a lot of data in regards to how my students scored compared to the previous year's class, which was taught in a more traditional style. I found that my flipped group performed approximately 5% higher on most assessments. But what I was more excited about was that I knew my students much better. I could tell you at any given moment exactly what they did and did not understand. I knew who needed help on any given topic and who might be a good resource for them—either another student or myself. I was amazed at how well my students were learning.

About a month into school, our board of education held a meeting at my school, and my principal asked if I would present. I was nervous, but I agreed. On the day of the board meeting, I had had a terrible time in the computer lab, and many kids were not as on-task as I would have liked. So I was a little disheartened when it came time to present, but I put my happy face on and gave my spiel. To be honest, I expected the board members to listen politely, then move on with the agenda. I was shocked when they started peppering me with questions. They were intrigued with the flipped classroom and wanted to know more. Their feedback was positive and encouraging. It was the pick-me-up I needed after a long day.

The Transformation Continues

About midyear, a journalist from our local newspaper got word of what I was doing and came in to interview me and my students. Around the same time, I also received an Action Research Award for the work I had done in my flipped classroom. In addition, my blog was starting to pick up steam, and I was getting more followers than I ever expected. I found myself feeling a little uncomfortable with all the publicity. I was getting all this positive PR, and yet I still didn't feel like we had reached our potential. Did I know my students' needs and strengths better than ever before? Yes. But I still felt undeserving of all the recognition I was receiving because I thought I had a long way to go.

Around that time I heard a question that started to shift my thinking: "What is the best use of my face-to-face time with students?" After reflecting on this question, I realized that while what I was doing was an improvement, I wanted more. My students needed to be pushed harder, and solving homework problems in class just wasn't cutting it. I felt there was still something missing. I wanted my students to master the material, I wanted my students to be deep thinkers, and I wanted my students to understand why math was relevant to their lives.

I liked the flipped classroom because it seemed as if you did your homework with your teacher at home! I never got stuck on a problem. Instead, I went back to the section of the video where she taught how to solve the problem. Then in class, we did our worksheet that used to be homework. What I liked and what helped me is that you had your teacher's help with both classwork and homework.

—*Erica, fifth grade student*

As the year progressed we continued to plug along, but I was unsure how to take the next step toward making our class time truly meaningful. The five million ideas that were floating around in my head started to solidify when I read a blog post by Brian Bennett titled "Redesigning Learning in a Flipped Classroom" (www.brianbennett.org/blog/redesigning-learning-in-a-flipped-classroom). His post made me think more deeply about what I was actually doing with my face-to-face class time. I realized I needed to do more meaningful activities with my students.

Supporting the Transformation

In my school district, I was the only person who was using the flipped classroom model. Most teachers had never heard of it. As supportive as my district was, professional development on the flipped classroom was not available. Then I entered two arenas that truly changed the course of my own professional development: blogging and Twitter.

I started a blog because I wanted a place to write honestly about my triumphs and struggles in my classroom. Through my years of undergraduate and graduate school, I was told multiple times how important reflection is to improve my teaching practice. This is great in theory, but by the end of the day, I was exhausted. The last thing I wanted to do was spend another few hours thinking about what happened during the day. But, I committed to sitting down every Sunday to write about my week at school. I immediately began to realize the importance of this process. By simply sitting down and writing out my thoughts, I was able to crystallize my thinking. The public nature of the blog gave me some accountability to really change. Blogging accelerated the change process faster than I ever would have dreamed.

I never expected to have people be inspired by what I wrote. I never expected to have a following. I never expected to be asked to write a chapter in a book about flipped learning. My only goal was to think about what I was doing in my classroom and figure out ways to improve. Another side effect of blogging that I did not expect was a sense of pride. I was humbled that my words were helping not only my students and me, but also other teachers. I preach to my students about the joy you can feel when you help others, and I was living proof. It was a powerful feeling to be a part of something that was impacting so many others.

In addition to blogging, I became more active on Twitter. At first I used it to spread the word about my blog. But it quickly turned into the best professional development I have ever been a part of. I started following the #flipclass hashtag. In following #flipclass, I was able to connect with hundreds of other teachers who were flipping their classes. I was no longer operating solo. I had a team. I finally had a PLN! If I was having a bad day, my tweeps were there to encourage me. If I needed motivation, I did not have to look far. If I needed help—you got it—my #flipclass tweeps were the first people I went to. #Flipclass is *full* of brilliant educators who are more than happy to share their experience and wisdom. If you don't know how to learn from Twitter, or even what a hashtag is, I encourage you to find a friend who can show you.

Via Twitter I was able to connect to other educators with philosophies similar to my own. Through those connections, I've had an opportunity to collaborate on a project called the Flipped Learning Journal (FLJ). In a nutshell, the FLJ (www.flippedlearningjournal.org) is a website that has several contributing authors, all of whom are currently teaching, who write about how the flipped classroom works for them. But the most powerful part of the FLJ is found at the bottom of the home page. There is an embedded link for you to go to if you are looking for a partner to collaborate with. By following that link, you'll find a list of educators all over the country who are using the flipped classroom model and who are looking to connect. There is no reason to work alone.

Yet another example of making global connections occurred shortly after Hurricane Sandy. My class had been blogging about math with John Fritzky, who teaches in New Jersey. When the class learned about Hurricane Sandy and where it struck, my students immediately became concerned about John's students because they lived directly in the danger zone. I was able to connect with John on Twitter and reassure the students that his class was OK, although many families had lost a lot during the storm. My class responded by asking what they could do. I still get goose bumps thinking about it. We ended up selling flowers at our music concert, and purchasing gift cards for some of the families in John's class. This happened around the holidays, and a gift card seemed like a good idea. The families who received the gift cards were touched that a group of students who lived a thousand miles away and had never met them had done what my class had done. My students will never forget that experience, nor will I.

Transforming to Flipped Learning

Through the end of the year, Flipped Class 101 (lecture at home, homework at school) was my go-to method. However, I was not completely satisfied with my students' progress. I was holding some children back by pacing them with the rest of the class. I was also doing my students a disservice by passing them on to the next unit when they did not have the previous unit mastered. How was that helping them? I spent the summer reevaluating my classroom time, and as I began my second year I was able to take my students deeper. I had graduated to flipped learning.

I liked the flipped classroom because when I did the video I could replay something I didn't understand. I loved this way because it helped me excel in math more than traditional math. It made me so good that I'm now doing seventh-grade math in sixth grade! My new math teacher is doing flipped math too, and I am so glad.

—*Nick, sixth-grade math student*

This year my classroom looks much different than last year. My units all begin and end with an inquiry project. One of my goals has been to connect math to the real world, and this is how I attempt to reach that goal. Every unit is broken up into learning goals, or "I can" statements. Each of those has one or two corresponding videos. After watching the videos, the students answer guiding questions. These questions are designed to be in the upper levels of Bloom's taxonomy. Then students come up with example problems. My version of flipped learning is more asynchronous, where students are allowed to pass out of concepts they already understand.

When students come to class, we have small group discussions over their guiding questions before they move on to practice problems. After completing these practice problems, the students take a quiz to prove mastery. If they do not pass, we work together on more practice and they try again, with a different quiz.

To some extent, students are working at their own pace. Unfortunately, this is not a perfect system, especially when students get behind. At what point do I move on when some students are still struggling with previous content? I wish I could tell you I have solved this problem, but I have not. I am still learning how to support my students through mastery. My classroom is a living, breathing entity. It changes constantly as we—my class and I—see things that need to be improved. That used to bother me, but I realize now that change is how we improve, and I am always looking for ways to improve.

In addition to the changes mentioned above, my students also started to make connections across the country with their blogs. We began blogging with the school in New Jersey and then blogged with a class in Texas. The blogging not only got the students writing about math, but they also had an audience, which was powerful.

Transforming My Teaching

When I think back to my pre-flipping days as a teacher, I see quite a transformation. Before, there was a lot of direct instruction going on. Now, students are working together so that everyone understands. Most are starting to take responsibility for their learning, and I play a much different role in the classroom. I now spend about five minutes at the start of class interacting with individual students so they can get busy on their next learning objective. The rest of the time students are working, and I am meeting with kids, one-on-one, every day. How powerful is that?! When I talk to parents about their child, I know exactly where they are academically, and what their strengths and weaknesses are. Bottom line, I know my kids, and I have the time to push them further than they knew was possible. Isn't that what teaching is all about?

A Student Teacher's Perspective

(Taken from Paige Laug's guest post, "Big Shoes to Fill," on my blog at http://flippedclassroom.blogspot.com/2012/04/flippingfrom-perspective-of-student.html)

If you were to ask me 12 weeks ago what I thought about a flipped classroom, my answer would have been a simple, "What?" I entered Mrs. Bush's fifth grade classroom [as a student teacher] not knowing how it worked or even if it worked, and to be honest, feeling a little skeptical. I was groomed to only think about

Continued

teaching in a traditional manner [with] the teacher standing in front of the students, delivering instruction. I quickly found that my comfort zone was about to be dissolved as I made my way into the realm of 21st-century teaching.

My first couple weeks of observing the students and Mrs. Bush uncovered many interesting things. First, the students were in the middle of NWEA/MAP (Measures of Academic Progress) testing which consumed all of Alpine's three [computer] labs. This meant that the flipped part of math had to be put on hold until testing was complete. I heard the students commenting on whole-group instruction during math, [calling it] "boring" and "confusing." I saw a lot of frustration and even heard one student say, "I miss the videos." This immediately sparked my curiosity as to what this whole flipped thing really entailed.

After MAP testing I was finally able to see how math worked in Mrs. Bush's classroom and let me tell you, I was so amazed! I observed students who never did their homework during the two-week MAP testing period, actually completing all of their homework once the videos were back in full swing. But more importantly, and probably the biggest element that the flipped classroom brought to life for me, was that Mrs. Bush and I were able to reach every single student and work with them one-on-one. Now, that's cool.

Okay, so Mrs. Bush makes it look easy. Let me enlighten you on how my first dabbles into the flipped classroom went.... After becoming familiar with all of the technology involved in creating the videos, I was ready to record...or at least I thought. I sat down with my notes (which were more like a script), took a deep breath and clicked, "record" only to immediately stumble over the first line! Five takes later I had finally gotten through the first part of the video and was ready to dive into the actual math lesson. Luckily for me, the process of recording became much easier after my first attempt.

Although my first video was finished, there were many more hiccups to come...like, what happens when the student teacher

Continued

Continued

forgets to embed the link for the video from Schooltube and the students can't view the video on Edmodo? Or, what happens when the student teacher unknowingly makes the video longer than the 15-minute allotted time and does not realize this until a student raises his hand in the lab and says, "the video just stops in the middle of the last problem!" I could have panicked, but thankfully for me there are two lessons that both traditional teaching and flipped teaching have taught me and that is to always have a Plan B and improvise!

These are just a few of the curveballs that the flipped classroom threw my way, but as I reflect upon my experiences I feel that I have gained so much. I have gained confidence in my abilities to teach math because I was able to plan, prepare, and deliver math lessons without the pressure of conducting whole-group instruction, which often is interrupted due to behavioral issues. I have gained a wealth of knowledge about all of the technology available out there, and furthermore, I have seen how the use of this technology can enhance and impact learning. Finally, I have gained an appreciation for teachers who "go out on a limb" and try something innovative. Mrs. Bush took a risk and with hard work, dedication, and courage, transformed her classroom into a place where students can learn math in ways they never have before. I cannot express how much this experience has impacted my life as a new teacher and as I set out on my own journey, I leave with one thought in mind: I have big shoes to fill.

Chapter 13

scaling innovation
with flipped
professional
development

KRISTIN DANIELS'
AND MIKE DRONEN'S STORY

Kristin Daniels, as an instructional and technology coach
with the public schools system in Stillwater, Minnesota,
successfully implemented the flipped learning model to
deliver professional development in her school district.
She is a Flipped Learning Network board member and
has developed a flipped learning course to be taught to
teachers using the flipped learning model.

Mike Dronen is the executive director of technology for
the Minnetonka Public Schools. He helped to design and
implement the flipped learning professional development
model for teachers and school administrators.

OUR JOURNEY INTO flipped learning began in the spring of 2011, shortly after Mike Dronen, then Stillwater's coordinator of educational innovation and technology, hired Kristin Daniels and Wayne Feller as full-time technology integration specialists for the nine elementary schools in the district. The hiring for these positions was the result of the 2005 Stillwater Technology Plan, which outlined the need to hire several staff members who could work directly with teachers on an ongoing basis to help increase student engagement and learning by integrating technology into instruction. The district has a firm belief that systematic change in teacher practice across the district would not be possible without full-time technology integration staffing.

Flipped professional development, or flipped PD, is what we call our ever-evolving model of professional development. This model, like the flipped classroom, is based on the idea of moving low-level instruction from the group learning space to the individual learning space. When applied to professional development, flipped learning means that teachers access digital content on their own so that face-to-face time can be used for reasons other than the typical sit-and-get training workshops. Flipped learning can be applied to a variety of professional development scenarios. Some consider flipped PD merely front-loading teachers with information before a group workshop or meeting. This is a great starting point, but the real impact of flipped learning occurs when learning becomes personalized. In Stillwater, similar to the successful transformation of many teachers in flipped classrooms, flipped PD has transformed the role of technology integration specialists into "technology and innovation coaches"—people who encourage and support innovative and transformative teaching practices. We wholeheartedly feel that this transformation would not have been possible without the changes we made to how we were spending our time with teachers, which ultimately led us to embrace the idea that coaches are needed for effective professional development.

Although we (Mike, Kristin, and Wayne) knew of one another through various technology groups in the St. Paul/Minneapolis area, the three of us had never worked together in the same organization. Mike had been in the district since 2005. He had not only built a strong technical infrastructure, but was carrying out the 2005 Stillwater Technology Plan and building an integration team that would work with teachers in the district. Wayne, a music teacher for over 35 years, had transitioned into working part-time in technology integration in the district before taking the role full time. Kristin arrived in Stillwater after leaving the classroom and working as a technology integration specialist with a 7–12 school and later with the local ISTE affiliate, TIES.

During one of our school visits in March 2011, we ended up in a conversation with Tom Hobert, principal of Afton-Lakeland Elementary School. The conversation started in a very typical way: Tom asked about technology in the classroom and what the "next thing" was that he should look into for his staff. We conveyed the critical point that it wasn't about the technology. We had seen it before: adding one more new tool would cause teachers to feel compelled to use it in the classroom, while they had barely mastered the tools that were already available to them. We knew that it was about providing teachers with effective professional development so that they could use technology to change the way they teach. So Hobert, in an extremely open manner, invited us to create and implement a model of technology professional development for his staff.

We were ecstatic at receiving this expansion of professional freedom to do our jobs in the district. With no desk or central location, we worked out of our backpacks. And we had just been given the opportunity to design and implement a professional development model at the school level. This would be the perfect opportunity to pilot a model that could be used throughout all nine elementary schools, and conceivably the entire school district.

Select, Copy, Paste

Traditionally, most of our professional development time was spent introducing new tools, showcasing possibilities, and showing teachers the "click here," "select," "copy," and "paste" components of each. These tools and techniques were taught in a vacuum that was not quite strong enough to pull in the context of pedagogy or the teacher's subject content. Before long, we could tell that our traditional demonstrations and "showcase" projects were not causing teachers to feel eager to start using their newfound knowledge in their classes the following Monday morning. But what we didn't know was what was behind this lack of enthusiasm.

Similar to students in a traditional classroom, our teachers were without our professional guidance at the very time they needed us by their sides: when they took their new knowledge of a tool or process and began to think about how they could integrate it into their classrooms. By necessity, our time with teachers remained focused on the exchange of ideas for creating engaging projects and activities, the application of the tool in the classroom, and the pedagogies that would be required. Our thinking and method of presenting information was a direct result of our understanding of the work that Mishra and Koehler (2006) put forth on the Technological Pedagogical and Content Knowledge (TPACK) framework for identifying and working with the different knowledge areas that teachers need in order to teach effectively with technology. Puentedura's (2013) Substitution Augmentation Modification Redefinition (SAMR) model suggests that just having the technology available doesn't help teachers realize its fuller ability to redefine instruction. These two frameworks helped tremendously, but neither suggested a method that we could use to effectively embed professional development.

Flipped Professional Development

Building from Experience

One of the most important questions we asked when creating our professional development model was "How do we want to spend our time with teachers?" After weeks of deep and reflective conversation about our experiences working with teachers, we identified the main components we felt would be vital to the success of a flexible professional development model. We outlined our ideas and drafted the mechanics of our first year of flipped PD.

We created a schedule for small-group, face-to-face, uninterrupted work time with teachers during the school day. In our experience, before- and after-school are very challenging times to work with teachers, because they have an endless to-do list. In a conversation with an elementary school principal a few weeks earlier, we had learned about a rotating substitute teacher model, and we decided we could use this model to relieve three teachers at a time. This allowed us to see up to 12 teachers each day, as the subs would rotate from one classroom to the next every two hours. These "workshop" groups, based on grade-level teams or topic interest, served as our monthly face-to-face time with teachers.

Later we discovered that, in a few of the workshop groups, the differences in technical ability frustrated the teachers. We made adjustments along the way, trying to minimize barriers to learning.

> I do want to work with colleagues on similar projects, but I would also like to work with colleagues who have similar technology skills. It is not a strength of mine and I get very frustrated when things go fast and I can't keep up and/or follow the facilitator.
>
> —*Teacher feedback, August 2012*

After our second year of flipped PD, we surveyed our teachers and asked them what component of our model was most beneficial to them. Four main benefits emerged: individualized coaching (38%); work time during the school day (29%); small group or individual sessions (16%); and support for implementing projects and taking risks (13%). The survey responses verified our observation that the greatest benefits of this model were the individual meeting time and the personalized coaching that the teachers receive.

> I really liked being able to work on things that I can use in my classroom. This option has allowed me to have help when I needed it most. The once-a-month schedule gave me some time to work on projects but then have some support the next month.
>
> —*Teacher response, flipped PD survey, May 2013*

We used technology to connect teachers and generate conversations. Teachers often work in isolation, and many still lack the skills to connect with others through online tools and networks. Even connecting teachers within the same district takes dedicated effort and persistence. We understood that working in isolation without the influence, encouragement, and camaraderie of professional colleagues limits one's growth potential. Connected educators benefit from the support of shared resources, experiences, and best practices. We connected all our teachers through Google Apps for Education. At every opportunity, we had them create and share documents with their colleagues.

> We have the opportunity to discuss some of the projects we are working on and are able to support one another and encourage expansion of ideas with our colleagues.
>
> —*Teacher response, flipped PD survey, May 2013*

To help teachers connect with other teachers in the district, we sought out teachers who were working on similar projects in flipped PD workshops and brought them together over the summer for additional collaborative time.

Summer PD Goal: Learn about different ways to create ePortfolios. Decide on model that is best for each teacher. Implement in 2012–13 school year. Record pros/cons and successes of ePortfolios. Share with others.

—*Notes from a collaborative document shared between five teachers across the district*

We provided online digital content for teachers to access outside of our workshop time. This allowed us to shift the time spent learning about the technology tools into the individual learning space so that our face-to-face time could be reserved for reflective conversation and deeper exploration of ways to use technology to transform the classroom experience. Basic requests for the simple "how-to" tutorials were made into videos. Teachers were able to view this digital content on their own time and at their own pace. For many of our teachers, even navigating to the place the videos were housed and getting instruction through video were new experiences.

Watching that video you sent me was awesome! And I was able to do everything I wanted to do before but was afraid to try. It was really fun to watch you show me how to do it on the video. That was a fabulous teaching tool. Thanks a million smiles!

—*Email from a teacher, sent after receiving and viewing a personalized video tutorial*

Prior to this, we had felt as though spending time with us was the only way that teachers were going to learn about the new technology tools. We redefined our role by simply changing how we spent our time with teachers. Most likely the same is true for many other flipped learning educators. Reflecting on this today, the impact this change has had on our lives is truly remarkable. Although we are into our third iteration, these components remain the foundation of our flipped PD model.

In June 2011, two months after we finalized our model of flipped professional development, ISTE released a white paper on the components of effective professional development. "Technology, Coaching, and Community Power Partners for Improved Professional Development in Primary and Secondary Education" outlined three components necessary for creating a powerful professional learning environment for teachers:

> ISTE recommends incorporating a three-pronged meth-
> odology to achieve 21st-century professional learning
> experiences, which will better prepare teachers to effec-
> tively help students learn. This methodology embraces:
>
> - An effective coaching model;
>
> - Online communities for greater collaborative idea
>   sharing; and
>
> - A fully embedded use of technology.
>
> By bundling these three factors into a singular profes-
> sional learning strategy, instructional leaders can
> develop a more powerful ongoing learning environment
> for teachers that bolsters PD and successfully prepares
> students when they enter the workforce. (ISTE, 2011)

The alignment of our flipped PD model with the ISTE white paper was remarkable. We proceeded with confidence as a team, knowing that our collective experiences about how people learn and why they take risks had shaped who we were as educators and how we wanted to work with our teachers. We recognized how we had arrived at the decisions we had made. Flipped PD was innovative. It was the result of being given the opportunity, time, space, and freedom to design.

Digital Resources and Personal Pathways

Although digital content had been a part of our work for many years, we knew that video would take on a new role in teacher learning as we approached our first year of flipped PD. We decided to organize our videos by topic area rather than by the tools being used, and grouped videos into four topic areas: communication, collaboration, creative media, and presentation. Each area included videos that were tool-specific and that showed a technical "how to." We also created videos that showcased projects created with these particular tools or processes. For example, in the collaboration strand, a video about Google Docs explained, step-by-step, how to share a document so that students and teachers could collaborate, edit, and review one another's work. The project showcase video in the collaboration strand showed how one classroom in the district used Google Docs to create a digital newspaper. The combination of these two different types of videos became a vital component of our work with teachers, because it provided context for the tools and allowed further exploration of the transformative power of technology in the classroom.

Throughout our first year, we were constantly tweaking how we used our digital resources. In the beginning, it was easy to send teachers to our Moodle course to view videos on certain topics. We were using high-quality screencasting software to produce videos, but production time was lengthy. Eventually the teachers' needs and interests outgrew the resources we had already created. We continued to make videos, but found ourselves creating them more spontaneously during the school year. The digital resources we were creating were becoming more personalized. We noticed that as we tailored resources to an individual's needs, we were able to move teachers further along than we had in the past.

Of course, not every teacher enjoys learning from video. We have received feedback like this:

> When asking for help in an area, written directions give the user or learner a way to go back and do it a second time to reinforce the skill.

and even this:

> The one part that I still do not understand is the access to tutorials. This would be something I would like to know more about and how to access those.

So some of our teachers are still becoming familiar with the idea of learning from videos, or even with learning where to find them! This is why we continue to tweak our model. How can we ensure that every teacher has a solid learning goal, and how can we provide them with an easy way to access digital resources? Basic technology navigation and file-management skills increase the potential for transforming a teacher into a DIYer (Do It Yourselfer). Maybe we will make a video for this!

Emerging Coach

Having time to work with teachers in small groups on a monthly basis allowed us to establish a trusting relationship with them. It was vital that we approached our relationships with teachers as equal partners. In his book *High-Impact Instruction*, Jim Knight (2012) talks about the importance of a "partnership approach" to professional learning. He states, "The top-down approach of telling professionals what to do and expecting them to do it just as they were told almost always engenders resistance."

When moving from a traditional model into a flipped learning environment, it's interesting to see the shift in roles. Through our close work with teachers, we slowly transitioned from a "stand and deliver" presenter to a coach, and found ourselves in close partnership with the teachers. However, the relationships did not begin that way. When the elementary teachers in Stillwater began flipped PD workshops, many were hesitant about how their time would be spent and what they would be asked to do, learn, and implement with precision and without failure. We could see a physical change in them once they realized that the workshops were intended to be a time for personal exploration, learning, and growth; a time to play; and a safe place to be vulnerable with their skills, hesitations, and fears. They began to relax and their wheels started turning. The workshops often ended with comments about how the time went so quickly and how the teachers wished they had more time "like this." Our end-of-year feedback included comments about coaching:

> The time I have spent in flipped PD has been extremely valuable to me! Flipped PD allows time to actually work on things as well as have a coach right at my side cheering me on, helping, and asking insightful questions.

and comments about taking risks:

> It has helped me to step out of my comfort zone and implement the projects I wouldn't have done without the support.

As we got to know each teacher's strengths and interests, it became easier to negotiate different personal pathways that would lead every teacher to his or her personal goal. For one teacher the goal was to create and maintain a classroom website, while for another it was to get her second-grade students blogging. Two completely different goals with two completely separate paths.

The impact of our flipped PD model was greater than expected, and the ripple that occurred after our work with teachers was noticeable. The influence that a confident and knowledgeable teacher has on his/her colleagues should not be underestimated. As we began to work more closely with teachers who were implementing projects, it became necessary to meet with them outside of workshop time. Stacey was a second-grade teacher who started to meet with us in the spring semester of our first year of flipped PD. By the fall of the next school year, she came to every flipped PD workshop with a to-do list already prepared.

At the close of one meeting, when only half the items on Stacey's to-do list had been crossed off, we asked her to set up a time to meet with us outside of workshop time. This started an intense learning period for Stacey as she dove headfirst into blogging with her second-grade students. We visited her classroom and encouraged her to learn alongside her students and to put them in charge of the tools and processes. She embraced the falls. She knew that each time she made a mistake she had learned something. She was not afraid and continued to step forward. Communication back and forth through email and in her flipped PD document guided Stacey to the things that she was seeking. Links to blog posts and video tutorials were shared with her.

Then one day, in passing, we had a conversation with the teacher who worked across the hall from Stacey. She was also interested in having her students start blogging! She was clearly energized by what she had seen happening in Stacey's room. This is the type of result from flipped PD that we had not anticipated. However, it led us to understand that when we affect the potential of an individual by supporting and encouraging creativity and risk-taking, we also affect the potential of the individuals around that person. Our sphere of influence increases. This energy is often unseen, and rarely harnessed. But we have witnessed the power of people. This has changed how we invest our time with teachers. No success is too small, or risk too big. This is necessary for innovation.

A Balancing Act

Imagine standing on the edge of a small platform. The ground is 1,000 feet below. A tightrope, stretching forward, is at your toes.

Your vision is focused on the tightrope. You know you need to move forward.

We started using the tightrope metaphor just after we began our work with teachers in the flipped PD workshops. We imagined that, at times, teachers felt like we were asking them to cross a tightrope high in the sky. We imagined that many teachers felt as though they were the last ones to understand something, acknowledging that even the students may have already skipped across the tightrope. By flipping our professional development, we had created an environment of personalized instruction for teachers. And we immediately discovered that, like students, many teachers were hesitant when asked to take risks associated with learning, especially when it came to learning about technology. We recognized their courage for being reflective practitioners and making changes to transform teaching and learning. Unlike our traditional role, most of our time was spent supporting and encouraging educators to take their first steps out on their own metaphorical "tightrope," with the focus, determination, trust, and vulnerability that were required to walk the line. This was extremely personal and rewarding work.

Cultivating Innovation

Innovation requires trust. Many of the people that encourage innovative ideas believe in the same things that Daniel Pink talks about in his book *Drive* (2009). They believe that in order to come to work every day and be motivated to do our best, we must have three things: autonomy, mastery, and purpose. When an organization honors its vision by hiring leaders who create this work environment, there is an energy felt throughout the organization. The energy and momentum that is experienced when people are motivated to create, improve, and innovate becomes contagious.

Conversations around innovation are becoming more commonplace. In Stillwater, changes to position titles reflect these changes—from "technology integration specialist" to "technology and innovation coach." This is all work to better align, coordinate, and in some cases combine the work of innovative teaching and learning efforts with technology.

Based on our experience with developing and implementing flipped professional development, it makes sense for a school district to provide a supported place where ideas can be "sandboxed" at a small scale in the hopes of discovering and developing future promising practices for learning. In a crowd-sourced and Twitter-fed landscape of ideas and promising practices, this kind of a small research and development effort can provide a place for ideas to be lightly managed and coordinated, and spread among innovative educators.

We are living with islands of innovation, and these islands of innovation are starting to spread. Many flipped learning educators talk about flipped learning as a bridge to something better. Neither the bridge (or the tightrope) is as scary as it may seem, nor is the innovation we encounter along the way. Flipped learning is a transition, from the first step to every step that follows. It's a way for teachers to make the transition to a different place in their educational journey. And in our experiences with flipped learning, teachers want to be in that place.

As for flipped PD, the transformations we have made as professionals cannot be undone. We have seen the impact that intentional content and coaching has on teachers. Flipped PD combines the best ideas for professional development. Personalized digital resources that are created for teachers, when combined with a coaching model of professional development, set the stage for highly efficient innovation.

Chapter 14

educational
sweet sauce

AT THE BEGINNING of this book, we noted that the world of education has fundamentally changed since we were in school. Instead of the information-scarce world we grew up in, our students are growing up in an information-saturated and globally interconnected world. This fundamental change needs to dramatically alter the way classes and schools operate.

The stories from each of these teachers reflect that change. Flipped learning has allowed them to get to the heart of teaching. They still teach their content, but they have gone through Flipped Class 101 and taken their classes deeper and further into flipped learning. What is remarkable is that they have each uniquely answered the One Question: What is the best use of your face-to-face class time? They all have their own individual stories of transformation, but the one commonality they share is how they have fostered great learning at the intersection of content, curiosity, and relationship.

The One Question is not just for teachers. We encourage administrators to consider: What is the best use of my face-to-face time with my staff? Often, administrators squander this valuable time. What if administrators flipped their faculty meetings? Instead of faculty meetings being used to disseminate information, what if they were rich discussions about best practices? During these meetings, are teachers disengaged? Are they checking their email or grading papers? Is this any different than students who are bored with their teacher lecturing and are on Facebook, or texting their friends? Could technology (even things as mundane as email) "deliver" content so that your face-to-face time is rich, rewarding, and powerful? A number of administrators who have implemented flipped learning tell us their faculty meetings are now deeper than ever before, and make much better use of the most valuable resource a school has: the creative minds of amazing professional educators.

As we have shared the flipped classroom and now the flipped learning story across the globe, we have been impressed with the dedication teachers exhibit to their students. Educators are a group of committed and caring people who want to do what is best for their students. Teachers recognize that some things need to change, but many just need a stepping-stone to help them move toward change. Many teachers on the brink of burnout are stuck in a content-heavy system where they are expected to deliver that content uniformly to all students simultaneously, with the content standards explicitly listed on the board.

Students sit in nice neat rows and all learn the same things on the same day. But when teachers honestly reflect on this practice, they find that students aren't actually learning at the same time; they are merely being exposed to content at the same time. These teachers are teaching how they were taught and are stuck in the paradigm in which they must be the fountains of knowledge. They realize the world has changed and they struggle to figure out how to connect to this generation of digitally connected and globally aware students.

Standards are not going away anytime soon, nor should they. According to Google CEO Eric Schmidt, humans are creating as much information every two days as we did as a species from our origin until 2003 (Siegler, 2010). The Siegler article was published in 2010, so that ratio may now be even more pronounced. Granted, what constitutes "information" in this context is up for discussion, but regardless of the actual numbers, the world is clearly not devoid of information. In fact, the difficulty in the world is no longer acquiring enough information, but knowing how to filter the abundance of information into relevant and usable bits. There was probably a time in which a human could know all there was to know about the world and could possibly even have read most of the published material in the world. That time is now long gone, so parents and educators must make a decision: do we want our students to know a lot about a little, or a little about a lot? Do we teach our students only set standards, or do we use those standards as a minimum requirement or framework for learning? Do we focus our students' attention toward the art of learning so they can navigate an increasingly complex world? Are some things more worthy of mastery than others, and how do we decide? The answers to these questions will vary based on various philosophical, scientific, and existential understandings of the world, but regardless of the answer, flipped learning has a role to play in the educational environment. It can help optimize the learning of content within the greater context of education, in whatever form it may take in any given school or other learning environment.

Flipped learning allows teachers to do what they do best: help students learn. And it does this by enabling teachers to deliver important content to individual students when students need it. The teacher no longer has to deliver content to students based on a rigid content calendar. Flipped learning, at a minimum, allows teachers to individualize the education of students through differentiation, and even allows for the personalization of education through choice, interest-driven education, and autonomy. Flipped learning is also flexible enough to meet the learning needs of students at all grade levels, to varying degrees.

Steve Kelly said it well: "How does an old teacher become better?" He knew things were broken, but didn't know how to take his students deeper or further. This theme was repeated over and over by our contributing authors. They knew that the system they were working in was broken and they needed a way forward. Each of them in their own way discovered Flipped Class 101 and dove in. They created videos, rearranged their classrooms, committed large amounts of time, and took a risk by trying something new. They were successful, but even so, they realized that there could be still more.

Though Flipped Class 101 changed their teaching practice, these individuals were still not satisfied. They took their students deeper and further and entered into the seemingly uncharted territory of flipped learning. And what did they discover? They discovered well-vetted teaching methodologies that have been around for a long time, such as project-based learning, Understanding by Design, inquiry learning, mastery learning, and many more. In many ways, the underlying ideas behind flipped learning are not new. However, the unique feature of flipped learning is that it provides a practical and achievable way for traditional teachers to take their students deeper and further into learning than they ever thought possible. Many teachers who have moved to flipped learning have told us how it has reinvigorated their careers. Some were ready to give up on teaching altogether. Others, like Delia Bush, were planning on moving into administration.

Educators long to do what is best for their students, but they have not had a simple way to do so. Some people have told us that the flipped classroom is such a simple idea, and they are right. We see the flipped classroom as a gateway to the richer experience of flipped learning. Brian Gervase is a high school mathematics teacher in Downers Grove, Illinois. Brian came to one of our early conferences in Colorado and he implemented Flipped Class 101, and did so for two years. Brian's students were successful, but he wanted to take his students to the next level. This past year he moved to the flipped mastery approach that we chronicled in our first book, *Flip Your Classroom* (Bergmann & Sams, 2012). He sent an email to Jon that said: "I have to say *this* is the game changer. My students and I are having a more enjoyable time than ever in class now...without even trying, the students all fall into their own comfort zones in how they learn best...some read...some scour videos and some just need to hear from me personally. It's been magic." Jon ran into him later at a conference and Brian said, "How did I miss this for so long? Now I can't tell people about the flipped classroom without telling them the other half: flipped learning. I feel like I have found the sweet sauce of education."

Don't we all want to find the "sweet sauce"? Yes! But we would like to push you even further and argue that there is more than one variety of educational sweet sauce. And since all students are different, they each need their own variety of educational sweet sauce. In an ideal flipped learning environment, teachers would develop a menu of educational choices for students. They could learn via video, or textbook, or website, or online simulation, or a hands-on activity, or a student-created project, or a real-world problem to be solved. And each teacher will develop the options based on the age of their students, the degree to which the students can handle choice and autonomy, and the type of learning resources that lend themselves to a particular subject area. Why then have we, for so long, served each student the same sauce?

Malcolm Gladwell, the author of *Outliers* (2008), and *Tipping Point* (2000), presented a TED talk in 2004 where he talked about spaghetti sauce. He tells the story of Howard Moskowitz, who was tasked with finding just the right flavor of Prego spaghetti sauce. Instead of finding *one* sauce that all people liked, Howard convinced Prego to make lots of different varieties of spaghetti sauce. Prior to Moskowitz, most food manufacturers were looking for the one recipe that most people would like. Moskowitz's contention was that instead of giving people one variety, a better way was to create many different varieties. When Prego took his advice, they made over $600,000,000—by giving people different choices. Howard's research showed that each person has individual preferences with regard to spaghetti sauce. Instead of a single choice based on someone else's preferences, people would rather have a variety of choices, a menu.

Educationally speaking, flipped learning is a way to provide a similar customization of the educational experience for each learner. Government and private entities have spent millions—if not billions—of dollars developing the one-size-fits-all education that is designed to meet the educational requirements of every student. However, no single system can meet this daunting task, nor should it. Each learner is different, and we need to honor each student's learning preferences and needs. We envision classrooms where content is valued, but where students have *choice* in how they learn. Flipped learning allows for this granular individualization of the classroom. The contributing authors of this book have moved away from the one-size-fits-all approach, and they are meeting the needs of *each* learner. Now we challenge you, our readers, to not only flip your classrooms, but, in the context of strong student-teacher relationships, to move deeper and further to flipped learning.

references

Bennett, B. (2012, May 16). Redesigning learning in a flipped classroom [Blog post]. Retrieved from www.brianbennett.org/blog/redesigning-learning-in-a-flipped-classroom/

Bergmann, J., & Sams, A. (2012). *Flip your classroom: Reach every student in every class every day.* Eugene, OR: ISTE/ASCD.

Biancarosa, C., & Snow, C.E. (2006). *Reading next—A vision for action and research in middle and high school literacy. A report to Carnegie Corporation of New York. (2nd ed.).*Washington, DC: Alliance for Excellent Education.

Bloom, B. (1956). *Taxonomy of educational objectives, handbook I: The cognitive domain.* Philadelphia, PA: David McKay.

Budin, H. (2011). Technology and democracy. Conference talk conducted from Teachers College, Columbia University, New York.

Budin, H. (2010). Changing roles of the citizen in American history. Lecture conducted from Teachers College, Columbia University, New York.

Colorado Department of Education School Performance. (2012). State performance framework for Discovery Canyon Campus [Data set]. Retrieved from http://cedar2.cde.state.co.us/documents/DPF2012/1040%20-%203%20Year.pdf

Dewey, J. (1916). *Democracy and education.* Institute for Learning Digital Classics. Retrieved from www.ilt.columbia.edu/?s=dewey+democracy

Driscoll, T. (2012). *Flipped learning and democratic education: The complete report.* Retrieved from www.flipped-history.com/2012/12/flipped-learning-democratic-education.html

References

Gladwell, M. (2008). *Outliers: The story of success.* New York, NY: Little, Brown.

Gladwell, M. (2000). *The tipping point: How little things can make a big difference.* New York, NY: Little, Brown.

Graham, S., & Perin, D. (2007). *Writing next: Effective strategies to improve writing of adolescents in middle and high schools—A report to Carnegie Corporation of New York.* Washington, DC: Alliance for Excellent Education.

Hattie, J. (2009). *Visible learning: A synthesis of over 800 meta-analyses relating to achievement.* New York, NY: Routledge.

Hattie, J. (2003, October) *Teachers make a difference: What is the research evidence?* Australian Council for Educational Research Annual Conference on: Building Teacher Quality. Retrieved from www.acer.edu.au/documents/Hattie_TeachersMakeADifference.pdf

Hattie, J. (1999, August 2). Influences on student learning. Inaugural lecture conducted from The University of Auckland. Retrieved from www.education.auckland.ac.nz/webdav/site/education/shared/hattie/docs/influences-on-student-learning.pdf

International Society for Technology in Education (ISTE). (2011). *Technology, coaching, and community: Power partners for improved professional development in primary and secondary education* [White paper]. Retrieved from www.iste.org/learn/coaching-white-paper

Kahne, J., & Westheimer, J. (2004, June 20). What kind of citizen? The politics of educating for democracy. *American Educational Research Journal, 41*(2), 237–269.

Kahne, J., & Westheimer, J. (2003, September). Teaching democracy: What schools need to do. *Phi Delta Kappan, 85*(1), 34–67.

Knight, J. (2012). *High-impact instruction: A framework for great teaching.* Thousand Oaks, CA: Corwin.

Kohn, A. (2007). *The homework myth: Why our kids get too much of a bad thing.* Cambridge, MA: Da Capo Press.

Marzano, R. J., & Pickering, D. J. (2007, March). Special topic: The case for and against homework. *Educational Leadership, 64*(6). Retrieved from www.ascd.org/publications/educational-leadership/mar07/vol64/num06/The-Case-For-and-Against-Homework.aspx

Maxwell, J. (2001). *The power of attitude.* Tulsa, OK: RiverOak Publishing.

Mishra, P., & Koehler, M. (2006). Technological pedagogical content knowledge: A framework for teacher knowledge. *The Teachers College Record 108*(6), 1017–1054.

Partnership for 21st Century Skills. (2011). *Civic literacy.* Retrieved from www.p21.org/overview/skills-framework/258

Pink, D. H. (2009). *Drive: The surprising truth about what motivates us.* New York, NY: Riverhead Books.

Puentedura, R. (2013) *SAMR: Moving from enhancement to transformation.* Retrieved from www.hippasus.com/rrpweblog/archives/2013/05/29/SAMREnhancementToTransformation.pdf

Siegler, M. (2010, August 4). *Eric Schmidt: Every 2 days we create as much information as we did up to 2003.* Retrieved from http://techcrunch.com/2010/08/04/schmidt-data

Skinner, B. F. (1938). *The behavior of organisms: An experimental analysis.* New York, NY: Appleton-Century.

Thorndike, E. L. (1905). *The elements of psychology.* New York, NY: A. G. Seiler.

Westheimer, J., & Kahne, J. (2004). What kind of citizen? The politics of educating for democracy. *American Educational Research Journal, 41*(2), 237–269.